GENEALOGICAL GLEANINGS

IN ENGLAND.

By HENRY F. WATERS, A.B.

BOSTON:
NEW-ENGLAND HISTORIC GENEALOGICAL SOCIETY,
18 SOMERSET STREET.
1885.

PREFACE.

By John T. Hassam.

———

The New England Historic Genealogical Society, through its Committee on English Research, has undertaken to make an exhaustive search of the English Records, on a plan never before attempted, for everything which concerns the family history of the early settlers of this country. For this purpose it has secured the services of the eminent antiquary Henry Fitz Gilbert Waters.

Mr. Waters sailed for England May 5, 1883, and at once entered upon his great work. Before a twelvemonth had passed he had accumulated a vast amount of historical and genealogical material, including abstracts of more than six hundred wills relating to American families, and he is still industriously engaged in adding to his invaluable collections. Some of the results of his researches, under the title of "Genealogical Gleanings in England," have been given to the public in the New England Historical and Genealogical Register, the organ of the Society. It has now been deemed advisable to reprint some of these "Gleanings" in a form more convenient for reference. The present volume includes the various instalments published in the Register from July, 1883, to April, 1885, inclusive.

It has been found impossible heretofore in most cases to satisfactorily establish the relationship between English and American families of the same name, and this failure to connect has been to the American genealogist the source of his greatest trouble. The searches now undertaken promise for the first time to meet and overcome this difficulty. The method adopted by Mr. Waters, so different from that of his predecessors, has, as was predicted, brought to light information which has escaped the attention of all other investigators. In this way only will it be possible to find and make accessible every clew which can serve to connect American families, distinguished or obscure, with the parent stock in England. The large number of Virginia wills contained in the present volume shows that this search is conducted in no narrow spirit, and that every American of English origin, in every part of our country, ought to feel an interest in this work.

In addition to these genealogical researches, Mr. Waters has made historical discoveries of the highest value. We owe to him the finding of the Winthrop map and the Maverick MS., two of the most important contributions made in our day to our early colonial history. For an account of the former the reader is referred to the Proceedings of the Massachusetts Historical Society for June, 1884 (XXI. 211), and the REGISTER for July, 1884 (XXXVIII. 342). The Maverick MS. was printed in the Proceedings of the Massachusetts Historical Society for October, 1884 (XXI. 231), and in the REGISTER for January, 1885 (XXXIX. 33). These discoveries have excited great attention among historical students, not only in this country but also in England.

The New England Historic Genealogical Society, having no fund at its disposal which could properly be used to defray the expense of this most important historical mission, has been obliged to rely upon the voluntary contributions of public spirited men to meet the cost of the work, and the responses to its appeals have always been prompt and generous. But it is necessary, for the successful prosecution of the undertaking, that money sufficient to carry it on uninterruptedly for a series of years should be obtained, and the committee confidently hope for further subscriptions for this purpose.

The index of the persons named in this volume is the work of Frank E. Bradish, Esq., a member of the Society.

Boston, April 2, 1885.

GENEALOGICAL GLEANINGS IN ENGLAND.

GREGORY COFFIN, of Stepney, co. Middlesex, mariner, shipped on board the William & Jane of London, Mr. John Baker commander, on a voyage to New England and Bilboe, by will dated 15 February, 1660, proved 20 August, 1662, appointed John Earle of Shadwell, mariner, his attorney, and left all his estate to the said John Earle and his wife. Joane Earle, whom he appointed joint executors. Laud, fol. 105.

JOHN COCKERELL, of Great Cogshall, co. Essex, clothier, made his will 14 July, 1662, proved 12 August, 1662. He bequeathed to his wife Mary all the lands and tenements in Bradwell, in the county aforesaid, which were her jointure; and also lands, &c., in Cressing, which he had lately purchased of one Mr. Jermyn and one Joseph Raven, during her natural life, and after her decease then to his son John Cockerell and his heirs forever. He devised to her also that part of the messuage which he had lately purchased of John Sparhauke, then in the tenure and occupation of Mistress Crane, for life, with remainder to son John, &c. The residue of his estate to son John at age of twenty-one years. He made bequests to two daughters, Mary and Elizabeth, and to the child his wife was then going withall. He appointed said wife executrix, and directed her to redeem the mortgage which he had made to Mrs. Hester Sparhauk of the messuage he then lived in, and which was in the occupation of the said Mrs. Crane.
Laud, 106.

BENJAMIN KAINE furnished an account of his goods and chattels, 16 October, 1654. Among the items was a tenement in Shoe Lane, and property in the hands of Mr. Coddington, his attorney, in Bow Lane, and in keeping of other persons (among whom a Mr. Walter Gibbons, cutler in Holborn). Thomas Blumfield spoken of, and called a brother of Mr. Withers. By his will, of same date, he gave his whole estate to his daughter Anna Kaine, except some particular legacies, viz., to his father Mr. R^t Kaine of Boston in New England, to whom he left (*inter alia*) a Japan cane with a silver head, which was in the trunk at Mr. Blumfield's, to his dear mother, to his cousin Dr. Edmond Wilson, to his Colonel, Stephen Winthrop, to Cornet Wackfield, to Mr. Mastin, to Mr. Richard Pery and his wife, to Mr. William Gray, late of Burchin lane; the said Gray and Pery to be trustees for his estate in England; to his servants John Earle and Thomas Lamb. The will was signed in Glasgow, in presence of Nicholas Wackfield and Richard Pery. On the sixteenth of May, 1662, emanavit comissio Simoni Bradstreet prox. consanguineo in hoc regno angliæ remanenti dicti defuncti, etc. Laud, 67.

[This was Benjamin, only son of Capt. Robert Keayne, of Boston, founder of the Ancient and Honorable Artillery Company. He married Sarah, daughter of Gov. Thomas Dudley. Gov. Simon Bradstreet, named in the probate, married another daughter, Anne (see REG. viii. 313; ix. 113; x. 130). Bradstreet sailed, November, 1657, for England, as the agent of the colony, and remained there three years, returning July 17, 1661. Probably the application for probate on Keayne's will was made before Bradstreet left England. For notices of the Keayne family, see REG. vol. vi. pp. 89–92, 152–8; xxxv. 277.—EDITOR.

See Savage Gen. Dict. iii. 1, where the date of Benjamin Keayne's death is incorrectly given. See also Suffolk Deeds, Lib. i. fol. 83 and 84.

John Morse, of Boston, in New England, salt-boiler, by deed of mortgage dated Nov. 9, 1654, recorded with Suffolk Deeds, Lib. 2, f. 180, conveyed to his uncle, Mr. Robert Keaine of said Boston, " my third part of that tennement or howse in shoe lane in London which comes to me by the right of my wife mary Jupe now mary morse which was left and given to hir by mrs Grace Jupe hir mother by will before hir decease with all the right title or Interest that myself and wife or either of vs haue therein," and also their interest in one half part of five certain tenements in Gravel Lane, in the Parish of St. Buttolph without Aldgate, London, to secure the payment of £32. See also fol. 86 and 182. See fol. 183 and 184 for a bond and an order from said John Morse to Mr. Simeon or Symon Smith of Southwark to pay "my Couzen major Benjamin Keajne" of London, £15 advanced by "my vnckell mr Robert Keajne" to pay for the passage of said Morse, his wife, and his wife's brother Benjamin Jupe from New England back to Old England. This sum was to be paid at the Golden Crown in Birchin Lane, London, on or before April 26, 1655, out of the rents belonging to his said wife, or brother Benjamin Jupe, remaining in the hands of said Smith as executor.—J. T. H.]

CAPTAIN HUMPHREY ATHERTON, 25 December, 1661, proved 3 July, 1662, by John Atherton, his brother and one of the executors. He named his brother Francis and his two sisters, Elizabeth Osborne, widow, late wife of Robert Osborne, and Anne Parker, wife of Richard Parker, of the city of Bristol. There was due to him by bond from Lieut. Col. Maurice Kingswell the sum of one hundred pounds, of which he ordered twenty pounds to be given to his worthy friend Mr. Richard Smith, one of the life guard to his Grace the Duke of Albemarle, to buy him a mourning suit and a cloak, thirty pounds apiece to his two sisters and ten pounds apiece to his two brothers, John and Francis Atherton, and also ten pounds apiece more which was owing unto him by Mr. William Walker at the Green Dragon in Cornhill, London. To the said Richard Smith he devised fourteen pounds owing to him by bill from Capt. Nathaniel Disborough. The residue of his estate, with arrears due from his Majesty for his service at Dunkirk, he left to his brothers, whom he named executors.

Laud, 94.

[It is singular that this Capt. Humphrey Atherton died about the same time as our Maj. Gen. Humphrey Atherton of Dorchester. The latter died Sept. 16, 1661, less than a year before his English namesake. For facts concerning the Atherton family, see REGISTER, ii. 382; x. 361; xxxii. 197; xxxv. 67.—ED.]

JOHN BURGES, the elder, of Westly, lying sick in Richman's Island, in New England, 11 April, 1627, proved 24 May, 1628, by Joanna Burges, alias Bray, relict and executrix. Besides his wife, he mentioned his three sons, Robert, John and William; and he enumerated, among other things, his bark, called the Annes, with her boat, tackling and provisions, and what she had gained that summer, his whistle and chain, and all his instruments that belonged to the sea.

Barrington, 45.

[Richmond's or Richman's island is situated near Cape Elizabeth, Maine. Walter Bagnall had a trading post there from 1628 till October 3, 1631, when he was killed by the Indians. The same year, Robert Trelawney and Moses Goodyeare of Plymouth obtained from the Council of Plymouth a grant which included this island. John Winter was their agent there. The papers relating to this plantation, fortunately preserved to this day and discovered by the late J. Wingate Thornton, A.M., are in press, edited by James P. Baxter, A.M., and will soon be issued as a volume of the Collections of the Maine Historical Society.—Ed.]

CAPT. JOHN WILCOCKS, late of Plymouth, now of Accomac, intending to go on service against the Indians, made his will, dated in Elizabeth City, Virginia, 10 September, 1622, proved the last of June, 1628. He named wife Temperance, his daughter in law, Grace Burges, legitimate daughter of his said wife, and his sisters Katherine and Susanna Wilcocks.

Barrington, 55.

EDWARD GREEN, late of Bristol, grocer, and now at present at Capt. Robert Dudley's in the county of Middlesex, in Virginia, 22 August, 1697, proved 9 August, 1698, by Robert Green, his brother and executor. He desired his body to be buried in a decent and christian manner at the discretion of John Barnard, then residing at John Walker's in King and Queen County in Virginia. The residue of his estate he left to his brother Robert Green of Bristol, haberdasher of hats. The witnesses to his signature were Robert Dudley, Senior, William Reynolds and Robert Dudley.

Lort, 186.

BENJAMIN WILLIAMS, of Stoake, near Guldeford, co. Surrey, schoolmaster, 2 July, 1695, proved 22 September, 1698, by Nathaniel Williams his brother and executor. To cousin Susanna Hall, John, Samuel and Daniel Hall, now or late of Whetenhurst in co. Gloucester, twenty shillings apiece, within six months after decease of the testator. To cousins Anna Cliffold (Clifford?), of Bisley, and her two brothers, Richard and Nathaniel Tindall of Nibley, and to my cousin Joseph Tindall, of Nibley, sometime of Trotton Hinton, ministers, ten shillings apiece, within six months, &c. To my cousins Samuel, Thomas and Benjamin Williams, of New England, and to my cousin Elizabeth Bird, of Dorchester in New England, and to the eldest child of my cousin Williams, of New England, deceased, in case there (are) any of them living, and also to the eldest child of my cousin Joseph Williams, deceased, in case he have left any living and who shall be living at the time of my decease, to every and each of the said last mentioned persons the sum of twenty shillings, within one year, &c. To the poor of the parish of Eastington fifty shillings, and to the poor of the parish of Whetenhurst fifty shillings, any poor people of my father's kindred principally recommended. To my brother in law Nathaniel Williams, of Brandley, in co. Worcester, and his heirs forever, all those my freehold, tenements, lands tenements and hereditaments, &c., in Eastington and Frampton, and elsewhere in Gloucestershire, and all the residue; he to be executor.

Note that the name Nathaniel is by my mistake omitted, and also the eldest child of my cousin Hannah Parmater is to be comprehended. B. W.

Lort, 208.

[The children of Richard Williams, one of the first settlers of Taunton, N. E., were 1. John, 2. Samuel, 3. Joseph, 4. Nathaniel, 5. Thomas, 6. Benjamin, 7. Elizabeth, wife of John Bird, 8. Hannah, wife of John Parmenter. See REG. v. 414*. All these children, except John, who may have died young, are named in the above will.

Emery, in his "Ministry of Taunton," i. 43-5, quotes "a manuscript of considerable antiquity," but evidently not written before 1718, which states that "Richard Williams was descended from a family of that name in Glamorganshire, in Wales, and found a wife in Gloucestershire, England." The same manuscript states that his wife was Frances Dighton, sister of Katharine, second wife of Gov. Thomas Dudley. Baylies, in his "Historical Memoir of New Plymouth," part i. p. 284, says there was a tradition that Williams was a relative of Oliver Cromwell. He also prints (i. 272) a letter from the Rev. Roger Williams, in which reference is made to "my brother." Baylies thinks this may be Richard Williams, of Taunton.

John Bird, the husband of Elizabeth Williams, was a son of Thomas Bird of Dorchester. See Bird Genealogy, REG. xxv. 21–30.—ED.]

THOMAS BEAVAY, waterman, of the city of Bristol, 21 Jan. 1656, proved by Mary Beavay, widow and executrix, 24 April, 1657. To be buried in the churchyard of St. Phillipps. To son Thomas Beavay, now a planter in Virginia, my best suit of clothes and all belonging to it. To my godson, Samuel Gosner, a small boat or twenty shillings in money. To godson Edward Martin the younger, twenty shillings. To godson Thomas Webb, twenty shillings. To wife Mary, the passage boat, with all the term of years that is yet to come.   Ruthen, 145.

EZEKIEL SHERMAN, of Dedham, clothier, the last of December, 1656, proved 12 May, 1657, by Martha Sherman, widow and sole executrix. To son Ezekiel one hundred pounds at age of twenty-one years. To daughters Grace and Hannah one hundred pounds each, at the age of twenty-one. To daughter now born eighty pounds at the age of twenty-one. To my brother John Sherman ten pounds within a year and a day after my decease. To Mary Sherman five pounds at the same time. After decease of wife Martha, son Ezekiel to enter on lands, &c. If he die without lawful issue, then the property to go equally among the daughters then living. Wife Martha to be executrix. The overseers to be Robert Stevens, of Dedham, my father-in-law, and Robert Stevens of Ardleigh, brother-in-law.

William Grindell one of the witnesses.   Ruthen, 147.

[Ezekiel Sherman probably was of the same family with the Rev. John Sherman, of Watertown, whose ancestors came from Dedham, co. Essex, England. See "Sherman Family," REG. xxiv. 66.—W. B. TRASK.]

WILLIAM SUMPNER, of Waltham Holy Cross, co. Essex, 12 February, 1656, proved 7 May, 1657, by Roger Sumpner, one of the executors. To daughter Susan Williams, daughter Mary Sumpner, son William; wife Jane and youngest son Roger executors. The overseers to be brother Roger Sumpner and brother-in-law William Sawdrie.   Ruthen, 148.

[There seems to be a similarity in early names between this family and that of the Sumner or Somner family of Bicester, co. Oxford, who settled in Dorchester, Mass., before 1637. See REG. viii. 128e; ix. 300.—W. B. T.]

JOHN MASON, of Mashburie, co. Essex, husbandman, 2 December, 1656, proved 7 May, 1657, by Sarah Mason, his widow and executrix. Real estate in Much Waltham to wife for twelve years and then to John Mason, the eldest son, he to pay certain legacies to daughters Mary, Lydia and Sarah Mason. Stileman's Croft, in Good Easter, Essex, to wife for six years, and then to son David Mason, he to pay to two (*sic*) other children, Abraham Arthur Mason and Samuel Mason, five pounds at age of twenty-one years.   Ruthen, 150.

ROGER BAKER, of Wapping, co. Middlesex, 15 August, 1676, proved 24 January, 1687, by Mary Johnson, alias Baker, wife of Thomas Johnson and daughter and residuary legatee of the testator named in the will. He mentions some land in Maryland, in Virginia, which he directs to be sold,

He leaves to his brother-in-law Abraham Hughs, of Ockingham, co. Berks, yeoman, ten pounds. The residue to two daughters, Houner Baker and Mary Baker, both under twenty years of age. Failing them, then to the four youngest children of his sister Mary Cleves, widow, ten pounds apiece, and the rest to such child or children as brother John Baker shall have then living.
Exton, 1.

JOHN HILL, of London, merchant, 14 December, 1665, proved 8 February, 1687. To wife Sarah one thousand pounds. To daughter Sarah one thousand pounds and a silver bason. To daughter Elizabeth eight hundred pounds and a silver "sully bub pott." To daughter Hannah eight hundred pounds and a silver sugar box. Wife now great with child. If it prove a son then he is to have land and tenements in Winthorpe and Croft and elsewhere in Lincolnshire, of the yearly value of twenty-four pounds, and six hundred pounds in money. Whereas my brother Valentine Hill, late of New England, deceased, did owe me at the time of my (sic) decease, above three hundred pounds, not yet satisfied, I give and bequeath the said debt unto the children of my said brother Hill and to the children of my brother-in-law Mr. Thomas Cobbett, to be equally divided amongst them, share and share alike. To my niece Bridget Cobbett five pounds. To cousin Garrett's children ten pounds, to be equally divided among them. To cousin Thomas Browne and his wife forty shillings, for rings. To cousin John Browne forty shillings. To brother Hutchinson and sister each forty shillings, and cousin Elizabeth Meredith twenty shillings, to buy rings. To my brother Nathaniel Hunt and brother Richard Hunt, each five pounds. To brother-in-law John Miles and to his wife, each five pounds, and to their son John Miles, five pounds. To my maid-servant Prudence, forty shillings if dwelling with me at time of my death. To my cousins Charles, Margaret and Katherine Watkins, each twenty shillings, for rings. To the poor saints in London ten pounds, to be distributed at the discretion of my overseers. To the poor of the parish where I now dwell, forty shillings. The residue to wife Sarah, who is appointed executrix. Friends Mr. William Allen, Mr. William Sawyer, and Mr. Robert Wakeling, overseers. Witnesses, Nathaniel Hunt and Charles Watkin.
Exton, 16.

[Valentine Hill was extensively engaged in real estate and other transactions in Boston, Lynn, Rumney Marsh, Dover, Oyster River and Pascataqua River, between the years 1637, when he was of Boston, and 1660. In 1651 he conveyed to Mr. Thomas Cobbett, of Lynn, styled "Clarke," afterwards minister of Ipswich, and others, all grants of land made to him, the said Hill, by the town of Dover, at Oyster River, and the saw-mills erected thereon. *Suffolk Deeds*, Lib. i. 182. See REGISTER, vii. 49, and Wentworth Genealogy, i. 138.—W. B. T.]

JOHN PARGITER, of St. Martins in the Fields, co. Middlesex, 8 February, 1687, proved 24 February, 1687, by John and Samuel Pargiter, sons and executors. To the four sons of my brother William Pargiter, deceased, viz., Robert, Edward, Samuel and William, and to his daughter Knight's children. To my cousin Frances Meade, wife to Mr. Francis Meade, of Battersea. To Mr. Thomas Pargiter, son to my brother Thomas Pargiter, deceased, to his son, my godson. To my sister Pargiter, his mother-in-law. To George Pargiter, his brother. To my cousin Sarah Louell at Virginia, by Yorke River, ten pounds. To Elizabeth, widow of cousin Robert Pargiter, deceased. To cousin Austin, of Hampton, and his wife. To cousin Benjamin Billingsby, bookseller, and his wife. To cousin Callendrine and his wife Mary. To my cousin Brewer. To my sister Blagrave. To Daniel and Deborah Blagrave. To Mr. Soffier, draper. To my grandson John Fleetwood and my grand-daughter Mary Fleetwood. My worthy friend Sir William Cowper, the elder. Sir Gerald Fleetwood (father of John and Mary). To my son John Pargiter, lands, &c., at Nordley wood, Ashley and Abbots Ashley, or any part of Shropshire, Pamber and Bramley in Hampshire, large house next the Northumberland House in the Strand, the Standard Tavern in the Strand, &c. &c. Son Samuel Pargiter.   Exton, 21.

JOHN ANTHONY, of Rhode Island, in America, mariner, 16 June, 1701, proved 10 December, 1703. To son John Anthony all the estate. Richard and Elinor Potts executors. Proved by Eleanor Potts.

         Degg, 205.

[Query.—Which John Anthony was this? See Anthony Genealogy, REGISTER, xxxi. 417.—ED.]

THOMAS READE, aboard the ship "Kingsoloman," now riding in the hope, being bound a voyage to Virginia. All my estate to loving brother William Reade, of the parish of St. Sepulchres, London, corn chandler, who is made executor. Signed 2 October, 1662, in presence of John Budd, scr. and Robert Bray. Proved by William Reade, 22 June, 1663.

         Juxon, 84.

ROBERT RAND, of Barham, co. Suffolk, 27 February, 1651, proved the last of March, 1651, and a commission issued to Jane Rand, the widow, no executor having been named in the will. To William Brooke, my grandchild, all my hooks and one hatchet and one pair of cobirons and one hale. To William Brooke, my son-in-law, all my wearing apparel and the "dobbe" house, and my cart and my biggest Danske chest and two brass pans and four pieces of pewter; and all the rest pewter that is mine to be divided among his children. To my son Robert, after my wife's decease, if he do come over, my best feather bed and my best bedstead. To wife Jane all the moveable goods, &c., "not disposed before of," and excepting three cows which are letten to Lionel Cooke until next Michaelmas, which, after decease of wife, are to go to son-in-law William Brooke.

         Bowyer, 64.

DENNIS GEERE, of "Sagust," in New England, 10 December, 1635, approved 6 August, 1637, before us, Tho. (sic) Winthrop Gov', Tho. Dudley dep Gov', Jo. Endecott. To wife Elizabeth three hundred pounds. To Elizabeth and Sarah Geere, my two daughters, three hundred pounds apiece. To cousin Ann Pankhurst so much as shall make her portion fifty pounds. To Elizabeth Tuesley twelve pounds to make up that eight pounds I owe her twenty. Roger Carver, of Bridhemson,* and John Russell, of Lewis, in Sussex, appointed overseers for estate in old England. My children to be paid at day of marriage, or at age of eighteen years. And whereas the Lord our God of his great goodness, since my coming into New England, hath discovered to me all usury to be unlawful, I do hereby charge my executor to restore all such moneys as any in England can make appear I have received from them by way of usury, whether it were 6 or 8 per cent, not thinking hereby to merit anything at the hands of God

* This, or Brighthelmston, is the old name for Brighton, as I am assured by J. C. C. Smith, Esq., who kindly called this and the succeeding will to my notice.   H. F. W.

but laboring hereby to attend my duty and manifest my distaste against every evil way. Of the estate in New England, to Thomas Topper five pounds, Thomas Braines three pounds, Thomas Launder three pounds, Benjamin Nye thirty shillings, Thomas Grenuill ten shillings, all which deducted and paid together with the sending my two servants with my child into England, the residue shall be employed to the advancement of such works as in the wisdom of my executors for that purpose shall seem good for the plantations settled within the Patent of the Massachusetts; and for the discharging of these legacies and sums, and the right ordering of my estate for the public good I appoint for my executors John Winthrop, the elder, and John Humphry, esquires, John Wilson and Hugh Peter, Preachers. Witnesses, Edmond Freeman and John Greene.

28 June, 1642. Emanavit comissio Edwardo Moonke avunculo Elizabethe Geere et Sare Geere filiarum dicti defuncti durante minori etate, &c. It appeared that the widow Elizabeth had departed this life.

Campbell, 79.

[Dennis Geere with his family embarked June 15, 1635, in the Abigail of London, Hackwell master, "having brought Certificate from the minister of Thiselworth," probably Isleworth in Middlesex. Those who embarked that day were Dennis Geere, 30; Elizabeth Geere, uxor, 22; Elizabeth Geere, 3; Sara Geere, 2, children; Anne Pancrust, 16; Eliz: Tusolie, 55; Constant Wood, 12." (REG. xiv. 315.) His fellow passengers, Anne Pancrust and Eliz: Tusolie, are no doubt the "cousin Ann Pankhurst" and "Elizabeth Tuesley" mentioned in the will. "Thomas Brane, husbandm. 40," and "Tho: Launder, 22," were also fellow passengers, having embarked in the Abigail, July 1, 1635. (REG. xiv. 318.) In the "Addenda" to Winthrop's Journal, under date of "1635, Dec. 10," among the "gifts bestowed upon the colony," is this entry: "Denis Geere of Sagus gave by his will (at the motion of Mr. Hugh Peter) £300."—ED.]

THOMAS GEERE, of the parish of Falmer, near Lewes, co. Sussex, 6 March, 1649, proved 25 April, 1650, by Dennis Geere, son and executor. To wife Mary. To eldest son Thomas Geere and his wife Mercy, and their children, Mercy and Mary. To grand-children Dennis and Richard Geere and grand child Thomas Geere. To the poor of Falmer and the poor of Stamer. Youngest son, Dionice Geere, executor. Friend John Russell, of Southover, near Lewes, and Stephen Towner, of Kingston, to be overseers. Witnesses, Richard Banckes and Tho. Russell.

Pembroke, 51.

DOROTHY PARKER, of Mildenhall, co. Wilts, widow, 10 October, 1649, proved 11 April, 1650, by Benjamin Woodbridge, one of the executors. To son Mr. Thomas Parker, of New England, two hundred pounds now in hands of my brother, Mr. Richard Stevens, of Stanton Bernard, co. Wilts, not doubting that if he die unmarried he will bestow what remains at his death, thereof, upon the children of my daughters Sarah Baylie and Elizabeth Avery. Of the other one hundred pounds in my brother Stevens' his hand I give five pounds to my son Mr. Thomas Bayly and the remainder to my daughter Sarah Bayly and her four children, John Woodbridge, Benjamin Woodbridge, Sarah Kerridge and Luce Sparhawke, equally. For the one hundred pounds due to me from my son Avery, for which his house was mortgaged, I bestow it upon my daughter Avery and her children. To my son-in-law Mr. Timothy Avery, &c. My loving daughter Sarah Bayly to be executrix in trust with her son, my grandson, Mr. Benjamin Woodbridge, executor, with his mother. Son Mr. Thomas Baylie and Cousin Mr. John Taylor to be overseers. Witnesses, John Barges and Anthony Appleford.

Pembroke, 54.

[An abstract of this will, made by the late Horatio G. Somerby for the Hon. Francis E. Parker of Boston, was published in the REGISTER, xxxii. 337. Mr. Waters has thought that a fuller abstract would be of service to the readers of the REGISTER. —J. T. H.

Mrs. Dorothy Parker was the widow of the Rev. Robert Parker, the famous Puritan author. Benjamin Woodbridge, the executor who proved the will, was the first graduate of Harvard College. See Woodbridge Genealogy. REG. xxxii. 292–6. See also the "Woodbridge Record," New Haven, 1883, large 4to., compiled from the papers of Louis Mitchell, Esq., by his brother Donald G. Mitchell, Esq. The will of the Rev. John Woodbridge, of Stanton, Wilts, the father of Rev. John and Benjamin Woodbridge, is printed in this work from a copy lately obtained in England.—ED.]

EDWARD BELL, of St. Brevells, co. Gloucester, 16 August, 1649, proved 21 January, 1649. He mentions nephew John Gorges, Esq. In a codicil, 20 August, 1649, he mentions lady Elizabeth Gorges of Ashton Phillips, Mrs. Mary Cutts, "my" godson Mr. Edward Perkins, Mr. Thomas Pole, &c. &c. He discharges sundry persons (among whom Mr. Wymond Bradbury, deceased) "of all debts owing by them to me or my brother William which became due unto me by his gift."   Pembroke, 3.

[I suppose that this Edward Bell was a brother of Ann, daughter of Edward Bell of Writtle, Essex. Ann Bell was the first wife of Sir Ferdinando Gorges, and her eldest son, John Gorges, probably the "nephew John Gorges, Esq." named in this will, was the father of Ferdinando Gorges, author of "America Painted to the Life." See Johnson's Wonder Working Providence, edited by William F. Poole, LL.D., and the notice of it by the Rev. Edmund F. Slafter in the REGISTER, xxii. 213–19. "Lady Elizabeth Gorges of Ashton Phillips" was no doubt the fourth wife and widow of Sir Ferdinando. See REGISTER, xxix. 42–7. Wymond Bradbury may be Wymond Bradbury of Wicken Bonant, co. Essex, whom the late John M. Bradbury, Esq., supposed to be the father of Thomas Bradbury, of Salisbury, Mass. (see REGISTER, xxiii. 262–6), but if so he died before 1650.—EDITOR.]

NATHANIEL PARKER, of East Berghoult, co. Suffolk, Esq., 5 August, 1684, proved 19 August, 1684. To be buried at the East end of the churchyard near the church of Great Wenham, co. Suffolk. He mentions his farm of Great Wilsey in Wrating, co. Suffolk. To nephew Philip Parker, Esq., son and heir apparent of Sir Philip Parker, Baronet, all my farm called the Priory in Great Wenham and East Berghoult, and the advowson of the church of Great Wenham, for life, and then to his son Philip. Nephew Calthorp Parker, son of Sir Philip Parker. Nephew Sir Philip Parker. Niece Mercy Parker, nieces Dorothy and Mary Parker, daughters of my late brother Sir Philip Parker, Knight. Niece Mary Parker, daughter of Henry Parker, Esq., my late brother. Nephew Henry Parker, son of said brother. My nephew Philip Gurdon, Esq. To John Gurdon, son of my nephew Mr. Nathaniel Gurdon. To Sir John Barker, Baronet. To my godson Winiff Sergeant. My god-daughter Elizabeth Walker. My god-daughter the daughter of my nephew Bernard Saltingstall. My nephew in law Anthony Gaudy, Esq., and my god-son Anthony Gaudie, son of the aforesaid, and his sister Winifred Gaudie. My cousin Elizabeth Garnish, widow.   Hare, 104.

JANE WILLIAMS, of Whetenhurst, co. Gloucester, spinster, 31 May, 1650, proved 30 June, 1655. To brother Samuel Williams my Scottish print bible. To my brother Richard Williams and my sister Elizabeth Williams that are in New England, each of them twenty shillings apiece. To Benjamin Williams and Nathaniel Williams, the two sons of my brother Samuel Williams, ten pounds apiece when they reach the age of twenty-one years. To John Hall, the younger, my sister's eldest son, ten pounds and a standing bedstead that is in his father's parlour chamber, my brother-in-law John Hall's. To Samuel, Daniel and Susanna Hall, the other three children of my brother-in-law, John Hall, twenty pounds apiece at 21. Brother-in-law John Hall to be executor.   Aylett, 292.

[It is possible that the Richard Williams, named above, as in New England, was Richard Williams of Taunton (*ante*, p. 3) ; but it is not probable. Six other persons by this name are recorded by Savage.—ED.]

WILLIAM GOODRICK, of Walton Head, co. York, 21 September, 1662, proved 25 January, 1664. My two daughters, Sarah and Elizabeth. My daughter Mary and her husband Matthew Elwald. My nephews Sir John Goodricke and Sir Francis Goodrick. My wife Sarah. My son William Goodrick.   Hyde, 4.

[See REGISTER, xxxvi. 384.—H. F. W.]

JOSEPH HOLLAND, citizen and clothworker of London, 25 December, 1658, with codicil dated 29 December, 1658, proved 17 January, 1658. To be buried on the south side of the christening pew in the parish church of St. Sepulchre, London, between my two former wives. To Elizabeth, my now wife, late the wife and administratrix of Jeffery Cumber, deceased. To son Joseph Holland the lease of my house in Green Arbour in said parish. To son-in-law John Perry and Johanna, his wife, my daughter, and their sons John Perry and Josias Perry and daughter Elizabeth Perry. To my said daughter Johanna, certain needle work "wrought by my first wife, her mother." To daughter Elizabeth, wife of Richard Bessy, in Virginia. To my son Nathaniel Holland, of Waterton in New England twenty pounds in goods ; to son Samuel Holland, in Virginia, thirty pounds in goods or money; and to each a bible. To son-in-law Miles Rich and daughter Prudence, his wife. To good friend Mr. John White, grocer, of above-named parish, and his wife. To Mr. John Andrewes in Fleet Lane. To my servant John Arnott. To the poor of said parish, in bread, twenty shillings, to such as Master Gouge will distribute unto. The executor to be Master John White; the overseer to be Master Andrews. The witnesses to the body of the will were Hen: Travers Scr: Ellen Booth (her mark). The witnesses to the codicil were Hen: Travers, John Arnatt and Thomas Bargett.   Pell, 9.

[The family of Nathaniel Holland of Watertown, named in this will, is found in Bond's Watertown, p. 302. Dr. Bond erroneously conjectures that he was a son of John and Judith Holland of Dorchester, Mass., and he has been followed by other writers.—ED.]

[I find a grant of land on record in the Virginia Land Registry Office, of 189 acres, to Edward Besse, on the south side of Chickahominy River, April 7, 1651, Book No. 2, p. 321. The names Arnott, Gouge, Booth, Perry and Travers appear in the early annals of Virginia. Francis Willis, the ancestor of the worthy Virginia family of that name, married, about the middle of the 17th century, Ann Rich.—R. A. BROCK, of Richmond, Va.]

MARGARET LANE, of London, widow, 16 January, 1661, with addition made 3 September, 1662. To be buried in the grave of my late husband, Edmond Lane, in the parish church of St. Dunstan's in the East, London. To my sister Martha, wife of William Eaton, now, I think, in New England, one hundred pounds within one year next after my decease. To her five children twenty pounds, to be equally divided amongst them, and also within the like time, to their said father or mother for their use, and whose acquittance shall be a sufficient discharge to my executor for the same. To my cousin Sarah Barett, daughter of my late brother Daniel Jenkin, deceased, and now wife of John Barett, twenty pounds. To her eldest daughter, Sarah Barett, thirty pounds, and to her son John Barett and her other daughter, Mary Barett, twenty pounds apiece. To the three children of my late sister Priscilla Haffioud, deceased, late wife of William Hammond, ten pounds apiece within one year after my decease. To Thomas Jenkins, eldest son of said deceased brother Daniel Jenkins. To my other cousin Daniel Jenkins, son of said deceased brother, &c. &c.

The addition, or codicil, mentions cousin Thomas Jenkins, of Minster, co. Kent, who is appointed overseer, the said 3 August (*sic*) 1662.

The witnesses to the will were Henry Travers, Scr. in Smithfield, Jo. Newland, Micah Machell and Samuel Fox, his servants.

Elizabeth Jenkin, relict and administratrix, with the will annexed, of Daniel Jenkins, deceased, executor of above will, received commission to administer on the estate of the above, 5 August, 1667.   Carr, 107.

["William Eaton of Staple, husbandman, Martha, his wife, three children and one servant," embarked for New England in 1637 (REG. xv. 29). They settled at Watertown (Bond's Watertown, p. 202). They had two children born in this country, making in all five children, the number named by Mrs. Lane.—ED.]

EDMUND MUNINGES, of Denge, co. Essex, the unprofitable servant of God, 2 October, 1666, proved 18 July, 1667, by Hopestill Muninges, executor. To wife Markiet ten pounds within one month after my decease, and the household goods which her father gave her, and that is to say, one bed, one table, cubbord, one guite (*sic*) chest, one brass pot, one dripping pan and four little platters. To second son, Return, twenty pounds within one year after demand be made for it. To third son, Takeheed, forty pounds within six months after my decease. To eldest daughter, Harry (*sic*) ten pounds within one year after demand be made for it. To second daughter, Rebecca, ten pounds. Eldest son, Hopestill, to be executor. If wife Markit prove with child, then to such child ten pounds at age of twenty-one years, &c. Testator made his mark in presence of William Cooch, John Spencer and Takeheed Muninge.   Carr, 95.

[Edmund Munnings, aged 40, came to New England in 1635, in the Abigail, Robert Hackwell, master, bringing with him his wife Mary, aged 30 years, daughters Mary and Anna, and son Mahalaleel, respectively nine, six and three years of age. He settled in Dorchester, where he had grants of land, among them that of Moon Island, "layd to Dorchester" by the General Court, June 2, 1641. This Island contained about twenty acres of land, and was used for pasturage, it may have been, for two and a half centuries. On the northerly side was a high bluff; southerly it was connected at very low water, by the bars or flats of the island, with the promontory of Squantum. This island is named on the Dorchester Records, in 1637 and 1638, "Mannings Moone." It is, however, no longer an island, having recently been joined to Squantum by an artificial isthmus in connection with the great Boston sewer, the reservoir of which is being built here.

Mr. Munnings had three sons, born and baptized in Dorchester, bearing the singular names of Hopestill, born April 5, 1637, Return, Sept. 7, 1640, and Take Heed, Oct. 20, 1642. The Dorchester Church Records say that Hopestill went to England. We have also evidence that the father returned and died in his native clime. Return removed to Boston. Goody Munnings, the mother, was admitted to the Dorchester church, 16. 2. 1641. On the "9 (8) 59, Mahallaeell Munings" was dismissed from this church "vnto ye new," or second "church at Boston, & dyed ye 27 (12) 59, being drowned in ye Millcreek at Boston in ye night."—Dorchester Church Records. He married Hannah, daughter of John Wiswall. The widow subsequently married Thomas Overman. By the inventory of the estate of Mahalaleel Munnings, made in 1659, and proved Jan. 30, 1660, occupying three large folio pages in volume three of Suffolk wills and inventories, pages 229 to 231, the last inventory in the book, it would appear that he invested largely in English goods, and was a prominent merchant of his day. In 1667 widow Munnings was taxed three pence, among those rated for lands at the neck in Dorchester, at a half penny per acre for the plow land. Mahalaleel went to England, it may have been with his father, and is doubtless the person who returned to New England in the Speedwell in 1656, Capt. Locke, master, notwithstanding the slight discrepancy in age, as given at the two arrivals.

The name of Edmund Munnings, on the 7th of 12 mo. 1641, is affixed to the list, consisting of seventy-one, of the inhabitants of Dorchester, who agreed that a rate of twenty pounds per annum should be paid out of the rents of Thompson's island towards the maintenance of a school in Dorchester. We are not certain that Mr. Munnings was there subsequent to 1641. On the 8th of March, 1663–4, his name stands the fifteenth on the list of rights in the New Grant of undivided land, which did belong to William Stoughton. Mr. Munnings had an interest in 10 acres, 3 quarters, 12 pole. Mr. Savage says Mr. Munnings " had probably gone home, I think, to Malden, co. Essex, there at least, was somehow connected with Joseph Hills, who before coming over had given M. £11 in a bill for bringing one bullock for the use of H." Maldon is a few miles only from Dengie, and is " locally in the hundred of Dengie." See REGISTER, i. 132 ; vii. 273 ; viii. 75 ; x. 176 ; xiv. 316 ; Fourth Report of the Record Commissioners, Boston, pages 29, 32, 106, 120 ; Savage's Genealogical Dictionary, iii. 255 ; Lewis's Topographical Dictionary of England, ii. 20 ; iii. 206 ; History of Dorchester, p. 68 ; King's Handbook of Boston Harbor, pp. 100, 106.—W. B. TRASK.]

JOHN NORRIS the elder, of Westminster, co. Middlesex, yeoman, 8 June, 1667, proved 4 (or 5) July, 1667. To son William Norris seventy-five pounds to make up the twenty-five pounds formerly given him to one hundred pounds, &c., and also house, &c., at Mooret-clack,* co. Surrey, which I bought of him, and a tenement at Tame in co. Oxford, held by lease. To son John Norris ninety pounds, to make up the ten pounds formerly given him to one hundred pounds, and a tenement at Mooretclack, bought of son William, &c. To grand child Annanias Andrews thirty pounds at age of twenty-one or day of marriage. To grand child John Andrews thirty pounds at twenty-one. To daughter Elizabeth Bell, now beyond the seas, forty pounds, if she be living and come to England to receive the same herself, and that Samuel Bell, her husband, shall not meddle or have to do therewith. To grand-child Edward Norris, son of Christopher Norris, thirty pounds, five pounds whereof to put him forth an apprentice, and the remaining twenty-five pounds, with the benefit and increase, at age of twenty-one years. Remainder to two sons, William and John Norris, equally.   Carr, 95.

Sir ROBERT PEAKE, Knight, citizen and goldsmith of London, 15 May, 1666, with codicil made 27 September, 1666, proved 26 July, 1667, by Gregory and Benjamin Peake. To my cousin and sometime servant, George Lyddall, in Virginia, gentleman, three hundred pounds in three years (one hundred pounds per year payable on Michaelmas day). To my sometime servant, Michael Tucker, in Virginia, husbandman, ten pounds. To servant Elizabeth Essington, of London, widow, twenty pounds. To my cousin James Waters, the son of Joseph Waters, fifty pounds. To my cousin —— Waters, relict of Samuel Waters, skinner, deceased, twenty pounds. To friend Doctor James Hide of Oxford, and his wife Margaret Hide, fifty pounds, and to their son Robert, my godson, fifty pounds. To my good friend and valentine Mary St. Loe, of the Parish of Dunstans in the East, London, widow, one thousand pounds in ten years (one hundred pounds a year, payable on Michaelmas day). To Mrs. Mary Burton, wife

* Mortlake.

of Mr. Thomas Burton of London, gentleman, and their son Robert, my godson, &c. To my godson Tristram Huddlestone, son of Nicholas Huddlestone of London, skinner, &c. To good friend Thomas Pulteney, of London, salter, and his wife, &c. To Edward Hunt, of London, vintner, and Elizabeth his wife. To my friend Edward Jerman. To good friend Richard Loans, of London. To John Peake, Esq., eldest son of Sir William Peake, Knight, of London, Alderman, and his brother Benjamin, second son of Sir William, &c. To Mrs. Elizabeth Vanbrugh, wife of Mr. Giles Vanbrugh, merchant, both my singular good friends—and to others.

Carr, 96.

[Much about the English family of Waters will be found in Emmerton and Waters's Gleaning from English Records, pp. 121–30.—ED.]

[In the Virginia Land Registry Office the following grants are recorded: George Lyddal, "Gentleman," 1750 acres in York County, Nov. 25, 1654; "Captain" George Lyddal, 2390 acres in New Kent County (formed from York County in 1654) Jan. 20, 1657. Book No. 4, p. 214. The name Lyddall is a favored Christian name in a number of Virginian families, notably in the Bowles and Bacon. I find on record in Henrico County court, in June, 1754, the will of Langston Bacon. Wife Sarah is named, and also as Executors, Nathaniel Bacon, Lyddal Bacon and John Williamson. John Lyddall Bacon, Esq. is at this date President of the State Bank of Richmond.—R. A. BROCK, of Richmond, Va.]

WILLIAM BURGES, of South River, County of Ann Arundell, Province of Maryland, 11 July, 1685. To son Edward Burges five thousand pounds of tobacco in casque within one year, provided he deliver to my executors one half of certain live stock that belonged to the estate of George Puddington, deceased. To William and Elizabeth, the children of said son Edward. To son George Burges five thousand pounds of tobacco in casque, within one year. To sons William, John, Joseph, Benjamin and Charles, and daughters Elizabeth, Ann and Susanna Burges. To daughter Susannah, the wife of Major Nicholas Sewall, five pounds in money and my seal ring. To my grandson Charles Sewall and my granddaughter Jane Sewall. To son William my messuage, &c., near South River, Ann Arundell county, which I purchased of one George Westall, and on a part whereof is a town called London. Wife Ursula to have the use of it till son William accomplish the age of twenty-one years. (It is again referred to as the town or port of London.) Also to son William a tract in Baltimore County, near land of Col. George Wells, containing four hundred and eighty acres. To son John a tract near Herring Creek, in Ann Arundell County, containing eight hundred acres. To son Joseph a tract lately bought of Richard Beard, gentleman, near the South River, &c., containing thirteen hundred and forty acres. To son Benjamin a tract near the Ridge, in Ann Arundell County, which I bought of Thomas Besson, containing three hundred acres, and another near the head of South River, containing four hundred acres. To son Charles my interest in land bought of Vincent Low, near the head of Sasafras River, in Cecil County, formerly granted to Nicholas Painter, since deceased, and containing sixteen hundred acres, also a tract lately purchased by me from said Vincent Lowe, on the south side of the Susquehanock River in said county of Baltimore, containing five hundred acres. (These sons appear to have been all under twenty-one years of age.) Wife Ursula to be executrix, and Major Nicholas Sewall, Major Nicholas Cassaway and Captain Henry Hanslapp, supervisors. The witnesses were Thomas Francies, Michael Cusack, John Harrison, William Elridge (his mark) and John Edwards.

5 July, 1689. Emanavit Comissio Micajæ Perry attornato unice depu-

tato per Ursulam Moore als Burges (uxorem Mordecai Moore) jam in com. de Ann Arundell in Provincia de Maryland comorand. relictam et executricem, &c. &c. Ent. 91.

THOMAS BRINLEY, of Datchett, co. Bucks, Esq., 13 September, 1661, with codicil of 16 October, 1661, proved 11 December, 1661. My third of tenements in the town of Newcastle upon Tyne, and two thirds of the manor of Burton in Yorkshire, to eldest son, Francis Brinley and his heirs. My half of the township or manor of Wakerfield, heretofore parcell of the Lordship of Raby, and my lands and tenements in Wakerfield, county and Bishoprick of Durham, purchased in the names of William Wase of Durham and of Robert Worrall, lately deceased, and of Michael Lambcroft, lately deceased, and of John Maddocke, of Cuddington, co. Chester, in trust for the use of me, the said Thomas Brinley, and the said Robert Worrall and our heirs and assigns forever, to my wife, Anne Brinley, during her natural life ; at her death to eldest son, Francis Brinley. My lands in Horton and Stanwell, in the several counties of Middlesex and Bucks, &c., by me purchased of Henry Bulstrode of Horton, to wife Anne for life ; then to my second son, Thomas Brinley, a lease of ninety-nine years. Certain other lands, &c., lately bought of James Styles, the elder, of Langley, to wife Anne ; at her death to my third son, William Brinley. A legacy to daughter Mary Silvester, widow, and her daughter, my granddaughter, Mary Silvester the younger, who are both left destitute of subsistence by the decease of my said daughter's late husband, Peter Silvester, &c. To the children of my daughter Grissell, the now wife of Nathaniel Silvester, gentleman, dwelling in New England, in the Parts of America, in an island called Shelter Island, one hundred pounds within one year after my decease.

The witnesses to the will were Robert Style and Rose Baker. In the codicil he bequeaths legacies to his brother Lawrence Brinley and Richard Brinley his son, both of London, merchants, to the intent that they shall with all convenient speed sell that half of said lands, &c. (in Wakerfield), for the best rate and value that they can get for the same, &c.

The witnesses to this codicil were William Wase, Budd Wase, William Carter and William Brinley. The will was proved by the widow, Anne Brinley. May, 193.

[Thomas Brinley, who made this will, was the father of Francis Brinley, who emigrated to Barbadoes, but, the climate not being "suited to his habits and constitution," came to New England and settled at Newport, R. I., as early as 1652. Francis Brinley wrote an "Account of the Settlements and Governments in and about the Lands of Narraganset Bay," which is printed in the Massachusetts Historical Collections, 1st S., vol. v. pp. 217-20. A catalogue of his library is printed in the REGISTER, xii. 75-8.

Brief genealogies of the Brinley family will be found in Bridgman's King's Chapel Epitaphs, 219-228, and in the Heraldic Journal, vol. ii. pp. 31-2. The former is by the Hon. Francis Brinley, now of Newport, R. I. From it we learn that Thomas Brinley, "one of the auditors of the Revenue of King Charles the First and of King Charles the Second," besides the children named above in his will— Francis, Thomas, William, Mary, widow of Peter Sylvester, and Grizzell, wife of Nathaniel Sylvester—had three other daughters who lived to be married, namely : Rose, who married Giles Baker, lord of the manor of Riple in Kent ; one, christian name unknown, who married William Coddington, governor of Rhode Island ; and the other, whose christian name is also unknown, who married Richard Hackle, Esq. Grizzell was baptized at St. James's Church, Clerkenwell, Jan. 6, 1635-6. Abstracts of the wills of Peter and Nathaniel Sylvester will be found later in this article.—ED.]

LAURENCE BRINLEY, citizen and haberdasher of London, 10 August, 1662, proved 11 December, 1662, by the oaths of Samuel and Richard

Brinley, sons and executors named in the will. The following bequests appear: to Mary Limbrey twenty pounds ; to Philip Limbrey, of Virginia, twenty pounds ; to my sister Susan Gregory, of Exon (Exeter), widow, ten pounds ; to my cousin Elizabeth Brinley, of London, widow, and her two daughters, twenty pounds apiece to buy them a ring ; to Master Calamy, my dearly beloved pastor and faithful minister of Jesus Christ, five pounds ; to poor Presbyterian ministers out of their places for conscience sake, thirty pounds, to be disposed of according to the discretion of my executors with Mr. Calamy ; to my daughter Jenne Jackson, the wife of ——, the sum of twenty pounds, and, in case Weaver's Hall money cometh in, eighty pounds ; to my daughter-in-law Elizabeth Earnly, widow, the sum of twenty pounds ; to my son Nathaniel Brinley fifty pounds when he cometh out of his time. I do constitute and appoint my two sons Samuel and Richard Brinley to be my executors, and give ten pounds apiece to them. The residue, &c., to my five children, viz., Nathaniel, Susannah, Hester, Philip and Isaac Brinley, according to equal proportions. My real estate of land in Ireland and England, after my decease, to be sold according to the uttermost value, for the payment of my wife's and the children's portions.

The witnesses to this will were William Webb, Richard Brinley and John Jackson.   Laud, 151.

Nathaniel, son of Laurence Brinley, of London, merchant, was a legatee to the amount of five pounds, under the will of Henry Hazlewood, citizen and currier of London, proved in the same year as the foregoing will.   Laud, 108.

[From Lipscombe's History of Buckinghamshire, published in 1847.] In an account of the church at Datchett are found the following copies of inscriptions on a slab in the floor of the nave :

Here lieth the body of Thomas Brinley, Esq., who was one of the auditors of the Revenue of King Charles the First and of King Charles y° Second. Born in the City of Exeter. He married Anne, youngest daughter of Wm Ware* of Petworth, in Sussex, gent., who had issue by her five sons and seven daughters. He dyed the 15th day of October in the year of our Lord 1661.

Here also lieth buried y° body of the above said William Ware,* who died the 19th of Sept. 1642, aged 62 years and 5 months.

Vol. iv. page 441.

[From Visitation of London, 1634, vol. i., printed by the Harleian Soc.]

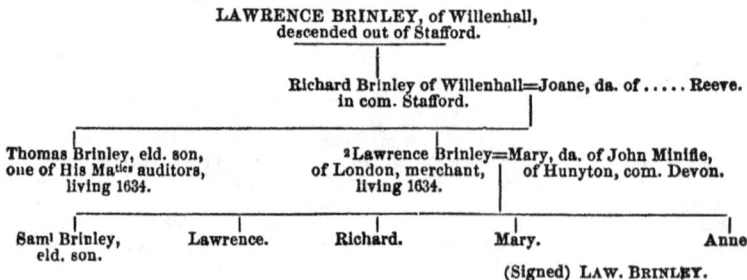

LAWRENCE BRINLEY, of Willenhall,
descended out of Stafford.

Richard Brinley of Willenhall=Joane, da. of . . . . . Reeve.
in com. Stafford.

Thomas Brinley, eld. son, one of His Maties auditors, living 1634.

²Lawrence Brinley=Mary, da. of John Minifie, of London, merchant, living 1634. of Hunyton, com. Devon.

Saml Brinley, eld. son.   Lawrence.   Richard.   Mary.   Anne

(Signed) LAW. BRINLEY.

* This is undoubtedly a mistake for Wase; for a pedigree of which family see Berry's Sussex Genealogies, p. 125, and Dallaway's History of the Western Division of Sussex, Vol. 2, Part ii. p. 123. It will be noticed that William Wase and Budd Wase were witnesses of Thomas Brinley's will.—H. F. W.

[From Randall Holmes's Heraldic Collections for Cheshire, Harleian MS., No. 2119 British Museum.]

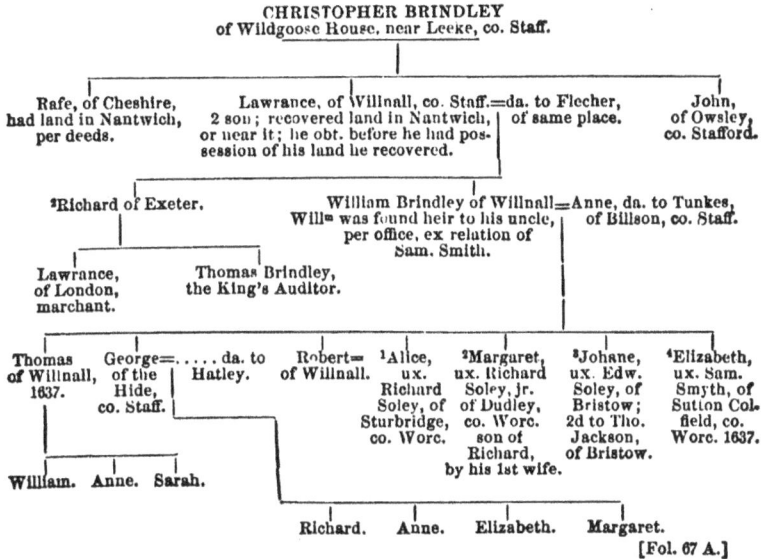

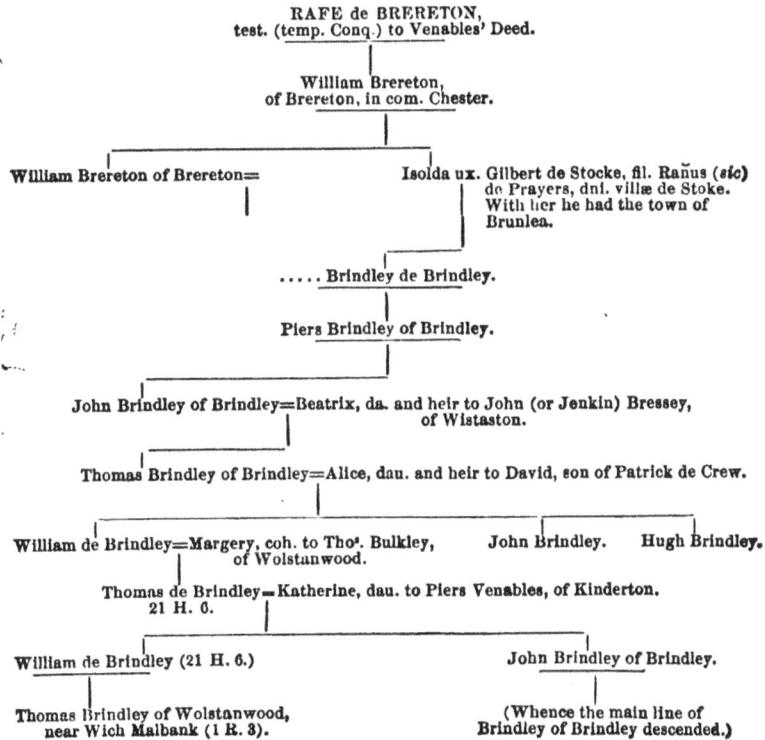

CHRISTOPHER BRINDLEY
of Wildgoose House, near Leeke, co. Staff.

Rafe, of Cheshire, had land in Nantwich, per deeds.

Lawrance, of Willnall, co. Staff.=da. to Flecher, 2 son; recovered land in Nantwich, of same place. or near it; he obt. before he had possession of his land he recovered.

John, of Owsley, co. Stafford.

²Richard of Exeter.

William Brindley of Willnall=Anne, da. to Tunkes, Will™ was found heir to his uncle, of Billson, co. Staff. per office, ex relation of Sam. Smith.

Lawrance, of London, marchant.

Thomas Brindley, the King's Auditor.

Thomas of Willnall, 1637.

George=..... da. to of the Hatley. Hide, co. Staff.

Robert= of Willnall.

¹Alice, ux. Richard Soley, of Sturbridge, co. Worc.

²Margaret, ux. Richard Soley, jr. of Dudley, co. Worc. son of Richard, by his 1st wife.

³Johane, ux. Edw. Soley, of Bristow; 2d to Tho. Jackson, of Bristow.

⁴Elizabeth, ux. Sam. Smyth, of Sutton Colfield, co. Worc. 1637.

William. Anne. Sarah.

Richard. Anne. Elizabeth. Margaret.
[Fol. 67 A.]

RAFE de BRERETON,
test. (temp. Conq.) to Venables' Deed.

William Brereton, of Brereton, in com. Chester.

William Brereton of Brereton=

Isolda ux. Gilbert de Stocke, fil. Rañus (*sic*) de Prayers, dni. villæ de Stoke. With her he had the town of Brunlea.

..... Brindley de Brindley.

Piers Brindley of Brindley.

John Brindley of Brindley=Beatrix, da. and heir to John (or Jenkin) Bressey, of Wistaston.

Thomas Brindley of Brindley=Alice, dau. and heir to David, son of Patrick de Crew.

William de Brindley=Margery, coh. to Tho⁴. Bulkley, of Wolstanwood.

John Brindley.   Hugh Brindley.

Thomas de Brindley=Katherine, dau. to Piers Venables, of Kinderton. 21 H. 6.

William de Brindley (21 H. 6.)

John Brindley of Brindley.

Thomas Brindley of Wolstanwood, near Wich Malbank (1 R. 3).

(Whence the main line of Brindley of Brindley descended.)

[Abstracts of deeds in evidence.]   William, son of Thomas de Brindley, gives to Rich[d] Reffs, parson of Bastomley, all his lands, tenements, &c., in the Hundred of Wich Malbank.   Dated at Wolstanwood on the Feast of Epiphany—21 H. 6.

A lease of a messuage in Rottenrow in Wich Malbank, by Thomas Brindley of Wolstanwood, near Wich Malbank, to Hugh Boston of the Wich, gentleman, dated 6 February, 1 R. 3.

A lease of Crofts in Copenhall and Wolstanwood, and a messuage and two crofts in Wighterson, near Nantwich, made by Thomas Brindeley of Wolstanwood aforesaid, to Hugh Boston, gent. aforesaid, of same date.

Mr. Garside to pay me for this pedigree for Mr. Sam. Smyth of Sutton Coldfield, 1637.   Ff. 40, 67 A. and 68.

PETER SILVESTER of London, merchant, now inhabitant in the parish of Saint James, Dukes Place, in London, 26 January, 1657, proved 11 February, 1657.   Whereas my dear mother, Mary Silvester, of London, widow, did oblige herself by promise to give unto me the sum of one thousand pounds of lawful money of England, for which said sum of one thousand pounds, &c., my said mother, at my request, hath this day become bound by obligation of the penalty of two thousand pounds unto Thomas Middleton of Stratford Bow, in the County of Middlesex, Esquire, conditioned for the payment of the said one thousand pounds within six years after the date of the said bond unto me or to Mary my now wife, &c. &c. I do give and bequeath the said sum to wife Mary.   To only daughter Mary six hundred pounds at the age of one and twenty years or day of marriage.   If she die in the mean time, then two hundred pounds of it to my dear and loving wife, one hundred pounds to my brother Nathaniel Silvester, one hundred pounds to brother Joshua Silvester, one hundred and fifty pounds to brother Giles Silvester, and fifty pounds to my sister Cartwright.   The said sum of six hundred pounds to be sent to my loving brother Constant Silvester, now resident in the Barbados, he to become bound for the payment, as above.   To each and every of my own brothers and brothers-in-law forty shillings apiece to make each of them a ring to wear in remembrance of me.   To my uncle Jeofrie Silvester the sum of twenty-five pounds.   To my cousin Joseph Gascoigne fifteen pounds.   To my Aunt Gascoigne five pounds, and to her daughter Anne Gascoigne five pounds.   To loving friend Richard Duke, scrivener, forty shillings to make him a ring.   To the poor of the parish of St. James, Duke's Place, five pounds.   Thomas Middleton, Esq., to be sole executor, and loving uncle Nathaniel Arnold overseer, and I give him fifty pounds.

The witnesses to the above were Edw: Warren, Hum: Richardson and Richard Duke, scr.   Wootton, 95.

GILES SILVESTER, of London, merchant, 2 March, 1670, proved 26 May, 1671.   To such child or children as my wife now goeth with, the sum of three hundred pounds at his, her or their age of one and twenty years, if sons, and at age of twenty-one, or on day of marriage, which shall first happen, if daughters.   To my nephew, Constant Silvester, the four pictures that were my late fathers.   The residue of the estate to loving wife, Anne Silvester, who is appointed executrix.   I entreat and appoint my dear and loving brother, Constant Silvester Esquire, and my good friend Redmaine Burrell to be overseers.   To each of them forty shillings, for rings.

Grant of administration on the estate of the above was made to Constant Silvester, natural and lawful brother of the deceased, the widow Anne Silvester having renounced the executorship.   Duke, 68.

CONSTANT SILVESTER made his will 7 April, 1671, proved 7 October, 1671, by Grace Silvester, relict and executrix. All my lands, plantations, houses and tenements in the island of Barbados, &c., to wife Grace and to Henry Walrond, Sen' Esq., brother of the said Grace, Col. Richard Hawkins, Samuel Farmer, Esq., and Mr. Francis Raynes (being all of the said island of Barbados) for one thousand years from the day of my decease, in trust, &c.; wife Grace to enjoy one moiety during her natural life, and my eldest son, Constant, to enjoy two thirds of the other moiety during his mother's life, and my second son, Humphrey Silvester, to have and hold the remaining third of said other moiety during his mother's life. After her death Constant to have two thirds of the whole, and Humphrey the remaining third. If there should be more sons, the eldest son (in that case) to have a double share, and each other son a single share. If wife Grace should marry again, then she to have one third, instead of one half, of the above described property. To daughters Grace and Mary two thousand pounds sterling each at day of marriage, or at age of twenty-one years, and, over and above that, the sum of one hundred pounds sterling each, to buy them a jewel at the age of sixteen years.

Item, I give and bequeath to my brother Nathaniel Silvester, his heirs and assigns forever, one sixth part of all the lands which I and my said brother hold in partnership in Shelter Island, upon the coast of New England; so that, whereas he had a third part of the said lands before, now he shall have a moiety. And the remaining moiety of the said lands I give and bequeath to my two sons before named, equally, and to the heirs of their bodies lawfully begotten, forever; and, for want of such issue, to my brother Joshua Silvester and the heirs of his body, forever; and, for want of such issue, to my brother Nathaniel, his heirs and assigns, forever. To brother Joshua Silvester eight hundred pounds sterling. To my sister Mary Cartwright a mortgage on the estate made over to me by her deceased husband, Isaac Cartwright, during her natural life, and after her decease to my nephew, Constant Cartwright, he paying out of the same to each of his sisters, Mary and Anne, two hundred pounds sterling at their day of marriage or arrival at age of twenty-one years, whichever shall first happen. To my nephew Richard Kett, six hundred pounds sterling, and sixty pounds sterling per annum so long as he shall remain upon my Plantation after my decease, to keep the accompts thereof and taking care no injury or prejudice be done to the estate by any without giving notice thereof to my trustees before-named.

Wife Grace to be executrix so long as she remain unmarried, then the other trustees, &c. To each of these fifty pounds sterling apiece to buy them what they shall think fit to remember me by after my decease.

The witnesses were Henry Walrond, Grace Walrond, Peter Blackler, Anne Guillett, Dorothy Marshall, Samuel Ainseworth, jun' and Will. Swepson.

17 June 1702 emanavit commissio Dominæ Gratiæ Pickering, uxori Domini Henrici Pickering, Baronetti, filiæ naturali et legitimæ dicti Constantii Silvester defuncti, etc. etc.   Duke, 124.

In the Chancel Aisle of the church in Brampton (co. Huntington), is a stone with this inscription: " Here lieth the body of Constant Silvester Esq" who departed this life the 2nd September, 1671." The church Register contains the following: " Mr Humphrey Silvester, son of Mr Constant

Silvester & Mrs Grace his wife, was buried April ye sixteenth 1673." "Mr Constant Silvester was buried the 4th day of September a: d: 1671."

Add. MS. 24493, Fol. 341, Brit. Mus. (Joseph Hunter's Colls.).

The following is an abstract of the last will and testament of NATHANIEL SYLVESTER of Shelter Island, proved 2 October, 1680. He calls himself the right, true and lawful owner and proprietor of one moiety or half part, in fee simple, of all that Island whereon he was then dwelling, formerly called Manhansack-Ahaqua-Shuwamock, now Shelter Island, &c. &c. also of one moiety or half part, in possession and reversion, of one other Island, formerly called Robert's Island. He gives and bequeaths to his endeared wife Grizzell Sylvester, Francis Brinley, James Lloyd, Isaac Arnold, Lewis Morris and Daniel Gould, all the above described property, and also the other moiety or half part of Shelter Island which is claimed in partnership by my brother Constant Sylvester and Thomas Middleton, or any part or parts thereof which may happen to fall due unto me from the said Constant Sylvester and Thomas Middleton by reason of the great disbursements made by me for the said moiety, &c., in their behalf since the year 1652 until this present year, and likewise by reason of the great sums of money which my brother Constant doth in particular stand indebted unto me, as per accounts doth appear, and furthermore by reason of the confiscation of the said moiety, &c. &c., by the Dutch men of war at their taking of New York with their fleet of nineteen men of war, they also taking and surprising the said moiety, &c. &c., as by the chief commanders of the said Dutch men of war their instrument of confiscation and Bill of Sale given unto me for the same, as doth at large appear, the said commanders also sending one of their men of war to Shelter Island where the Captain landed with about fifty soldiers, taking possession of the said moiety, &c., and to strike the greater dread in my family they beset my house, the better to obtain the money which they forced from me and myself constrained to pay to prevent their suing of said moiety, &c. &c. The above described property is to be held in trust for certain purposes. Reference is made to his wife's jointure, as by a deed left in hands of brother William Coddington of Rhode Island may at large appear. My children to be brought up in the fear of God, and to have such education bestowed upon them as may be conveniently gotten in these parts of the world, and as shall seem meet to my endeared wife, their mother, &c. My brother Joshua to be conveniently maintained both with diet, lodging, clothing and necessaries, decent and becoming him, as hitherto he hath enjoyed, that he may in no manner of way want, and in no wise put off from the Island, unless he shall think good to live elsewhere, &c. To son Giles (certain property); to son Nathaniel; to son Peter; to daughter Patience at age of twenty-one or marriage; to daughter Elizabeth at twenty-one or marriage; to daughter Mary at twenty-one or marriage; to daughter Ann at twenty-one or marriage; to daughter Mercy at twenty-one or marriage. To sons Constant and Benjamin at twenty-one. Son Nathaniel (a minor) to have certain bricks lying at Thomas Moore Senior's farm and at the Oyster Pond. Son Peter (also a minor) to have part of the said bricks. Property at Southold spoken of. The executors of the above will to be wife Grizzell Sylvester, brother-in-law Francis Brinley, son-in-law James Lloyd, cousin Isaac Arnold, Lewis Morris and Daniel Gould.

The witnesses were John Colling, Ann Colling (by mark), Peter Aldritch and Jaques Guillott. These made deposition 2 October, 1680, under authority given by the Governor 2 September, 1680.

Additional MS. 24493, Fol. 344, British Museum (Joseph Hunter's Collections).

[On the 9 of June, 1651, Thomas Middleton, Thomas Rouse, Constant Sylvester and Nathaniel Sylvester, purchased Shelter Island, on the east end of Long Island, for sixteen hundred pounds of good merchantable Muscovado sugar, from Stephen Goodyeare, of New Haven, who had purchased it May 18, 1641, from the agent of the Earl of Sterling. Full particulars of the transactions of Nathaniel Sylvester in relation to Shelter Island will be found in Thompson's Long Island, vol. i. pp. 364-9. Nathaniel Sylvester died in March, 1680, according to Thompson, who gives an account of his descendants. Savage, in his Genealogical Dictionary (iv. 99), says : " There is no slight reason to believe this Nathaniel to be the son of the celebrated poet Joshua Sylvester, translator of the divine rhapsodies of Du Bartas.'' I do not know what reason Mr. Savage, who was a cautious genealogist, had for thinking so. It is possible that he was a son, or more likely a grandson.—ED.]

SAMUEL WARD, the elder, of Ipswich, clerk, 19 October, 1639, proved 24 April, 1640, by Nathaniel and Joseph Ward, sons of the deceased and executors of his will; to whom he left all his books, all his loadstones, shells, papers, pictures and maps. Item—I will and bequeath all that money which doth belong to me upon the house where I now dwell, situate in Ipswich aforesaid (which money was given by many gentlemen and townsmen my friends), to be equally divided between them and their heirs forever ; also all my lands and houses in Brickelsea, both free and copy, equally, &c. &c., on condition that every year during the natural life of Deborah, my loving wife, and Samuel Ward, my eldest son, they pay to the said Deborah and Samuel twenty pounds a year apiece,—to either of them at four times or terms in the year,—upon the feast-day of the Nativity of our Lord God, upon the feast day of the Annunciation of our Blessed Lady St. Mary the Virgin, upon the feast day of St. John the Baptist, and upon the feast day of St. Michael the Archangel, by even and equal portions, &c., at the now dwelling house of Mr. Robert Knapp in Ipswich ; or, in lieu of said twenty pounds a year to son Samuel, to keep and maintain him in a comely and decent manner for and during his natural life, at the election and choice of the said Nathaniel and Joseph. To my mother forty shillings yearly, to be paid her at her now dwelling house in Weathersfield, quarterly. My watch to my daughter Deborah, and my fair English Bible, printed anno domini 1633, to my said daughter Deborah, only my wife to have the use of said bible during her life. Sundry chattels to daughter Abigail, after decease of wife. All the plate and wearing clothes to son Nathaniel. My Greek Testament, of Robert Stephens print, to my brother John Ward. My best gloves to my son Robert Bolton. A Greek Testament to son John Bolton. To Margaret my maid, twenty shillings. To John Boggas, my servant, ten shillings. To the poor of the parish of St. Mary Tower and of St. Mary Key in Ipswich, either of them twenty shillings apiece. To Mr. Robert Knapp, my ancient friend, a pair of gloves of five shillings price, or a book of the same value.

The witnesses to the signature were Thomasin Willis and Daniel Ray.

Coventry, 47.

[The Rev. Samuel Ward, B.D., the maker of the above will, was the town preacher at Ipswich, and a celebrated Puritan author. He was the eldest son of the Rev. John Ward of Haverhill, in Suffolk, and brother of the Rev. Nathaniel Ward, author of the Massachusetts Body of Liberties, or code of laws adopted in 1641. Samuel Ward married, January 2, 1604-5, Deborah Bolton, widow, of Isleham, Cambridgeshire. It seems from this will that she had two sons, Robert and John Bolton, by her first husband. For further details of his life, see a brief memoir of Rev. Samuel Ward, appended to the editor's memoir of the Rev. Nathaniel Ward (Albany, 1868). An abstract of his will, furnished by the late Col. Chester, will be found on pages 154–5 of that work.—ED.]

MARGARET SIMONDS, late widow of John Simonds, late of Kunckles Alley in London, deceased, her nuncupative will, August, 1665 ; To daughter Margaret Burton, who is now beyond the seas. Proved 6 March, 1667, by Margaret Burton. \   Hene 36.

TIMOTHY SNAPE, London, yeoman, one of the sons of Edmond Snape, late of the parish of St. Saviors, in Southwark, co. Surrey, clerk, deceased, being bound forth on a voyage to Virginia in the parts beyond the seas, executed his will 10 September, 1624, proved 9 July, 1629. He names brothers and sisters, Samuel, Nathaniel and John Snape, Hannah, now wife of John Barker, citizen and haberdasher of London, and Sarah Snape, spinster.   Ridley, 67.

SAMUEL IVE, of Portsmouth, 13 July, 1667, proved 17 August, 1667, by John Ive, brother and executor. To sister Sarah Putland, of Strood, wife of Elias Putland, four score pounds. To brother John Ive. To Mary Alderidge or any other of our kindred. To my brother Thomas Ive twenty pounds. To Mary Alderidge, my sister's daughter, twelve pence. To Robert Reynolds, carver, all my working tools and the time of my servant John Rauly which he has yet to serve, only six months of the time I do give to the said John Rauly. To Mʳⁱˢ Reynolds what goods I have in the house, except my desk and trunk of linen and wearing clothes, which I do give to my brother Thomas Ive if he live to come home ; or, else, to my brother John Ive, to whom all the residue.   Carr, 107.

[Much about the Ive family will be found in Emmerton and Waters's Gleanings from English Records, pp. 60–1.—ED.]

WILLIAM QUICKE, citizen and grocer of London, 26 October, 1614, proved 21 January, 1614. He mentions daughter Apphia, wife Elizabeth, daughter Elizabeth, daughter Debora, brother Nicholas Quicke and his children, the rest of brothers' and sisters' children, kinswoman Mary Marshall the younger, brother-in-law Thomas Hodges, merchant taylor, &c.

" I give and bequeath to and amongest my three daughters aforesaid, all my pte of all such landes, tenements and hereditaments as shall from time to time be recovered, planted and inhabited eyther in Virginia or in the somer Ilandes heretofore called the Bermoodas togither wᵗʰ all such mynes and mineralls of gold, silver and other mettalls or treasure, perles, precious stones or any kinde of wares and merchandices, cõmodities or profitts whatsoever which shalbe obtayned or gotten in or by the said voyages and plantations according to the adventure and portion of money that I have employed to that use."   Rudd, 1.

[John Smith, in his " Generall Historie," Ed. 1626, page 126, gives the name of William Quicke in the List of the Adventurers for Virginia.—R. A. BROCK, of Richmond, Va.]

NATHANIEL WARDE, of Old Winsor, co. Berks, Doctor in Divinity, 3 December, nineteenth of K. Charles, proved 11 February, 1667. He mentions wife Susanna and marriage contract, a bond of one thousand pounds unto Mʳ Thomas Hanchett and Mʳ Solomon Smith, in trust for said wife. Son Nathaniel to be executor. The witnesses were Robert Aldridge, Elizabeth Reynolds and (the mark of) Edward Stokes.   Hene, 26.

SMALEHOPE BIGG, of Cranbrooke in the County of Kent, clothier, 8 May, 1638, proved 3 October, 1638, by John Bigg. Brother John Bigg, of Maidstone, to be executor. To the poor of Cranbrooke ten pounds. To my Aunt Mary Bridger of West Peckham and her two sons, Robert and Thomas Betts; to my kinswomen, the wife of William Hunt of Brenchley, Anne Bottinge of Brenchley, widow, and the wife of John Saxby of Leeds; to Judith, wife of Thomas Tadnall, late of Dover; to Godfrey Martin of Old Romney and his sisters; to the children of Robert Pell of New Romney, jurat, deceased.

To my kinsfolk Thomas Bate, of Lydd, James Bate, Clement Bate, the wife of William Batchelor, John Compton, Edward White and Martha his wife, all which are now resident in New England, twenty shillings each. I give ten pounds to be distributed to them or to others in New England by my mother and my brother John Stow. To Peter Master of Cranbrook who married my sister. To my mother Rachell Bigg one hundred pounds. Lands &c. at Rye in County Sussex to my wife Ellin. To my sisters Patience Foster and Elizabeth Stow in New England. To Hopestill Foster, son of my sister three hundred pounds. To Thomas and John Stow, sons of my sister Stow two hundred pounds each. To Elizabeth Stow and the other three children (under age) of my said sister Stow. Lands in Horsmonden to my brother John Bigg. Lands at Wittersham, Lidd and Cranbrook to Samuel Bigg, my brother's son, at the age of twenty-three years. My friends John Nowell of Rye, gentleman, James Holden and Thomas Bigg the elder, of Cranbrook, clothiers, to be overseers. To my cousin Hunt's children and John Saxbey's children; to the two sons of my Aunt Betts; to my cousin Bottenn's children; to my cousin Pell's children, viz., Joan Pell, Elizabeth Pell, Richard Pell and Thomas Baytope's wife.

After a hearing of the case between John Bigg, brother and executor of the one part, and Hellen alias Ellen Bigg (the relict), Patience Bigg alias Foster, wife of Richard Foster, and Elizabeth Bigg alias Stow, wife of Richard (*sic*) Stow, testator's sisters, of the other part, sentence was pronounced to confirm the will 4 April, 1639 (the widow having previously died, as shown by date of probate of her own will which follows).

Consistory Court, Canterbury, Vol. 51, Leaf 115.

ELLEN BIGGE, of Cranbrooke, widow of Smalehope Bigge, of Cranbrook, clothier, 24 November, proved 12 February, 1638. To be buried in Cranbrooke Cemetery, near my husband. To Samuel Bigge, son of my brother John Bigge, of Maidstone. Lands and tenements at Rye in the County of Sussex to my only sister Mary, wife of Edward Benbrigg, jurat, of Rye, for her life, remainder to her son John Benbridge; to Anne Benbridge, alias Burrish, and Elizabeth and Mary Benbrig, daughters of my aforesaid sister Mary. To John Benbrigg, clerk, Thomas Benbrigg and Samuel Benbrigg, sons of my deceased sister Elizabeth; also her daughters Anne Benbrigge, alias Puttland, and Elizabeth Benbrigg (the last named under age). My said sister Mary Benbrigg and her son John Benbrigg to be executors. To Peter Master, son of my brother Peter Master, of Cranbrooke; to my sister-in-law Katherine Master. To William Dallett (son of my dec'd sister Bridgett) and his son (under age). To William Edwards, son of my sister Mercy. To Thomas Pilcher, Elizabeth Pilcher alias Beinson, Judith Pilcher alias Burges, and Anne Pilcher, son and daughters of my uncle John Pilcher of Rye, deceased. To Mary, wife of Robert Cushman and their son Thomas (under age). James Holden of

Cranbrooke, clothier, and my brother-in-law Peter Master of Cranbrooke, mercer, to be overseers.

Archdeaconry, Canterbury, Vol. 70, Leaf 482.

Will of JOHN BIGG, of Maidstone, co. Kent., jurat. begun Aug. 17, 1640, finished March 27, 1641, probated Feb. 7, 1642.

Mr. Andrew Broughton, Ex'., friends James Bolden of Cranbrook and Thomas Lamb of Staplehurst, overseers. Legacies to Roger Ball, John Bowden, William Whetston, Samuel Browne, Samuel Skelton, widow Clarke, widow Peirce, Susan the wife of Daniel Clarke my ancient servant, William Lawraman, William Ayerst, Richard Weller Sen'., of Cranbrook, —Cheeseman, my porter and fetcher in of my water, old goodman Greensmith of Loose, widow Darby of Staplehurst, old goodman Humphry or his wife of Harresham, widow Warren late of Sandwich, Mr. Harber Minister of Raish beside Mallinge, Mr. Elmeston schoolmaster of Maidstone, Mr. Goodacker and Mr. Bramston, brother to widow Charleton of Loose, "two poore godlie ministers, I think of Sussex," Damarys Wilson now living with me and her father and mother, Mary Tatnell daughter of Thomas T. now living with me and her sister Judah Tatnell.

Also to Packnam Johnson, now living with me, my sister Johnson his mother, my cousin Milles widow, living at Raysh, my cousin Botten, widow, living at Brenchley, my aunt Bredger of Peckham, my cousin Hunt's wife of Brenchley, my cousin Saxbey's wife of Leeds, my cousin Gaskyne and my cousin Betes living about Lengly. My mother Bigg, my sister Foster, my brother Stowe, all these living in New England. Hopestill Foster, Thomas Stowe, John Stowe, Nathaniel Stowe, Samuel Stowe, my brother Stowe's two daughters, Elizabeth Stowe, Thankful Stowe.

My wife Sibella Bigg. Elizabeth Pell dwelling with me. My cousin Beatupes wife of Tenterden. Marie Terrie in New England. My cousin Godfrey Martyne, my cousin Smith's wife of Ladomi, late Saltman. My cousin William Boysse. John Crumpe, son of Thomas Crumpe. My brother Beaccons. Cousin Yonge of Canterbury. My brother Peter Masters of Cranbrooke and his four children. My cousin James Bate of New England. My cousin Lyne of New England. Clement Bate and William Bachelor. Edward Whitt, John Compton, John Moore, Thomas Bridgden, Goodman Beale that went from Cranbrook and my cousin Betts there. My brother Robert Swinocke and his wife. Mr. John London. My mother Mrs. Dorothie Maplisden, my brother Mr. Jervis Maplisden and his wife, my brother Mr. Nynion Butcher and his wife, Mr. Thomas Swynocke, my brother in law, Mr. Wilson and his wife, my brother Wildinge, Mrs. Marie Duke. Mr. Elmeston of Cranbrook. James Holden of Cranbrook. My brother Smallhope Bigg, late of Cranbrook. My brother Beaccon's will. Mr. William Randolph. Mr. Robert Drayner.

Crane, 11.

A copy of this will was printed in the REGISTER, xxix. 256.—H. F. W.

[See will of Christopher Gibson, Suffolk Probate Records, vi. 64. He and Hopestill Foster, Jr., married sisters, daughters of James Bate.

For the foregoing abstracts of the wills of Smalehope Bigg and his widow, Mrs. Ellen Bigge, the readers of the REGISTER are indebted to the kindness of Joseph Eedes, Esq., who has, moreover, given me numerous clews and references to other

American names, to be followed up hereafter. Indeed all my fellow workers here are constantly exhibiting proof of that good will and kindly fellowship which my experience, in America as well as England, has shown me to be characteristic of the brotherhood of antiquaries.   HENRY F. WATERS.

By an instrument dated Sept. 10, 1653, recorded with Suffolk Deeds, lib. i. fol. 318, Hopestill Foster of the one part and Thomas, Nathaniel and Samuel Stowe of the other part, all of New England, for the purpose of ending the "many & vncomfortable differences" which have arisen concerning the wills of their deceased uncles Mr. Smallhope Bigg and Mr. John Bigg both of the County of Kent in old England, and which "haue occasioned much trouble each to other p'tio & likewise vncomfortable suits att Lawe," agree that each party shall "enioy what they now enioy namely Hopestill ffoster or his assignes the one half of all those lands In Crambrooke Withersham & Lidd wch m^r Smallhop [ ] Bigg gaue vnto Samuell Bigg his Brothers Sonne & Thomas Stowe and his sonne John as heires to John Stowe his Uncle deceased And Nathaniell & Samuell Stowe the other half of the said land and likewise quietly & peacably to enioy the lands of m^r John Bigg of 60^li a yeare or thereabou^ts, wch hee deuided as by his will is exp^rsed Unto Hopstill ffoster 15^li a yeare, John Stowe 15^li a year, Thomas Nathaniell & Samuell ye remainder."—JOHN T. HASSAM.

Smallhope Bigg, in his will, mentions sisters Patience Foster and Elizabeth Stow. They were the wives of Hopestill Foster of Dorchester (see Dorchester Antiq. Society's Hist. Dorch., p. 118) and John Stow of Roxbury (see the Apostle Eliot's Ch. Records, REGISTER, xxxv. 244). Of the kinsmen whom he names, Edward White, Dorchester, Mass., had married in 1616, at St. Dunstan's Church, Cranbrook, Kent, Martha King, according to a pamphlet printed in 1863, entitled, In Memoriam Lieut. W. Greenough White ; John Compton was probably the person of the name who settled at Roxbury (REG. xxxv. 244), and William Batchelor may have been the Charlestown settler who had wives Jane and Rachel (Wyman's Charlestown, i. 42). Clement Bate settled at Hingham (Barry's Hanover, p. 245) and James Bate at Dorchester (Hist. Dorch. p. 106). For the parentage of the latter, see REGISTER, xxxi. 142.

John Bigg in his will (REG. xxix. 259), mentions as persons "that went from Cranbrook," "Edward Whitt [White], John Compton, John Moore, Thomas Brigden and Goodman Beale."—EDITOR.]

THOMAS BELL, senior, of London, merchant, 29 January, 1671, proved 3 May, 1672, by Susanna Bell, his relict and sole executrix.

I give unto Mr. John Elliott, minister of the church and people of God at Roxbury in New England and Captaine Isaac Johnson, whom I take to be an officer or overseer of and in the said church, and to one such other like godly person now bearing office in the said church and their successors, the minister and other two such Head Officers of the church at Roxbury, as the whole church there, from time to time, shall best approve of successively, from time to time forever, all those my messuages or tenements, lands and hereditaments, with their and every of their appurtenances, scituate, lying and being at Roxbury in New England aforesaid, in the parts beyond the seas—To Have and To Hold to the said Minister and Officers of the said church of Roxbury for the time being and their successors, from time to time forever,—In Trust only notwithstanding to and for the maintenance of a Scoole-master and free schoole for the teaching and instruction of Poore mens children at Roxbury aforesaid forever, And to and for no other use, intent or purpose whatsoever.

Whereas my son Thomas Bell did pay unto me the sum of three hundred pounds which he received in marriage with his wife, I therefore give, &c., over and besides two hundred pounds formerly given him, the sum of twelve hundred pounds within twelve months after my decease. If he be dead then to his wife Jane the sum of five hundred pounds. To grand child Clement Bell three hundred pounds at the age of one and twenty. To grand child Thomas Bell three hundred and fifty pounds ; to grand child

Simon Bell one hundred and fifty pounds at one and twenty. Whereas I
gave in marriage with my daughter Susan to John Wall deceased the
sum of three hundred pounds and afterwards the sum of four hundred
pounds to M[r] John Bell her now husband, I do give to M[r] John Bell and
to said Susan his wife the sum of eighty pounds between them. To grand
child John Wall the sum of one hundred and twenty pounds at the age of
one and twenty. To Simon Baxter, my son-in-law, and Sarah his wife
eighty pounds, and for Edward and Simon their sons, and to Sarah and
Susan Baxter, my grand children, one hundred pounds apiece at age of one
and twenty or on day of marriage, &c. To my daughter Mary Turpin,
wife of John Turpin; to Edward Bell, son of my brother Edward, at age
of twenty one years; to Elizabeth and Sarah Bell, at age of twenty one;
to Susanna ——, late wife of Edward Bell, and to her two children which
she had by the said Edward; to the poor of the parish of Allhallows Barking, London, where I now dwell, &c.

I do hereby give and bequeath unto Thomas Makins, my sister's son, in
New England, the sum of twenty pounds and to the other child of my said
sister, whose name I remember not, twenty pounds. And to all the children of my sister Christian, on her body begotten, who married one Chappell* or Chapman, I give and bequeath twenty pounds apiece, &c. To my
cousin Ann Bugg, widow, an annuity of three pounds for life. To cousin
Thomas Wildboare (my cousin Sarah's son) ten pounds at age of twenty
one, and to Susan, her daughter, ten pounds. To said cousin Sarah Wildboare the sum of twenty pounds, and her husband to have no power over it.
A legacy to M[r] Isaac Daffron. The sum of one hundred pounds to be distributed among poor necessitous men late ministers of the Gospel, of which
number I will that that M[r] Knoles and M[r] John Colling, both late of New
England be accounted. Legacies to the said M[r] Knoles and M[r] Samuel
Knolls his son, M[r] John Colling and one M[r] Ball. To my cousin M[r] John
Bayley of little Warmfield, in co. Suffolk and his wife and daughter Mar-
tha and his other four children; to my cousin William Whood and his wife;
to my uncle's daughter of S[t] Edmundsbury whose husband's name is John
Cason; to Mary Bell, daughter of brother Bell. Houses in Grace church
St., London, to wife Susan for life, then to son Thomas. I omit to give
anything to his daughter.   Eure, 56.

[Thomas Bell of Roxbury and his wife " had letters of Dismission granted & sent
to England an° 1654 7mo," according to the Apostle Eliot's records (REG. xxxv.
245). Thomas Meakins and his wife Catherine were admitted to the church in
Boston, Feb. 2, 1633–4. His son Thomas settled in Braintree, and thence removed
to Roxbury and Hadley (Savage). " M[r] Knoles and M[r] John Colling," mentioned
as " ministers of the Gospel," were the Rev. Hanserd Knollys and the Rev. John
Collins. Knollys preached at Dover, N. H., awhile, and returned in 1641 to England. He died in London, September 19, 1691, aged 93. See his Life and Times,
London, 1692, and articles by A. H. Quint, D.D., in the Congregational Quarterly,
xiii. 38–53; and by J. N. Brown, D.D., in Sprague's Annals of the American Pul-
pit, vi. 1–7. A society in England for publishing Baptist historical works was
named for him. The Rev. John Collins, graduated H. C. 1649, returned to England, was chaplain to Gen. Monk, and afterwards pastor of an Independent Church
in London, where he died, Dec. 3, 1687. (See Sibley's Harvard Graduates, i. 186–
91.) He was a son of Edward Collins, of Cambridge, N. E., who with sons Daniel,
John and Samuel and daughter Sible, are mentioned in 1639, in the will of his brother Daniel Collins, of London. (Emmerton and Waters's Gleanings, p. 20.) Mr.
Waters sends us, as confirmatory of his queries four years ago, in Emmerton
and Waters's Gleanings, p. 21, about the Collins family, the two following short
pedigrees :

* Perhaps William Chappell of New London. [(See Savage's Gen. Dict. i. 363.)—H. F. W.

Sam¹ Bedle of Wolverston, Suff.═Abigail, dau. of .... Collins in com. Essex.

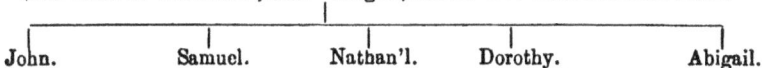

John.	Samuel.	Nathan'l.	Dorothy.	Abigail.

Have we not here, Mr. Waters adds, Abigail widow of Samuel Bedle, wife of William Thompson, sister of Daniel Collins, Dorothy daughter of above and first wife of John Bowles, and Abigail her sister wife of Michael Powell?

John Collyns of London, Salter═Abigail, dau. of Thos. Rose of Exmouth, co. Devon, 3d wife.

Daniel Collyns of London, merchᵗ. 1633, s. p.═Sibil, dau. of Thos. Francklyn of London, goldsmith.

—EDITOR.]

NATHANIEL EELES, of Harpenden in the County of Hartford, 28 March, 1678, with codicil of 9 April, 1678, proved 12 February, 1678. To wife Sarah one third of household goods and the lease of Denhames house and land, and the money made of her lands at Boringdon, now in the hands of Mʳ Combes of Hemsted, for her natural life, and my watch and largest English bible in folio, with annotations thereon, in two volumes, and Deodate's Annotations, and all the books I have of Mʳ Carill upon Job, &c. Certain property to three daughters at day of marriage or age of twenty four years. To son Nathaniel ten pounds and my sealing ring, he having formerly received his portion, for which I have a writing under his hand. To son John ten pounds, he having received his portion and part formerly, the said ten pounds to be paid to him within one year after my decease, or be then or as soon as may well be after sent over to him into Virginia, if he be then living; and if he die before the time limited for the payment thereof to him, I give the said ten pounds unto my son Nathaniel. To son Isaac my lease of Denhames, with the rents and profits thereof, after the decease of my wife, and all my books, he to pay ten pounds unto my son Daniel within one year after the decease of my wife. To sons Jacob, Joseph and Jeremiah, to each one hundred and fifty pounds for to educate, maintain, and put them forth to callings and for the setting them up in their trades after they shall have served up their apprenticeships or times with them to whom my wife shall put them; and the like sum of one hundred and fifty pounds to son Daniel for the same ends and purposes.

The portions to my four sons last named shall be paid unto them at their ages of twenty four years or when they shall have served out their apprenticeships and need the same to set up with, at the discretion of my wife. To daughter Sarah two hundred pounds; to daughters Rebecca and Mary one hundred and fifty pounds each; and to every of my sons and daughters I give a practice of Piety (a book so called) and Mʳ Alley his Treatise of Conversion and Mʳ Baxter his call to the unconverted, and a new bible to such as need the same. To my very loving brother Mʳ William Eeles and my dear and loving sister Mⁿ Foster, both which I appoint to be overseers of this my will, I give twenty pounds to each of them and desire them, by all the love they ever bare to me, to give my destitute and afflicted wife the best assistance, counsel and advice they can in all cases, from time to time, as need shall require. To loving sisters Mⁿ Eeles and Mⁿ Pearse, to each of them ten pounds, to buy them rings. My dear and loving wife Sarah to be sole executrix. The one hundred pounds in Mʳ Coombe's hand is of right my wife's during her life.

The witnesses to the will were William Eele, John Eeles, Will: Eeles junʳ and Jos: Marlow. All but the first named were witnesses to the codicil.   King, 16.

[In Calamy and Palmer's Nonconformist's Memorial (1802), Vol. II., page 306, under the head of Harden, in Hertfordshire, we learn that Mr. Nathaniel Eeles (of Emmanuel College, Cambridge) was born at Aldenham in that county, of good parentage. Having prosecuted his studies till he was senior bachelor and then studied two years at Utrecht, he was ordained a Presbyter, returned to England and preached at Caddington in Bedfordshire. In 1643 he was called by the people of Harding to be their preacher. There he continued till the year 1661, when he was ejected. He preached in private in sundry places till 1672, when he took out a license for his own house at Harding, where he preached, gratis, to all who would come. He died 18 December, 1678, aged 61, leaving, we are told, a wife and ten children.—H. F. W.
I do not know of any present representative of the name Eeles in Virginia. I find that Samuel Eale and John Stith received a grant of 500 acres in Charles City Co., Va., in 1652. Va. Land Registry, Book 5, p. 268.—R. A. B.]

MARMADUKE GOODE, of Ufton, in Berkshire, clerk, 5 September, 1678, proved 20 February, 1678, by Samuel and Mary Goode, executors. To brother Samuel Goode all that messuage or tenement, with the appurtenances, lying in Sulhamsteed Abbots and South Bannister which I hold by lease from Francis Perkins Esquire, to said Samuel to enjoy the same during his natural life; and, after his death, I give the said messuage &c. to my niece Mary Goode, the daughter of my brother John Goode, to enjoy for the remaining term of the said lease. To my brother John Goode, citizen of London, & to Susanna his now wife all my house, tenement, lands and hereditaments &c. in Sylchester in the County of Southhampton, which I purchased of John Carter of Sylchester, and after their decease, to my nephew Marmaduke Goode, son of the said John Goode, he to pay to his sisters, Elizabeth, Susanna and Anne, forty pounds apiece within twelve months after he shall be possessed of the said lands and premisses at Silchester. To my brother William Goode my messuages or tenements, &c. called or known by the name of the Heath lands or heath grounds, situated, lying & being in the several parishes of Ufton and Sulhamsteed, in the county of Berks, and which I lately purchased of Richard Wilder of Theale in the parish of Tylehurst, in the said County of Berks, innholder, during his natural life and afterwards to my nephew Robert Goode, son of the said William Goode and his heirs forever, he to pay to his two sisters, Elianor and Mary, forty pounds within twelve months, &c. To my sister Mary Haines and her two maiden daughters fifty pounds apiece within one year after my decease; to my brother John Goode in Virginia ten pounds within twelve months after my decease, according to the appointment of my brother John Goode, citizen of London; to my brother Thomas Goode, in Ireland, ten pounds (in the same way); to my sister Ann Wickens of Upton ten pounds; to my servant Alice Payce ten pounds; to my servant Hugh Larkum five pounds. All the rest of the property to brother Samuel Goode and niece Mary Goode, daughter of my brother John Goode, who are appointed joint executors.
The witnesses were Samuel Brightwell and Robert King.
                                                                    King, 17.

[By family tradition John Goode came to Virginia from Whitby, England, about 1660, with his wife, and purchased the plantation of one Gough (situated on the south side of James River, about four miles from the city of Manchester) which he named "Whitby." His descendants have intermarried with many prominent families of Virginia, including the Harrisons, Blands, Turpins, Gordons, Scotts, Cookes and others. Col. Thomas F. Goode and Hon. John Goode of Virginia, and Prof. G. Brown Goode of the Smithsonian Institution, are descendants of John Goode. " Whitby " is now the property of A. D. Williams, Esq., Richmond, Virginia.— R. A. B.]

MARY HOSKINS, of Richmond in the County of Surrey, widow, 30 July, 1678, proved 28 February, 1678. To my dear mother Anne Githins, widow, all my plate and linen and diamond locket and five hundred pounds within three months after my decease. To M[rs] Mariana Carleton, the wife of Matthew Carleton, gentleman, my best diamond ring and twenty pounds. Ten pounds apiece to be paid to the three children of my late deceased brother John Githins in Meriland, Philip, John and Mary Githins. To Mary Evererd, daughter of Robert Evererd of Godstone, five pounds and five pounds to Richard Nye, whom I placed with M[r] Taw. Twenty pounds to be laid out in placing two boys to trades, whereof one to be of Oxted and the other of Godstone. All my houses in the Maze in Southwark, held of S[t] Thomas Hospital and all other personal estate, &c. to my loving brother William Githins, Gentleman, whom I appoint executor.

The witnesses were Thomas Jenner, Richard Smith (by mark), Winefrut King of Petersham and Jeoffrey Glyd. King, 19.

The pedigree of the Hoskins Family of Oxted is given in various MSS. in the British Museum. The marriage of any Hoskins with the testatrix named above has not been found.

[The name Everard has had most prominent representatives in Maryland, Virginia and North Carolina, and is a favored Christian name in the distinguished Meade family of Virginia.—R. A. B.]

ANNE JONES, of S[t] Clement Danes in the County of Middlesex, widow, 20 February, 1676, proved 6 February, 1678. To Bridget Waite, wife of William Waite (certain household effects) and the lease of my house wherein I now dwell, she paying the rent, &c. All the rest to my son Thomas Daniell who is in Virginia, beyond the seas. And I do hereby make my said son Thomas Daniell full and sole executor, and my friends Charles Stepkin Esq. and M[r] Richard Southey overseers, they to keep the estate in trust for my said son Thomas Daniell. In case he die before he comes from beyond the seas, then I bequeath to Edward Jones and Patience Jones, son & daughter of John Jones, of the parish of S[t] Clement Danes, taylor, five pounds apiece; and all the rest of my estate to Mark Workman and Elizabeth Workman, son and daughter of Mark Workman, late of the parish of S[t] Mary Magdalen, old Fish Street London, deceased, equally.

The witnesses were Richard Southey, Jun[r]. John Searle and Ro: Stone. King, 19.

[I find of record in the Virginia Land Registry, Book No. 8, p. 428, a grant of 130 acres in the Counties of Isle of Wight and " Nanzimond," Va., to Owen Daniell, in 1695.—R. A. B.]

ROBERT LUCAS, of Hitchin, in the County of Hertford, in his will of 13 January, 1678, proved 14 February, 1678, speaks of land purchased of William Papworth of New England, lying close to land which was heretofore that of the testator's father, Simon Lucas, deceased, and lands heretofore the lands of William Willis. King, 21.

[Query. Where did William Papworth reside ?—ED.]

ANTHONY ROBY, of the Province of Carolina, 6 December, 1686, proved 11 July, 1688. To mother Early Roby, in England, all my estate in Carolina or elsewhere; if she be dead then to her next heirs then living. My friend Andrew Percivall Esquire, of the said Province, to be sole executor. The witnesses were David Harty, James Wyatt and John Shelton.

Exton, 99.

JOHN REED, mariner, 4 April, 1688, proved 6 July, 1688. I bequeath all my concerns aboard the ship Richard, of London, John Reade Master, riding at anchor in the York River, to my loving wife Mary Reade of Bristol. I desire my loving friend Capt. Trim, commander of the ship Judy, riding at anchor in York River, to take accompt. The witnesses were Benjamin Eyre, George Lodge and Charles Perkes.

Exton, 99.

[John Read was granted 145 acres in Gloucester Co., March 18, 1652. Va. Land Registry Office, Book 5, p. 280. There are grants within a short period thereafter to Alexander Argubell and James Read or Reade.

The Eyres have been continuously seated in Northampton Co., Va., from the 17th century. They early intermarried with the Severns, Southeys and Lyttletons, and these latter names are now favored Christian names in the family.—R. A. B.]

HENRY WOODHOUSE, of the parish of Linhaven, of lower Norfolk in Virginia, 29 January, 1686, owned to be his will 31 January, 1686-7, and proved 24 July, 1688. To eldest son Henry Woodhouse my plantation where I live (containing five hundred acres, and described); to second son, Horatio, property called Moyes land (adjoining the above); to son John (other real estate); to son Henry two negroes Roger and Sarah; to daughters Elizabeth and Lucy, daughter Mary, wife of William More, and daughter Sarah, wife of Cason More.   Exton, 102.

[I find the following grants of land to the name Woodhouse, of record in the Va. Land Registry Office : Thomas Woodhouse, 200 acres in James City Co., March 24, 1644, Book No. 2, p. 1 ; *Henry Woodhouse*, 200 acres in Lynhaven parish, Lower Norfolk Co., April 5, 1649, p. 167 ; the same, 275 acres in same, May 11, 1652, Bk. No. 3, p. 254 ; the same, 749 acres in the same, April 3, 1670, Book No. 6, p. 357, Hamond Woodhouse, 340 acres in Charles City Co., April 20, 1669, Book No. 6, p. 216.—R. A. B.]

MICHAEL GRIGGS, of County Lancaster, Colony of Virginia, gentleman, 17 April, 1687, proved 10 September, 1688. To my father-in-law Robert Schofield. To wife Anne Griggs the residue. The witnesses were William Lee, Richard Farrington and William Carter.

The above will was proved at London "juramento Annæ Bray, als Griggs (modo uxoris Richardi Bray) relictæ dicti defuncti et executricis," &c.

Exton, 117.

[William Lee was doubtless the son of Col. Richard Lee, the founder of the distinguished family of the name in Virginia.

The name Bray is of early seating in Virginia. John Bray received a grant of 200 acres in " Worrosquinack " Co., June 4, 1636. Va. Land Records, Book No. 1, p. 362. His descendants intermarried with the Harrison and other prominent families. The Brays intermarried early also with the Plomer, Plommer, Plummer or Plumer family.—R. A. B.]

JOHN CURTIS, of Boston, Co. Middlesex, New England, mariner, belonging to Majesty's ship the English Tyger, appoints Robert Chipchace in County Middlesex, Old England, his attorney and sole executor, 31 January, 1689–90, in presence of Thos. Coall and Thoˢ Browne. Proved 3 December, 1690, by Robert Chipchace.   Dyke, 200.

ELIZABETH BRETLAND, late the wife of William Bretland, deceased, Barbados, 6 October, 1687. Legacies to daughters Elizabeth Taylor and Millecent Acklam; to grandson Peter Jones; to grandsons John and Jacob Legay. I give and bequeath to my brother Adam Coulson's children, of Reading near Boston, in New England, the sum of one hundred pounds, to be equally divided among them or the survivor of them.

Cousin Edward Munday and M'r John Mortimer of London, merchants, to be executors of the will.

Item I give unto my brother Adam Coulson's children, of Reading, near Boston, in New England, one negro woman, by name Sarah, being my own proper purchase, or to the survivor of them, to be sent to them the first opportunity after my decease. I leave, according to the desire of my dear husband, Mr. Edward Munday, to my three daughters, Elizabeth, Millecent and Mary, thirty five pounds of silver, at twelve ounces to the pound.

Friends, Capt. Elisha Mellowes and Mr. John Hooker, to be executors for that portion of the estate in the Barbados.

The witnesses made deposition as to this will 3 April, 1689. It was entered and recorded in the Secretary's Office, 17 February, 1689. Proved in London 5 December, 1690.   Dyke, 199.

[Adam Colson, of Reading, Mass., married Sept. 8, 1668, Mary, daughter of Josiah Dustin. He was schoolmaster there from 1679 to 1681. He died March 1, 1687. See Eaton's Reading, p. 58, and Savage.—ED.]

ROBERT HATHORNE, the elder, of the parish of Bray in the county of Berks, yeoman, 15 February, 1689, proved 16 February, 1691. He left all his estate to his son Robert Hathorne, the younger, of the parish of Bray in the county of Berks.   Fane, 49.

[The testator of the above will was doubtless a brother of Major William Hathorne of Salem, Massachusetts, ancestor of the distinguished writer Nathaniel Hawthorne. (See Emmerton & Waters's Gleanings from English Records.)—H. F. W.]

EDWARD GADSBY, of Stepney, in the county of Middlesex, mariner, bound out to sea "with M'r Penn to Virginy" in the Charity of London, appointed John Duffield, citizen and barber-surgeon of London, his attorney, &c. 30 January, 1692, proved 28 April, 1696. He wished all his estate to be given to his brother Samuel Gadsby, of Woodborough, in the County of Nottingham, basket-maker.   Bond, 47.

DANIEL JOHNSON, of Lynn in New England, trumpeter, 22 June, 1695, appointed Patrick Hayes of Bermondsey in the County of Surrey, victualler, to receive and collect his bounty or prizemoney, pursuant to their Majesties' Gracious Declaration of 23 May, 1689, and all such money, &c. as should be due to him for service in any of their Majesties' ships, frigates or vessels or any merchant ships, &c. He gave and bequeathed all unto his beloved children (without naming them) equally to be divided among them. Proved 6 April, 1696.   Bond, 51.

[There was a Daniel Johnson at Lynn, Mass., who married March 2, 1674, Martha Parker, and had Abigail, born April 21, 1675, Stephen and Nathaniel, twins, born Feb. 14, 1678, Sarah, born July 5, 1680, Elizabeth, born March 7, 1682, and Simon, born Jan. 25, 1684 (Savage).—ED]

JOHN ROLFE, of James City in Virginia, Esquire, 10 March, 1621, proved 21 May, 1630, by William Pyers. Father-in-law Lieut. William

Pyers, gentleman, to have charge of the two small children of very tender
age. A parcell of land in the country of Toppahannah between the two
creeks over against James City in the continent or country of Virginia to
son Thomas Rolfe & his heirs; failing issue, to my daughter Elizabeth; next
to my right heirs. Land near Mulberry Island, Virginia, to Jane my wife
during her natural life, then to daughter Elizabeth. To my servant Robert
Davies twenty pounds.

The witnesses were Temperance Yeardley, Richard Buck, John Cartwright, Robert Davys and John Milwarde.   Scroope, 49.

[It would appear that John Rolfe was three times married, his first wife bearing him in 1609 one male child, which died on the Island of Bermuda. His second
wife was Pocahontas, and his third Jane Pyers, or Poyers, of the text, the mother
of the daughter Elizabeth. The son Thomas appears to have married in England,
having issue Anthony, whose daughter Hannah married Sir Thomas Leigh of co.
Kent, the descendants of that name and of the additional highly respectable names of
Bennet and Spencer being now quite numerous. Died prior to 8 Nov. 1682. See
Richmond Standard, Jan. 21, 1882.

The witness Richard Buck (sometimes rendered Bucke) was doubtless the minister of the name at Jamestown, who died sometime prior to 1624, leaving a widow,
and children—Mara, Gershom, Benoni and Peleg.—R. A. B.]

Sir GEORGE YARDLEY, 12 October, 1627, proved 14 February, 1628.
To wife Temperance all and every part and parcell of all such household
stuff, plate, linen, woollen or any other goods, moveable or immoveable,
of what nature or quality soever, as to me are belonging, and which now
at the time of the date hereof are being and remaining within this house in
James City wherein I now dwell. Item, as touching and concerning all
the rest of my whole estate consisting of goods, debts, servants, " negars,"
cattle, or any other thing or things, commodities or profits whatsover to
me belonging or appertaining either here in this country of Virginia, in
England or elsewhere, together with my plantation of one thousand acres
of land at Stanly in Warwicke River, my will and desire is that the same be
all and every part and parcell thereof sold to the best advantage for tobacco and the same to be transported as soon as may be, either this year or the
next, as my said wife shall find occasion, into England, and there to be
sold or turned into money, &c. &c. The money resulting from this (with
sundry additions) to be divided into three parts, of which one part to go to
said wife, one part to eldest son Argoll Yeardley, and the other part to
son Francis & to Elizabeth Yeardley equally.

The witnesses were Abraham Peirsey, Susanna Hall and William Clayborne, Scr.

A codicil, dated 29 Oct. 1627, was witnessed by the same scrivener.
                                                          Ridley, 9.

Commission to administer on the estate of Sir George Yeardley, late in
Virginia, deceased, was issued 14 March, 1627-8, to his brother Ralph
Yeardley during the absence of the widow, relict, Temperance Yeardley, in
the parts beyond the seas, &c.   Admon Act Book for 1628.

[From the Calendar of State Papers, Colonial Series (London, 1860), we learn
that Governor Francis West and the Council of Virginia certified to the Privy Council, 20 December, 1627, the death of Governor Sir George Yeardley and the election
of Captain Francis West to succeed him in the government. In July, 1629, Edmund Rossingham sent in a petition to the Privy Council stating that he was agent
to his uncle Sir George Yeardley, late Governor of Virginia, who dying before any
satisfaction was made to the petitioner for being a chief means of raising his estate
to the value of six thousand pounds, Ralph Yeardley, the brother, took administra-

tion of the same. He prayed for relief and that his wrongs might be examined into. This was referred, July 11, 1629, to Sir Dudley Diggs, Sir Maurice Abbott, Thomas Gibbs and Samuel Wrote, late commissioners for that plantation, to examine into the true state of the case. Annexed is the report of Gibbs and Wrote, made 25 Sept. 1629, describing in detail the petitioner's employments from 1619, and awarding three hundred and sixty pounds as due to him in equity ; also an answer by Ralph Yeardley, administrator, &c., to Rossingham's petition. In January or February, 1630, Rossingham sent in another petition praying for a final determination. In it he styles Ralph Yeardley an apothecary of London. On the nineteenth of February the Privy Council ordered Ralph Yeardley to pay two hundred pounds to the petitioner out of his brother's estate, twelve hundred pounds having already come into the administrator's hand.

Captain Yeardley was chosen Governor of Virginia in 1618, in place of Lord De la Warr, who is said to have died in Canada, and he departed immediately thither with two ships and about three hundred men and boys. On the twenty-eighth of November Chamberlain writes that Captain Yeardley, "a mean fellow," goes Governor to Virginia, two or three ships being ready. To grace him the more the King knighted him this week at Newmarket, "which hath set him up so high, that he flaunts it up and down the streets in extraordinary bravery, with fourteen or fifteen fair liveries after him." He arrived in Virginia in April, 1619, and is said to have brought the colony from a very low state to an extremely flourishing condition. He was governor again 1626-27.—H. F. W.

Colonel Argoll Yeardley married Sarah, daughter of John Custis, of Northampton Co., Va., a native of Rotterdam and the founder of the socially distinguished family of the name in Virginia.

"Colonel" Francis Yeardley (died August, 1657) married Sarah the widow of Adam Thorowgood and of John Gooking, the latter being her first husband.

The name Yeardley, or properly Yardly, is still represented in the United States, but I know of none of the name in Virginia.

One Abraham Piersey, or Percy, was treasurer of the colony of Virginia in 1619. He may have been the father of the first witness. The other witness was doubtless Col. William Clayborne, or Claiborne, as it is now rendered, the son of "the rebel" of the same name, who had the command of a fort in New Kent county in 1676 (Major Lyddal serving with him), and who distinguished himself in the Indian wars of Bacon's Rebellion. There was of record in King William County, Va., a certificate of his valorous service, signed by Gov. William Berkeley and attested by Nathaniel Bacon (senior, of the Council) and Philip Ludwill.—R. A. B]

EDWARD COLE, of East Bergholt, in the county of Suffolk, clothier, 18 August, 1649, proved the last of May, 1652. To wife Abigail ; to youngest son Peter Cole ; to my two daughters Sarah and Mary Cole ; to the children of my son Edward Cole; to my grandchildren in New England twenty pounds.

The witnesses were John Layman and Richard Royse.

Bowyer, 103.

ROBERT FEVERYEARE, the elder, of Kelshall in the county of Suffolk, yeoman, 24 June, 1656, proved 5 September, 1656. To wife Elizabeth. Frances Brothers of Kelshall owes me on bond. To Edmund Feveryeare, my brother, the sum of forty shillings within six months after my decease. To William Feveryeare, my brother, three pounds. To Margaret Feveryeare, my sister, forty shillings within six months, &c. To Margery, my sister, wife of Robert Goodwin, forty shillings within twelve months, &c. ; also eight pounds within twelve months, &c. To Anne, my sister, wife of John Miles, five pounds within six months, &c. To Richard Eade, mine uncle, twenty shillings ; to Mary Minstrell, my former servant, twenty shillings within six months, &c. To Robert Goodwin, the elder, my new suit of apparel. To Henry Minstrel, the elder, a legacy. Brother William and wife Elizabeth to be executors and residuary legatees. Berkeley, 333.

CLEMENT CHAPLIN, of Thetford, in the county of Norfolk, Clerk, 16 August, 1656, proved 23 September, 1656, by Sarah Chaplin his relict and sole executrix. To wife, Sarah, all my houses and lands in Hartford and Weathersfield in New England, to her and her heirs forever. Loving brother Thomas Chaplin of Bury St Edmunds in old England, and my kinsman Mr. William Clarke, of Rocksbury in New England to be supervisors. Witnessed by Elizabeth Gurnham (her mark) and John Spincke.

Berkeley, 332.

[The testator of the above will, son of William Chaplin " of Semer " (see the Candler MS. No. 6071 of Harleian Collection, British Museum), we are told was a chandler in Bury, went over into New England, and was one of the elders in the congregation whereof Mr. Hooker was minister. His wife Sarah was one of five daughters and co-heiresses of —— Hinds, a goldsmith in Bury. Her sister Elizabeth was wife of Thomas Chaplin (mentioned above), linen draper in Bury, alderman and justice of the peace for the County of Suffolk, her sister Margaret Hinds was married to George Groome of Rattlesden, Justice of the Peace, Abigail Hinds was married to Richard Scott of Braintree (who married secondly Alice Snelling), and Anne Hinds was married to —— Alliston. Mr. Chaplin had, besides the brother Thomas whom he names, a brother William of Blockeshall, who had issue, a brother Richard, of Semer (sine prole), a brother Edmund of Semer, who had many children, and a brother Capt. Robert Chaplin of Bury, who had issue. A sister Martha is said to have been married to Robert Parker of Wollpit, who went into New England, another sister, whose name is not given, was wife of —— Barret of Stratford, and mother of a Thomas Barret, and a third sister (also unnamed) was married to —— Smith of Semer. Alderman Thomas Chaplin had a daughter Anne who was married to Jasper Shepheard, an alderman of Bury, and a daughter Abigail married to Robert Whiting of —— in Norfolk.—H. F. W.]

JOHN SMITH, citizen and merchant tailor of London, by reason of age weak in body, 17 December, 1655, proved 20 October, 1656, by Sarah Whiting, daughter and executrix. To wife the sum of five pounds in money, as a token and remembrance of my love, and I will and appoint that it shall & may be lawful for her to dwell and abide in my dining-room and wainscot chamber belonging to my dwelling house in the old Bailey, London, by the space of three months next after my decease ; and I confirm the indenture bearing date 30 August, 1654, between me and Thomas Fitz Williams, of the one part, and my said wife, known by the name of Sarah Neale, and Vincent Limborowe, of the other part, &c. &c. To the children of my loving daughter, Sarah Whiting, ten pounds apiece towards putting them out to be Apprentices, &c., and also forty pounds apiece to the sons at twenty four years of age and to the daughters at twenty one.

Likewise I give to the children of my cousin William Smith, in New England, and Mary, his now or late wife, the sum of three pounds apiece, to be paid to them, the said children, at the ages as above is limited to my grandchildren, &c. &c.

Legacies to brother Thomas Smith and to the daughter of James Smith, son of brother Thomas. To grandchild John Whiting, son of daughter Sarah Whiting, the half part of certain lands, tenements, &c. in Hogsden, alias Hoxden, in the County of Middlesex, and to the male and female issue of the said John ; failing such issue, then to grandchild Nathaniel Whiting, &c. &c. ; with remainder to grandchildren Robert and Stephen Whiting ; then to Samuel Whiting, another son of my said daughter, &c. The other moiety to grandchild Nathaniel Whiting ; then to John ; then to Robert and Joseph ; then to Stephen Whiting. Legacy to son-in-law Timothy Whiting.

Berkeley, 337.

[There was a Nathaniel Whiting in Dedham who had sons John, Samuel and Timothy.—H. F. W.]

JOSIAS FIRMIN, the elder, of Nayland, Co. Suffolk, tanner, 27 August, 1638, proved the last of November, 1638. To the poor of Nayland. To wife Anne, houses and lands in Nayland and also in Stoke next Nayland (called Noke meadow in Stoke), then to Gyles Firmin my youngest son and his heirs, but if he die before he arrives at twenty four years of age. then to the rest of my children. Lands in Stoke called Edmondes Field, after death of wife, to eldest son Josias Firmin and his son Josias, my grand child. To John Firmin, my son, ten pounds within one year after my decease. To my daughter Mary, now wife of Robert Smith, forty five pounds. To daughter Martha Firmin one hundred pounds at age of twenty one. To daughter Sara Firmin tenement, &c. at Foxyearth, co. Essex, which I purchased of one Thomas Partridge, &c., to said Sara at age of twenty years. To grand child, John Firmin, son of Josias Firmin. Sons Josias and Gyles and my three daughters. Executors to be wife Anne and son in law Robert Smith of Nayland, mercer. Lee, 146.

[See abstracts of wills and extracts from parish registers relating to the name of Firmin in Emmerton and Waters's Gleanings, pp. 34-9.—ED.]

JOSE GLOVER, of London, being by the providence of God forthwith to embark myself for some parts beyond the seas, 16 May, 1638, proved 22 December, 1638, by Richard Daveys, one of the executors, power being reserved for John Harris, another executor. To my dear and loving wife all my estate, &c. both in New England and old England for life, she to maintain and liberally educate all my children. After her decease the property to go to two eldest sons, Roger and John, equally. To my three daughters, Elizabeth, Sara and Priscilla, four hundred pounds apiece (then follows a reference to a decree and order of the court of chancery), my three daughters to release to Edmond Davyes Esq. and Thomas Younge, merchant of London, at day of marriage or arrival at full age, all their interests, &c. in tenements, &c. in Dorenth* and Stone in co. Kent, &c. To my ancient, faithful servant John Stidman fifty pounds. To all my brothers & sisters that shall be living (except my sister Collins) five pounds. To friend Mr Joseph Davies and his wife five pounds apiece. The executors to be John Harris, my loving uncle, warden of the College of Winchester, and Richard Davies, my ancient loving friend. The witnesses were E. Davies, Joseph Davyes, Thomas Yonge, Samuel Davyes & John Davyes. Lee, 176.

[See the article by J. Hammond Trumbull, LL.D., on the christian name of Mr. Glover, in the REGISTER, xxx. 26-8. His will, from a copy preserved on the Middlesex Court Files, is printed in full in the REGISTER, xxiii. 136-7.—ED.]

Sir ROBT CARR, of Ithall, co. Northumberland, knight. All estate in America, &c. to eldest son William Carr, the other estate in England being formerly settled. To James Deane, my now servant and his heirs, for and in consideration of his service, a plantation within any of the six islands granted unto me, except in Carr's Island. This having been read to him, 29 May, 1667, he did declare, &c. Proved 16 July, 1667, when commission was issued to William Carr, natural son and lawful heir and principal legatee named in the will of Sir Robt Carr, knight, lately of Carr's Island, in New England, in the parts beyond the seas. Carr, 90.

[See notice of Sir Robert Carr, with remarks on his will, in the REGISTER, xxiv. 187.—ED.]

* Darent.

NOWELL HILTON of Charlestown, co. Middlesex in New England, mariner, appoints his trusty and loving kinsman Nathaniel Cutler, of the parish of Stepney in co. Middlesex, sawyer, his attorney, &c. The amount due for my service done or to be done on board of any of his Ma^{tes} ships, vessels or frigates, &c. Signed 6 October, 1687, in presence of Mary Story (her mark), Cuthbert Stoy (*sic*) and Samuel Sapp, at the two Anchors and three Stars on Wapping Wall.   17 September 1689 emanavit comissio Nath^{ll} Cutler, &c.   Ent, 123.

[Nowell Hilton, the testator, was born in Charlestown, May 4, 1663. He was a son of William Hilton of Charlestown by his second wife Mehitable, a daughter of Increase Nowell. After the death of his father his mother married (2) 29: 8th, 1684, Deacon John Cutler. Timothy Cutler, a son of Deacon John Cutler, married, Dec. 22, 1673, Elizabeth Hilton, a sister of the testator. See the articles entitled "Some of the Descendants of William Hilton," REGISTER, xxxi. 179. See also Wyman's Genealogies and Estates of Charlestown, 255, 257, 504, 710. This will was printed in full in the REGISTER, xxxii. 50.—JOHN T. HASSAM.]

THOMAS GOLLEDGE, his will in form of a letter written from Charde in Somerset, 10 May, 1645, and addressed to his wife Mrs. Mary Golledge at Chichester ; proved by Mary Colledge, 1 June, 1648.

"My Deere Wyffe I am now goinge in the service of my Lord and Master Jesus Christ. I knowe not howe hee will dispose of my fraile lyfe in breife I shall desire thow wilt take all fitt opportunity yf the Lord soe dispose to leave thee wth out an husband as to transport my sweete poore innocent children into New England or some such place voyd of Trouble because the Lord ys ready to shoote his fiery darts of wrath against this sinfull land and yo^u wthout an husband and they wthowt a ffather may suffer the black darknesse of Egiptian Popery or Athisme pray sell what of mine is to bee sould for though I cannot wthowt helpe of a lawyer make a fformall will yet my desire in breife ys that thow bee my sole executor & have full power."   Essex, 98.

Notes on Abstracts previously printed.

JOSEPH HOLLAND.   Will Dec. 25, 1658.   [Page 9.]

[We have received the following note from Prof. Arthur L. Perry, LL.D., of Williams College :

If Mr. Waters's abstract of the will of Joseph Holland of London, citizen and clothworker, discredits one conjecture of Dr. Bond in his history of Watertown, it strikingly confirms another conjecture of that author in the same volume. A John Perry died in Watertown in 1674, aged 61. Another John Perry of Watertown married Sarah Clary, of Cambridge, Dec. 1667. Bond says the first John was "probably father" of the second John. Joseph Holland's will makes that guess a certainty. He leaves bequests "*to son-in-law John Perry and Johanna his wife, my daughter, and their sons John Perry and Josias Perry and daughter Elizabeth Perry.*" In another clause : "To my said daughter Johanna certain needle work wrought by my first wife, her mother." In another clause he leaves twenty pounds in goods "*to my son Nathaniel Holland of Waterton in New England.*" The first John Perry was therefore brother-in-law of Nathaniel Holland, and the second his nephew. The Perrys came to Watertown eight years (1666) after this will was drawn (1658). They were clothworkers, i. e. weavers and tailors, like the Hollands in London. The London names, John and Johanna and Josiah and Joseph, were kept up constantly among the Perrys in Watertown and after their removal to Worcester in 1751, and some of them are not even yet disused as christian names in the family. It is a matter of record in the family Bibles that the two Perrys came to Watertown from *London*. Inferentially, therefore, but certainly, they were among the heirs mentioned in Joseph Holland's will.

That will was drawn before the great fire of London in 1666. The mother of Mrs. John Perry the elder was already buried in St. Sepulchre Church in 1658 ; and the good Joseph Holland, citizen and clothworker, directed that his own body should be buried " on the south side of the christening pew " of that parish church.

A grandson of the second John Perry, Nathan, became deacon of the old South Church in Worcester in 1783, and continued in that office till his death in 1806 ; his son Moses succeeded in the office immediately, and continued in it till his death in 1842 ; and his son Samuel succeeded his father and sustained the office thirty-five years longer, making ninety-four years of continuous service in one family.

ARTHUR L. PERRY,
Seventh generation from first John.]

NATHANIEL DOWNEINGE of London, gentleman, 7 May, 1616, proved 14 May, 1616, by his wife Margaret Downeinge. To be buried in the parish Church of St. Dionis Backchurch, London, or elsewhere it shall please my executrix. To the poor of St. Dionis and of St. Gabriel Fanchurch, London. To my brother Joseph Downeinge, now dwellings in Ipswich, in the County of Suffolk, twenty pounds. To my sister Abigail Goade, wife of John Goade, skinner, twenty pounds, and to their son, John Goad, forty shillings to make him a cup. To my sister Susanna Kirby, wife of John Kirby, skinner, twenty pounds. To my mother in law Mary Cellyn, widow, ten pounds and the " Hope [hoop] Ringe " which was my mother's. To my brother Joshua Downinge the seal ring of gold that I do wear on my hand. And to my brother Emanuel Downeinge I give the like ring of gold of the same value & fashion. The residue to my wife Margaret Downeinge, whom I make sole executrix. Whereas I am now seized in fee of and in the late dissolved monastery of the " Fryers Carmelites, or the Whitefryers," in Ipswich in the County of Suffolk, with the appurtenances, &c. —this to wife Margaret and her heirs forever.   Cope, 48.

Sir GEORGE DOWNING of East Hatley, in the County of Cambridge, Knight and Baronet ; 24 August, 1683, with codicil added 7 July, 1684 ; proved 19 July, 1684. My body to be interred in the vault which I have made under the chancel at Crawden, alias Croyden, in the county of Cambridge, by the body of my wife Frances. Son George Downing, Esq., and son William named. Houses in or near King Street, in the city of Westminster, lately called Hampden House, which I hold by long lease from the Crown, and Peacock Court there, which I hold by lease from the Collegiate Church of St. Peter, Westminster ; all which are now demolished and rebuilt, or rebuilding, and called Downing Street. To Edward Lord Viscount Morpeth and Sir Henry Pickering,* Baronet, my son-in-law, in trust, &c. Bequests to sons Charles and William Downing, and to three daughters, Lucy, Mary and Anne, at age of twenty-one years or day of marriage. The guardianship and custody of the persons of these three daughters entrusted to my dear daughter Frances Cotton. Bequests to daughter Cotton's children, Francis, John and Thomas, and to Elizabeth and Frances, the two daughters of my late daughter Pickering deceased ; also to nephew John Peters, niece Lucy Spicer, nephew Joshua Downing and Mr Edmond Woodroffe, one of my clerks in my office in the Exchequer.   Hare, 139.

* This Sir Henry Pickering was son and heir of Sir Henry Pickering of Whaddon, who was created a Baronet 2 January, 1660. He was of Barbados in 1695, and had two wives, Philadelphia, daughter of Sir George Downing, by whom he had two daughters, Mary and Anne (who both died without issue), and secondly, Grace, daughter of Constant Silvester, Esq. (See REG. xxxvii. 385.) At his death, in 1705, the title became extinct. (See Add. MS. 24493, British Museum.)—H. F. W.

This Indenture made the Thirteenth day of Sept. Anno Dom̄. one thousand seuen hundred and in the twelfth yeare of the Reigne of our Soue-
raign Lord William the third, by the grace of God of England, Scotland,
ffrance and Ireland King, defender of the Faith &cᵃ. ——

Between Charles Downing of London in the Kingdome of England
Esqʳ of the one part and Thorndike Procter of Salem in the Countey of
Essex within his Majᵗⁱᵉˢ Province of the Massachusetts Bay in New England in America, yeoman, on the other part [then follows the ordinary
phraseology of conveyance of a tract of three hundred acres in Salem
which was] formerly the farme of Emanuel Downing of Salem aforesaid
Gent: Deceased, Grandfather of the said Charles Downing, purchased by
the said Emanuel Downing of one Robert Cole unto whome the same was
granted by the said town of Salem one thousand six hundred thirty and
five* [together with other parcels of land which had belonged to Emanuel
Downing. And the grantor warrants the purchaser that he may hold
these premisses] free and clear or well and sufficiently Indemnified saued
and kept harmless of and from all and all manner of former and other gifts,
grants, bargaines, sales, leases, releases, mortgages, Joyntures, Dower,
Judgments, Executions, Extents, wills, Entails, ffines, fforfeitures, titles,
troubles, charges and Incumbrances whatsoever had, made, done, committed, knowledged or suffered by the said Charles Downing, Sʳ George Downing, Baronᵗ, late father of the said Charles, and the abouesaid Emanuel
Downing or any of them.

This Indenture was signed by the grantor, Charles Downing, Esqʳ, and
his wife, Sarah Downing, and their seals affixed on the day and year first
abovewritten.   Deeds of Essex Co., Mass., Book 7, Lvs. 7 to 10.

The will of Sir George Downing, Knight of the Bath & Baronet, providing (in default of male issue to his cousin) for the foundation of a new
college in the University of Cambridge, "which college shall be called by the
name of Downing College," was dated 20 December, 1717, and proved 13
June, 1749.   Lisle, 179.

[The foregoing extracts show clearly enough the connection of this family with
New England, a family whose name, associated as it is with a street in which has
been, for so many years, the official residence of the Prime Minister of England,
the centre of the greatest and most wide-spread empire of modern times, and with a
college in one of the most famous universities of the world, is known wherever the
English language is spoken, and bids fair to last so long as English history shall be
read.

From some MS. notes furnished me by my very obliging friend Mr. T. C. Noble,
whose authority on matters connected with the history of the great metropolis
of the world and its surrounding parishes is unquestioned, I find that Sir George
Downing was rated for a house in "New Pallace" (New Palace Yard, Westminster) for twenty years previous to 1683, that in 1728 the rentals of the whole of
Downing Street (for assessment) amounted to less than £1000, and in 1828 the total
was £3000. At the present time (1883) the whole street is occupied by the offices
of the government and the residences of the First Lord of the Treasury, Chancellor
of the Exchequer, &c. From the "Memorials of Westminster," by the Rev. Mac-
kenzie E. C. Walcott, we learn that "The official residence of the First Lord of the
Treasury formerly belonged to the Crown : King George I. gave it to Baron Bothmar,
the Hanoverian Minister, for life. After his death King George II. offered the house
to Sir Robert Walpole, who only accepted it upon the condition that it should be
attached to the Premiership forever. Since that time, therefore, Downing Street is
inseparably connected with the name of every successive Prime Minister of England." Chapter III. of the Appendix to these Memorials gives us additional information, including a list of the successive occupants of the official residence down

* This must be a mistake for 1638. (See Book of Grants, Salem, edited by William P.
Upham, Esq.)—H. F. W.

to July 6, 1846. " Sir Robert Walpole accepted it in 1732, and came to reside here 22 Sept. 1735." " In the small waiting-room of No. 14, for the first and only time in their lives met Sir Arthur Wellesley and Lord Nelson ; the latter was well known to Sir Arthur from the prints in the shop windows ; they conversed together for some minutes ; on parting Lord Nelson went out of the room and asked the name of the stranger whose conversation and appearance had made a deep impression upon him."

I am informed by William H. Richardson, Esq., F.S.A., who is now annotating " The Annals of Ipswiche, by N. Bacon,"* that George Downing, who was un-doubtedly the father of Emanuel and Nathaniel Downing, was master of the Gram-mar School, Ipswich, about the years 1607 to 1610. His son Emanuel, baptized in the parish church of St. Lawrence, Ipswich, 12 August, 1585, married at Groton, Suffolk, 10 April, 1622, Lucy (baptized 27 January, 1601), daughter of Adam Win-throp, Esq., and sister of Governor John Winthrop. Mr. Downing was a lawyer of the Inner Temple, London, Attorney in the Court of Wards, and seems to have lived in the parishes of St. Bridget and of St. Michael, Cornhill. He came over to New England in 1638, took up his abode in Salem, was admitted into the church 4 November of the same year, and frequently represented the town in the General Court of the colony. The date of his death is not known, nor has any record yet been found of any will made by him. We have seen what became of his farm in Salem. His town residence was conveyed, 8 August, 1656, by Lucie Downing of Salem, with consent of Emanuel Downing her husband (as is recited in the deed) to their son Lieut. Joseph Gardner, as the dower of their daughter Ann on her mar-riage with Lieut. Gardner. It was described as a messuage or tenement in Salem situated upon four acres of ground entire, having the Common on the east, the street or highway that runs from the meeting-house to the harbor on the south, and the lane that goes to the North River on the West. This property comprises the various estates now included between St. Peter, Essex, Newbury and Browne Streets. Lieut. Gardner and his wife sold various lots at either end to sundry members of the Gardner family, and to Deacon Richard Prince and Mr. William Browne, Jr. The house, which stood where the residence of the late Col. Francis Peabody stands, remained as the homestead of Mrs. Gardner. After the untimely loss of her first husband, who was killed in the great Swamp Fight, 19 December, 1675, she took for a second husband Simon Bradstreet, Esq. ; but by the terms of the marriage contract of 2 May, 1676, the ownership of the homestead remained with her. It was afterwards commonly known as the Bradstreet house, and was torn down in 1750, having previously been used as a tavern. On page 75 of the first vol-ume of the REGISTER, and on page 185 of the fourth volume of Historical Collections of the Essex Institute, may be seen an engraving representing this house, in which Sir George Downing probably passed his boyhood while under the tuition of the Rev. John Fisk, preparing for entrance into Harvard College, from which he was graduated in that famous first class of 1642. For a long account of him and his family, and a list of his published works, see Sibley's Harvard Graduates, vol. i. pp. 28-51.

Nathaniel Downing, brother of Emanuel and uncle of Sir George, was baptized in the church of St. Mary at the Tower, Ipswich, 8 October, 1587. He married, 6 May, 1613, Margaret, daughter of Doctor Daniel Selyne (or Selin), a French phy-sician, who died 19 March, 1614-15, and in his will (Rudd, 28) mentions his son-in-law Nathaniel Downing. Mr. Downing seems to have had one son, Daniel, bap-tized at St. Dionis Backchurch, 5 April, 1614, and buried five days afterwards.

In the Whitehall Evening Post of Febr. 11, 1764, is this letter :

" To the Printer &c.   Sir

By the death of Sir Jacob Garrard Downing Bar^t an estate of about 5 or 6000 pr annum falls to the University of Cambridge, to build a college, to be called Downing College. The late Sir George Downing, of Gamlingay, in Cambridge-shire, Bar^t, having left it to the late Sir Jacob Garrard, and his Heirs male ; & for want of such Issue, to the rev. Mr Peters, late Lecturer of St Clement-Danes & his Heirs male : both of whom having died without such Issue, the Estate descends as above. The Original of the Family was Dr Calibut Downing, one of the Preachers in the Rebel Army, & a great man with Rump : and his son, afterwards Sir Geo: Downing & the first Baronet of the Family, was made Envoy from Cromwell to the States-General, and got a great Estate, owing to this Incident. When King Charles

* The valuable MS. referred to in note, pp. 197-8, vol. xxxvii. REG.

the 2d was travelling in Disguise in Holland, to visit the Queen Mother, attended only by Lord Falkland, & putting up at an Inn, after he had been there some Time, the Landlord came to these strangers and said, there was a Beggar-man at the Door, very shabbily dressed, who was very importunate to be admitted to them ; on which the King seemed surprised, & after speaking to Lord Falkland, bid the Landlord admit him. As soon as this Beggar-man entered, he pulled off his Beard (which he had put on for a Disguise) & fell on his knees, & said he was Mr Downing, the Resident from Oliver Cromwell ; & that he had received Advice of this intended visit from his Majesty to the Queen ; and that, if he ventured any farther, he would be assassinated ; & begged secrecy of the King, for that his Life depended upon it, & departed. The King was amazed at this, & said to Lord Falkland, How could this be known ? there were but you & the Queen knew of it. Therefore the Queen must have mentioned this to somebody who gave Advice of it to his Enemies. However, the King returned back, whereby this Design was prevented. Upon this, after the Restoration, Sir George Downing was rewarded, made a Baronet & Farmer of the Customs, &c. &c., whereby this large Estate was raised.

Besides the above Estate of Sir Jacob Garret Downing Bart. which devolves on the University of Cambridge, another fine Estate, with a handsome house at Putney, falls to his Lady."

In the London Chronicle of Jan. 9, 1772, is this Article :

" We are assured that the Heirs at Law [B. P. Ewer of Bangor who married a Barnardiston] of Sir Jacob Downing Bart have applied for a Royal Charter to found & incorporate the College at Cambridge. A spot is fixed upon for erecting this edifice, which is a spacious Piece of ground, fit for the Purpose, on the South Side of the Town, opposite the Physic Garden, & between Pembroke & Emanuel Colleges. A Design is preparing & Application making to the Owners of the Ground which belongs to several Bodies Corporate ; & as soon as an Act of Parliament can be obtained to impower them to sell, this noble Benefaction will be carried into immediate Execution."—H. F. W.

The English genealogical works which attempt to give the ancestry of Sir George Downing, baronet, give it erroneously. The error seems first to have been promulgated by Anthony a Wood in his Athenæ Oxoniensis, published 1691–2, where, in an account of Dr. Calybute Downing, the Puritan writer, son of Calybute Downing of Shennington, Gloucestershire, Sir George is called his son. The error has been copied into several Baronetages. Dr. Downing's ancestry has been carried back through his grandfather, Arthur, of Lexham in Norfolk, to his great-grandfather Geoffrey Downing of Norwich, who married Elizabeth, daughter of Thomas Wingfield. There are no indications of a relationship between this family and that of George Downing of Ipswich, Suffolk, who, as Mr. Waters shows, was father of Emanuel, the father of Sir George. Savage names Mary, wife of Anthony Stoddard; James ; Anne, wife of Capt. Joseph Gardner and afterwards of Gov. Simon Bradstreet ; John ; and Dorcas, as other children of Emanuel Downing ; and there was probably also a son Joshua (Mass. Hist. Coll. 4th S. vi. 79). Emanuel Downing announces his intention to leave New England in the fall of 1654 with Gen. Sedgwick (Ibid. p. 84). He was living as late as Sept. 6, 1658, in Edinburgh (Ibid. p. 86). His wife was living in England, June 27, 1662 (Ibid. p. 544). The place and date of death of neither are known. Interesting letters from Emanuel Downing and other members of his family, are printed in the volume of the Mass. Hist. Coll. cited.

Henry Downing, father of Col. Adam Downing, distinguished as an officer in William III.'s army in Ireland, may have been, as represented by Burke (Ext. and Dorm. Baronetage, ed. 1844, p. 163 ; Landed Gentry, ed. 1853, i. 453), a son of Dr. Calybute. We find no evidence that Sir George had a brother Henry.

It is not probable that Wood obtained his information from the family, for the deed of which Mr. Waters gives an abstract proves that Charles Downing, son of Sir George, knew that his grandfather's name was Emanuel so late as 1700, eight years after the publication of Wood's Athenæ. The following letter, copied for us by G. D. Scull, Esq., of Oxford, England, from the original, shows that Wood, while engaged on his work, applied to the Rev. Increase Mather for information about the Downings, but with little success :

" Sir

I have yours of 20th Instant. There never was any Dr Downing in New England. It is true yt Sir George Downing (who was knighted by Charles 2nd) had his education in ye Colledge there ; but had no other degree there besides yt of

Bachelor of Art. Nor do any in that colledge proceed further than Master of arts after seven years standing, as 'tis in Oxford and Cambridge. We never (which is pity) had any Doctors. I am ashamed to tell you that I cannot procure any further account concerning non conformist writers. I have really laboured to gratify you to my power. I heartily wish there were more publick spirits in the world.

Sir   Your servant,   I. Mather.

London July 23—1691.

To Mr Anthony Wood near Merton College in Oxford."

An equally inexplicable error will be pointed out in this article when we come to the will of Sir William Phips, who is represented in English books to be ancestor of the present Marquis of Normanby. Both errors have years ago been pointed out by our countrymen. The second volume of Hutchinson's Massachusetts, which was reprinted in England in 1768, gives the true christian name of the father of Sir George Downing.—Editor.]

Thomas Warnett, now of James City in Virginia, merchant, 13 February, 1629, proved 8 November, 1630, by Thomazine Warnet, relict and executrix. To Mrs Elizabeth Pott one Corfe and crosse cloth of wrought gold and to Dr John Pott (1) five thousand of several sorts of nayles. To Francis Pott four score pounds of tobacco which he oweth me. To Mr Francis Boulton, minister, one firkin of butter, one bushel of white salt, six pounds of candles, one pound of pepper, one pound of ginger, two bushels of meal, one rundlett of ink, six quires of writing paper and one pair of silk stockings. To John Johnson's wife six pounds of soap, six pounds of white starch and one pound of blue starch. To John Browning's wife one thousand of pins, one pair of knives carved with two images upon them, twelve pounds of white starch and two pounds of blue starch. To the wife of Mr John Uptone one sea green scarf edged with gould lace, twelve pounds of white starch and two pounds of blue starch. To my friend Mr Thomas Burges my second best sword and my best felt hat. To John Grevett's wife one pair of sheets, six table napkins, three towels and one table cloth marked with T. W., six pounds of soap, six pounds of white starch and one pound of blue starch. To Thomas Key's wife one gilded looking glass. To Sargt John Wane's (2) wife four bushels of meal and one rundlett of four gallons of vinegar, one half pound of "threed" of several colours, twenty needles, six dozen of silk and thred buttons, one pewter candlestick & one pewter chamberpot. To Roger Thompson's wife one half bushel of white salt, one pound of pepper and one jar of oil. To Benjamin Symes (3) one weeding hoe. To George Muleston one "howing" hoe & one axe. To John Goundry one bar of lead of twenty pound weight and three pound. To John Hattone one black felt hat, one suit of grey kersie, one shirt marked T. W., four pairs of Irish stockings, two pairs of my own wearing shoes, one bar of lead and six pounds of powder. To John Southerne (4) six pounds of candles, one Poland cap furred and one pair of red slippers. To Michael Batt (5) his wife two bushels of meal.

The rest of my temporal estate in Virginia, my debts being paid and legacies paid & discharged, to wife Thomazine, whom I appoint executrix. Friends John Southerne and James Stome overseers. To the former one black beaver hat and gold band, one doublet of black chamlet and one pair of black hose; and to James Stome my best sword and a gold belt.

The witnesses were Francis Boltone (6) & John Southerne.

Scroope, 105.

[The following, from Harl. MS. (Brit. Mus.), 1561, f. 142, undoubtedly gives the pedigree of the testator of the above will, and indicates his place of residence before his migration.

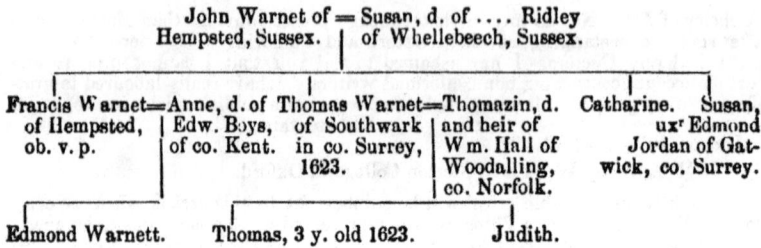

John Warnet of = Susan, d. of .... Ridley
Hempsted, Sussex. | of Whellebeech, Sussex.

Francis Warnet=Anne, d. of   Thomas Warnet=Thomazin, d.   Catharine.   Susan,
of Hempsted, | Edw. Boys,   of Southwark | and heir of   ux' Edmond
ob. v. p. | of co. Kent. in co. Surrey, | Wm. Hall of   Jordan of Gat-
              | 1623. | Woodalling,   wick, co. Surrey.
              | | co. Norfolk.

Edmond Warnett.   Thomas, 3 y. old 1623.   Judith.

                                                    H. F. W.

1. Dr. John Pott, the legatee mentioned, was doubtless the John Pott, A.M.,
M.D., physician for the colony of Virginia, who arrived with his wife Elizabeth in
October, 1621, in the ship George. He was appointed on the recommendation of
Dr. Theodore Gulston, the founder of the Gulstonian lectureship of Anatomy, still
maintained by the London College of Physicians. In the Virginia Land Records,
Book No. 1, p. 8, he appears as a grantee, on August 11th, 1624, of three acres of
land in "James Cittie," and is mentioned as a "Doctor of Physicke" and a member of the "Councill." Francis West, the governor of the colony and a younger
brother of Lord Delaware, departing for England March 5th, 1628, Dr. Pott succeeded him as governor, and so served until some time in March, 1630, when he
was superseded by Sir John Harvey. Pott was then arraigned for pardoning Edward Wallis, condemned for murder and cattle stealing. This was the first trial by
jury in the colony. Pott was found guilty and confined to his plantation at Har-
rope, now Williamsburg, until the King's pleasure could be ascertained. Governor Harvey forwarded the recommendation of the Council for his pardon, and Mrs.
Pott crossed the ocean and pleaded her husband's cause. The commissioners to
whom the petition was referred reported to the King that "condemning him for
felony was very rigorous, if not erroneous," and recommended that he should be
restored to liberty and his estate, and the practice of his profession.

2. I find in the State Land Registry a grant of 300 acres to John Wayne (rendered in the Index, Waine) in Charles River County (as the County of York was first
called), May 10th, 1638. Book No. 1, p. 560.

3. It may be recalled that Benjamin Symmes is reported in 1648 as having
founded in the colony a free school, which he endowed with two hundred acres of
land, a good house, forty milch cows and other appurtenances.

4. There is a grant also of record to John Southerne, "Gent." (in all probability
him of the will), of twenty-four acres in "James Cittie," September 1st, 1627.
Book No. 1, p. 55.

5. Michaell Batt appears as a grantee of one acre of land in "James Cittie Island," September 20th, 1643, Book No. 1, p. 890. Grants also appear contempo-
raneously to John, William and Henry Batt, Batte or Batts, as the name is variously rendered. The descendants of William and Henry Batte (as the name now ob-
tains), brothers, are quite numerous in Virginia, and of high respectability.

6. The Rev. Francis Boulton, Boltone or Bolton, as the name is variously rendered, who had been recommended by the Earl of Southampton for some vacant parish
in Virginia, arrived in the colony in the ship George, as above, and was assigned to
Elizabeth City, to reside with Captain Thomas Newce.—R. A. BROCK, *of Richmond,
Virginia.*]

WILLIAM PEPPERELL of St. Stephens by Launceston, in the County of
Cornwall, 5 June, 1655, proved 15 October 1655, by Jane Pepperell, his
widow, and William Pepperell, his son. Daughter Alice (under 12) and
Jane Pepperell, second son Robert, wife Jane, son Thomas (under 12) and
eldest son William. Richard Call my brother-in-law, John Roe of Launceston, Thomas Facy of St. Thomas, and Robert Pepperell my brother (of
whose unfained affection and fidelity I have had long and frequent experi-
ments), to be overseers. The witnesses were Nevill Blighett, Will Blag-
don and Nicholas Dodge.   Aylett, 387.

[The testator could not have been the grandfather of Sir William Pepperrell, bart., the captor of Louisburg Possibly he may have been his great-grandfather. William Pepperrell, the father of the baronet, was born about 1646, having died Feb. 13, 1733-4, in his 87th year. Usher Parsons, M.D., in the biography of the son (Boston, 1856), states that the father was born in Tavistock, Devonshire: but ten years later (REGISTER, xx. 1) he calls him a native of Wales. The Wentworth Genealogy (ed. 1878, p. 307) calls him a native of Cornwall. "Tradition," according to Dr. Parsons, "says that he spoke broad Welsh, as Boll and Woll for Bill and Will." He had three sisters. One married a Phillips, another a Gilbert, and the third, Grace, died unmarried. His children were Andrew, Mary, Margery, Joanna, Miriam, William the baronet, Dorothy and Jane. For an account of the descendants of the baronet, among whom is Edward Walford, M.A., of London, Eng., editor of the *Antiquarian Magazine*, see REGISTER, xx. 1-6.— EDITOR.]

GEORGE FENWICK, of Worminghurst, co. Sussex, Esquire, 2 February, 1656, with codicil of 9 March, 1656, proved 27 April, 1657, by Elizabeth Fenwick, daughter and executrix. To wife Katherine, &c. &c.; to my most natural and dear mother, M⟨r⟩ Dorothy Clavering; to brother Claudius and his heirs male my lands in Brenckborn and Nether Framlington in the county of Northumberland; to my nephew Thomas Ledgard and his heirs male land in Thirston and Tillington in Northumberland; to my sister Ledgard and my sister Cullick each fifty pounds; to my brother Ledgard and my brother Cullick, each ten pounds; to my sister Cullick's children one hundred pounds apiece; to my niece Clifton fifty pounds, and to niece Bootflower's boy fifty pounds; to my daughter Elizabeth and daughter Dorothy; to Ralph Fenwick, a scholar of Christ Church, Oxford, ten pounds a year; to my daughters land in Sussex that descends to them from their uncle Edward Apsley, Esquire, deceased.

The above he declared to be his will 10 March, 1656. In the codicil he bequeaths to his sister Cullick and her children all his estate in New England; and also five hundred pounds to the public use of that country of New England if " my " loving friend Edward Hopkins think fit. He makes bequests to his friend Robert Leeves and to his servant Moses Fryer. To Dame Elinor Selby of Barwick he leaves ten pounds and desires her to undertake the education of Dorothy. His father-in-law Sir Arthur Hesslerigg to accept the mean remembrance of forty shillings to buy a ring. He also mentions his cousin Lawrence and his wife, his cousin Strickland and his lady, his ancient acquaintance and dearly beloved friend Sir Thomas Widdrington, his dear and good friend M⟨r⟩ Edward Hopkins, late warden of the fleet, his friend Aaron Gourdon, Dr. of Physic, his friend M⟨r⟩ Tempest Milner, alderman of London, and the latter's kinsman Robert Key, his father-in-law, M⟨r⟩ Claveringe, and Thomas Burrell of Brinckborn, Northumberland. He gives six pounds per annum to Tristram Fenwick for life, forty shillings to M⟨r⟩ Ogle of Leith in Scotland, and twenty shillings to the widow Clarke of Weldon.   Ruthen, 138.

[The family of Forster, of Newham, from which Col. George Fenwick and his sister Mrs. Elizabeth Cullick derived their descent, are said by Mundy to be descended out of the house of Forster of Etherston. In this latter family the baptismal name of Reignold often occurs, suggesting the possible origin of Reginald Forster of Ipswich. They bore *Argent, a chevron vert between three bugle-horns stringed sable*. " these verses were sett about the Armes," says Mundy:

> " let us derly them hold
> to mind ther worthynes
> that wch our parent's old
> hath left us to posses."

Col. Fenwick's first wife and the mother of his children, was Alice, relict of Sir John Botteler, knight, and daughter of Sir Edward Apsley of Thackham in county Sussex, knight. One of her sisters, Elizabeth, was the wife of Sir Albert Morton, Secretary of State to King James. His second wife, Catherine, was eldest daughter of the famous Sir Arthur Hazelrigg of Noseley Hall, in Leicestershire. The monument erected to the memory of Col. Fenwick in the church at Berwick, which he is said to have been principally instrumental in building, shows that he died 15 March, 1656. It will be noticed that his sister Elizabeth, wife of Capt. John Cullick, does not appear on the following pedigree, probably not having been born until after 1615, when the visitation was made. The " sister Ledgard " was Mary, wife of Thomas Ledgard.

The following pedigree is extracted from Richard Mundy's copy of Visitations of Northumberland, 1575 and 1615, Harl. MS. 1554, ff. 20, 54 :

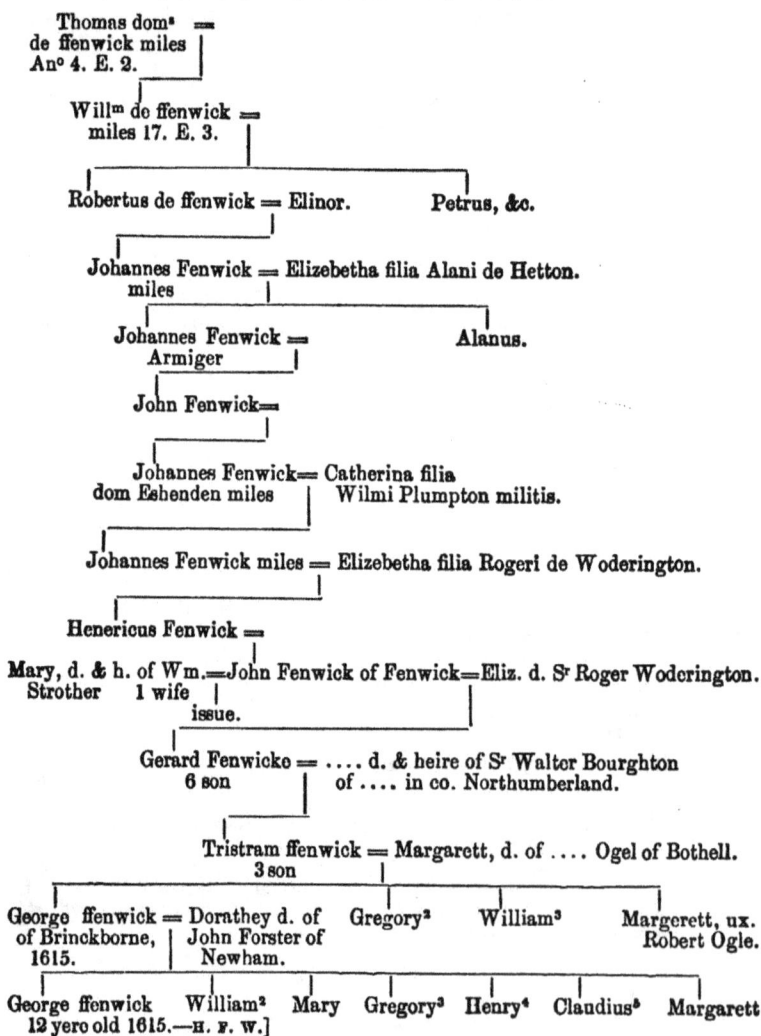

Thomas domᵃ =
de ffenwick miles
Anº 4. E. 2.

    Willᵐ de ffenwick =
    miles 17. E. 3.

Robertus de ffenwick = Elinor.   Petrus, &c.

Johannes Fenwick = Elizebetha filia Alani de Hetton.
    miles

Johannes Fenwick =   Alanus.
    Armiger

John Fenwick=

Johannes Fenwick= Catherina filia
dom Esbenden miles   Wilmi Plumpton militis.

Johannes Fenwick miles = Elizebetha filia Rogeri de Woderington.

Henericus Fenwick =

Mary, d. & h. of Wm.=John Fenwick of Fenwick=Eliz. d. Sʳ Roger Woderington.
Strother   1 wife   issue.

Gerard Fenwicke = ... d. & heire of Sʳ Walter Bourghton
    6 son   of .... in co. Northumberland.

Tristram ffenwick = Margarett, d. of .... Ogel of Bothell.
    3 son

George ffenwick = Dorathey d. of   Gregory²   William³   Margerett, ux.
of Brinckborne, John Forster of   Robert Ogle.
1615.   Newham.

George ffenwick William² Mary Gregory³ Henry⁴ Claudius⁵ Margarett
12 yero old 1615.—H. F. W.]

WILLIAM HATHORNE, of Binfield in the County of Berks, yeoman, 18 May, 1650, proved 2 May, 1651, by Sara Hathorne, the widow and executrix. To the poor of the parish of Binfield twenty shillings, to be distributed on the day of my burial. To Robert Hathorne, my son, all that my messuage or tenement now in the tenure of my brother-in-law John Lawrence, situate and being in Bray, in the County of Berks, together with all barns, stables, outhouses, orchards, gardens, backsides, easments, profits and hereditaments thereto belonging; and also that my cottage closes and parcels of land, pasture and meadow, lying and being in Bray aforesaid, and hereafter particularly mentioned. That is to say, one barn with two orchards and five closes of pasture and meadow called Neatherhouse barn, neathouse mead, the two Butts, Bishopps cloase and the backside, containing in all eighteen acres, more or less, lying together near unto the said messuage and abutting upon Oakely Greene towards the North,—(other lots, of four acres and of eighteen acres respectively, abutting upon Oakely Green towards the South), one cottage, with a hay house and backside, late in the tenure of Richard Braiser, containing one acre, more or less, abutting upon Okely Greene aforesaid towards the North; also one close and one pidle of pasture ground called Godlers, containing seven acres, adjoining to a lane leading out of Okeley Greene into Didworth Green towards the South, to have unto the said Robert Hathorne my son & his heirs forever, upon trust, &c.—that they shall give and pay unto William Hathorne, my eldest son, his executors or assigns, the sum of one hundred pounds of lawful money of England within two years next after my decease, and unto John Hathorne, my son, &c., twenty pounds within three years, &c. Item, I give unto Nathaniel Hathorne, my son, twenty shillings in money. Further unto John Hathorne twenty pounds, if living, otherwise to his wife and children, within one year next after my decease. To Edmond Hathorne, my youngest son (thirty acres and more in Bray) upon the trust and confidence and to the end, intent and purpose that the said Edmond Hathorne, my son, his heirs or assigns, shall give and pay unto Elizabeth, my daughter, the wife of Mr Richard Davenporte, her executors or assigns, the sum of forty pounds of lawful money of England within two years next after my decease. To Anne, my daughter, wife of Hugh Smith, twenty shillings, and to Elizabeth, her daughter, five shillings. To Robert, Sara, Anne and Katherine, the children of my son-in-law Philip Lee, five shillings apiece.

The residue, my debts being paid, my funeral expenses discharged and this my last will and testament in all things duly performed, to Sara Hathorne, my wife, whom I ordain and make sole executrix.

The witnesses were John Sowthey als Hayle, Thomas Dyer and Robert Southey als Hayle.   Grey, 87.

SARA HATHORNE (by mark) of Binfield in the County of Berks, widow, 5 September, 1655, proved 14 March, 1655, by Nathaniel Hathorne, son and sole executor. To the poor of Binfield twenty shillings, to be bestowed on such as have most need, at the discretion of my executors, on the day of burial. To Robert Hathorne, my son, a round table in the chamber over the Hall, with a drawer to him, a great joyned chair in the parlor, my elm chest in the chamber over the parlor, a great pair of andirons standing in the parlor, two pillow beares, one of them Holland pillow beare and the other of them a flaxen pillow beare, two silver spoons, one of my best joined stools in the hall, a cupboard cloth wrought with blue at the ends and a great brazen candlestick. To Anne, my daughter, the wife of Hugh Smith, my best feather bed and bolster belonging to him, a feather pillow, two blankets, my green rug, my green sea curtains and valians to them, two pair of my better sheets, the fourth part of all my pewter, my lesser brass pot and pothooks, my little skillett, all my wearing apparell, three of my bigger milk bowls, a low leather chair, my best green matted chair, the biggest chest that was her fathers and ten pounds of lawful money of England. To my two grandchildren Anne Lee and Katherine Lee, twenty shillings apiece. To all the residue of my grandchildren, that is to say, Sara Hathorne, Elizabeth Hathorne and Elizabeth Hathorne, Susanna Hathorne, Nathaniel Hathorne, William Smith and Elizabeth Smith, the several sums of ten shillings apiece. To Anne Middleton, my late servant, ten shillings.

The residue to son Nathaniel Hathorne, who is to be sole executor. The witnesses were John Yonges and Henrie Otwaie (by mark).

Berkley, 34.

[The foregoing will of William Hathorne of Binfield confirms the guess made in 1879, as to the English home of the American family of Hathorne, and the inter-marriage of Lieut. Richard Davenport, of New England, with that family. (See Gleanings from English Records, &c., by Emmerton and Waters, Essex Institute, Salem, Mass., where sundry abstracts of English wills may be found, and paternal and maternal pedigrees of the distinguished author Nathaniel Hawthorne.) Binfield, Bray and Oakley Green are all in the North Eastern part of Berkshire, a little West and South West of Windsor. From a History and Antiquities of the Hundred of Bray, by Charles Kerry, London, 1861, I learn that there was a manor of Cruchfields and Hawthorne, that a William Hawthorne was one of the tenants of "Queen Lease" in the parish of Bray and Manor of Bray, 1650; in the "Rentall of the Manor of Bray, 1650," William Hawthorne is charged one pound per annum for all lands holden of the manor, Thomas Hawthorne is charged three shillings, the heirs of Robert Hawthorne five shillings, and William Hawthorne, Jr., five pence. In "The Assert Rent of Bray, 1658," under the title "Oakley," I find "Robert Hauthorne for house and lands," six shillings four pence, "Thomas Hauthorne ditto," three shillings three pence half penny, and "Henery Hauthorne for lands," seven shillings. William Hawthorne was one of the church wardens in Bray, A.D. 1600. By Indenture dated 10 January, 6 James (1609), Sir John Norris confirmed unto William Goddard, William Hathorne, Thomas Westcott and five others, and their heirs, all those piddles or parcels of ground severally lying in certain hamlets and tithings of the parish of Bray in the county of Berks, whereupon small cottages and other edifices were erected and built, containing in the whole, by estimation, five acres," &c., in trust for the "relief of such poor, impotent and aged persons as from time to time thereafter should be dwelling within the said parish, and to the intent that the poorest and most aged and impotent persons of the said parish should be provided for ever of houses and habitation." By an Indenture dated 14 January, 1621, it appears that William Hawthorn and Thomas Westcott, who were the surviving trustees. associated with themselves eight other substantial inhabitants of the parish as feoffees in trust, &c. By Indenture of feoffment bearing date 1 September, 1657, it appears that Thomas Wilcox was the surviving trustee. On page 110 of the History may be found "The Legend of Hawthorn," which narrates the finding of two pots of gold on Hawthorn Hill, near Cruchfield (but a little way from Binfield), and on page 111 sundry notices of the name of Hawthorne, gathered from court rolls, registers and other authentic sources; from which it appears that John Hothorn died 1520, leaving Henry Hothorn his son and heir. Henry died 1531, leaving Roger his son and heir. In 1535 a field of Thomas Hothorne adjoined one held by John Bysshop in "Cryche-feld." In 1533 Thomas Hothorne was appointed collector for the lands he (Bysshop) held called "Chaunters" by the yearly rent of twenty shillings nine pence. William Hothorn died 1538, leaving William his son and heir. William Hawthorne was a copyhold tenant 1601 and church warden 1600–02. Thomas Hawthorn jun. purchased "Brownings" in Holyport, 1602. John Hawthorne held a coppice at Binfield called "Picking's Points," 1605. One of this family married Anne, daughter of Gilbert Loggins, circa 1605. And Robert Hawthorne's name occurs 1656 to 1664.—H. F. W.]

NATHANIEL HATHORNE, of Cookham in County Berks, gentleman, 27 September, 1652, proved 29 July, 1654, by Martha Hathorne, the relict and executrix. To wife Martha eight hundred pounds in lieu of her jointure and thirds, &c. My manor of South Braham* in the county of Somerset. Estates in the counties of Devon, Somerset and Berks. My four brothers-in-law, Thomas Loggins, John Whistler, Ralphe Whistler and Thomas Whistler, gentleman. My three own sisters, Elizabeth, Mary and Anne, and John Laurence, the husband of Anne. My son-in-law William Mattingly and Jone his wife. My kinsman William Eldridge and Judith his wife. Anne Winche, the wife to my nephew John Winch. My nephew William Winche. The poor of Cookham and South Braham. Wife Martha to be executrix, and two loving kinsmen, Dr. Daniel Whistler of Gresham College, and John Winche, of London, haberdasher, to be overseers. One of the witnesses was John Hathorne. Alchin, 251.

[This testator was, of course, brother to the foregoing William Hathorne and uncle to the American immigrant.

It is with a peculiar satisfaction, it must be confessed, that the compiler of these Gleanings, himself a native of Salem, has at last been able to prove beyond a doubt whereabouts in "Our Old Home," that elder England beyond the seas, we must look for the ancestry of the most widely known among the distinguished sons of old Salem, the most original of the prose writers of our New England, and the one whose writings are most native to her soil; a satisfaction tinged with the regret, however, that the discovery was not made in the great writer's life-time. We can easily imagine with what delight he would have made a pilgrimage into Berkshire, how gladly he would have loitered about Binfield and Bray, Cruchfield and Oakley Green, making new sketches to illustrate his English Note Book, and how eagerly his quaint and vivid fancy would have seized even upon the scanty materials offered to it in the Legend of Hawthorn Hill and its pots of gold, to weave therefrom a story that should rival in weirdness any of his "Legends of New England."

The eldest son and namesake of William Hathorne of Binfield, and first American ancestor of the distinguished writer, was, next to Governor Endicott, by far the most important personage in the civil history of Salem during the first generation. By sheer force of natural talent and commanding character, this son of a plain English yeoman easily came to the front rank among the many wise and active New England men who were then engaged in the tremendous and to them solemn task of founding a state, opening up the wilderness, treating with "the barbarious Heathen," justly and peaceably if possible, but with fire and sword if need be, allotting lands to the new comers in proportion to their means and ability and to the numbers of their families, establishing offices of record, settling disputes, levying taxes, making provision for meeting-house and school-house, regarding justice and morality, a careful religious training and the free education of all, as the only sure basis of good order and sound government, the only firm and stable foundation whereon to erect the superstructure of a mighty new state. In all this work Major William Hathorne bore a prominent part, whether as an enterprising and prosperous merchant, a trusted citizen and deputy, an honored speaker of the House, a wise and influential magistrate in the highest court, or an active and successful commander in the wars; and his career illustrates most happily the wonderful capacity of the Anglo-Saxon race, that imperial race of modern times, its adaptability and readiness to cope with new conditions of life, to adjust itself to strange and heretofore untried surroundings, its plain and homely common sense, its union of native practical sagacity and sound judgment with a love of law and order, and at the same time a spirit of adventure, which has made Great Britain not only the most prosperous of nations, but the greatest colonizing people in the world, the mother of Nations, and which is so conspicuously manifested in the marvellous career of her daughters, the "Greater Britain" in America and Australia and elsewhere throughout the world wherever a love of enterprise or any other cause has led its people to settle and plant new homes.—H. F. W.]

* Probably South Bruham (or Brewham) in the Hundred of Bruton.—H. F. W.

Sir WILLIAM PHIPS, Knight, of Boston in the county of Suffolk, Province of Massachusetts Bay, in New England, 18 December, 1693, sworn to by Dame Mary Phips 10 September, 1696; proved 29 January, 1696. To brother James Phips or his heirs, the sum of five shillings. To my dear and entirely beloved consort Mary Phips, and to her heirs forever, all my estate, real and personal, &c. &c., with power to alienate by deed of gift, will or codicil. If she should die without having, by will, disposed of my estate, &c., it shall all descend and fall to my adopted son, Spencer Phips als Bennett and the heirs of his body. If he should die without issue surviving, what is left shall be equally divided and shared, one half thereof by my sisters Mary, Margaret and the heirs of my sister Anne deceased, or their heirs forever, and the other half in like manner, to the relations of my beloved consort, reserving only out of the whole estate one hundred pounds current money of New England, which my said relations and the relations of my said wife shall cause to be paid unto John Phipps, son to my brother John Phipps deceased, or to his heirs, if this clause be not repealed by my wife aforesaid. If my dear consort should die before my said son is come to age or is married, then I do nominate and appoint my friends Capt. John Foster, Esq., and Capt. Andrew Belcher of Boston, merchants, to be trustees of my estate and guardians to my said son, until he shall be of full age or married.

The witnesses were John Phillips, John White, John Hiskett, Josiah Stone and John Greenough.   Pyne, 15.

FRANCIS PHIPPS, the elder, of Reading, in the county of Berks, mentions (inter alios) son Constantine Phipps, in his will proved 1668.

Hene, 69.

[A flattering sketch of the mathematical and inventive ability of Sir William Phips—our governor during the time of the witchcraft delusion; with a copy of the epitaph from his monument in St. Mary Woolnoth's Church in London, are given in "The Peerage of Ireland," by John Lodge, vol. vii. p. 84, of the edition of 1789, edited by Mervyn Archdall, as a prelude to the history of the ancestry of Lord Mulgrave; which is followed by the statement that Sir William Phips was father of Sir Constantine Phipps, Lord Chancellor of Ireland from 1710 to 1714, who was grandfather of the first Baron Mulgrave.

Sir William (whose will is given above) was son of James Phips, a gunsmith, who came from Bristol, England, and settled near the Kennebec River. Cotton Mather states that James had twenty-one sons and five daughters. Sir William mentions in his will but one brother and three sisters, and having *no* child adopts his wife's nephew, afterward known as Spencer Phips, who lived and died in New England. Sir Egerton Brydges copied the statement from Archdall and incorporated it in his celebrated edition of Collins's Peerage (1812), but having noticed later the Life of Sir William Phips by Cotton Mather, corrects the statement in an appendix, so far as Sir *Constantine* was concerned, by suggesting that Spencer Phips, the adopted son of Sir William, was the true ancestor of Lord Mulgrave. Debrett, in his annual Peerage, carried the original story for years, but finally left it out entirely. Burke substituted "cousin" for "father," still keeping Sir William Phips for the "figure-head" of the family by saying he was cousin of Sir Constantine. Savage (1861) Vol. iii. p. 422, calls attention to the "preposterous fable," and quotes "Smiles's Self-Help, p. 169," as a present example of its continuance. The Heraldic Journal (1865), Vol. i. pp. 154-5, contains a full and interesting account of this "popular error." The latest promulgation of the old story which has come to my sight is in an elegant volume purchased by the Boston Athenæum during 1881, "Picturesque Views of Seats of Noblemen, &c.," by Rev. F. O. Morris, no date, but evidently a *very* recent publication, Vol. ii. pp. 11 to 12, with a view of Mulgrave Castle, the seat of the Marquis of Normanby.

This magnificent place was inherited by Constantine Phipps (a grandson of Sir Constantine previously mentioned) from his maternal grandmother, whose paternity was a question of historic doubt.

Catherine Sedley, created Countess of Dorchester *for life*, was the acknowledged mistress of James II.; the keeper of his privy purse, Col. James Graham, also had intimate relations with her. It happened that her daughter—Lady Catherine Darnly—bore an exact resemblance to his daughter, the Countess of Berkshire. Col. Graham was not inclined to deny the paternity, while the mother asserted that her daughter "need not be so proud, as she was *not* the King's child, but Col. Graham's." (Jesse's Lives of the Stuarts, Vol. iii. p. 508.)

Lady Catherine Darnley was married first to the Earl of Anglesey, from whom she was divorced; she then married the Duke of Buckingham. From him she received Mulgrave Castle, and she gave it to Constantine Phipps, the son of her daughter by her first husband.

This Constantine Phipps was created Baron Mulgrave *of the peerage of Ireland* in 1768, but the titles have accumulated upon his descending line until the present head of the family is "Marquis of Normanby, Earl of Mulgrave, Viscount Normanby and Baron Mulgrave of Mulgrave, co. York, *in the Peerage of the United Kingdom;* Baron Mulgrave of New Ross, co. Wexford, *in the Peerage of Ireland.*" The armorial bearings are quarterings of those of James II.! and of Sir William Phips!

Mr. Waters has found a father for *a* Constantine Phipps, and we hope the whole question of relationship to Sir William (if any existed) will be fully settled soon. Dr. Marshall in "The Genealogist," Vol. vi., gave new material as to the marriages and children of the first Constantine.—J. C. J. BROWN.

From Hist. and Antiquities of Reading, by the Rev. Charles Coates, LL.B., London, 1802, p. 445, we learn that there was a tradition that Sir Constantine Phipps, the ancestor of the Mulgrave family, was born at Reading.—H. F. W.]

SYMON BRADSTREETE, citizen and grocer of London, 22 February, 1627, proved 28 February, 1627, by Samuel Bradstreete. Daughter Margaret, now wife of Edmond Slater, citizen and mercer of London, married without my love, leave or consent. My nephew, Samuel Bradstreete, to be residuary legatee and sole and absolute executor.   Barrington, 14.

[Simon Bradstreet, the "Nestor of New England," who was governor of Massachusetts, 1679–86 and 1689–92, was probably related to the testator. Gov. Bradstreet used on his will a seal with these arms: On a fesse three crescents, in base a greyhound passant (REGISTER, viii. 313). The tinctures are not indicated. The arms of Sir John Valentine Bradstreet, baronet, descended from Simon B. of Kilmainham, co. Dublin, Ireland, created a baronet in 1759, are, Arg. a greyhound passant gules; on a chief sable three crescents or.

The father of Gov. Bradstreet was named Simon, according to the statement of the Rev. Simon B. of New London (REG. ix. 113). Cotton Mather, who does not give the christian name, says that he was "a minister in Lincolnshire who was always a nonconformist at home as well as when preacher at Middleburgh abroad" (Magnalia, ed. 1702, Bk. ii. p. 19; ed. 1853, vol. i. p. 138). Gov. Bradstreet, according to Mather, was "born at Horbling, March, 1603." He died at Salem, March 27, 1697, "æt. 94," according to the inscription on his monument (REG. i. 76). He was bred at Emmanuel College, Cambridge, A.B. 1620, A.M. 1624, came to New England in 1630, being then secretary of the Massachusetts Company. He married first, Anne, daughter of Gov. Thomas Dudley, by whom he had eight children—Samuel, Dorothy married Rev. Seaborn Cotton; Sarah wife of Richard Hubbard; Rev. Simon, Hannah or Ann, wife of Andrew Wiggin; Dudley, John, and Mercy wife of Nathaniel Wade. He married secondly Mrs. Anne (Downing) Gardiner. See memoirs, REGISTER, i. 75–7; viii. 312–13. Lists of descendants of him and his gifted wife, the first female poet in New England, including some eminent American writers, are printed in the REGISTER, viii. 312–25; ix. 113–21.—EDITOR.]

JOHN SEDGWICKE, of the parish of St Savior's, Southwark, in county Surrey, brewer, 27 November, 1638, proved 5 December, 1638, by Martha Sedgwicke, widow and executrix. To be buried in the parish church of St Savior's. To wife Martha two thousand pounds of money and certain personal property at my house at Barnes in county Surrey, late in the occupation of Mr Hubland deceased. To my mother Elizabeth Sedgwicke, of Woburn in the county of Bedford, widow, the sum of five hundred pounds in money within one year after my decease. But if she die before the expiration of said year, then two hundred and fifty pounds of that money to be given to my wife and the other two hundred and fifty pounds to be at the disposal and ordering of my said mother to such of her children as she shall think most meet, at her own will and pleasure. To my sister Mary Houghton, now wife of Robert Houghton, and their daughter Martha, my god-daughter, the sum of one hundred and fifty pounds within one year, &c. To my brother William Sedgwicke, minister of Farnam, near Bishops Starford, fifty pounds within one year, &c. "Item I give and remitt to my loving brother Robert Sedgwicke, of Charlestowne in new England Thirtie and eight pounds which hee oweth mee by bill and fourty shillings to buy him a ring." To my father and mother in law, Edward and Joan Wicke, of Leighton in the county of Bedford, the sum of five pounds each; to sister Joan Wicke ten pounds; to brothers Matthew, Mark and Thomas Wicke ten pounds apiece; and to brother Luke Wicke thirty pounds; all within one year after my decease. To my friend and brother Nicholas Crisp, citizen and girdler of London, ten pounds, and to his wife Sarah Crisp, ten pounds within one year, &c. To the poor of the parish of Woburn in the County of Bedford, the sum of twenty pounds, &c., it being the parish in which I was born. To the poor of the town of Leighton twenty pounds. To the poor of the Liberty of the upper ground, on the Bankeside, in the parish of St. Saviors, ten pounds. To ten poor godly ministers of God's word the sum of forty pounds, to be distributed at the discretion of my overseers. To Mʳ Nicholas Morton, minister of the parish of St. Saviors, forty shillings to preach my funeral sermon. To Mʳ James Archer, minister also of the said parish, forty shillings. To my uncle, Mr Stephen Sedgwicke, brewer, five pounds to buy him a ring. To servant Nathaniel Barrow five pounds. Wife Martha to. be executrix, and kinsmen and friends Edward Wicke, Stephen Sedgwicke, Nicholas Crisp and Robert Houghton to be overseers.   Lee, 181.

[Robert Sedgwick, named in this will as brother of the testator, was a prominent man in early New England history. It is noteworthy that Sarah Sedgwick, second wife of Gov. John Leverett (Reg. xxxv. 348), who has been supposed to be a sister of Robert, is not mentioned here. Robert Sedgwick settled in Charlestown as early as 1636, was one of the founders of the Artillery Company in 1638, was chosen Major-General, the highest military office in the colony, May 26, 1652; went to England and was appointed by Cromwell commander of the expedition which captured in 1654 the French posts in Acadia. He was sent as a commissioner to Jamaica after the capture of that island (Reg. ante, p. 24), where he died May 24 (Drake), or June 24 (Palfrey), 1656. His children were Samuel, Hannah, William and Robert (Wyman's Charlestown). His widow Joanna became the second wife of Rev. Thomas Allen of Charlestown, whose first wife was Anna, widow of John Harvard, founder of Harvard College. Descendants have been distinguished in literature and in civil and military life.—Editor.]

Notes on Abstracts previously printed.

Constant Sylvester. (*Ante*, p. 17.)

Grace Sylvester.—In the Register for October last, page 385, Mr. Waters gives an abstract of the will of Constant Silvester, made in Barbadoes in 1671. In this will the testator gives his two daughters, Grace and Mary, "two thousand pounds each on the day of their marriage, besides One hundred pounds each to buy them a jewel at the age of 16 years." The following deposition, made by the mother of these two young ladies, has been transcribed from the "Proceedings in the Spiritual Court of the Diocese of London," and brings to light an interesting episode in the annals of the family of Sylvester :

"12 Die Menses Decembris Anno Dom̄ 1685 which day appeared p'sonally Grace Sylvester, widdow and Relict of Constant Sylvester, Esquire, dec^d and by vertue of her oath deposed that about Ten years since her husband being dead, her affaires called her into Barbadoes ; she left her children, vizt one Sonn and two daughters under the care and tuition and government to Anne Walrond her sister, who dyed in ffebruary last, as she was informed and she was likewise informed y^t one Mr John Staples being an acquaintance of this deponents sonn Constant Sylvester, thereby became acquainted with Grace Sylvester this deponents daughter and pretended to make his addresses to her in the way of marriage and the same (as this deponent was informed) Came to the Knowledge of the said Anne Walrond & she forbad the said John Staples to come to the said House and he thereupon did desist and she doth farther depose that she this deponent arrived at London on the 28th of September last and after such her arrivall Sir Henry Pickering Bar^t made courtshipp in the way of marriage to her this Deponents daughter Grace Sylvester and he made also his addresses to this deponent therein to whom she gave her consent, upon Information of his Quality, State and Condition and after some tyme the said Mr John Staples came to her this deponents lodgings in St James S^t vizt. on or about the 8^d day of Novr last and in the p'sence of this Depon^t, Henry Walrond Senr Esqre and severall other p'sons the said m^r John Staples told this deponent that he understanding that her daughter Grace was speedily to be married to Sir Henry Pickering and he thought good to acquaint this deponent that her daughter could not justly p'ceed in the s^d match, for she was by promise engaged to him or to that effect and he being asked, when, where, and in whose p'sence, he answered, in the Mall in St James and that her sister Mary and Mrs Mary Seaman were with them, but were either soe much before or behind them that they could not heare theire discourse and the s^d Grace Sylvester being then p'sent absolutely denyed that she made any such p'mise, but declared that she told him that she would never marry any p'son wth out her mothers consent and approbation, or to that very effect, whereupon the s^d John Staples replyed that the p'mise made to him had that condi̅ō̅n and the s^d Grace denying any p'mise, the s^d John Staples said that this was noe more than he expected and in a little tyme after departed, but im̄ediately before his departure had some private discourse with Henry Walrond Senr Esq^t and this depon^t findeing that her s^d daughter Grace Sylvester was noe wayes engaged to the s^d John Staples nor had any kindness for him, This dep^t did consent that the said Sir Henry Pickering should pursue his addresses to the s^d Grace her daughter which he did accordingly and hath obteyned the affections of her s^d daughter and there was and is an agreement made between them by and with the Consent of this dep^t and that order was and is given for drawing up writings and settling of a Joynture and preparation for the marriage between him the s^d Sir Henry Pickering and the s^d Grace to be solemnized before any —— or Inhibition was served on the said Grace which was not served as she believeth untill the fourth of this Instant—December and upon designe (as this dep^t doth verily believe) by the s^d John Staples to gett some money or other sinister end. In witness whereof she hath hereunto sett her hand.

GRACE SYLVESTER.

12 Decemb. 1685.   p' fata Gratia Sylvester }
     vidua jurat coram me,   Th° Exton. }

Henry Walrond, Sen[r] also made a deposition similar to the above, and also adds that Staples in a private discourse with him said "he knew the Consent or promise made to him, was no such promise, as thereby to oblige her, meaning the s[d] Grace, to marry him, or to make null or void her marriage to any other person, but he could thereby putt a stopp, or hindrance if he pleased to her marriage with any other person and desired this deponent (Henry Walrond) to consider thereof."

Sir Henry Pickering was the only son of Sir Henry, the first Baronet, of Whaddon, co. Cambridge, by Elizabeth, daughter of Sir Thomas Vinor, 1st Baronet, Lord Mayor in 1653. He succeeded his father in 1667-8, and married first the daughter of Sir George Downing, Bart., of East Hatley, co. Cambridge; second, Grace Sylvester, by whom he had no children. He resided in Barbadoes, where he died in 1704-5. With him the Baronetcy became extinct.—G. D. SCULL, *of Oxford, England.*

ABSTRACT of the last Will and Testament of the most reverend Father in God Edmund Grindall, Archbishop of Canterbury, made 8 May, 1583, and proved 15 July, 1583. All other wills revoked (except one bearing date 12 April, 1583). My body to be buried in the choir of the parish church of Croydon, without any solemn hearse or funeral pomp. To her Majesty the Queen the New Testament in Greek of Stephanas his impression. To my next successor the pictures of Archbishop Warham and of Erasmus and all such instruments of music and other implements as were bequeathed and left unto me by my predecessor that last was. To Lord Burghley, the Lord High Treasurer of England that my standing cup which her Majesty gave unto me at New Years Tide last before the date hereof. And I make him supervisor, &c. (Gifts to sundry other legatees.) To my faithful friend M[r] Nowell, Dean of Paul's, my ambling gelding called Gray Olyphant. To the poor of the town and the lower part of the parish of S[t] Beghes; to the use of the parish church of S[t] Beghes. To M[r] Doctor Gybson. To William Woodhall, my nephew (*inter alia*), "my blacke straye nagg called Nixe." To Mr. Wilson my chaplain (certain books) and the advowson of the parsonage of Wonston in the diocese of Winchester if it shall fall void in his life time; if not, then to M[r] Robinson, now provost of Queen's College, Oxford. To my nieces Mabell, Anne, Barbara and Frances, the daughters of Robert Grindall, my brother. To my nieces Dorothy, Katherine, Elizabeth and Isabell, the daughters of Elizabeth Woodhall, my sister, late deceased (fifty pounds to each). To the children of Mabel, daughter of my sister, fifty pounds, to be divided amongst them at the discretion of William Woodhall, their uncle. To my niece Woodhall a bowl. To my niece Isabell Wilson, one other bowl, double gilt, without a cover. To Edmond Woodhall, my godson. To my niece Frances Younge, widow. To John Scott, Esq., steward of my household. To my servant William Grindall, my servant William Hales (and other servants named). To John Sharpe. To my loving friend master Thomas Eaton and his wife. To M[r] William Strycland, M[r] Atherton, John Browne, fellow of Pembroke Hall, Cambridge, M[r] Redman, Archdeacon of Canterbury.

I ordain & constitute William Redman, Archdeacon of Canterbury, John Scott, Esq., Steward of my Household, and William Woodhall, my nephew, executors.

Clause, referring to a Free Grammar School, to be founded in St. Beghes in the county of Cumberland, blotted, and "stroken" out 3 July, 1583, about 11 A. M.

A codicil bequeathing to Mr Redman, Archdeacon, &c., all his antique coins of the Roman Emperors. To Mr Wilson, his chaplain, his watch. He did forgive his niece Ann Dacres, widow, &c. &c. Rowe, 39.

Sñia pro allocacõe coñ̃pi bonorum Reuĩendissimi prĩs Edĩ Grindall nup Cant Archipi defti—in judicio inter Alexandrū Willson Mariam Willson et Aliciam Willson nepotes ex sorore dc̄i defuncti partem hm̃õi negotiū promoveñ ex una et Johannem Scott Armigerum executorem superstitem testamenti siue ultime voluntatis dc̄i defuncti partem contra quam hm̃oi negotium promovetur necnon Mabillam Windor ffranciscum Dacres Elenam Dacres Dorotheam Dacres aĩs —— Barbaram Raper ffranciscam Latus Johēm Wilkenson Robertum Wilkenson Dorotheam Bowman Dorotheam Willson Johannem Gibson Thomam Gibson Edmundum Willson Willum Willson Johannem Willson Thomam Willson Mariam Willson Mariam Sheafe et Isabellam Willson proximos consanguineos dc̄i defuncti in specie ac omnes et singulos alios jus titulum aut Interesse in bonis dicti defuncti habeñ aut pretendeñ in genere ad videndum compūm dc̄i defuncti exhiberi et in debita Juris forma iustificari ltñ̃e citāt etc. etc.

Lecta lata et promulgata fuit hec sñia diffinitiua etc Tertia sessione Termini Pasche die Jovis decimo octauo vizt die menss Maii Anno Domini millesimo sexcentesimo nono. Dorset, 60.

[This celebrated puritan Archbishop, the son of William Grindall, was born at St. Bees, in the County of Cumberland, in 1519. He was fellow, president and master of Pembroke Hall, Cambridge, and filled successively the Sees of London, York and Canterbury. He died July 6, 1583, and was buried in the chancel of Croyden church, where are his monument and epitaph. The free school of St. Bees was incorporated by Queen Elizabeth in the name of Edmund Grindall, Archbishop of Canterbury, and the school and master's house were built by his executors. The founder's donation was fifty pounds a year, twenty pounds whereof he appointed to be paid to the master of Pembroke Hall, Cambridge. By the foundation the master of the school is to be a native of Cumberland, Westmoreland, Yorkshire, or Lancashire, and is to be nominated by the Provost of Queen's College, Oxford. King James 1. augmented this foundation. Lord Bacon says he was the gravest and greatest prelate of the land. (Hutchinson's His. of Cumberland.)—THOMAS MINNS.]

JAMES WOODHALL of Walden in the county of Essex, yeoman, 21 February "in ye thirtith yere of the raigne of oure Soueraigne Ladie Elizabeth," &c., proved 30 June, 1601. My body to be buried at the discretion of my executor. To William Woodhall, my son-in-law and Mary his wife, my daughter, all my lands and tenements, both free and copy hold lying within the parish church of Littlebury in the county of Essex, and to their heirs forever, "in consideration of ye great kindness which I have found in him towards me and for a Remuneration of his fatherly goodnes and charges and benevolence bestowed upon the children of William Bird deceased, his said wyves late husband." To the same all that my messuage wherein I now dwell, situate in Walden aforesaid, in a street there commonly called Threshwell hundred, &c., two acres I bought of William Pumfrett, two parcels I bought of Thomas Crofte, one and a half acre of land lying between the land I bought of Thomas Crofte and the lands of George Nicholls Esq., two acres of land in Windmill lane which I lately bought of John Crofte, two and a half acres of land I bought of Richard Chapman, lying on Windmill Hill, &c., and my two houses in Duck Street, in the parish of Walden, (one) now in the tenure of Richard Austen, the other late in the tenure of Davy Hodson. James Woodhall, eldest son of the said William Woodhall, my godson, Edmond Woodhall (second son) and William Woodhall (third son). Certain land at the Sandpits, next the land lately Richard Plommers. Land near William Shelford, land near Thomas Howard, bought of William Bowling. To William Bird and George Bird, sons of my daughter Mary. To Mary Bird, one of the daughters of my said daughter and now the wife of John Kyng, clerk and canon of Windsor. To Debora Woodhall, a daughter of William and Mary Woodhall and every of the other sons and daughters of the said William and Mary, viz. Elizabeth, Mary, Edmond, Dorothy, Jane, Katherine and Johane Woodhall. Whereas Johane my wife, after my marriage had with her, did faithfully promise that she would not claim any title of dower, &c. To Robert Nicholls, her son, and to James, her son, and Henry, her son. William Bird, my daughter's eldest son, to be the overseer of this my will.

The testator's signature was Jamys Woodhall. The witnesses were William Willson, clerk, John Kyng, clerk, and James Crofte Not. Publique.

In a codicil, made 29 August, 1596, referring to his wife's dowry and the bequests to Robert, James and Henry Nicholls, her sons, and to the children of William Woodhall of Walden Esq., his son-in-law and daughter Mary his wife, we learn that "synce that tyme it hath pleased god to blesse hym with one sonne more named Grindall Woodhall," &c. The witnesses to this codicil were William Bird, George Bird, John Sharpe, Robert Longe No. Pub., William Lawe and Josaphat Webbe.

In another codicil, bearing date 22 March, 1598, he makes bequests to his wife and to the poor of Walden. The witnesses to this were George Bird, Thomas Bird, William Burroughs, John Sharpe and John Rice.

Woodhall, 1.

WILLIAM WOODHALL, of Walden in the County of Essex Esq., 30 May First of James, proved 29 November, 1604. To be buried in the parish church of Walden, either on the North side of the church in a place where I appointed or else by my father-in-law and my son James, at the discretion of my executor.

"Nowe whereas my wife and I haue bin mareyed this foure and thirtie yeres and I haue had nott onely by her many children but alsoe haue founde her a moste kinde and loving wief I should farr forget myself if I should nott soe prouide for her as she may haue sufficient," &c. &c. I leave unto my said wife, according to her father's will all such lands as he hath bequeathed unto her, lying either in the parish of Walden or Lytlebury. To John, Archbishop of Canterbury (certain bequests) humbly beseeching his Grace to be good and favorable to my son Edmund whom I leave behind me to succeed in my office. To loving cousin Doctor Duff, M^r of the Requests and Dean of the Arches. To my dear and faithful brother Mr William Wilson. To Doctor Birde and Michael Woodcock (spoken of in another place as "son Woodcock"). "I had a purpose to bestow my sonne William Woodhall either at the study of the common lawe or at the Universitie of Oxforde; but pceiving his tabackicall humor I see he hath nott anie minde either to the one or to the other, And therefore for anythinge I see he must be a souldyer or servingman both places commendable for a younge man especially if he may haue a pipe of tobacco. And to that ende least a farther inconuenience mighte followe for his better maintenaunce I giue unto the said William the place wherein Thomas Lynne was," &c. &c. "Nephew John Wilkinson now in London," referred to.—"Son Grindall Woodhall to be an apprentice either with a merch^t Venturer or some other good trade." My three eldest daughters, Debora Calton, William Burroe and Michael Woodcock. My four other daughters, Mary, Jane, Katharine and Jone Woodhall.

" Memorandum that on Thursday being Ascensõn day and the second daie of June 1603 betweene the howers of seauen and eight in the fore-noone the testator within named lieing in his bed in his chamber within Mr Chayre's house in Pawles church-yarde London did with his owne hande subscribe his name to every leafe of this Will being fiue in nomber," &c.

The witnesses were Jo: Lawe not. pub., William Birde, Antho: Calton, George Birde, Rich. Theker, Christopher Yowle, Robert Longe, William Cooke and Timothy Paget. Harte, 86.

[The following pedigree from Harleian MS., 1541, fol. 55, in the British Museum, shows the connection between Archbishop Grindall and the Woodhalls, whose wills follow his :

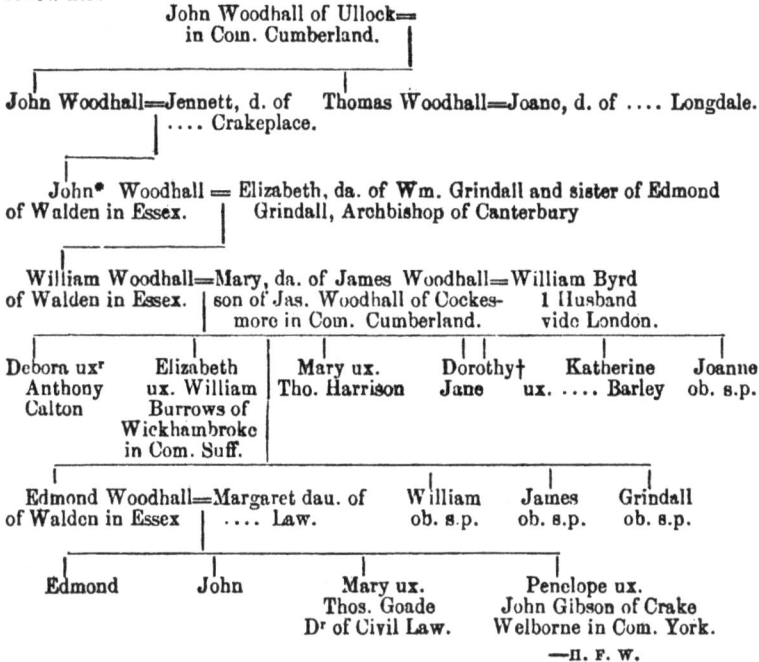

John Woodhall of Ullock═
in Com. Cumberland.

John Woodhall═Jennett, d. of   Thomas Woodhall═Joane, d. of .... Longdale.
.... Crakeplace.

John* Woodhall ═ Elizabeth, da. of Wm. Grindall and sister of Edmond
of Walden in Essex.   Grindall, Archbishop of Canterbury

William Woodhall═Mary, da. of James Woodhall═William Byrd
of Walden in Essex. son of Jas. Woodhall of Cockes- 1 Husband
more in Com. Cumberland.   vide London.

Debora ux^r Anthony Calton	Elizabeth ux. William Burrows of Wickhambroke in Com. Suff.	Mary ux. Tho. Harrison	Dorothy† Jane	Katherine ux. .... Barley	Joanne ob. s.p.

Edmond Woodhall═Margaret dau. of of Walden in Essex .... Law.	William ob. s.p.	James ob. s.p.	Grindall ob. s.p.

Edmond	John	Mary ux. Thos. Goade D^r of Civil Law.	Penelope ux. John Gibson of Crake Welborne in Com. York.

—H. F. W.

In Lipscomb's County of Buckingham is an interesting account, tracing one branch of the Woodhall family from Walter De Flanders, Lord of Wahal, alias Woodhal, 20 William the Conqueror, and giving the coat of arms.

In the Chapel of Eton College is a Latin inscription in memory of " Jane Goad dau. of Edmund Woodhall aged 34 1657 the mother of 3 sons & 2 daughters." (v. iv. p. 312, 486.)

In the church of Walden in Essex, are epitaphs of the following persons : James Woodhall, Assistant and Treasurer, died 1529 ; William Woodhall, Esq., Register of the Prerogative Court of Canterbury, died 1603 ; Mary, daughter of James Wood-hall, first wife to William Byrd, afterwards married to William Woodhall. She died 1613. William Byrde, Gent., d. 1568. (Salmon, His. of Essex, p. 142.)—T. M.

I have a conviction that the Birds mentioned in the abstracts of the wills of the Woodhalls et al., were of the same lineage of William Byrd, of " Westover,"

* Willm Woodhall had evidently been written first, in the same ink as the rest of the pedigree, and John Woodhall written over this in blacker ink.—H. F. W.
† Dorothy became the wife of Michael Woodcock. (See Cussans' Herts, vol. ii. p. 149.) H. F. W.

James River, Va., whose parents were John and Grace (Stagg, or Stegge) Byrd, (or Bird, or Birde), of London. The christian names John, Thomas and William, appear to be favored ones in his pedigree. William Byrd, the first of the name in Virginia, came thither a youth as the heir of large landed estates of his maternal uncle Colonel Thomas Stegge (as he wrote it), whose will is dated 31st March, 1690, and it is presumed that Byrd arrived in the latter part of the year. If the arms are given of the Bird legatees under the Woodhall wills, the family identification would be of easy solution.—R. A. Brock.]

EDMUND WOODHALL, Esq. Registrar of the Prerogative Court of Canterbury, 25 January, 1638, proved 3 February, 1638. My body to be decently interred, near the bodies of my two wives, in the "Ile" belonging to me in the church of Little Munden in the county of Hartford, "there to sleep free from further molestačŏn till it be awaked at the last day by the Angels trumpe with a Surge—Arise thou that sleepest & come to Judgment." I will that the like monument be there erected for me as I did set up for my father in the church of Walden, but my desire is that my funeral may be without any great cost, my will & meaning being that only my children and two sons in law have mourning provided for them; the charges of my funeral not to exceed fifty pounds. My two eldest daughters, Mary Goad, now wife of Thomas Goad, Doctor of Laws, and Dame Penelope Gibson, the now wife of Sir John Gibson the younger, Knight. To Bridget Woodhall, my third daughter, one thousand pounds and to Jane Woodhall, my youngest daughter, the like sum, at four & twenty years of age or day of marriage. Son Edmond and son John (who appears to be at King's College, Cambridge). Brother-in-law Alexander Southwood, gentleman. Brother mr. Michael Woodcock. Cousins and friends Nicholas Hawes Esq. and John Wilkinson gentleman.

" And soe Lord Jesu come quickly."   Harvey, 20.

WILLIAM WILSON, Canon of St. George's Chapel, Windsor Castle, 23 August, 1613, proved 27 May, 1615. To be buried in the chapel near the place where the body of my dear father lies. If I die at Rochester or Cliff, in the County of Kent, then to be buried in the cathedral church of Rochester, near the bodies of wives Isabel and Anne. To my cousin Collins, prebendary at Rochester. To the Fellows and Scholars of Martin College, Oxford. My three sons Edmond, John and Thomas Wilson, daughter Isabel Guibs and daughter Margaret Rawson. My goddaughter Margaret Soffiers which my son Soffiers had by my daughter Elizabeth, his late wife. To my god-son William Sheafe, at the age of twenty one years. Son Edmond, a fellow of King's College, Cambridge, eldest son of me, the said William. To son John the lease of the Rectory and Parsonage of Caxton in the County of Cambridge, which I have taken in his name. To Thomas Wilson, my third son. Son Edmond to be executor and Mr Erasmus Webb, my brother-in-law, being one of the Canons of St. George's Chapel, and my brother, Mr Thomas Woodward, being steward of the town of New Windsor, to be overseers.

The witnesses were Thomas Woodwarde, Joh. Woodwarde, Robert Lowe & Thomas Holl.

In a codicil, dated 9 May, 1615, wherein he is styled William Wilson Doctor of Divinity, he directs his son Edmond to give to his son John forty pounds and to his wife forty marks, he gives to Lincoln College Oxford ten pounds towards a Library, and mentions son-in-law Mr Doctor Sheafe and daughter Gibbes. To this Thomas Sheafe was a witness, amongst others.

In another codicil, of 12 May, 1615, he says, I have provided for the husband of my daughter Isabel Gibbes a place in Windsor, in reversion, of some worth. His signature to this codicil was witnessed by David Rawson and William Newman. Rudd, 36.

[Rev. William Wilson, D.D., of Merton College, Oxford, was also a prebendary of St. Paul's and Rochester cathedrals, and held the rectory of Cliffe, in the county of Kent. In 1584 he became canon of Windsor in place of Dr. Will. Wickham promoted to the see of Lincoln, being about that time chaplain to Edmund (Grindall), Archbishop of Canterbury. He married Isabel Woodhall, daughter of John and Elizabeth Woodhall of Walden in Essex, and niece of Archbishop Grindall. He was buried in St. George's Chapel, Windsor Castle, near the body of his father, William Wilson, late of Wellsbourne, in Lincolnshire, Gent.

His eldest son, Edmund Wilson, M.D., of London, gave the infant colony of Massachusetts one thousand pounds sterling about 1633, which was invested in arms and ammunition. See Mass. Colonial Records, v. 1, p. 128, and 2d Mass. Hist. Soc. Collections, v. 8, p. 228.

His second son, Rev. John Wilson, of Christ's College, Cambridge, married Elizabeth, daughter of Sir John Mansfield and sister of the wife of Mr. Robert Keayne, the first commander of the Artillery Company of Massachusetts, and in 1630 accompanied Winthrop's company to New England, and became the first minister of the First Church in Boston, dying in office in 1667. For a fuller account of him, see Mather's Magnalia, vol. ii. p. 275. For his will, see REGISTER, vol. xvii. p. 343-4.

His daughter Margaret married for her first husband David Rawson, of London, and was the mother of Edward Rawson, secretary of the Massachusetts Colony from 1650 to 1686. For her second husband she married William Taylor. For a further account of them, see the Taylor Family, prepared by the late Col. Chester for Mr. P. A. Taylor.—T. M.

Since these abstracts were in type, the editor has received from Mr. Waters abstracts of the wills of Edmund Wilson, M.D., of William Taylor his brother-in-law, and of William Taylor, son of the latter. They will appear in another number.—EDITOR.

The following notes, taken from the History and Antiquities of Berkshire, by Elias Ashmole, Esq. (Reading, 1736), give the inscriptions found by that famous antiquary in the Chapel of St. George, Windsor Castle, relating to this family.

On the North Side lies a Grave-stone, on which, in Brass Plates, is the Figure of a Man, and this Inscription.

To me to live is Christ, and to dye is Gain.
Philip. I. 21.

Here underneath lies interr'd the Body of William Wilson, *Doctour of Divinitie, and Prebendarie of this Church by the space of 32 yeares. He had Issue by Isabell his Wife six sons and six daughters. He dy'd the 15th of May, in the Year of our Lord 1615, of his Age the 73. beloved of all in his Life, much lamented in his Death.*

Who thinke of Deathe in Lyfe, can never dye,
But mount through Faith, from Earth to heavenly Pleasure,
Weep then no more, though here his Body lye,
His Soul's possest of never ending Treasure.

On another small Brass Plate, on the same Grave-stone, is the following Inscription.

Neere unto this Place lyes buried William Willson, *the third Son, Who, after a long Trial of grievous Sickness, did comfortably yield up his Spirit in the Yeare of our Lord* 1610. *of his Age* 23. Pp. 305-306.

On a Brass Plate, on a Grave-Stone Northward of the last,* is this Inscription.

William Wilson, *late of* Wellsbourne, *in the County of* Lincolne, *Gent. departed this Lyfe, within the Castle of* Windsor, *in the Yeare of our Lord* 1587. *the* 27th *Day of August, and lyeth buried in this Place.* P. 309.

* The "last" monument referred to is a white marble monument erected to the memory of Henry Somerset, Duke of Beaufort, at the east end of a small chapel, dedicated to the Virgin Mary, in the south-west corner of the church.

Arms of " Will'm Wilsohn, of Welborne, per Norroy flower, 1586."

Per pale argent and azure three lions' gambs barways, erased and counterchanged. Crest:—*A lion's head erased argent guttée de sang.*

Harleian Coll., No. 1550, Fol. 192, British Museum ; Richard Mundy's copy of the Visitations of Lincolnshire, 1564 and 1592.

—H. F. W.]

JOHN WILKINSON, of London, gentleman, 3 May, 1614, acknowledged 27 May, 1628; acknowledged again 18 June, 1634; with three codicils, dated respectively 18 June, 1634, 11 October, 1638, and 21 March, 1638 ; proved 12 September, 1639. To my brother Robert Wilkinson the land whereon he now dwelleth, at Preston Howes, pish of St. Bees, in the county of Cumberland. Sister Jeane Pyper, wife of William Pyper, mariner. Sister Mary Wilkinson and brothers Henry and James Wilkinson.

"I do give and bequeath unto the Right Worshipfull my loving uncle William Wilson, Doctor of Divinity, five pounds, and to every one of my loving cosens, his children, twenty shillings apiece." To my loving uncle Henry Bowman and every one of his children by my aunt, the right Worshipful, the lady Margaret Gibson, my good Aunt, &c. The right Worshipful Sir John Gibson, Knight, my loving cousin, and his now wife and virtuous lady, the lady Anne Gibson. My cousin Thomas Gibson and his brother Edward Gibson. The right Worshipful my loving kinsman William Byrd, Doctor of the civil laws. My loving kinsman Mr Thomas Byrd, his brother. My loving kinsman Mr George Byrd. My loving cousin Mrs Elizabeth Burroes and every one of her children. My loving cousin Mrs Dorothy Woodcocke, wife of Mr Michael Woodcocke, and every one of her children. My loving cousin Mrs Jane Warren, wife of Francis Warren. My loving cousin Katherine Barley. My loving cousin Mr William Woodhall. My loving cousin Grindall Woodhall. My dear and loving cousin Edmund Woodhall Esq. & my loving cousin his wife, and his two daughters, Mary & Penelope Woodhall. Mr John Law, Actuary, and Mrs Ann Law, his wife. My loving friend John Sharpe of Walden. My cousin Robert Wilkinson, of Everdale, in the county of Cumberland. The poor of Preston Howes, where I was born. My loving cousins Mary Wilson and Aylce Wilson. Michael, Anthony and George Calton, sons of my cousin Debora Calton deceased. Edmond Calton, another son, when master of arts.

In the first codicil he mentions his friend & kinsman Mr William Wilkinson, mercer in Pater Noster Row, cousin Mrs Grace Pyne, Jane Warren, deceased, and the children of brother Edward Bowens. Friend William Sharpe and his three sisters. To Ralph Brownerigg, Doctor in Divinity, a seal ring of gold. Nephew John Wilkinson goldsmith of London, son of brother James. The children of my sister Mary Bowen. My cousin Alice Swallowe and her husband Mr Thomas Swallowe, my cousin. Others mentioned.   Harvey, 151.

Dame MARY ROWE, widow of Sir Thomas Row, Knight, late citizen and alderman of London (and evidently a sister of William Gresham deceased and of Edmond Gresham), by her will of 21 March, 1579, proved in the year 1582–3, bequeathed to William Wilsonn, parson of Cliff, als Clyve, in Kent, a ring of gold, of three pounds or three pounds in money, and to his wife a ring of gold or its equivalent in money.   Rowe, 1.

EDWARD RAWSON, of Colbrooke, in the parish of Langley Marris, in the County of Buckingham, mercer, 16 February, 1603, proved 4 May, 1604. To my wife Bridget Rawson for and during her natural life, my house and tenement and the appurtenances, &c. lying in Colbrooke, now in the occupation of Edward Whitlock, and, after her decease, unto David Rawson my son and to the heirs male of his body lawfully begotten; and, for want of such issue, unto Henrie Rawson, my eldest son, & to the heirs male of his body lawfully begotten; and, failing such issue, to the right heirs of me, the said Edward, for ever. To son Henry all that house called the "Draggon" and the two shops thereunto adjoining, lying and being in Colbrooke aforesaid, and to his heirs male, &c., with remainder to son David & his lawful issue, &c.; and failing such issue, unto Raphe Warde, my brother-in-law and his heirs for ever. To the said David Rawson, my son, the sum of two hundred pounds at his full age of one and twenty years. Henry Rawson, also a minor. My executors, at their costs and charge, shall bring up my said son David in some reasonable learning until he may be fitt to be putt to apprentice unto some good trade or mystery. My brother Henry Rawson doth owe me fifty pounds.

Wife Bridgett and son Henry to be executors, and friends John Bowser, gentleman, Raph Warde, Philip Bowreman and George Charley to be overseers. Harte, 40.

DAVID RAWSON, citizen and merchant tailor of London, a most unworthy servant of Jesus Christ, 15 June, 1616, proved by his widow Margaret Rawson 25 February, 1617. My goods, &c. shall be divided into three equal & just parts and portions according to the laudable custom of this honorable city of London. One of the three parts to Margaret Rawson, my loving & well-beloved wife. One other part to William and Edward Rawson and such other child or children as I shall hereafter have or as my wife shall be with child withall at the time of my decease, to be equally divided amongst them all, part and part alike. The other third part I reserve towards the payment of legacies, gifts and bequests, &c. To William Rawson, my eldest son, a double gilt salt and a standing cup with a cover, double gilt, and half a dozen of Postle spoons and two double gilt spoons, and a silver porringer, a silver spoon and a silver bowl. To Edward Rawson, my son, a great standing bowl, double gilt, and six silver spoons, and two double gilt spoons, "which was given him by those which were his witnesses at his christening," and a silver bowl. All the rest of the plate to my wife. To the relief of the poor of the Town of Colbrooke, in the County of Buckingham, where I was born, the sum of five pounds of lawful money of England, to be paid within one year next after my decease. To John Emery, son of John Emerie of Colbrooke, clark, deceased, five pounds, to be paid him on the day when he shall be made a freeman of the city of London. To William Fenner, a poor scholar in Pembroke Hall in Cambridge, five pounds within three years after my decease. To David Anngell, my godson, five pounds at the age of twenty one years. To John Nayle, the son of Nicholas Nayle, of Iver in the County of Buckingham, five pounds on the day he shall be made a freeman of the city of London, if he take good courses. To the poor people at my funeral the sum of forty shillings. To John Anngell, clothworker, forty pounds, & to Alexander Dubber, clothworker, forty shillings, which I will shall be deducted out of such money as they shall owe unto me at the time of my decease (if any

be). Item, I give unto my godson Edward Rawson, the son of my brother Henry Rawson, the sum of ten pounds to be paid unto him at his age of
twenty one years.

I give and bequeath to my dear mother, Bridget Woodward, the sum
of ten pounds, which I desire her to give to Mr Winge and Mr Foxe, forty
shillings apiece, if she so please. To my sister-in-law, Jone Rawson, the
sum of forty shillings to make her a ring, and to my sister-in-law Isabel
Gibbs the like sum of forty shillings to make her a ring, and to my sister-
in-law, Elizabeth Wilson, the like sum of forty shillings to make her a
ring; which said four legacies so given to my mother and three sisters I
will shall be paid within one year next after my decease. Item, I do give
& bequeath to my brother-in-law, Thomas Wilson, the sum of five pounds,
to be paid within one year, &c.; and to Andrew Warde, son of my uncle
Raphe Warde, the sum of five pounds, to be paid him at his age of twenty-
one; and to my uncle John Warde the sum of forty shillings, if he be living
at my decease. To my master, Mr Nathaniel Weston, the sum of forty shillings to make him a ring, and I desire him to be assisting to my executrix to
help get in my debts. To Isabel Sheafe, daughter of Doctor Sheafe, three
pounds, to be bestowed in a piece of plate and given her at her age of twenty one years or at the day of her marriage, which ever shall first happen.
To my son Edward Rawson, over and above his said part, the sum of one
hundred pounds; and to my apprentice Matthew Hunte, the sum of six
pounds, thirteen shillings and four pence, to be paid unto him on the day
he shall be made a freeman of the City of London ; and to William Beard
and John Samford, my apprentices (the like sums & on the like conditions).

If all my children die the portions shall remain & come to Alexander
Rawson, the eldest son of my said brother Henry Rawson (if he be then
living); but if he die then to John Rawson and Edward Rawson, two other
of the children of my said brother, &c. equally. The Residue to wife Margaret and son William. I constitute my loving friends, Mr Thomas Woodward, of Lincoln's Inn, in the County of Middlesex, Esq., my father-in-
law, my brother Henry Rawson and Edmond Wilson, Doctor of Physic,
and John Wilson, master of Arts, my brothers-in-law, overseers and give
them five pounds apiece. If wife should die then the above to be executors during the minority of my said sons William and Edward. The witnesses to this will were John Wilkinson & Arthur Viger scr.

In a codicil made 27 November, 1617, he bequeaths to daughter Dorothy
Rawson, besides her (child's) portion, the sum of one hundred pounds at
her age of twenty one or day of marriage ; to sister Anne Wilson, the wife
of brother Thomas Wilson, the sum of forty shillings ; to uncle John Warde
the sum of seven pounds, thirteen shillings and four pence and some of my
cast apparell ; to my cousin Elizabeth Glover the sum of twenty shillings ;
to cousin Jane Lawrence twenty shillings ; to Isabel Cave twenty shillings ;
to Aunt Fenner ten shillings ; to Mr Frogmorton forty shillings ; to Mr.
Houlte twenty shillings ; to Mrs Jane Bartlett ten shillings ; to Mrs Martin
of Windsor ten shillings ; to cousin Dorothy Sheafe a piece of plate of
fifty three shillings price ; all these legacies to be paid within one year and
a half next after my decease by my executrix.

The witnesses to the codicil were John Wilkinson & John Hill.

Meade, 15.

[These wills carry the pedigree of Edward Rawson, secretary of the Massachusetts Colony from 1650 to 1686, back two generations. They give his father David

Rawson of London, and his grandfather Edward Rawson of Colebrook. For a memoir of Secretary Rawson, with a portrait, and a genealogy of his descendants, see REGISTER, vol. iii. pp. 201-8 and 297-330; also The Rawson Family, editions of 1849 and 1875.—EDITOR.

In Lipscomb's Buckingham is the following mention of the Rawson family. In 1540 Sir John Rawson is Grand Prior in Ireland of the Knights Hospitallers. Sir Michael Stanhope, Knt., knighted at Hampton Court, 37 Henry VIII., governor of Hull, &c., married Anne, daughter of Nic. Rawson, Esq., of Aveley, Essex. Ob. 20 Feb. 1587. The ancestress of the noble families of Earls Stanhope, Chesterfield and Harrington. Richard Rawson, LL.B., was presented rector of Beaconsfield, 26 July, 1525, by John Scudamore, Esq. He was Canon of Windsor and Archdeacon of Essex; and rebuilt the parsonage here where his arms remained in 1728. He died 1543. James Rawson, inst. vicar of Wingrave, 8 August, 1508. Edward Rawson, inst. Rector of Hedsor, 13 May, 1664; also vicar of Wooburn. Edward Rawson, presented vicar of Wooburn, 5 Feb. 1662. John Rawson, presented vicar of Turville, 5 Dec. 1532. V. i. p. 265, 479; v. iii. p. 195, 536, 580, 637, 631. (See also Maskell's History of Allhallows Barking, in London, p. 47.)

The wife of Edward Rawson of Colebrooke, mother of David Rawson of London, and grandmother of Edward Rawson of Boston, Mass., married for her second husband Thomas Woodward of Lincoln's Inn.—T. M.]

WILLIAM RAWSON of the town of Northampton, Notary Publique, 4 May, 1603, proved 27 February, 1604. To be buried in S[t] Gyles church, Northampton, near to the door of the pew where I use to sit. To Joane Glover my sister ten shillings and to every one of her children ten shillings apiece which I will shall be paid to her husband to their uses; and he shall have the use thereof until the said children accomplish the age of one and twenty years. To my brother Richard his children ten shillings apiece in same manner and form as is above rehearsed concerning my sister Glover's children. To Mary my eldest daughter, one "gymold Ringe" of gold, with a sharp diamond in it. To Elizabeth my daughter a little gold ring enamelled that the lady Cromwell gave her mother, with the poesie (*Decreui in aeternum*) in it, which rings are in the keeping of Martha now my wife. I will and charge these my said children to keep the said rings so long as they shall live in remembrance of their good mother, my late wife Francys. My children William, Mary, Thomas, Elizabeth and Timothy. To son James my greatest silver bowl; to William my second silver bowl; to Thomas my best silver salt parcel gilt; to Timothy a stone pot garnished with silver double gilt and six silver spoons which I bought of M[rs] Warde. My eldest daughter Mary. My three youngest children, Mary, Frances and Melior. My wife Martha, her father Christopher and mother Alice and brother Robert. My cousin William Ive. My brother-in-law M[r] Francis Morgan of Kingsthorp. Son James to be executor. Hayes, 11.

[Although in the above will there is no direct reference to the family of Secretary Rawson, yet the mention of the names Glover and Warde has led me to save it for printing. (See will of Secretary Rawson's father, who speaks of a cousin Glover and of the Warde family.)—H. F. W.]

RICHARD PERNE, of Gillingham in the County of Dorset, Gentleman one or two days before his death. All to wife; only my eldest son to have an eldest son's part. Wife to be executrix, and Mr. Edward Rawson and my uncle Foyle to be overseers. Sworn to 10 April, 1636, by Edward Rawson, Mary Perne and Jane Clark (by mark). Proved 17 May 1636, by Rachael Perne, widow, relict of the deceased. Pile, 59.

RACHEL PERNE of Gillingham in the County of Dorset, widow, 31 March, 1656, proved 13 November, 1656, by John Perne, son and executor. My body to be buried in the parish church of Gillingham. I am possessed of a living called Easthaimes in Gillingham, as by a lease bearing date 12 October, 12th of late King Charles, under the hand & seal of William, Lord Stowerton, for and during the term of four score and nineteen years, if I, the said Rachel, and Richard Perne and John Perne, my sons, or either of us, shall live so long; and am also possessed of the lawful right of a certain ground called Wagger and one other ground called Ramsleare, allowed and assigned unto me for & in lieu of the fee fostership; and of & in certain lands called Linches, by virtue of a lease and assignment to me made by John Tyse, clerk, for a long term of years, if William Bull, Thomas Bull and Joane Bull, sons & daughter of Edward Bull, shall so long live; and of two acres of mead in Combermeade, by virtue of a lease and other assurances to me made for divers years to come, which said two acres were heretofore the lands of one Augustine Matthew; and of one acre of allotment heretofore allowed and assigned to the said two acres, &c. in lieu of common upon the dissaforestation of the late forest of Gillingham; and of five acres of meadow or pasture upon the top of Bowridge Hill, now in the possession of Richard Gornish, baker, &c. All the above to John Tyse of Orcheston St. George in the County of Wilts, clerk, Simon Crocker, of Winterborne Stoake in said County of Wilts, clerk, and John Greene, of the parish of St. James in the said county of Dorset, gentleman, &c., upon the trust and to the intents following, that they shall permit and suffer my eldest son, Richard Perne, to take & receive the rents, &c. for so long time as he shall live; and after his death, &c. such woman as shall be his wife at the time of his death, so long as she shall live; then the child or children or grandchild or grandchildren of the said Richard Perne; In default of such then John Perne (in the same way). I give to the said Richard Perne half my plate and half my household stuff and half my bacon and half my cheese in my house at Easthaimes and half my stock of bees there in my beefold or garden at Easthaimes and all my timber and wood at Easthaimes, except the two woodpiles abutting against the great meade there at Easthaimes and one of my cheese steanes and all my doors with their locks and keys, loose boards, "gice" planks, about or belonging to my said house of Easthaimes, ——— my biggest white mare and great colt and all the panes of glass about or upon my windows of my house at Easthaimes. To John Perue (certain property similar to a portion of the above) and also my lease which my husband took of Mr William Whittaker the elder deceased, with all my right and title in the same. To my son-in-law John Tyse one shilling.

"Also I give and bequeath unto my sonne in Lawe Edward Rawson one shilling." To daughter Marie Tyse thirty pounds and the goods that I formerly delivered to my said daughter which are now in her house at Orcheston St. Georges aforesaid. "Also I give and bequeath unto my daughter Rachell Rawson the summe of ffortie pounds of lawfull monie of England to be paid at Mr Webb's house in London unto such friend as my daughter Rachell Rawson shall nominate or appoint to receive it for her." To grandchildren John Tyse and Mary Tyse, ten shillings each, to daughter Rachell Rawson's children the sum of ten pounds to be divided among them according to the discretion of my said daughter,—& likewise to be paid at Mr Webb's house aforesaid. To my brother Peter Greene twenty shillings to buy him a ring, to sister Anne Stagg, six pounds, to be paid by forty shillings yearly, to Marie Tyse my great bible, to maid servants Alice Clemont, Anne Frippe and Margerie Bateman, to the minister or the curate of the parish & to the poor of the parish. Son John Perne to be sole executor.

The witnesses were Richard Perne, Mary Tyse, John Hiscock (by mark), Alice Clement (by mark) and Anne Fripp (by mark).

Berkley, 405.

[It seems probable from the following pedigree of Stagg of Little Hinton, printed in Hutchins's Hist. of Dorset, vol. i. p. 55, from the visitation book 1623, that the maiden name of Rachel Perne was Green.

2 Margery, dau. of = William Stagg=1 Maud, dau. of Thomas Pain, of
—— Mathews.   of Ashton.   Winterbourne, c. Wilts.

1. William   2. Giles Stagg=Margery, dau. of John Powlden,
                       of Little Hinton.   of Durweston.

1. Wm. Stagg=Mary, d. of   2. Giles Stagg=Anne, dau. of —— Green.
           —— Bartlett.   of ditto.

Margaret.   Mary.

—T. M.]

Sir HENRY LELLO of Ashdon in the County of Essex, Knight, 7 January, 1629, proved 18 January, 1629. To be buried in the church of St. Brides als Bridgett, London, in the "Isle" of the said church where my predecessors, Wardens of the Fleet, have been buried, if I depart this life in London. If in Ashdon, then in the parish church there. I do give and bequeath to my most Honble and loving friends the gifts, sums and bequests hereafter named. To the Right Honorable Thomas, Lord Coventrie, Lord Keeper of the Great Seal of England, my great Beaserstone. To my loving friend, Dr William Paske, twenty nobles. To Mr John Eldred the elder twenty pounds. To Mr Binge five pounds. To Mr James Ingram twenty pounds and also, as a token of my love to him, my "cristall cabonite," lying now in a chest in the fleet, for his great respect and good service done unto me and in hope of his future care of the place for my executor. To Mr Robert Bailey twenty pounds. To my brother in law Edmund (sic) Hopkins twenty pounds. To my kinsman Cuthbert Macklyn twenty pounds, to his wife five pounds and to his son Henry five pounds. To the said Cuthbert Macklyn the office of Chamberlain of the Fleet during his life, with this direction that who shall execute the clerk's place shall be in the nomination of my very loving friend Mr James Ingram and my executor, because it shall be well executed. To John Lello, my godson and kinsman, twenty pounds at his setting up of shop to begin his trade. To the servants at Ashdon. To the poor of Clenton, where I was born, ten pounds. To the poor of Ashdon, if I die there, five pounds. To Abigail and Margaret, my sister Hopkins' daughters, two hundred pounds apiece, and to Patience and Judith, other two of her daughters, which are already preferred by me in marriage, to Patience one hundred pounds and to Judith fifty pounds. To Edward Hopkins, my nephew, all my adventure in the East India Company. And whereas I have already given him four hundred pounds for which I am indebted and stand bound for the payment thereof unto Benjamin Eldred, if before my decease I shall not have paid and discharged the same then I do ordain my executor to pay it or so much as shall be unpaid at my decease.

I give unto my sister Katherine Hopkins, the wife of Edward (*sic*) Hopkins, all my lands, tenements and hereditaments in Clenton and Clun in the County of Salop, during her natural life, and, after her decease, to Matthew Hopkins her son, to him and his heirs forever. Further, whereas I and John Eldred aforenamed purchased the Fleet and keeping the Palace of Westminster jointly, to us and our heirs forever, since which said purchase the said John Eldred, for and in consideration of the sum of eight thousand pounds, &c. &c. hath released all his right, title and interest of the said office and keeping of the Palace of Westminster to me and my heirs forever, and for non-payment of the said eight thousand pounds at the several times aforementioned I have made to him a lease for three score and ten years, as by the said lease doth likewise appear, whereof the " counterpaine " is amongst my writings, now for the payment of the said sum of eight thousand pounds, as all my debts and legacies, I do ordain and appoint Henry Hopkins, my nephew, whom I do make my sole executor, to see paid and discharged. In consideration whereof and for the due accomplishment of the same I do give and bequeath unto the said Henry all that my manor or capital messuage called the Fleet, otherwise " the King's Gaole of the Fleete," situate in the parish of St. Brides London, with the office of " Boarden of the Fleete," &c. &c., and also the keeping of the Palace of Westminster, called the old and new Palace, with the benefits and rents of the shops and stalls in Westminster Hall and without &c. &c., in as large and ample manner as I and M͏ͬ Eldred had and purchased the same from Sir Robert Tirrell, Knight. Also I give unto the said Henry Hopkins my farm or messuage of Thickho, in the County of Essex, and all my lands, tenements and hereditaments belonging to the same, &c. ; provided that if the said Henry Hopkins do sell the office of the Warden of the Fleet, for the performance of this my last will and follow not the course I have by the same set down then I do, by this my will, appoint him to pay out of the said purchase money to his brother Edward Hopkins two hundred pounds, to his brother Matthew Hopkins two hundred pounds and to every one of his four sisters before named one hundred and fifty pounds apiece. I advise him to continue the execution of the office in M͏ͬ James Ingram, &c. &c., because he is a sufficient and able man for the place, well acquainted therewith and one that I have always found very honest and most ready to do me any service for the good of the office.

Bequests are made to the poor of St. Brides, to my servant Robert Freeman, my loving friend James Weston Esq., my loving friend Sir Paul Pindor, Knight, to M͏ͬ John Eldred's son Nathaniel, my godson, to my servant John Lightborne, and his son, my godson, to the children of Josias Piggott, to my kinsman Willowe Eve and to his wife Judith, my niece.

The witnesses were Robert Holmes, Edward Hopkins and Virgill Reynolds.   Scroope, 6.

HENRY HOPKINS, Esq͏ͬ. Warden of the Fleet, 30 December, 1654, proved 24 January, 1654, by Edward Hopkins, brother and sole executor.

I desire to lie in my own ground in S͏ͭ Bride's church, near my uncle and predecessor Sir Henry Lello, if I expire in London or near thereunto ; to which parish I give & bequeath five pounds if I be buried there. Of my temporal estate,——first, because there is the greatest need, I give and bequeath to my sister Judith Eve thirty pounds per annum, with that stock I have at Ashdon and household, provided that none of it may come into her husband's hands but be disposed of for her own subsistence. I will that my executor defray the charges of the commencement of our nephew Henry Dalley at Cambridge and allow him some competent means for his subsistence until he obtain some preferment there or abroad. I will that my executor take special care of our dear sister Margaret Tompson and her two children, with two more of sister Dally's, according as the estate will arise to and according to their several deserts, which are very different, and so are their necessities. And this I reserve the rather to him because he is equally related with me unto them all. To master James Jackson, fellow of Clare, that ten pounds which his brother, master Richard Jackson, oweth me and all that household stuff he possesseth of mine in Clare Hall. I give unto Henry Hopkins, now at Barbadoes, ten pounds; unto my godson William Hall, the son of William Hall at Lackford, one silver tankard which is now in my possession at the Fleet. To my loving friends Doctor Thomas Paske, master James Ingram, Doctor John Exton, Doctor William Turner, Dr Robert King, Doctor John Leonard, Doctor Cornelius Laurence, Master William Hall of Lackford, Master John Sicklemore, Master Charles Jones, Master John Fifield, Master Charles Bushie, Master Jackson, Master Peele, Master Moungague (*sic*) Newso and Master Wilson, fellows of Clare Hall, Master Thomas Hall of the Exchequer, Master Thomas Rivett, Master Thomas Newcomen, Master Cutbert Macklin, Master Henry Walthew, to each of them a ring of thirty shillings price, with this motto inscribed—*Præ eo non pereo.* The like I give to my loving cousins, Mr John Harris of Elton, Master Edward Mathewes of Burraton and my brother, Master William Lowe of Hereford. To the poor of the parish of Elton, where I was born, ten pounds, to be disposed of at the discretion of my executor and my cousin John Harris. To my servant Richard Walker five pounds and I will that my executor continue him in the place of Tipstaff of the Exchequer as long as he behaves himself well. To my servant Matthew Pitt the place he now holds of Tipstaff in the Common Please, during his good behavior, and ten pounds in money, with all my wearing clothes & do commend him to the care of my executor as judging him very fit his employment here as long as he continue it. I give unto Thomas Lell the son of Thomas Lello, draper, ten pounds; unto Mistress Bridget Exton, the daughter of my most loving friend, my crimson damask canopy and my best crimson quilt.

I do make and constitute my dear and loving brother Edward Hopkins, merchant, sole executor, &c.; and to my said executor all that office of Warden of the Fleet and Keeper of the Palace of Westminster in as ample a manner as I had it from my uncle Sir Henry Lello, Knight. To my said brother and executor all that my farm of Thickho, in the parish of Ashdon, to him and his heirs forever——and all else, &c. &c.

Henry Hopkins.

" There haue bin many interlinings but all of my owne hand."

H. Hopkins.

The witnesses were William Ball, Henry Nevill and John Milett.

Aylett, 41.

EDWARD HOPKINS, esquire, at his house in London, 7 March, 1657, proved 30 April, 1657, by Henry Dalley, nephew and sole executor. If any debts shall appear to be due in New England that they be paid out of my estate there. As for the estate I have in New England (the full accompt of which I left clear in my books there, and the care and inspection whereof was committed to my loving friend Capt. John Culleck) I do in this manner dispose. To eldest child of M[rs] Mary Newton, wife of M[r] Roger Newton of Farmington and daughter of M[r] Thomas Hooker deceased, thirty pounds; and also thirty pounds to eldest child of M[r] John Culleck by Elizabeth, his present wife. To Mrs. Sarah Wilson, the wife of M[r] John Wilson, preacher of the gospel, and daughter of my dear pastor, M[r] Hooker, my farm at Farmington, &c. To M[rs] Susan Hooker, the relict of M[r] Thomas Hooker, all such debts as are due to me from her upon the Account I left in New England. The residue of my estate to my father, Theophilus Eaton, Esq., M[r] John Davenport, M[r] John Culleck and M[r] Goodwyn, in trust, &c.—to give some encouragement in those foreign plantations for the breeding up of hopeful youths in a way of learning, both at the Grammar School and College, for the public service of the country in future times.

Of the estate in England one hundred & fifty pounds per annum to be paid to M[r] David Yale, brother to my dear distressed wife, for her comfortable maintenance and to be disposed of by him for her good, she not being in a condition fit to manage it for herself; this income to be paid in quarterly payments. The thirty pounds per annum given me by the will and testament of my brother Henry Hopkins, lately deceased, to be given to our sister M[rs] Judith Eve, during her natural life, and to be made up to fifty pounds per annum. To my sister M[rs] Margaret Thomson fifty pounds within one year after my decease. To my nephew Henry Thomson, eight hundred pounds, whereof four hundred pounds to be paid him within sixteen months after my decease, and the other four hundred pounds within six months after the decease of my wife. To my niece Katherine Thomson, but now Katherine James (over and above her portion of five hundred pounds formerly given her), the sum of one hundred pounds. To my nieces, Elizabeth and Patience Dallye, two hundred pounds each, provided they attend the directions of their brother or aunts, &c., in disposing of themselves in marriage. To brother M[r] David Yale two hundred pounds; to brother M[r] Thomas Yale two hundred pounds; to my sister M[rs] Hannah Eaton two hundred pounds. Within six months after the decease of my wife the sum of five hundred pounds to be made over into New England according to the advice of my loving friends Major Robert Thomson and M[r] Francis Willoughby (for public ends, &c.). Twenty pounds apiece to M[r] John Davenport, M[r] Theophilus Eaton and M[r] Culleck; a piece of plate of the value of twenty pounds to my honored friend M[r] Wright; (a bequest) to my servant James Porter; to my friends Major Robert Thomson and M[r] Francis Willoughby twenty pounds each in a piece of plate; to my servant Thomas Hayter; to my sister Yale wife of David Yale twenty pounds; to John Lello, a youth with sister Eve, twenty pounds; to my nephew Henry Dally, M.A. in Cambridge, my land and manor in Thickoe in the County of Essex and I appoint him executor, and Major Robert Thomson and M[r] Francis Willoughby overseers, of my will.

Ruthen, 141.

Edward Hopkins, governor of Connecticut, one of the early settlers of Hartford, an abstract of whose will is given above, was born in Shrewsbury, England, in 1600, and died in London, March, 1657. For action of the General Court of Connecticut in relation to his legacy to Theophilus Eaton and others, trustees, see Colonial Records of Connecticut, edited by J. H. Trumbull, vol. i. p. 374; and for correspondence in relation to it, see the same volume, page 578. The £500 for " public ends " was paid to Harvard College under a decree in chancery in 1710. With it a township of land was purchased, which was named Hopkinton in honor of the donor. See Savage's notes on Winthrop's New England, vol. i. 1st ed. pp. 228–30; 2d ed. pp. 273–5, where large extracts from the will of Gov. Hopkins are made. It seems from the wills here abstracted that he was the son of Edward or Edmund Hopkins, that his mother was Katherine, sister of Sir Henry Lello, and that he had two brothers, Henry and Matthew ; and four sisters, Abigail, Margaret, Patience and Judith. For an account of the insanity of his wife, see Winthrop's New England, vol. ii. 1st ed. p. 217 ; 2d ed. p. 266. Another early settler of Hartford was John Hopkins, who could not have been a brother of Gov. Edward, though he may have been related. He was the ancestor of President Mark Hopkins of Williams College, and of the late Mark Hopkins, Esq., an enterprising citizen of San Francisco, Cal.—EDITOR.]

THOMAS YALE of London, merchant, the poorest of what is stamp'd with my Creator's image and most unworthy his mercy ; 29 September, 1697 ; proved 17 January, 1697. As to my temporal estate here, in India, and elsewhere, &c. To my dear mother Mrs Ursula Yale and my beloved brother Mr Elihu Yale. The hereditary estate in the county of Denbigh to my brother Elihu Yale's male issue, if he have any. Failing such, then to the heirs male of my uncle Thomas Yale, in New England and to his right heirs forever.

The Revd Doctor John Evans of London and Mr Robert Harbin of London to be trustees and overseers.

Then follows an account of his estate. Lort, 26.

July, 1721. Undecimo die emi̅t com̅i̅o Catharinæ Yale viduæ Relc̅æ Elihu Yale nup p̅õae Sc̅i Andreæ Holborn in Com̅ Middxiæ ar̅i defti he̅ntis etc. ad adm̅istrandum bona jura et credita dc̅i defti de bene etc. jurat.

Adm̅c̅o de bo: non etc. emi̅t mense Febr̅ii 1727.

Admon. Act. Book 1721 P. C. C.

[The name Ursula here given as that of the testator's mother, shows that he and his brother Elihu, the founder of Yale College, were sons of David Yale and not of Thomas, as has been asserted (REG. iv. 245 ; Savage's Gen. Dict. iv. 666). This agrees with the entry on the register of the private school of William Du Gard, where Elihu (there written *Eliah*) is called the son of David (REG. xiv. 201). Du Gard had previously been head master of Merchant Taylors' School, London.— EDITOR.]

ROBERT THOMSON (residence not stated in will), 14 April, 1691. To my wife, in addition to her jointure, my household stuff, plate, coach and horses and five hundred pounds; and, during her natural life, the profits of my houses, lands and stock at Gelford in New England, the rents of my farm at Culpho and Felsham, in the county of Suffolk, and of that bought of Mr Denham in Kent. I give unto my wife and son Joseph five hundred pounds to dispose as they know is my mind without being accountable to any. I will that there be not above three hundred pounds expended on my funeral in mourning and all other expenses. I will that what is expended on those one thousand apiece (which I have by deed settled on my daughters Ashhurst, Clark, Miller and Duckinfield) of land at Nipmugg in New England be made up a one hundred pounds to each for their further settlement, as Mr Staughton shall direct. To my grandson William Thompson, son of my deceased son William, during his natural life, after he shall attain the age of twenty five years, Esham in Lincolnshire, with its appurtenances, bought of my cousin Oldfield, and the farm in Kent bought of Mʳ Denham, and that, in the mean time, my executors receive the profits and lay them out in land for his use as aforesaid; and this in discharge of the twelve hundred pounds which my executor is to pay : after his decease to his first son, then to the second son (and so on); failing male issue, to my grandson Joseph, son of my son Joseph (in the same order, &c.); then to my daughters that shall be living, during their natural lives, and after their deaths to such of their sons as are or shall be baptized Robert. Whereas upon my son William's marriage I did settle several lands in Yorkshire and Kent upon my brother Glover and son Clarke in trust, &c. &c.

On examining Mʳ Richard Bradly's account of Kintledg, I found an overweight which, for the reasons writ in my waste book, may be my just right, yet, least there should be an error, I will that his heirs or executors be paid the sixty four pounds. I give unto each of my grandchildren (except Joseph Ashurst) that shall be living at my death, when they marry or come of age, fifty pounds. My dear wife & son Joseph to be executors.

The witnesses were Ann Cunliffe, Henry Scoupholme, John Rooke and William Watson.

The testator declared it to be his will 12 March, 1693. Signed and delivered in presence of Henry Scoupholme, Mary Watson and A. Hatway. Proved by Joseph Thomson, 6 December, 1694. Confirmed by decree 3ᵈ Session Trinity, 1695. The receipt of the original will acknowledged by Joseph Thomson 13 July, 1695.   Box, 42.

Sententia pro valore Testamenti Roberti Thompson, nuper de Stoke Newington in comitatu Middlesexiæ armigeri defuncti etc. etc. in judicio inter Franciscam Thompson, relictam, et Josephum Thompson, filium, dicti defuncti, executores hujusmodi negotium promoventes, ex una, et Dominam Elizabetham Ashurst (uxorem domini Willielmi Ashurst, militis) Mariam Clerke (uxorem Samuelis Clerke armigeri) Annam Miller, viduam, et Dominam Susan Duckingfeild (uxorem Domini Roberti Duckingfeild Baronetti), filias naturales et legitimas dicti defuncti, ac Guilielmum Thompson nepotem ex filio ejusdem defuncti, partes contra quas idem negotium promovetur, &c. &c. 1695.   Irby, 201.

In connection with the foregoing it may be well to note that Thomas Sprigg of London, merchant, in his will of 19 May, 1675, proved 14 January, 1678, appointed Mr Maurice Thomson, Col. George Thomson, Sir William Thomson and Major Robert Thomson his executors and trustees, &c.   King, 10.

[Major Robert Thompson of London purchased of the Rev. Henry Whitefield of Guilford, Ct., who returned to England in 1651, his property in that town including the famous "stone house" built in 1639—one of the oldest buildings in New England now standing. The property remained in Thompson's family "to the great detriment of the town till October 22, 1772, when Andrew Oliver, Esq., of Boston, as attorney for Thompson's heirs, sold it all to Mr. Wyllys Elliott for £3000 of the current money of Massachusetts." (Smith's Guilford, p. 92.) Savage (Gen. Dict. iii. 288) conjectures that Thompson married a sister of Gov. Hopkins. We see by the Hopkins wills that the governor had a sister Margaret who married a Thompson; but the names of her children, Henry and Katherine, are not found as the children of Robert Thompson in the probate of his will. It is possible, however, that they and their mother died after 1657 and before 1691. Several letters from Major Robert Thompson are printed in Hutchinson's Collection of Papers. Winthrop, in his History of New England, under 1639 (vol. i. p. 307 of 1st ed., p.

370 of 2d ed.), states that "a fishing trade was begun at Cape Ann by one Mr. Maurice Tomson, a merchant of London." (See also Mass. Colony Records, i. 256.) This was probably Maurice, eldest brother of Maj. Thompson, son of Robert of Watton, and grandson of Maurice of Cheshunt. "He was Governor of the East India Company in the reign of King Charles the First, as was also his brother Sir William in the reign of King Charles the Second." His son, Sir John Thompson, bart., was created Baron Haversham, May 4, 1696. (Collins's Peerage, ed. 1741, pp. 230–233.) For other facts concerning Major Thompson and his brothers and their families, see Collins's Peerage, as cited. See also Wotton's Baronetage, iv. 488.—EDITOR.

[From Hartfordshire Pedigrees.]

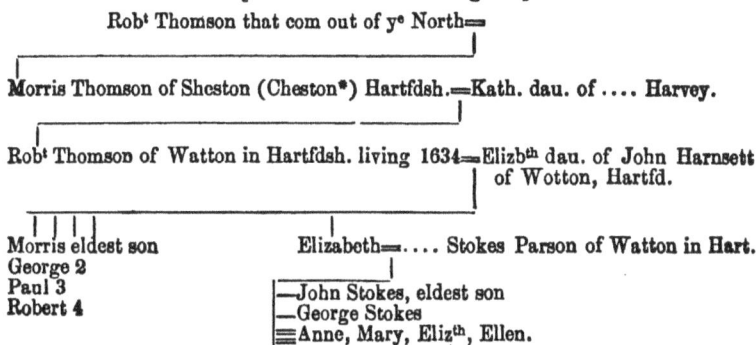

Robt Thomson that com out of y^e North⚌

Morris Thomson of Sheston (Cheston*) Hartfdsh.⚌Kath. dau. of .... Harvey.

Robt Thomson of Watton in Hartfdsh. living 1634⚌Elizbth dau. of John Harnsett of Wotton, Hartfd.

Morris eldest son	Elizabeth⚌.... Stokes Parson of Watton in Hart.
George 2	
Paul 3	—John Stokes, eldest son
Robert 4	—George Stokes
	⚌Anne, Mary, Elizth, Ellen.

Harl. MS. 1234, fol. 124, and Harl. MS. 1547, fol. 11.

—H. F. W.]

HANNAH WALLIN, alias Poulter, of St Andrews Undershaft, London, spinster, 15 March, 1661, proved 7 August, 1663, by Joseph Alston.

To be buried in the parish church of St. Mary Hill, London, as nigh to the place where my dear brother John Wallin als Poulter was buried as conveniently may be with such charge of my funeral as is answerable to my degree and estate, with the remainder of my estate which is hereby undisposed of, which I have purposely left sufficient to perform the same in a handsome and plentiful manner. To Mr Joseph Alstone of London, Norwich merchant, and Mary his wife ten pounds apiece. To Joseph, Edward, Isaac and Clare Alstone, children of said Joseph and Mary, five pounds apiece, the sons at the age of twenty one years and the daughter at the age of twenty one or day of marriage. To Mr Edward Ashtone, kinsman of the said Joseph Ashtone (sic) the father, and unto Thomas Spring servant unto the said Joseph Ashton, the father, five pounds apiece within six months after my decease. To John Baldridge, son of Mr Baldridge, now dwelling with the said Joseph Alstone the father, five pounds at the age of twenty one. To my kinsman Thomas Hunt, the elder, thirty pounds within six months after my decease. To his son Thomas Hunt five pounds at the age of twenty one. To my god-daughter Hannah Hunt, daughter of the same, twenty pounds at the age of twenty one years or day of her marriage. To my kinsmen Edward and John Hunt, brothers of the said Thomas Hunt the elder, ten pounds within six months. To Elizabeth ——,

* My friend Mr. Eades suggests that Cheshunt may be intended, he having seen the name in this form before.—H. F. W.

Collins gives Cheshunt as the residence of this person.—EDITOR.

sister of the said Thomas Hunt the elder, ten pounds within six months. To my cousin John Poulter of Hitchin, in the county of Herts, forty pounds within three months after my decease; and to Mary Poulter his daughter twenty pounds at the age of twenty one or the day of her marriage.

Item I give and bequeathe unto Thomas Poulter (being now at Virginia or some parts beyond the seas), brother of the said Mary Poulter, the sum of ten pounds of like lawful money, to be paid unto him within six months next after my decease. To the son and daughter of my cousin Isaac Poulter, late of Hitchen aforesaid deceased, whose names I know not, five pounds within six months. If they die, then amongst the children of my cousin John Poulter equally. To the poor of the parish of St. Andrew Undershaft three pounds; to the poor of the parish of Hitchen, where I was born, five pounds. To my cousin Katherine, wife of my cousin Thomas Hunt the elder, to Mary Poulter, daughter of my said cousin John Poulter, and to my cousin Elizabeth ——, sister of my said cousin Thomas Hunt the elder, all my wearing apparel.

The executors to be Mr Joseph Alstone the father and Mary his wife. When the will was proved by the former, power was reserved for the latter.   Juxon, 112.

This family of Poulter, or Pulter, were long settled in Hitchin in Hertfordshire. They bore—*argent, two bendlets Sable, in the sinister chief a Cornish chough of the Last.* Crest—*Out of a ducal coronet Azure a demi bear rampant Ermine.*

SAMUEL PURCHAS, rector of St Martins near Ludgate, 31 May, 1625, proved 21 October, 1626. Five pounds to the poor of Thaxted where first I received light. To my son Samuel all that messuage and tenement in the parish of Thaxted which I lately bought of Absolon Onion, &c. A portion lately bought of my brother William Purchas and by him purchased of one —— Kent als Reynolds, who formerly had bought of Absolon Onion, unto Martha my daughter and her heirs, also lands near a hamlet called Beyton End, which were lately belonging to my father George Purchas, of pious memory, in the parish of Thaxted, now in the tenure of my brother William. My wife Jane to have the use of the said lands so long as she shall continue a widow. If my son & daughter die without issue these premises shall descend to Daniel Purchas, son of my brother William, with remainder to Samuel, son of the said William. If my brother William's posterity should fail then to the heirs of my brother George Purchas, i, e. to his eldest son John. In defect of issue of brother George then to Samuel, son of my brother Thomas Purchas of Eastwood and to his heirs forever.

My library and all my books, globes, maps and charts unto Samuel my son, except all those books or works or any part of them whereof I have been the author, namely my Pilgrimage, Pilgrim and Pilgrims, of which he hath already had one printed copy of each of them. The other printed books thereof now in my custody or now due or hereafter to be due upon reckonings from Mr Fetherstone I reserve & bequeath to the performance of my will. One of each to my daughter Martha, my brethren George and William and to my brother in law William Perkins, to each of them one entire work of my Pilgrims in four books. Wife Jane to be executrix. Brethren George & William and William Perkins to be overseers. My seal ring to my son Samuel.   Hele, 137.

[Samuel Purchas, rector of St. Martins, Ludgate, London, and author of Purchas his Pilgrimage and Purchas his Pilgrimes, was born in Thaxted, Essex, about 1577, and died in London probably in 1626. For an account of him and his writings, see Allibone's Dictionary of Authors, vol. ii. p. 1706. See also Drake's Dictionary of American Biography, p. 745 ; and Notes and Queries, London, 1867, 3d S. xi. 57. For notices of his son Samuel, rector of Sutton, Essex, also an author, see Allibone's Dictionary, and Notes and Queries, 1868, 4th S. ii. 541.

It seems, from the following note by Dr. Perkins, of Salem, that the christian name of the father of the author of the " Pilgrimes " was George.—EDITOR.

" William Perkins, merchant taylor, who is mentioned in the will of Samuel Purchas, was the son of George Perkins of Abbots Salford in the county of Warwick, yeoman, by his wife Katherine ; he was baptized January 1, 1579. He married first, Katherine ———, May 22, 1603. She died Sept. 18, 1618. He married second, Mary, daughter of George Purchas of Thaxted, in the county of Essex, March 30, 1619. She died Oct. 29, 1629 (REGISTER, x. 369). This Mary must have been a sister of the testator, Samuel Purchas, and of ' Brethren William and George.' William Perkins had, by his first wife Katherine, a son (inter al.) William, born Aug. 25, 1607, who immigrated to N. England about 1630-1, and whose name appears in various places in our early history as Rev. William Perkins. He was first in Boston and afterwards in Weymouth, Roxbury, Ipswich, Gloucester, and last in Topsfield, where he died, May 21, 1682. He was a man of education and very varied accomplishments. He has descendants now living in Topsfield and elsewhere. His daughter Mary was the second wife of Oliver Purchase, of Lynn.—
G. A. PERKINS.]

MARGARET STONE, wife of Simon Stone of St. Andrews Holborn, gentleman, and relict and executrix of John Fawne, late of St. Buttolph without Aldergate, London, gentleman, deceased, did, about the beginning of May, 1605, and about "sevenights" before her death and at divers other times, &c. make her test. nuncupativ. Her husband the said Simon Stone to have the keeping and bringing up of her daughter Judith Fawne.

The above will was proved 23 May, 1605, by Simon Stone.

Hayes, 35.

THOMAS FOULKS, planter, lying in Princess Ann's county in Virginia, 1 August, 1692, proved 19 Sept. 1692. I do leave my plantation in Princess Ann's County in Virginia & all my servants & my stock & all other things belonging to it, also in cash 250ll sterling which is now in the hands of John Vicary mariner living in the city of Bristol, to the said John Vicary, my sole executor.

Wit: John Barwick, Edward Cocks, John Vicary.
Confirmed per sententiam 31 October, 1692.

Fane, 141.

[William Fookes, an ancestor probably of the testator Thomas Foulkes, received a patent of 450 acres of land lying on " Nanzamond " river, November 24th, 1636. Va. Land Records, Book No. 1, p. 399. The name, variously rendered: Foulkes, Fowlkes, Folkes, and Foulks, is quite numerously and respectably represented in the states of Virginia and North Carolina.—R. A. BROCK.

JOSEPH WADE (called also Ward) of Boston in New England, on board the ship Mary, 21 October, 1691, proved 17 October, 1692. He speaks of clothes lent to John Trinby, 4* to Mr Collins the waterman at Barbadoes, 6* lent to William Jewry, messmates Thomas Linch, Valentine Baker, William Barten & George Golden. All money goods & chattells in New England left to Frances Gibbs of Boston aforesaid spinster.

Wit: John Marshall, Edward Mobryd, Richard Hazard. Fane, 193.

JONE COLE, of the city & County of Exon, spinster, 12 September, 1687, proved 16 February, 1693. Referring to will of husband John

Cole, left with her when he took a voyage to America, intended for the city Philadelphia; to Alice Stoker's children, to William Home, to Fortuna Martin's brothers and sisters. Residue to Fortuna Martin, kinswoman. James Kearle executor of husband's will & mine.   Box, 28.

JOHN LARABEE of New England (evidently a mariner) appoints Elizabeth Crawford of London his attorney, &c. 30 April, 1694. Proved 19 June, 1694.   Box, 130.

RICHARD CHARLETT in the Province of Maryland in the County of Calvert, in Pawtuxen River, in Swanson's Creek, 28 August, 1686, proved 4 April, 1694. To cousin Hannah Kings forty pounds, to cousin Richard Kings ten pounds. All the rest to my brothers & sisters. Brother Richard Kings to be executor.   (Signed) Richard Charlet.

Wits: Philip Rogerson, Thomas Vuett, Ann Rogerson, William Goode.
                                                                Box, 72.

MARY GODWYN of Lyme Regis in the County of Dorset, widow, the last of March, 1665, proved 6 June, 1665. To the poor of Lyme Regis five pounds upon condition that my body is permitted to be buried in the church of Lyme Regis aforesaid without a sermon or the Service Book in such order as is therein appointed. To my three cousins William, James, Ynatius, the sons of my brother William Hill, in New England, one hundred & fifty pounds, to be equally divided amongst them. To John Tyderleigh, & Susan & Mary Tytherleigh, children of Nathaniel Tytherleigh of Lyme Regis & to Grace, wife of the said Nathaniel & to Nathaniel their son, ten pounds each. To my sister Elizabeth Kerridge five pounds (& some land) to cousin William Hill of Lyme, son of my late brother Benjamin Hill & to Mary his now wife & Benjamin their son & their four daughters, at ages of one & twenty years. To cousin Joane Berry, wife of John Berry. To sister Martyn. To Mr Wyatt, clerk. To M^n Thomazine West, wife of Mr Walter West. To Henry Fry of Weyford, my sister's son & to his daughter Elizabeth. To my cousin John Shute, to my cousin Anne Whitfield, to Elizabeth Sprake, daughter of my cousin William Kerridge, to Mary Hoare, my now servant, to James Gollopp of Taunton, to Mr Bartholomew Westley, to M^n Sara Kerridge, late wife of Mr John Kerridge of Wooten, to my sister Paveatt, to my cousin Mr John Kerridge who lives in Lyme churchyard, to Grace, daughter of mr. Nathaniel Tyderleigh, to William & Samuel Courtney, sons of William Courtney, one of my executors, to Elizabeth daughter of my cousin John Whetombe (sic), to my cousin Elizabeth Hart, to the widow Isaacke, the widow Hockett, the widow Pike & John Palmer's wife, to my cousin Judith, sister of my cousin Ann Whitfield, to my cousin Mary Fry of Woathill, to M^n Elizabeth West, wife of Mr Gabriel West, to Mr Richard Farrant's two children. To Mr John Farrant, Mr Robert Burridge & Mr William Courtney all my right, title & interest in the dwelling house & garden, with the appurtenances wherein I do now live in Combestreete, the issues & profits thereof to be to the use of such and to be given & disposed to such poor outed and ejected ministers from time to time as they shall think fit & in their judgments have most need & best deserve the same. All the residue to the said three whom I make executors.

                                                                Hyde, 61.

[The above will answers the query printed in the REGISTER (vol. xxxv. p. 184). The widow of William Hill and mother of William, James and Ignatius, became the wife of Mr. Edmund Greenleaf (ancestor of the New England families of that name) who, in a paper appended to his will and recorded in the Suffolk Registry at Boston (B. 7, L. 112), says: " When I married my wife I kept her grandchild, as I best remember, three years to schooling, diet & apparel; and William Hill, her son, had a bond of six pounds a year, whereof I received no more than a barrel of pork of 3^{li} 0. 0. of that 6^{li} 0. 0. a year he was to pay me, and sent to her son Ignatius Hill to the Barbadoes, in mackerel, cider & bread & pease, as much as come to twenty pounds, and never received one penny of it. His aunt gave to the three brothers 50^{li} apiece—I know not whether they received it or no; but I have not received any part of it.   Witness my hand   Edmund Greenleaf."

" Besides when I married my wife she brought me a silver bowl, a silver porringer and a silver spoon. She lent or gave them to her son James Hill, without my consent."—H. F. WATERS.

See Mr. Appleton's article on the Greenleaf family in the REGISTER for July, 1884 (xxxviii. page 299).

Mrs. Sara Kerridge, named by Mrs. Godwyn, was perhaps Sarah, sister of the Rev. John Woodbridge of Andover, Mass., and of the Rev. Benjamin Woodbridge, whose name heads the list of the graduates of Harvard College. (REG. xxxii. 337, 342; xxxvii. 240.) Sarah Woodbridge married, Dec. 27, 1632, John Kerridge (Mitchell's Woodbridge Record, p. 9), probably the Rev. Mr. Kerridge of Wooton Fitz-Paine, Dorset, who was ejected in 1662 and died soon after (Palmer's Nonc. Mem., ed. 1778, p. 487). His son John Kerridge, M.A., of Corpus Christi College, Oxford, was for a time schoolmaster at Abingdon, Berks; thence went to Lyme Regis, where he was ejected as a schoolmaster; was afterwards pastor of a dissenting church in Culleton, Devonshire, and died April 15, 1705 (Ibid. p. 460).—ED.]

JOSEPH TILDEN citizen & girdler of London, 1 February, 1642. To my brother Freegift Tilden five pounds, to my niece Sara Smyth ten pounds, to my sister Lydia Tilden, late wife of my brother Nathaniel Tilden, ten pounds, and to her two daughters who are married in New England twenty nobles apiece. The livery of the company of Girdlers whereof I am a member to attend my corps to burial. To the said company for poor members and widows ten pounds. To the poor of Smallhead Street in the parish of Tenterden, Kent, three pounds for the poor at the discretion of Mr Thomas Huckstropp. To the widow Hamond three pounds. To the widow Prestwich of Lambheth in the County of Surrey thirty shillings, to Jane Ranndall a diaper table cloth with the napkins belonging to it, to my maid servant Margaret Smart ten shillings, to my nurse five shillings, to the poor of the parish of St John Baptist, London, the several legacies following i. e. the widow Armefield thirty shillings and to the rest of the said parish fifty shillings, to be distributed among them at the discretion of my brother Thatcher. To Hudnall the hairdresser of our parish twenty shillings. My nephew Joseph Tilden, son of my brother Nathaniel Tilden, to be sole executor. My brother Hopestill Tilden to be administrator in trust for the use of the said Joseph until he shall take upon him the executorship and I give to the said Hopestill ten pounds for his pains. To my brother George Thatcher the half year's rent due next Lady day for my lands in Sussex. George Thatcher to be overseer.

(Signed) Jos Tillden.

Wit: Henry Randall Francis Helmes Val: Crome.

By a codicil he bequeaths the residue to nephew Joseph Tilden.

Letters of administration were issued 18 March, 1642, to Hopestill Tillden, brother of the deceased, during the absence of Joseph Tillden, executor named in the will & now dwelling in the parts beyond the seas.

Crane, 28.

[Elder Nathaniel Tilden, brother of the testator, settled in Scituate, Mass. For an account of him and his descendants, see Deane's History of Scituate, pp. 353–5. One of his descendants is the Hon. Samuel J. Tilden, formerly governor of the state of New York, and the democratic candidate for president of the United States in 1876 (see Register, vol. xxxviii. p. 6).—Editor.]

Thomas Spelman of Virginia, gentleman, declared his will that his daughter Mary Spelman in Virginia should have all that he had here in England & what ·he had in Virginia his wife should have, in presence of Jane Bridges (her mark) Mary Rowe (her mark) & Fran: Spelman. Letter of administration was granted 24 April, 1627, to Francis Spelman natural and lawful brother of the said Thomas Spelman lately of Truro in the county of Cornwall deceased, &c. &c. during the absence of Hannah Spelman the relict of the said deceased in the parts of Virginia then dwelling, &c.   Skinner, 40.

[Thomas Spilman, of "Kicoughton in the corporacion of Elizabeth Citty," received a grant of fifty acres, his "first personall divident" as an "ancient planter, * * * to be augmented and doubled by the Company," December 1st, 1624. *Va. Land Records*, Book No. 1, p. 35.—R. A. Brock.

Query. Was this Thomas Spelman a relative of Henry Spelman, whose "Relation of Virginia," 1609 (see Register, xxvii. 332), was edited by J. F. Hunnewell and printed for him in 1872? The author of the Relation was a son of Sir Henry Spelman, the antiquary, whose pedigree will be found in Blomefield's Norfolk, 2d ed. vol. vi. pp. 150–5.—Editor.]

Ralph Hooker, of Barbadoes, 14 March, 1663, proved 27 May, 1665. To my good friend and neighbor Mr Judith Pinney eight hundred and twenty one pounds eight shillings and three pence which she oweth me, and also one hundred thousand pounds of Muscovado Sugar. And for the remainder of her debt to me my executors to forbear to call on her for it until February next, excepting only the debt which she owes me as executrix of Mr Robert Challoner deceased, which I desire may be paid this year. To my friends Capt. Jeremy Egginton, Mr John Knight, Mr Stephen Spicer, Mr John Bawdon and Mr John Sparks each a ring with a death's head, value three pounds sterling. To my friend Dr Peter la Rous fifty pounds sterling to buy himself a ring. To Mr Jeoffrie Body two thousand pounds of Muscovado Sugar. To Thomas Peake one thousand pounds of Muscovado Sugar. To Edward Russell my servant one half piece dowlas. To my cousin Mr James Woods of London merchant, ten pounds sterling and to his wife ten pounds sterling. To my cousin Mrs Woods, relict of my cousin John Woods deceased ten pounds sterling and to her son John Woods five pounds sterling. To my cousin Edward Hooker his children that are alive in England five pounds sterling each. To my cousins Robert & Edward Boys, my cousin Soane & her sister & my cousin Anne Boys, to each of them five pounds sterling.

Item I give and bequeath unto my young cousin Peter Bennett the son of Richard Bennett of New England (the which Peter was my own sister's son) the sum of one hundred pounds sterling, to be paid him when he shall accomplish the age of eighteen years of age. To my poor kindred in England one hundred & fifty pounds sterling, to be distributed by my cousin James Woods, something of it to be given to my aunt Webbe her children of Ottebourne, if any alive, my cousin Edward Hooker of Chilcombe can inform. For goods consigned to Capt. Samuel Davis & myself he to make returns to the principals in London, but not to meddle or intermeddle with any of my other consignations. A reference to goods sold in this island on account of Sir Andrew Riccard & Co. To Capt. Davis five pounds sterling and a horse. To my friend Capt. William Porter ten pounds & a gold hat band & my best beaver if he please to wear it for my sake. To Hugh Lewis three pounds sterling to buy him a ring. My executor to confer with Mr Stephen Spicer who is administrator with me about Mr John Williams' estate. Reference to shipments home to Mr Mico on ac't of John Williams deceased,—much more sugar than I have received on ac't. My executor may employ Mr Jeoffery Body on my books and accounts. He knows the accounts between Mr John Knights & myself and also about Mr John Williams' estate, Mr John Lewis' estate and all the accounts in my books. My loving cousin John Hooker, now residing in the Island of Barbadoes, to be sole executor and my cousin James Woods of London, merchant, to be overseer in trust.

Wit : John Hawkesworth, Josias Cox, John Watkins.

Barbadoes —— By the Deputy Governor.

This Fifteenth day of April, 1664, personally appeared before me Major John Hawkesworth & Mr Josias Cox & made oath that they saw Major Ralph Hooker sign, seal & publish the foregoing Writing, &c. &c.

Henry Willoughby.

A true copy of the Original recorded in the Secretary's Office of Barbadoes attested 17 August, 1664.   Edward Bowden Dep: Secretary.

Hyde, 50.

[The Richard Bennett, referred to in the above will, said by Savage to have been of Salem in 1636, afterwards of Boston, had a wife Sybil, the mother of his children, whose maiden name is here shown to be Hooker, and a second wife Margaret. His will of 21 June, 1677, with a codicil of 6 July, 1677, was proved at Boston 8 September, 1677. In it he mentions grandchild Susanna Bennett, daughter of son Peter, wife Margaret Bennett, son Jonas Clarke and Susanna his wife, and cousin Anthony Bennet of Bass River, New England. (Suffolk Probate Registry, B. 6, p. 195.)—H. F. W.]

ELIZABETH VANSOLDT of Whitegate Alley in the parish of Buttolph Bishopsgate London, widow, 7 September, 1665. Five pounds to be spent about my funeral. To my son Abraham Vansoldt in Virginia or elsewhere twenty pounds within three months after my decease (and certain moveables). Legacies to daughter Mary Wills, cousin Mrs Judith Bonnell of the Old Jury, daughter Anne White (*inter alia* two pictures made & drawn for my brother Stripe & his wife), grand child James White, & loving friend Thomas Parker of Walbrook London & his wife. My loving son James White to be full and sole executor.

James White having died, letters of administration were granted 12 October, 1665, to Anna White.   Hyde, 126.

Notes on Abstracts previously printed.

Sir WILLIAM PHIPS, Knight (*ante*, pp. 46).

The following inscription on a monument in St. Mary Woolnoth Church, between Lombard and King William Street, London, is contributed to the REGISTER by A. M. Haines, Esq., of Galena, Ill.

" Near this place is interred the body of Sir William Phipps, Knight; who in the year 1687 by his great industry, discovered among the rocks near the banks of Bahama on the north side of Hispaniola a Spanish plate-ship which had been under

water forty four years, out of which he took in gold and silver to the value of
£300,000 Sterling; and with a fidelity equal to his conduct, brought it all to London, where it was divided between himself and the rest of the adventurers. For
which great service he was knighted by his then Majesty King James II.; and
afterwards, by the command of his present Majesty, and at the request of the
principal inhabitants of New England, he accepted of the government of the Massachusetts, in which he continued to the time of his death; and discharged his
trust with that zeal for the interest of his country, and with so little regard to his
own private advantage, that he justly gained the good esteem and affections of the
greatest and best part of the inhabitants of that Colony.
" He died the 18th of February, 1694, and his Lady, to perpetuate his memory,
hath caused this monument to be erected."

ROBERT THOMPSON.—The following notes, appended by Mr. Waters to
the will of Major Thomson (*ante*, pp. 65–6), were accidentally omitted in
the last number:

[Information of Hugh Squier. Heard three men of quality, one seemingly a
Dutchman, rejoice that the Dutch had done so well, and attribute it chiefly to the
care and diligence of Maurice Thompson and his brother Major, in supplying them
with information of the motions of the English fleet; they said these men served
much better than Scott for his thousand guilders a year. Finds that Maurice Thompson was always violent against kingly government, was intimate with the Protector, sat on some of the high courts of justice, and sentenced some beheaded lords to
death, so that he is incapable of bearing any office. He was a poor man in Virginia, but got a great estate, chiefly from the king's party. He, Hugh Peters and
Nich. Corsellis, a Dutchman, went over in the beginning of the war to collect
money in Holland for the distressed Protestants in Ireland, and was always in great
favour with the Dutch. As to Major, can hear of no one of that name but a rich Mr.
Major, who married his daughter to the Protector's son Richard, but he is no brother of Maurice Thompson, so thinks they must mean his brother Major Rob.
Thompson, who was so great with Cromwell that he had nearly married his daughter: he began with nothing, rose high enough to purchase 2,200l a year in bishops'
lands, and lost it on the Restoration, so that he brags that he hates not the persons
but the office of bishops; he is bold, full of malice, and embittered against government; he was six or seven years a navy commissioner for the Protector, so that
he knows all the ways of the navy, and is thus able to commit this treason. Thinks
their houses should be searched, and Council should consider whether to seize them.
Asks directions in case he should again meet the three men whose discourse he
heard. [2 pages with postscript in cypher undeciphered.] Westminster, 24 June,
1666.
Account of two other brothers of these Thompsons: George, who lost his leg
fighting against the King, but got a great estate. When the army had fallen into
the posture of a brand-iron, with the Rump in the middle, threatening a battle royal,
Haslerigg and Morley to support the Rump, and Lambert and his party to pull them
down, this Col. George Thompson was with some thousands in St. George's-in-the-
Fields, Southwark, and with Bibles in their hands, and good swords also, they declared for King Jesus, which signified what they pleased, except King Charles.
" Endorsed Col. G. Thompson, of Southwark, a Millenary, &c." 24 June, 1666.
                    Calendar of State Papers, Domestic Series, 1665–1666.
The great interest taken by this family in the affairs of the British Colonies of
North America, and the important parts played by them (directly or indirectly) in
the management of those affairs, as shown by the State Papers, would seem to warrant the giving of so much space to this account of them. From this family were
derived the baronial house of Thomson Lords Haversham, created 4 May, 1696, and
extinct on the death of Maurice, the last Baron Haversham in 1744, a family closely
allied, by intermarriages, to the house of Annesley, Earls of Anglesey. Of the children of Major Robert Thomson, the testator of the foregoing will, Elizabeth became
the wife of William Ashhurst, son of Henry Ashhurst,* an eminent merchant of
London, descended from an old Lancashire family. This William was himself Lord

---

* Of this Henry Ashhurst, Morant (vide History of Essex, ii. 296) says: " He had the
chief hand in settling the corporation for the Propagation of the Gospel in America, of
which he was treasurer; and also zealously promoted the translation of the Bible into the
Indian language. He dyed in 1680."—H. F. W.

Mayor of London in 1693, one of the representatives of the city in several parliaments, received the honor of knighthood from King William III., and died 12 January, 1719 ; his lady survived till 22 March, 1723. His brother Henry was created a Baronet in 1688. Her sister Mary was the wife of Samuel Clarke, Esq., of Snailwell in the county of Cambridge (of Kentish stock), who was created a Baronet 25 July, 1698, and died 8 March, 1719. Another sister, Susan Thomson, was the second wife of Sir Robert Duckenfield, of Duckenfield Hall, Cheshire, created a Baronet 16 June, 1665, who died Nov. 1729.—H. F. W.]

JOHN SCOTCHFORD of Brenchlie in the county of Kent, clothier, 26 December, 1600, proved 16 January, 1600. To be buried in the parish church of Brenchley. To the poor of the parish. To Jasp Saxbie, Henry Alchin and Lawrence Bycie, to every of them ten shillings. To my servants. To every one of my godchildren twelve pence apiece. To John Scotchford my uncle ten shillings. To Laurence Briggenden ten shillings. To Jone, my sister, wife of Richard Browne, forty shillings, and to her son, Noe Stone, three pounds. To every one of the children of the said Jone, my sister, ten shillings. To my sister Martha, wife of Richard Glydd, twenty shillings. To her son John my godson, twenty shillings, and to the rest of her children ten shillings apiece. To every one of my daughters, Elizabeth, Anne, Margaret, Mary and Martha, one hundred pounds at one and twenty years of age or day of marriage. To my daughter Elizabeth, at the age of one and twenty years, the sum of ten pounds, which ten pounds was given her by her grandmother, my mother. To my wife Elizabeth one hundred and fifty pounds within one year after my decease (and other bequests made to her).

To every one of the daughters of John Bigge two shillings, and to his son Hope Bigg ten shillings ; to Mary wife of John Bett ten shillings ; to Mary wife of George Stacie ten shillings ; all within twelve months after my decease. To my mother nine pounds ten shillings yearly (in quarterly payments) &c. To George Saxbie, my uncle, twenty shillings, and to William Saxbie, my uncle, ten shillings ; both within three months after my decease. To Edward Henshall, vicar of Brenchley, twenty shillings. The residue to my son Thomas Scotchford and his heirs forever. John Saxbie and Robert his son, both of Brenchley, clothiers, to be my executors. Richard Glidd, of the parish of Brightling, in the County of Sussex, yeoman, and John Maynard of Brenchley, yeoman, to be the overseers.

The witnesses were Edward Henshall, Script. and John Maynard.

Woodhall, 40.

[The testator of the above will was probably the ancestor of John Scotchford, town clerk of Concord, who married Susanna (perhaps) daughter of George Meriam, and died 10 June, 1696. The will is at any rate of interest as relating to the Bigg family.—H. F. W.]

NINION BUTCHER, of Mary Aldermanbury, London, 25 February, 1658, proved 13 October, 1660. To the poor of the parish of Staplehurst. To eight poor people of the parish of Marden five shillings apiece, and to ten poor people of the same parish two shillings apiece. To Mrs Lawrence, widow, twenty shillings, to Mrs Southen forty shillings, and to Henry Parsons ten shillings. To eight poor people of the parish of Aldermanbury five shillings apiece, and to eight more poor people two shillings and sixpence. To my loving daughter Elizabeth Houlden five hundred and fifty pounds if my said daughter is living in twelve months, &c. if not then to her children at their respective ages of eighteen years. To my sister Rebecca Glover five hundred pounds within one year, if my sister is living, if not then to her children at eighteen. To my daughter Mary Pointell five hundred pounds in one year, &c. if alive, if dead then to her children at their several ages of eighteen. To my grand children, Elizabeth Butcher, fifty pounds at eighteen, William Butcher, twenty pounds at one and twenty, and Hannah Butcher twenty pounds at eighteen. To my grandchildren, James Houlden, fifty pounds at one and twenty, and Mary Houlden, fifty pounds at eighteen. To my grandchildren, Rebecca Glover, fifty pounds at eighteen, and Thomas Glover, twenty pounds at one and twenty; and twenty pounds to every other child of my daughter Glover's that shall be born before my death, and to be paid at eighteen if daughters and at one and twenty if sons. To my grandchildren, Judith Pointell, forty pounds at eighteen, Daniel Pointell, twenty pounds at one and twenty, and Edward Pointell, twenty pounds at one and twenty. To my reverend Pastor Mr Edmund Calamy four pounds within 6 months. To every one of my brother William's children that shall be alive six months next after my decease twenty shillings. To my kinswomen Mary and Elizabeth Sheefe twenty shillings apiece at eighteen. To my kinsman Thomas Butcher of Staplehurst twenty shillings in twelve months. To my kinsman Richard Butcher twenty shillings in twelve months. To my cousin Tunnell twenty shillings a year during natural life. To my cousin Elizabeth Busnell twenty shillings in twelve months. To my cousins Joseph, Samuel and Caleb Swinoke twenty shillings apiece in twelve months. To my cousin Elizabeth Crosse, in Southwark, twenty shillings in twelve months. To my cousin Mary Hasleden twenty shillings in twelve months. To my loving sister Johnson forty shillings in twelve months. To Mr Bland and his wife ten shillings apiece in twelve months. All my lands to my son John Butcher and his heirs forever, and the residue to him. My three daughters, Elizabeth Houlden, Rebecca Glover and Mary Poyntell. Grandchildren Elizabeth and Hannah Butcher, daughters of son John. Son John Butcher to be executor and sons Daniel Poyntell, Francis Willoughby and Thomas Glover to be overseers.   Nabbs, 176.

[I suspect Thomas Glover (husband of Rebecca) was son of John Glover of Dorchester.—H. F. W.]

JOHN IVE of Naylonde, in the county of Suffolk, clothier, 4 Dec. 1618, proved 17 June, 1619. To wife Anne the house wherein I dwell, for and during her natural life. Friends William Forth, gentleman, and Thomas Blythe to be executors. To my eldest son John Ive twenty pounds within one year after the decease of my wife. My son Thomas Ive of London oweth unto me forty pounds by a bond bearing date 9 January, 1617. To my son Myles Ive the sum of five pounds to be paid unto him within one year after the decease of my wife. To my son Ambrose fifteen pounds, within one year, &c. To my two daughters Anne and Mary five pounds apiece, &c. To my grandchild John Ive, son of my son Thomas, three pounds at the age of one and twenty years. To every one of my grandchildren, the children of my son John, Miles and Anne, now living, twenty shillings apiece, the sons at twenty-one and daughters at eighteen. The younger children of my son Thomas. The children of my son Miles. The children of my daughter Anne Frost.

The witnesses were Edmund Wells, John Smyth and Richard Robinson.
                                        Parker, 57.

EDMUND CHAPLIN of Little Waldingfield in the County of Suffolk and the Diocese of Norwich, gentleman, 6 October, 1618, proved 8 February, 1618, by John Wincoll and Thomas Brian, with power reserved for the widow Martha Chaplin to act. To my grandchild Edmunde Chaplin, eldest son of my late son Edmunde, my messuage called Lyons, in Whatfield, Suffolk, at the age of five and twenty years. To grandchild William Chaplin, another son of said Edmund and to Ursula and Elizabeth Chaplin, his daughters (minors). To John Wincoll, my grand child, at the age of fourteen, Anne Wincoll, my grand child, at sixteen, John Wincoll, my son in Law, Awdry Wincoll, my daughter, his wife. Thos. Brian my son in law and Martha Brian, my daughter, his wife. John Howe of Melford, my nephew, and Judith his wife. To my friend Mr Thomas Iles of Hammersmith, Middlesex, gentleman, a ring of gold (value forty shillings) desiring him, of all kindness, to stand good grand father and friend unto the young poor fatherless children of my late son and his son-in-law Edmund Chaplin and his wife Anne the daughter of Mr Iles. If interred at Little Waldingfield, then, &c. If interred at Lindsey, &c. To Pernell Wilkinson, wife of Wilkinson the elder, and to the widow Mallard, both of Little Waldingfield, five shillings apiece. A bequest to four household servants of John Wincoll. All the residue to wife Martha, appointed executrix, with sons John Wincoll and Thomas Brian.

The witnesses were George Wincoll, Francis Wincoll and Joseph Briaute. Parker, 40.

Sententia pro confirmaçone testi Edmundi Chaplin dēf in judicio inter Johannem Wincoll et Thomam Bryant partes hm̄oi negotium promoventes ex una et Martham Chaplin aĺs Bryant filiam n'raĺem dicti defuncti Edmundum et Wĺĺm Chaplin nepotes, Ursulam et Eliz. Chaplin neptes ex filio eiusdem defuncti, etc. 21 June 1619. Parker, 56.

Testamentum nuncupativum THOME AYRES, of the parish of Froome in the County of Somerset, broadweaver, 14 January, 1638. To the church there three shillings and fourpence; to the poor six shillings and eight pence. Having a debt of five pounds, eight shillings due him by bond from one Nathan Doale, of Brooke in com. Wilts, his will was that Symon Ayers, his brother, should have that debt to his own use; also his wearing apparel and a piece of new green cloth which lay in the chest, of five yards; also his broad loom unto Simon Ayers and William Ayers, his brother Simon Ayers his children, to each the moiety. A cupboard at his father's to Anne Ayers, daughter of Simon Ayers. His wife consents to these legacies. Witnesses John Lacie and Richard Eyers.

A commission issued forth 20 March, 1638, to Mary Ayers, the relict. Harvey, 54.

SYMON EYRE of Osmington in the County of Dorset, yeoman, 29 April, 1659, proved 4 October, 1660, by William Eyre. To wife Joan and son William Eyres, &c. To my daughter-in-law Mary Eyres the sum of three score pounds which was promised her at the marriage of her unto my son Symon Eyres, provided the portion promised by her friends in marriage be truely and duely paid and for those children she had by my son Symon. To my four grand children twenty shillings to be divided equally amongst them. Son William to be executor and my good friends Robert and Henry Godshall to be overseers. One of the witnesses was a John Eyre. Nabbs, 182.

NATHANAELL SMITH, 19 February, 1650. "I dispose of my money and goods that is now in new England and elsewhere in wise and manner following." The sixty three pounds in Mr George Corwin's hands due by bond, twenty pounds of it to my kinsman Thomas Edwards, eighteen pounds to my sister Ruth Halford, ten pounds to Mr John Nicolls, flaxman, five pounds to my cousin Nathaniel Edwards and ten pounds to my uncle John Smith. The money in James Brown's hand and that which is in Master Makepeace his hand, Brown's being eight or ten pounds and Mr Makepeace's four pounds ten shillings, my will is that my sister Hanna Mellowes shall have, &c. The linen that I have I do give the napkins, towells and tablecloths and one half the sheets to my kinsman Thomas Edwards and the other half of the sheets to my sister Hanna Mellowes in New England. Linen of mine in my brother Mr. Samuel Wandley's hands I do freely bestow it upon him. Also if there should be any allowance for the plundered estate, one half whereof is due to me, I do give one half to my brother Mr Samuel Fisher and the other half to be distributed between my sister Walford and my sister Wandley. My kinsman Thomas Edwards and cousin Nathaniel Edwards to be administrators.

The witnesses were Samuel Brinsmeades and Samuel Oliver.

20 March 1650 emanavit cõmissio Thomae Edwards et Nathanaeli Edwards, consanguineis dicti defuncti, ad administrand̃ bona jura et credita dict. defuncti iuxta tenorem et effectum testamenti ipiũs defuncti, eo quod dictus defunctus nullum omnino in hujusmodi testamento nominaũit Executorem etc.   Grey, 53.

[In the Massachusetts Archives, at the State House in Boston (B. 15, No. 70), may be found a copy of this will. Another copy is in the Court House at Salem, among the records of Ipswich Court, 1651, in the present office of the Clerk of Courts for the County of Essex. I have (scanty) minutes of what seems to be an earlier will, made 1 January, 1648 (Mass. Archives, B. 15, No. 72), in which the testator mentions William Halford, " my brother Andrew Halford's sonne," cousin Nathaniel Wandley, cousin Hannah Mellowes to have the linen and Abraham Mellowes my books, my brother Edward Mellowes and my brother Samuel Wandley to be executors.—H. F. W.]

EDWARD APSLEY of Apsley in the County of Sussex. The yearly profits of all my real and personal estate, in Sussex, Middlesex and Kent, to my brother George Fenwick, till my nephew Edward Fenwick attain the age of twenty one years. Then my will is that he should change his name to mine; and so I give to him the said Edward Fenwick als Apsley all mine estate, both real and personal, he paying to his father one hundred pounds per annum during his life, to Jo: Apsley, son to my cousin Jo: Apsley of Pulberrow fifty pounds per annum during his life, to my servant Margaret Moyse twenty pounds per annum, to Thomas Stringer, my servant, ten pounds per annum, to Moses Fryer ten pounds per annum, to be paid to him at the house his father-in-law, Mr Evernden, now lives in, to Jo: Adams als Humphrey ten pounds per annum and a lease for twenty one years of all the lands he holdeth of me, at the rents he now payeth, to the town of Steyning five pounds per annum, to Sir Thomas Middleton one hundred pounds. To Sir Arthur Heislerige two either of my stone horses or mares. To Duncombe Colchester such of my geldings as he shall choose and twenty pounds, ten pounds by the year. To my cousin Richard Coldicott one hundred pounds. I would have one hundred and fifty pounds paid to Mr Bartholomew; Mr Pierce knoweth where he liveth. Other bequests.

There issued forth letters of administration, 13 August, 1652, to Sir Arthur Haslerigg, one of the members of the right honorable the Parliament of the Common Wealth of England, and a "legatary" named in this will, for that the said deceased named no executor, the pretended will or "scrowle" of the said deceased, bearing date 11 October, 1651, being declared and decreed null and void. Bowyer, 215.

[See will of Col. George Fenwick, *ante*, p. 41.—H. F. W.]

NATHANIEL ELES late of Harden in the County of Hartford, husbandman (nuncupative) 26 July, 1653, proved 18 February, 1653. To every one of the children of Mʳ William Eles twenty shillings apiece. To John Eles, son of the said William, a two and twenty shilling piece of gold over and above, &c. To every one of the children of Mʳ Nathaniel Eles twenty shillings apiece. It was his will that Richard White who liveth with Mʳ Nathaniel Eles should have all the money due unto him from goodman Salmon. To the two sisters of the said Richard White the rents of his house and lands till his brother John's son shall come to age. To the poor of Harnden and Essenden twenty shillings apiece to each parish if his money would hold out. To Mʳˢ Wilton and Mary Smith twenty shillings apiece. To goodwife Lewis one shilling. To his brother's daughter all the remainder of the money in his chest. To his brother's son his house and lands when he cometh of age. To his sister in-law a bond which is in his chest. Master William Eles to be sole executor. Alchin, 179.

[See will of Nathaniel Eeles, *ante*, p. 25.—H. F. W.]

RICHARD CROUCH (by mark) of the parish of St. Gyles without Cripplegate, London, Brewer's Servant, 27 October, 1660, proved 29 November, 1660. My body to be buried at the discretion of my executrix.

Imprimis I give and bequeath unto my brother William Crouch in New England beyond the seas one shilling of English money, to be paid unto him within one twelvemonth next after my decease if the same be demanded. To my sister Elizabeth Ayres, wife of Richard Ayres, the sum of twelve pence of like money if the same be demanded in twelve months. The residue to my loving wife Anne Crouch, who is to be executrix.

The witnesses were William Howe, Daniel How and Thomas Gill, Scr. Nabbs, 206.

[William Crouch, of Charlestown, married Sarah, daughter of Barnabas Lamson, of Cambridge. See Wyman's Charlestown, pp. 251, 597; Paige's Cambridge, p. 597.—EDITOR.

In connection with the above it may be well to notice the will of Peter Lidget of Boston, merchant, made 10 February, 1670–71, with a codicil dated 21 April, 1676, proved 5 May, 1676. (Suff. Reg. Prob., B. 6, pp. 160–162.) The following persons are named : My wife Elizabeth, my daughter Elizabeth, wife of John Usher, my only son Charles, my daughter Jane, my three children, the three children of my sister Elizabeth Cornel, lately deceased, viz: Peter, Mary and Robert, my sister Mary Smith's two children, John and Peter, they living in Essex, to be paid in London, my three kinswomen, cousin Crouch of Charlestown, cousin Cooke of Cambridge and cousin Rice of Sudbury, the three children of my aunt Lampson, my grandchild Elizabeth Usher, jr. My son Charles to marry Mʳˢ Bethiah Shrimpton.—H. F. W.]

THOMAS BURNELL, citizen and clothworker of London, 5 July, 1661, with a codicil bearing date 19 August, 1661, proved 2 October, 1661, by the oath of Hester Burnell his widow.

Remembering the saying of St. Jerome which soundeth daily in mine ears, *Surgite mortui et venite ad judicium.*

If I die in London, to be buried within the chancel door of the parish church of Allhallows Barking, near Tower Hill, under the gravestone there lying where my dear brother John Burnell and his virtuous wife Mary (of worthy memory) lie buried.   But if it shall please the almighty God that I shall die at Stanmore Magna then my desire is that I may be buried there in the vault within that chancel door of the said parish church where the bones of my dear deceased father and mother lie buried, at the discretion of my loving and dear wife Hester Burnell.   To my she cousin Hasell, my nephew John Burnell Senr, and his three sisters, An, Katherine and Elizabeth, and to the three sons of my deceased brother William Burnell, viz: Thomas, John and Henry Burnell; also unto my sister Rewse, my two nephews John and Richard Ball and their five sisters, An, Barbara, Jane, Margaret and Elizabeth, my cousin Sarah Edlin and also my cousin William Pindar, jun^r, for his help for the getting in of mine estate,—to all of them the sum of thirty pounds apiece.   Also I give unto my nephew John Morley, resident in New England, and to his sister-in-law, the wife of his brother Thomas Morley deceased, the sum of ten pounds apiece, and unto her son Thomas Morley, both resident in or about Hamburgh, together with all the children of my nephews John Burnell, Senr, and Thomas and Henry Burnell, lawfully begotten in wedlock, that shall be living at my death, the sum of five pounds apiece.   To my loving and dear wife fifty pounds.   Also unto her loving brother, Henry Wollastone, Esq. and his son Henry, my brother-in-law Robert Smyth, my nephew Doctor Richard Ball, my cousin Doctor William Pindar, my cousin Thomas Reeve, my cousin James Gough, my nephew John Burnell, sen^r, my cousin Doctor Coe, Bourcheirs and Rudyere, my cousins Thomas and Henry Burnell, and all their wives, also my sister Rewse, my cousin Anne Young and her sister Allett, and my cousin Sarah Edlin, widow, also unto my cousin John Ball, Esq. and my cousin William Robinson and my cousin John Cooke; also unto my cousins Doctor Trench and Doctor Deake and Doctor Winter and their wives, and old Mrs Churchman, the sometime bedle's wife of Marchant Taylor's Hall; to all the sum of six pounds apiece towards their mourning.

My copyhold land and houses in Stanmore Magna, in the County of Middlesex unto my wife for and during her natural life.   Whereas I have lately purchased another house and land lying in or near upon Weald Green in the parish of Harrow upon the Hill, called or known by the name of Brookes, another field, wood ground and springs called Sander's Hill, and now both in the tenure and occupation of John Dancer; and also my present house and garden wherein I now dwell here in London, &c. &c., with five other tenements, all lying in the court or alley called Nunn's Court or Alley, in the street or parish of St. Stephens, Coleman Street, London, (and other leases, &c.) ;—all these to my wife for life; and then to my nephew John Burnell, Senr, my chief house and lands lying in Stanmore Magna, called and known by the name of Fiddles (and a lot of other lands there-to my said nephew for life, then to his wife, if he do marry again, and his children equally, during the natural life or second marriage of his said second wife, if he marry again, then equally among his children and their heirs forever; failing such issue, equally among the children of the three daughters of my eldest brother John Burnell long since deceased.   Also, after my wife's decease, I give, &c. to my nephew Thomas Burnell, eldest son of my brother William Burnell deceased, my two thirds of the house and land he now lives in, called, &c. Buggs, for life, then to his wife and children during her life or second marriage, then to the children.   To my nephew John Burnell, jun^r now resident in the East Indies (estate in Harrow, &c). To my nephews John and Richard Ball (the house, &c. in London). Legacies to godson Burnell Ball, son of said nephew Richard Ball, to my brother Robert Smyth, my brother Thomas Wollaston and my brother-in-law Justice Henry Wollaston.

The witnesses to the will were Robert Fenn, Peter Whitinge and William Pindar, Jun'. It was published by the said Thomas Burnell for his will 19 August, 1661.

In the codicil he names his nephew Thomas Burnell, citizen and haberdasher of London, nephew Henry Burnell, citizen and leatherseller of London and his three daughters, Elizabeth, Mary and Barbara, nephew John Burnell, citizen and clothworker of London, now in the East Indies, nephew William Pindar, citizen and clothworker of London and niece Elizabeth Gough, wife of James Gough.

The witnesses to the codicil were John Mosse, Notary Public, and Edward Bullocke.   May, 150.

[Stanmore Magna lies at the extremity of the County of Middlesex, towards Hertfordshire, from which county John Morley probably came, as shown by his will, wherein he disposes of real estate in Cheshunt, Hertfordshire. John Burnell, Esq., was lord of the manor of Stanmore, and died in 1605. His widow Barbara was lady of the manor for twenty-six years. After her death it was for some time the property of her son Thomas Burnell, Esq., as we learn from Lyson's Environs of London (vol. 3), in which also are given the arms of this family :—*Sable on a bend Or three escallops of the field.*—H. F. W.]

JOHN ASTWOOD, of Milford in the Colony of Newhaven in New England, 27 June, 1654, proved 31 August, 1654, by his son Samuel Astwood.

To my loving wife Sarah Astwood all my estate in New England whatsoever it be in household stuff or cattle or debts, to be disposed by her as she shall see meet for her own proper use. Of my estate here in England, in Abutley, I do give my brother William Astwood ten pounds sterling within one year after my decease. To my loving mother five pounds sterling and the use of two rooms of my house so long as she please. To my brother Robert Astwood do I give five pounds sterling within two years after my decease. To John Rute do I give ten shillings after my decease. The rest of my property to my executor. My son Samuel to be sole executor. The witnesses were Nicholas Hudley and Robert Swan (by mark).
                                                        Alchin, 505.

[See REGISTER, xiv. 304 ; xxxv. 245.—EDITOR.]

PETER CUSHING, citizen and turner of London, 2 February, 1663, proved 12 January, 1664. To wife Godly Cushing (referring to contract with John Greenhill of London and William Newbold of London, gent.). The messuage or tenement wherein I now dwell, in or near Broad Street, London, and other tenements. To my brother Thomas Cushing. To ten ministers (who are named). To the "M', Warden and Cominalty of the Mistery or Arte de lez Turnors," London, whereof I am a member. To Abigail Phillips, Margaret Bull and Sarah Norris, my god-daughter. To my loving friend Francis Gillow of Stratford Bow, in the county of Middlesex, gent. To Martha Gamlin, now wife of Henry Gamlyn and daughter of the said Francis Gillow. To my sister Katherine. To William and Robert Cushing, sons of my brother William Cushing. My loving friend M' William Devonshire. My God daughter Sarah Norris, the daughter of David Norris, in St. Clement's Lane. To my wife's kinsman, Richard Hill, twenty pounds. My loving brother Theophilus Cushing. My brother William Cushing's youngest daughter. To Anne Cushing, daughter of my said brother William.

"I give and bequeath unto each one of the children of my nephew Daniell Cushing, son of my late brother Matthew Cushing, which shalbe living at my death fiftie pounds a peece." To Deborah Briggs, wife of Matthew Briggs, one hundred pounds.—all within twelve months next after the decease of my wife Godly. The residue to my brother Thomas Cushing. The tenement in Bread Street which I purchased of William Swayne, Esq. Loving friends Arthur Remington, Thomas Hartley and William Greenwood to hold property in trust. After payment of debts, legacies, annuities, &c. the residue to my said nephew Daniel Cushing and to Jeremy Cushing, Matthew Cushing and John Cushing, sons of the said Matthew "Cushion," my brother deceased.

The witnesses were Francis Gillow, Henry Woods, John Dawson and Thomas Stevens.   Hyde, 3.

[See REGISTER, x. 79, 173.—H. F. W.]

ELIZABETH HAILES of Lower Shadwell in the parish of Stebunheath als Stepney, in the County of Middlesex, widow, 28 September, 1664, proved 22 March, 1664, by Thomas Parker and William Bugby, the executors. My executors to invite such a number of my christian friends as they shall think fit to accompany my corps to my funeral, and to disburse and lay out for the accommodation of those friends the full sum of thirty pounds. To my cousin Thomas Parker twenty pounds, and to my cousin Ann Parker, his wife, twenty shillings. To my cousin John Parker, son of my said cousin Thomas Parker, thirty pounds. To my cousin Thomas Little ten pounds; to Elizabeth Little, his wife, thirty pounds; and to Mary Little, his daughter, ten pounds. To my grandchild William Bugby, five pounds. To my cousin John Foster, of Tower Hill, and to ——, his wife, five pounds apiece. To my cousin William Foster, at New England, the full sum of ten pounds of like lawful money. To my cousin —— Graves, of Tower Hill, widow, twenty shillings. To my cousin Elizabeth Harris ten pounds, and to her daughter ——, my husband's goddaughter, four pounds. To my cousin —— Appleby, of London, Beavermaker, and to ——, his wife, five pounds apiece. To my cousin Isaac Foster's daughter, four pounds; to my cousin Elizabeth Parsons twenty pounds; to my cousin Martha Goodwin twenty pounds; to my cousin John Hutchinson twenty pounds. To my said cousin John Hutchinson's five sons (that is to say) John, Henry, Edmond, Thomas and George Hutchinson, ten pounds apiece. To my cousin Ann Barber, widow, twenty pounds, to her daughter Susan, now the wife of Robert Aldons, ten pounds, and to the children of the said Susan ten pounds. These legacies to be paid within one month next after my decease to the several respective legatees, or to so many of them as shall demand the same; they to give absolute discharges of any further claim to mine or my deceased husband's estate.

To my cousin Thomas Parker the full sixteenth part of the good ship William and Elizabeth, of London, &c. &c., of which ship he the said Thomas Parker, under God, at the date hereof, is master. To Jane Bugby, the wife of my aforesaid grandchild William Bugby, my full two and thirtieth part of the good ship called the Owners Adventure, of London, &c. &c., of which ship, under God, the said William Bugby, at the date hereof, is master. To my aforesaid cousin John Parker my other two and thirtieth part of the aforesaid ship. Twenty pounds amongst the poor of Shadwell, to be "distributed to and amongst the Auntient poore and such as are not Idle, drunken or of badd conversation," within one month next after my decease. Twenty pounds to another division of Stepney, respect being first had to aged poor seamen and their families in want.

My loving cousin Thomas Parker and my loving grandchild William Bugby to be my executors, and my loving friends Mr John Hall and Mr Day to be the overseers. Two twenty shilling pieces of gold to be given to Doctor William Clarke, minister of Stepney, for his pains to preach my funeral sermon, if he shall please to undertake the same. To my nurse Margaret Wybrow forty shillings.

The witnesses were John Hulme, Elizabeth Hill, Raph Matthews and William Bissaker.   Hyde, 25.

ROGER GLOVER of London, merchant, being now at the Island of Meavis, 14 November, 1636, proved 5 Sept. 1637. William Hawkins, citizen and waxchandler of London, to be overseer. Goods, &c. in the Increase of London to be disposed of for the advantage of Richard Rowe of London, merchant, my loving brother Richard Glover of London, merchant, and my loving sisters Elizabeth and Sara Glover, whom I appoint, &c. executors. Debts due in the Indyes and debts formerly due in any part of the West Indyes. To my niece Elizabeth Glover, daughter of my loving brother Joss: Glover fifty pounds. To William Rowe, son of the said Richard Rowe, thirty pounds. To my niece Elizabeth Pemmerton forty pounds. To John Worcester ten pounds. To my friend Capt. Thomas Sparrowe, Governor of the Island of Meavis two thousand weight of tobacco. To Mr George Upcote of the same Island five hundred weight of tobacco. To Nicholas Godsalve, Secretary, three hundred pounds of tobacco. Debts due from Thomas Littleton late Governor of the abovesaid Island. To James Littleton, his son, one hundred pounds.

The witnesses were Thomas Sparrow, John Worcester, Thomas Hinde and Nicholas Godsalue, Secr.   Goare, 126.

THOMAS NELSON of Rowlay in the County of Essex in New England, being by Providence called now to make a voyage into Old England "this sixt of Sextilis, here called August, 1648." To wife Joane for her natural life my mill, millhouse, &c. in Rowlay and all that ground near unto the said mill, lately in the occupation of Joseph Wormehill, and all my upland and meadow or other ground between Rowley Oxe Pasture on one part, the common on another part and the Mill River and the Brook that goeth from the town on the other part,—all containing fifty acres more or less, provided she make no claim to any other part of my houses, lands, &c.,—also two acres of ground in the Pond field next Mrs Rogers, during her natural life (leaving out the pond), to build her an house. The reversion of said mills, &c. I give amongst my children and their heirs, as well that child which my wife is withall as the rest. To my eldest son Philip Nelson a double portion, and to son Thomas Nelson and daughter Marie Nelson and the child or children she is withall their equal parts. Richard Bullingtam (*sic*) Esq. and my honored uncle Richard Dūmer gen^t shall have the education of my son Philip Nelson and Thomas Nelson and the proportions of both their estates, &c. for their education and maintenance, till they come to the age of twenty-one years, &c. My uncle Richard Dummer to have the education of my daughter Marie Nelson and the other children. To my son Philip Nelson the sum of ten pounds which was given him by my aunt Katharine Witham and is in my hands, &c. Mr Richard Bellingham and my uncle Richard Dūmer to be executors. I would intreat M[r] Ezekiell Rogers of Rowly and M[r] John Norton of Ipswich to be overseers. Signed Dec. 24th, 1645, in presence of Jeremy Howchin and Ezechiell Northens.

I Thomas Nelson being about to return to Rowland in New England do by these present test-my confirming of my last will and testament which I made and left in New England with my wife's uncle M[r] Richard Dumer.

—— My youngest child Samuel Nelson being born since that will was made, &c. &c.

The witnesses were Henry Jacike a̅l̅s̅ Jesse, Daniel Elly (by mark), Sara Appleyard (by mark).

The above will was proved 21 February, 1650, by Richard Dummer one of the executors, power being reserved for Richard Bellingham, the other executor, &c.   Grey, 30.

[See Essex Co. Court Papers, vol. iii. Nos. 65 and 70.—H. F. WATERS. This will was also proved and recorded in the Suffolk County Probate Court. An abstract is printed in the REGISTER, iii. 267-9. An account of Thomas Nelson is printed in the REGISTER, xxxv. 271 ; see also pp. 261, 267, 269.—EDITOR.]

BENJAMIN WOODBRIDGE of Englefield, in the county of Berks, 25 October, 1684 (nuncupative) in presence and hearing of Dame Elizabeth Alleyn, M[rs] Mary Alleyn and M[rs] Mariabella Charles. He bequeathed all to his wife Mary. As no executor was named, Letters of Administration were issued to his widow 3 April, 1685.   Cann. 51.

[His name stands first on the list of graduates of Harvard College. See REGISTER, xxxii. 293.—EDITOR.]

PARGITER.

London y[e] 2[d] of August 1654

Brother Francis —— I beinge now intended by divine providence for Ireland desireinge in my absence that you would be pleased to receive and open whatsoever letters shall come to mee from beyound Seas, or from freinds here ; And for what goods of mine or others that shalbe consigned to mee from the Barbadoes or elcewhere I request you to enter them in the custome house and take them up and to dispose of them at price Currant (except you see anie probability to advance by keepinge of them which I leave to yo[r] discretion And withall you may please to take notice that I stand indebted to the Account of John Washington (as per Account sent him thirty eight pound tenn shillings and tenn pence, which monies is to pay the fraught of Servants to the Barbadoes in case his freinds have or shall provide anie to send him And for the dischargeinge of part of this debt I herewith leave you a bond of Thomas Pargiter's for twenty and three pounds payable to mee the Sixth day of September next, but since hee made this bond to mee I have had of him to the value of aboute Seaventeene shillings Soe rests due but twenty two pounds and three shillings. The rest (or this if his occation require it sooner) I desire you wilbe pleased to disburse for mee And to pay yo'selfe out of the proceeds of such goods of mine as shall come to your hands There is likewise due from mee to my cosen Robert Wards account five pounds which monies as soone as you shall have soe much monies of mine in your hands I then desire it may be paid to James Yeates for my Cosen Robert Wards Account I likewise leave one bill of Ladinge for my cosen John Washington's goods shipt in the Advice M[r] Robert May which I desire may be sent him the verie next shipp after M[r] Mays that shall goe for the Barbadoes And if M[r] Lapsey will doe mee the favour (as hee hath promised mee) which is to lett mee have aboute halfe a dozen hoggs heads of his Virginia Tobacco at price Currant to Satisfie the debt of thirty two pound Seaventeene shillings and eleaven pence which hee owes mee I shall then desire my Cosen Thomas Pargiter the groser, or some others of Judgment whom you shall thincke fitt to looke it over that it be found marchantable and good and worth the monie And then desire you to receave it and shipp it out in his name for Waterford or Dublin in Ireland And this is all the materiall at present: only (in case of mortallity) I then bequeath to you the hundred and fifty pounds now restinge in my brother Robert Pargiters hands for which a yeares interest was due to mee in may last And there is three pounds tenn shillings and nine pence due to mee from my nephew William Pargiter And I doe stand indebted unto Thomas Pargiter's brother who lives at Wardington five pounds And five pounds more to my ffather which hee lett him have long since And for what other estate of mine shalbe cominge to mee from beyound Seas together with the ffifty pounds my brother ffrancis Smith hath of mine upon a mortgage I doe as before (only in case of mortallity) bequeath it to my brother William Parogiter and my brother Ezechiell Pargiter to bee equally devided betweene them. Soe wishinge you health and prosperity in all your affaires I take leave and rest Your Loveinge brother to Comand Theodor Pargiter.

Commission or Letters of Administration issued 20 May, 1656, to William Pargiter and Ezekiel Pargiter, natural and lawful brothers of the deceased. Berkeley, 164.

[What is known of this John Washington who was in Barbadoes just before the emigrant ancestor of George Washington settled in Virginia?—EDITOR.]

Letters of Administration on the estate of JOHN LLOYDE, late in Virginia, deceased, granted 27 August, 1653, to his daughter Mary Lloyde.
Admon Act Book P. C. C., 1653, fol. 24.

[Though I have not met with the name of John Lloyde in early record or print of Virginia, the following data of others of the same name may prove of interest. The State Land Registry Office presents of record, grants to Cornelius Lloyd, 800 acres in Elizabeth City county, June 2, 1635; 400 acres on the west branch of Elizabeth River, March 13, 1636; 100 acres on the east side of Elizabeth River, Dec. 22, 1636—Book No. 1, pp. 394, 359 and 406 severally. Cornelius Lloyd of London, merchant, Wm. Tucker, Maurice Tompson, George Tompson, William Harris, Thomas Dobson, James Stone and Jeremiah Blackman, mariner, 8000 acres in Charles City county, February 9, 1636, Book No. 1, p. 410. Edmund Lloyd, 400 acres in James City county, May 20, 1636, Book No. 1, p. 359. Humphrey Lloyd, 250 acres in Charles River county, November 6, 1637, Book No. 1, p. 523. Cornelius Lloyd was a member of the House of Burgesses from Lower Norfolk county, March 2, 1642-3, Oct. 1, 1644, and Nov. 3, 1647. "Leftenant Colonel" Cornelius Lloyd appears as a burgess from Lower Norfolk county, May 6, 1652, and July 5, 1653.—Hening's Statutes, I. pp. 239, 283, 340, 373 and 379. Edward Lloyd as burgess from Lower Norfolk county, Feb. 17, 1644-5.—Hening, i. p. 289.—R. A. BROCK, Richmond, Va.]

Letters of Administration on the estate of ROBERT BOUGHTON the younger, late in New England, bachelor, deceased, issued to his father Robert Boughton, 31 January, 1655.
Admon Act Book P. C. C., 1656, fol. 6.

Letters of Administration on the estate of SAMUEL FRYE, late in Virginia, bachelor, deceased, issued 12 March, 1655, to his mother Ann Frye, widow. Admon Act Book P. C. C., 1656.

[The following grants of record in the Virginia Land Registry Office may have some connection with the testator Samuel Frye:—To William Frye, 250 and 500 acres in James City county, May 20, 1637, and Aug. 29, 1643, Book No. 1, pp. 421 and 906; to Joseph Farye, 250 acres in Charles City county, May 27, 1638, Book No. 1, p. 561.—R. A. BROCK, Richmond, Va.]

Letters of Administration on the estate of ANDREW GILLIARD, in ship King of Poland, late in Virginia, deceased, issued 2 April, 1656, to John Pulling, cousin German.   Admon Act Book P. C. C., 1656.

Letters of Administration on the estate of MARGARET GIBBONS, late of New England, but at her death of Plymouth in County Devon, issued 28 February, 1656, to Jerusha Rea, now the wife of Capt. Thomas Rea, natural and lawful daughter of the deceased.

Admon Act Book P. C. C., 1657.

[This was Margaret, widow of Maj. Gen. Edward Gibbons. See REGISTER, viii. 276; ix. 346; Savage's Gen. Dict. ii. 245; Wyman's Charlestown, i. 406.—ED.]

Letters of Administration on the estate of RICHARD PATE, late in Virginia, deceased, issued 30 October, 1657, to John Pate, his brother's son.

Admon Act Book P. C. C., 1657.

[The following grants are of record in the Virginia Land Registry Office :—Richard Pate, 1141 acres, of land on the north side of York River, Dec. 12, 1650, Book No. 2, p. 271.   John Pate, 1000 acres in Rappahannock county, Dec. 31, 1662, Book No. 5, p. 201.   The name Pate is numerously represented in Virginia at the present day.—R. A. BROCK, Richmond, Va.]

FRANCIS ANTHONY, Doctor of Physick, 25 May, 1623, proved 19 June, 1623.   To be buried in the parish church of St. Bartholmewes.   My lease at Barnes I bequeath to my beloved wife, consisting of mansion house, garden, orchard, &c., late in the occupation of Thomas Erskins, and ten pounds a year to be paid out of my dwelling house in St. Bartholmewes, during her natural life, and all moneys in the hands of Sir Stephen le Sure, Knight, and Mr Richards.   To my daughter Martha, as her dowry money, three hundred pounds.   The inheritance of this my dwelling house in St. Bartholmewes to Francis my son, my copyhold lands, &c. in Barnes to my youngest son Charles.   Other estates to eldest son Francis.

To my sons Francis, John and Charles all that state of mine in Virginia, together with all disbursements of all and singular such moneys as the Company have received from me for thirty shares, and all the appurtenances in Southampton Hundred there, to be divided amongst them by equal portions as long as they shall be living, "and so to the longest liver of them three." · To my wife the basin and ewer of silver and all such other plate as was in her possession at the time of my marriage with her.   To my daughter Vickars twenty pounds a year.   To my son Charles twenty pounds a year during the term of the lease at Barnes.   To my daughter Smith and my daughter Martha each twenty pounds, in the same manner. To John and Charles, my sons, all my books equally except my written books, which I bequeath to Charles.   To them I give and bequeath all my medicines equally.

I appoint my wife and Sir Stephen le Sure, Knight, my executors, and Mr Humfrey Selwood overseer.

The testator made his mark 26 May.   Probate was granted to Elizabeth Anthony the relict and one of the executors, power being reserved for the other.   On the 17th of March, 1629, commission issued to Sir Stephen le Sieur, Knt, the other executor.   Swann, 60.

FRANCIS ANTHONY of London, gentleman, 11 Aug. 1623, proved 18 Aug. 1623.   To be buried in the parish of St. Gyles without Crepelgate, London.   To wife Judith Anthony all those two leases of the mansion house, &c.

&c. situate, lying and being in Barnes in the County of Surrey, sometime in the tenure of one Thomas Erskins, and my right, title, interest, &c. in the same by virtue of the last will and testament of Francis Anthony, my father deceased, on condition she do suffer my mother in law Elizabeth Anthony to enjoy such part of the same mansion house and premisses as by the last will and testament of my said father she is appointed to enjoy, and that she pay such legacies as are or shall be due to be paid to my said mother for her dower, my brother Charles Anthony, my sister—Robinson, my sister—Smith and my sister Martha, out of the same two leases, &c. or out of my messuage or tenement in the tenure of John Anthony my brother, situate, lying and being in the parish of Great St. Bartholmewe near West Smithfield. To my son Edmond Anthony all my said messuage or tenement in Great St. Bartholmewe, &c. to hold forever; but if my said son Edmond shall depart this present life before he shall accomplish his full age of twenty and one years then to Elizabeth Anthony my daughter. If both die before accomplishing the age of twenty one then to my said wife Judith for and during the term of her natural life, my wife to receive the rents, &c. until they attain their several ages, as aforesaid. To my said daughter Elizabeth one hundred and fifty pounds at her age of twenty one or day of marriage. To Sara Russha my daughter in law fifteen pounds due me by bond from my brother Charles Anthony within four years next after the date hereof. To my said wife all the arras hangings, the best taffata bed, &c. To the poor of St. Gyles without Crepelgate ten shillings. The residue to my wife Judith whom I appoint executrix. My brother John Anthony, Doctor of Physicks, and Edmund Bollyvant to be overseers.

Wit: John Wandley Scr., Edward Leche, John Duesh.

Swann, 87.

, [Frauncis Anthoyne obijt one Wensdaye the 13 of August buryed in St Giles Criplegatt before the Pulpett the 15 of ye same 1623 wt 7 escochens.—*Harleian MSS.* 1754, f. 63.—H. F W.]

EZEKIELL CULVERWELL, of London, clerk, 5 July, 1630, proved 9 May, 1631. To Nicholas Piccard my kinsman ten pounds. To Katherine my kinswoman ten pounds. To Mrs Johnson, wife to Frederick Johnson, five pounds. Item to Margaret Chevers, for herself and her son Ezekiell, ten pounds. To John Hudson, student at the University in Dublin, forty shillings. To Josiah, son to Martha Wilson, five pounds. To old Alice Grinder twenty shillings. To old Ellyn Smith, a maid, forty shillings. To Ezekiell Washbourne, son of Robert Washbourne, five pounds. To my daughter Sarah one hundred pounds to her own use. To Benedict, son of my daughter Sarah Barfoot, two hundred pounds. To poor faithful preachers and godly poor students in either University one hundred pounds.

For all my English books (my bible in quarto excepted, which I give to Martha Wilson) I leave to my executrix for her own use. All my Latin books I will to be divided in three parts, equally as may be, and then, by lot, to give to Nicholas Piccard one lot, to Josias Wilson another lot, a third lot to Ezekiell Cheuers. The residue to my daughter Sara, whom I appoint sole executrix. Wit: Arthur Harbur.

Reg. of Commissary Court of London (1629–34), fol. 147.

[Ezekiel Culverwell, a Puritan divine and author, was curate of Felsted in Essex, but in 1583 was suspended for not wearing the surplice; was afterwards rector of Stambridge magna in the same county, of which living he was deprived about 1609, his successor having been instituted March 27 of that year. He was afterwards curate of St. Antholin's, London. The register of that church, contains this entry under the year 1631: "April 14, Mr Ezekiel Culverwell, minister, bur." Biographical sketches are printed in Brook's Puritans, iii. 512, and Davids's Nonconformity in Essex, p. 125. See also Newcourt's Repertorium, ii. 542; Register of St. Antholin (Harl. Soc.), p. 65. Brook and Davids give the titles and dates of his works; as does also Allibone in his Dictionary of Authors, i. 458.—EDITOR.

Ezekiel Cheever, one of the legatees named in the foregoing will, was doubtless the famous master of the Boston Latin School. He was born in London, Jan. 25, 1614, came to Boston in New England in 1637, and died there Aug. 21, 1708, in the ninety-fourth year of his age. For a biographical notice of him and an account of his family, see the articles entitled " Ezekiel Cheever and Some of his Descendants," in the REGISTER for April, 1879 (xxxiii. 164), and April, 1884 (xxxviii. 170).—JOHN T. HASSAM.

In vol. i. p. 395 London Visitations (edited by Dr. Howard and Col. Chester), appears the marriage of Thomas Horton, of London, merchant, a^o 1634, 3d son to Margaret, dau. of Lawrence Culverwell.—J. C. J. BROWN.]

JAMES HOLT of Virginia, planter, 8 December, 1629, proved 12 May, 1631. To my son James Hoult all and singular my goods, catells, chatells, household stuff and all my houses and ground and all other things which I have or may have in Virginia or elsewhere; and also all the servants which are or shall be mine in Virginia, and all the time that they have yet to serve with me; only to my servant William Bond one year of his time. To my servant Richard Bawinton four years of his time. My executors to be Nathaniel Flood, planter, Henry King, planter, Theophilus Berrestone, planter.

Wit: Theophilus Berrestone and Peter Perkins.

Emanavit commissio W^{mo} Donne, curatori ad lites Jacobi Houlte, &c. (for the reason, it appears, that those named executors in the will were beyond the seas).

Reg. of Commissary Court of London (1629–34), fol. 150.

[The following grants from the Virginia Land Registry Office may be informatory in connection with the above.

Randall Holt, 400 acres in James City county, Sept. 18, 1636 ; Thomas Holt, 500 acres in New Norfolk county, May 22, 1637 ; Robert Holt, 700 acres in James City county, July 23, 1640.—Book No. 1, pp. 386, 423 and 727.

John Fludd, 2100 acres in James City county, May 12, 1638, Book No. 1, p. 548. John Flood, " Gentleman," " an antient planter," 1100 acres in James City county, June 7, 1650—" Mary Flood, John Flood, John Lawrence and John Connaway," being among the " head-rights."—Book No. 2, p. 227. Francis Flood, 300 acres on York river, April 1, 1651, Book No. 2, p. 318. John King, 300 acres in Charles River county, Dec. 10, 1642 ; " Anne his wife, Katharine Kallaway, Thomas Clary, Phillip Neale, Alice Smith and Alice Cooke," " transports " or " head-rights "; John King, 500 acres in York county, Nov. 9, 1649.—Book No. 2, p. 192. John King, 200 acres in " Gloster " county, October 10, 1651, Book No. 2, p. 345.—R. A. BROCK, Richmond, Va.]

———————

Notes on Abstracts previously printed.

THOMAS SPELMAN (*ante,* p. 72).

[The Thomas Spelman (Spilman) of Virginia, an abstract of whose will is found in the Genealogical Gleanings of Henry F. Waters, in the REGISTER of July, 1884, p. 323, came to Virginia in A.D. 1616, when he was about sixteen years of age. His wife Hannah, when about eighteen years old, arrived in A.D. 1620. In the Muster of Inhabitants, taken in January, 1624–5, and published in *Hotten's Lists,* Thomas was then listed as twenty-four years old and his wife as twenty-three. The daughter Mary, in England, in 1627 could not have been more than six years old. Spilman in 1625 had four white servants in his employ, and lived at Kecoughton in

Elizabeth City Corporation, now Hampton. At the same time there was another Thomas Spilman living at James City, twenty-eight years of age, who came in A.D. 1623, and was a servant of Richard Stephens, who arrived in the ship George with him. Stephens was for several years a prominent colonist.—From Rev. EDWARD D. NEILL, of St. Paul, Min.]

RACHEL PERNE (*ante*, pp. 60–61).

[I may add from my own family papers, that "John Tyse, clerk," son-in-law of Richard and Rachel Perne, mentioned on p. 60, had two children, John and Mary. The former, I think, died unmarried; but Mary married, first, John (or Nicholas) Goddard, of Gillingham, and, secondly, in 1681, William Weston, of Weston in Stalbridge, both in Dorsetshire. She died about the year 1725, having had an only son, John Goddard of Gillingham, who died in 1702, leaving, by his wife Martha Cox, who predeceased him, Mary Goddard, sole heiress. She became in 1717 the wife of William Helyar of Coker, co. Somerset, eldest son of William Helyar of Coker, M.P. for Somersetshire in 1714, and from this marriage is descended the present Horace Augustus Helyar of Coker Court, Secretary of the British Embassy at the Hague.—*Letter of the Rev. Charles J. Robinson, M.A., of West Hackney, London, England.*]

THOMAS BROWNE, 17 April, 1663, proved 17 July, 1663. List of Property &c. viz :—on board the Samuel, Jemaico, one half of fifty thousand pounds of Sugar, the other half belonging to George Thompson. Goods coming per George Ladd. I left behind, in hands of George Thompson, &c. I have in Abraham Brown's hands, in New England, one hundred and fifty pounds. I have in brother William's hands about one hundred pounds. I have in Virginia employment fifty pounds, &c.

For the hundred pounds to brother William, I freely forgive him. To my sister Joane Browne twenty pounds, besides ten pounds I owe her. To my cousin Joane Browne ten pounds. Which sums I desire may be paid out of the sugars I have in Barbados. The balance; to my son Thomas, God sending him to age, one third, and two thirds to my wife Priscilla Browne.

Wit: Argent Tuttle, William Browne.   Juxon, 89.

[Abraham Browne, an early settler of Watertown, is supposed by Bond, in his history of that town, to be a son of Thomas Browne of Swan Hall, in the parish of Hawkedon, co. Suffolk, by his wife Joan. A tabular pedigree of this family from John Browne, alderman of Stamford, co. Lincoln, in 1376 and 1377, is found in that book, pp. 116–17.—EDITOR.]

JOHN PEMERTON (by mark) of Lawford in the County of Essex, weaver, 9 September, 1653, proved 25 March, 1654, by John Beeston, sole executor. For my worldly goods being in New England, in the custody of Hercules Woodman, living in Newbery in the County of Essex, or his assigns, I give and bequeath unto my daughter-in-law Deborah Gofe, there born, and to her heirs forever, and all my moveable goods which I now possess in this England, both within doors and without, whatsoever. I make and ordain my loving kinsman and faithful friend, John Beeston of Dedham, my executor. My debts to be paid within six months next after my decease. My desire is likewise that if my said daughter-in-law should happen to die without heirs that then all the forementioned estate should be equally divided, that is, for my means in New England, to my brother James Pemerton and to my sister Robinson, to be equally divided between them. And for such my other goods my desire is that they may be divided equally between my three brothers, William, Richard and Thomas.

The witnesses were William Winge, John Stud and Thomas Boston.
                                                       Alchin, 191.

[The above will throws light upon the family of the Reverend Ebenezer Pemberton, minister of the old South Church in Boston, 700–1717, the testator evidently
being his uncle John, who was of Boston 1632, and afterwards of Newbury. Savage suggests that he may have been living in Winnesemit in 1662; but that sug-
gestion is disproved, not only by this discovery but also by a document among the
Massachusetts Archives (B. 15, No. 43), wherein John Pamerton of Winnesimmet
distinctly calls himself (14 April, 1662) son of James, of Malden.   H. F. W.

The name of "Hercules Woodman, of Malford [probably Christian-Malford, Wilt-
shire], mercer," appears in the list of passengers who embarked "aboute the v^t of
Aprill 1635" in the James of London, William Cooper, master. (See REGISTER,
xiv. 333.) He settled at Newbury. His true name was Archelaus, at least that is
the name he went by in this country.

Another person by this surname, namely, Edward Woodman, settled at Newbury, Mass., about the same time as Archelaus. He was deputy from Newbury and
held other important offices. A genealogy of the Woodman family by a descendant,
Cyrus Waterman, A.M., was published in 1874. The author supposes that Edward
Woodman came from Corsham in Wiltshire, about eleven miles from Christian-Malford. No connection has been traced between Edward and Archelaus Woodman.

Who was the Deborah Goffe named as born in New England?—EDITOR.]

RICHARD LARDNER of Portsea, in the County of Southampton, merchant, nominated Mr Urian Oakes of Southweeke, Southampton, gentleman, and Mr Thomas Mills and Mr John Mills, of Portsmouth, overseers
to the carrying out of his will, proved 1670–71.   Duke, 64.

ALICIA LISLE of Moyles Court in the County of Southampton, widow,
9 June, 1682, with codicil of same date, proved 11 November, 1689. To
the poor of the parish of Ellingham two pounds within one year after my
decease. I have settled upon Thomas Tipping of Wheatfield in the County
of Oxford, Esq., and Christopher Warman of Milborne Weekes in the
County of Somerset, gentleman, their heirs and assigns, the reversion and
inheritance of the moiety of the manor of Moyles Court, alias Rockford
Moyles and over-Burgatt and several other manors, lands, tenements and
hereditaments in the said County of Southampton and in the County of
Dorset and elsewhere, mentioned in an indenture tripartite, dated 19 Feb.
1678, to be conveyed to William Tipping, Esq., for five hundred years, who
hath since conveyed and assigned over his interest, &c. to the said Thomas
Tipping and Christopher Warman; which said conveyance is in trust for
the payment of certain debts in a schedule thereunto annexed, &c. &c. The
overplus (after payment of such debts) to my worthy friends, the said William Tipping and Mrs. Frances Tipping his sister, Richard Lloyd, citizen
and linen-draper of London, and Triphena his wife, to hold forever upon
this especial trust, &c. to discharge my funeral expenses and pay debts, &c.
and to pay unto my daughter Anne twelve hundred pounds at the age of
one and twenty years or day of marriage, to pay unto my grandaughter
—— Hore, daughter of my daughter Bridgett, now in New England, the
sum of one hundred pounds at age of one and twenty or day of marriage,
to pay unto my daughter Mary one annuity or yearly rent of six pounds
during her natural life, but if said daughter Mary marry against their consent said annuity shall cease, to pay to daughter Mabella Lisle an annuity
of forty pounds (under same conditions). The residue to be distributed
among my daughters or daughters' children as they (the trustees) shall
think fit. To cousin Judah Rie ten pounds within two years after my decease. To William Carpentar, my servant, thirty pounds (in two years).
In the codicil she bequeaths to daughter Margaret, now the wife of M^r
Whitaker, seventy pounds (in two years). Witnesses Anne Tipping, William Withrington, John Swan and Abiah Browne.   Ent, 159.

[I am indebted to Henry Marillier, Esq., for the reference to the above will.

The following pedigree is from Berry's County Genealogies, County of Hants, pages 173-175.

ARMS.—*Or, on a chief az. three lions rampant, of the field.*
CREST.—*A stag statant ar. attired or.*

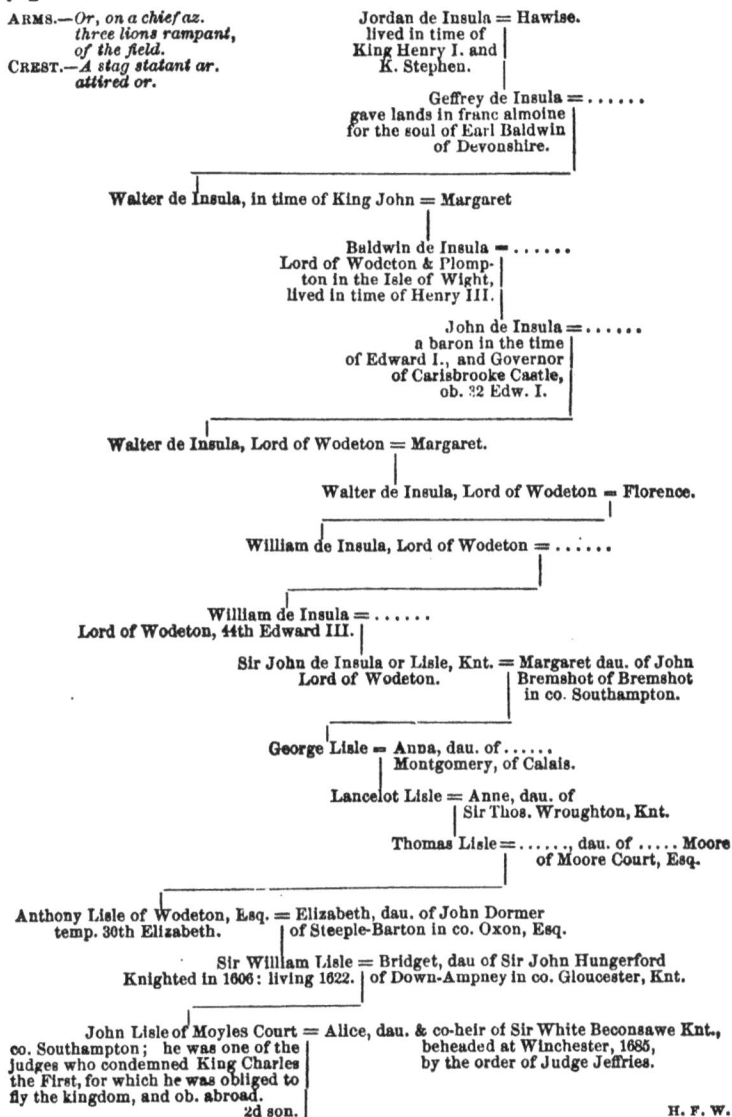

Jordan de Insula = Hawise.
lived in time of
King Henry I. and
K. Stephen.

Geffrey de Insula = ...
gave lands in franc almoine
for the soul of Earl Baldwin
of Devonshire.

Walter de Insula, in time of King John = Margaret

Baldwin de Insula = ...
Lord of Wodeton & Plomp-
ton in the Isle of Wight,
lived in time of Henry III.

John de Insula = ...
a baron in the time
of Edward I., and Governor
of Carisbrooke Castle,
ob. 32 Edw. I.

Walter de Insula, Lord of Wodeton = Margaret.

Walter de Insula, Lord of Wodeton = Florence.

William de Insula, Lord of Wodeton = ...

William de Insula = ...
Lord of Wodeton, 44th Edward III.

Sir John de Insula or Lisle, Knt. = Margaret dau. of John
Lord of Wodeton. Bremshot of Bremshot
in co. Southampton.

George Lisle = Anna, dau. of . . . . . .
Montgomery, of Calais.

Lancelot Lisle = Anne, dau. of
Sir Thos. Wroughton, Knt.

Thomas Lisle = ..., dau. of . . . . . Moore
of Moore Court, Esq.

Anthony Lisle of Wodeton, Esq. = Elizabeth, dau. of John Dormer
temp. 30th Elizabeth. of Steeple-Barton in co. Oxon, Esq.

Sir William Lisle = Bridget, dau of Sir John Hungerford
Knighted in 1606: living 1622. of Down-Ampney in co. Gloucester, Knt.

John Lisle of Moyles Court = Alice, dau. & co-heir of Sir White Beconsawe Knt.,
co. Southampton; he was one of the beheaded at Winchester, 1685,
Judges who condemned King Charles by the order of Judge Jeffries.
the First, for which he was obliged to
fly the kingdom, and ob. abroad.
2d son.

H. F. W.

Mrs. Bridget Hoar (daughter of John and Alicia Lisle and widow of Leonard Hoar, president of Harvard College) married 1686, Hezekiah Usher, Jr., who died *s. p.* July 11, 1697. She died May 25, 1723. See Usher Genealogy, REG. xxiii. 410-13.—EDITOR.]

THOMAS COTTON, of Pond Street, Hampstead, in the County of Middlesex, gentleman, 9 May, 1730, proved 11 August, 1730, by Bridget Cotton, his widow, and Thomas Cotton, his son. To dear wife Mrs Bridgett Cotton, who for many years has been a dear and tender wife to me and a faithful partner with me in all my joys and sorrows of life and a tender mother to all my dear children, &c. I appoint her executrix, in conjunction with my son Thomas Cotton, as soon as he shall become of age, which will be, God willing, on the 20 July next ensuing. To wife I give and bequeath whatever money, bonds, leases or estates that yet belong unto me in any wise upon the death of our dear Honoured mother, Mrs Bridgett Usher, late of Boston in New England, left in trust with the Honoured Judge Sewal or others. At her decease all my effects, &c. to be equally divided between our two dear children Thomas Cotton and Alicia Cotton. For, as our eldest son Mr Leonard Cotton wherever he at present is has long ago received from me far above the property of worldly goods I had to bestow upon my children, I only give him ten pounds.

The witnesses were Edward Morton, Anne Tanton and Eleanor Brearecliff.   Auber, 152.

[The following pedigree is from Add. MS. 24458 (Brit. Museum), p. 54.

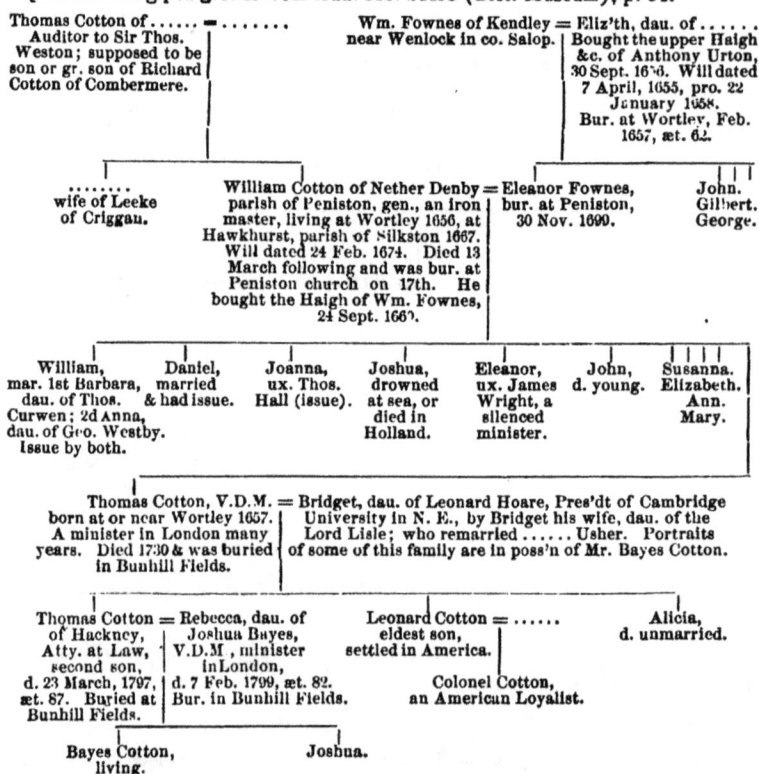

Thomas Cotton of ...... ■ .... Auditor to Sir Thos. Weston; supposed to be son or gr. son of Richard Cotton of Combermere.

Wm. Fownes of Kendley = Eliz'th, dau. of ...... near Wenlock in co. Salop. | Bought the upper Haigh &c. of Anthony Urton, 30 Sept. 16_6. Will dated 7 April, 1655, pro. 22 January 1658. Bur. at Wortley, Feb. 1657, æt. 6_.

.... wife of Leeke of Criggau.

William Cotton of Nether Denby = Eleanor Fownes, parish of Peniston, gen., an iron | bur. at Peniston, master, living at Wortley 1656, at 30 Nov. 1690. Hawkhurst, parish of Silkston 1667. Will dated 24 Feb. 1674. Died 13 March following and was bur. at Peniston church on 17th. He bought the Haigh of Wm. Fownes, 24 Sept. 166_.

John. Gilbert. George.

William, mar. 1st Barbara, dau. of Thos. Curwen; 2d Anna, dau. of Geo. Westby. Issue by both.

Daniel, married & had issue.

Joanna, ux. Thos. Hall (issue).

Joshua, drowned at sea, or died in Holland.

Eleanor, ux. James Wright, a silenced minister.

John, d. young.

Susanna. Elizabeth. Ann. Mary.

Thomas Cotton, V.D.M. = Bridget, dau. of Leonard Hoare, Pres'dt of Cambridge born at or near Wortley 1657. | University in N. E., by Bridget his wife, dau. of the A minister in London many | Lord Lisle; who remarried ...... Usher. Portraits years. Died 1730 & was buried | of some of this family are in poss'n of Mr. Bayes Cotton. in Bunhill Fields.

Thomas Cotton = Rebecca, dau. of of Hackney, | Joshua Bayes, Atty. at Law, | V.D.M , minister second son, | in London, d. 23 March, 1797, | d. 7 Feb. 1799, æt. 82. æt. 87. Buried at | Bur. in Bunhill Fields. Bunhill Fields.

Leonard Cotton = ... eldest son, settled in America.

Colonel Cotton, an American Loyalist.

Alicia, d. unmarried.

Bayes Cotton, living.

Joshua.

Mrs. Bridget Cotton is mentioned by her step-father, Hezekiah Usher, of Boston, in his will, recorded in Suffolk Co. Probate Registry (B. 11, p. 318), in which, after speaking in very strong terms of his wife, he goes on to say : " But as for her daughter Bridget, if her mother had not been so undermining and over-reaching for her I should a been willing to have done what I could for her and I do give her the tumbler with the armes of a spread eagle with two heads but I think one head for a body is enough." This doubtless refers to the arms of the Hoare family. If so, is it not the earliest sign of their use in New England?

In Massachusetts Archives at the State-House in Boston (Book 8, No. 22), in the case of Samuel Sewall, surviving trustee to Mrs. Bridget Usher, *vs.* Winthrop, may be found a certificate from the Rev. Joshua Richardson, Rector of the parish church of Allhallows on the Wall, London, 1692, showing that Mr. Thomas Cotton of Peniston in the County of York, and Mrs. Bridgett Hoar of the Parish of St. Buttolph, Bishopsgate in the city of London, were married 21 June, 1689. And, in the same volume (No. 67) is a deposition made by Henry Newman that Mrs. Bridgett Hoar, daughter of Madame Usher, is the wife of Mr. Thomas Cotton, &c. H. F. W.

I do not find the name Cotton among the patentees of land in the Virginia Land Registry Office. The following extracts from the Parish Register of Sussex County, Va., 1737-1775, in which the entries are made alphabetically by Christian, not surname, may however be of some interest to the Cotton family of New England.

Amelia dau.	of John	and	Lucy	Cotton	b. Dec. 1, 1739.
Sarah "	"	"	"	"	b. Sept. 24, 1741.
Ephraim son	"	"	"	"	b. Dec. 13, 1747.
Drury, son	Thos.	"	Jane	"	b. Aug. 10, 1741.
Mary dau.	Thos.	"	Jean	"	b. Apr'l 3, 1743.
Frederick son	Joshua and Susanna			"	b. June 11. 1760.
					Sponsors: Drury, Henry & Eliza Cotton.
Jesse son	"	"	"	"	b. Dec. 28, 1758.
Drusilla dau.	"	"	"	"	b. Dec. 9, 1763.
Howell son	"	"	"	"	b. Mch 3, 1765.
Edmund son	"	"	"	"	b. Mch. 30. 1769.
					Sponsors : Thos. Whitfield, Wm Sola & Eliza Hight.
Susanna dau.	"	"	"	Cotton	b. Oct. 3, 1775.
Becky dau.	Richard	&	Betty	Cotton	b. Mch. 29, 1756.
Cary son	"	"	"	"	b. Mch. 12, 1765.
Jane dau.	"	"	"	"	b. Apl. 14, 1762.
Sally dau.	"	"	"	"	b. June 2, 1748-9.
Seth son	"	"	"	"	b. Nov. 1, 1750.
Weaver son	"	"	"	"	b. July 2, 1768.
Betty dau.	Henry	"	Sarah	Cotton	b. Jan. 3, 1762.
Thomas son	"	"	"	"	b. May 2, 1766.
John son	Seth	"	Rebecca	"	b. Oct. 22, 1772.
William son	"	"	"	"	b. Nov. 6, 1769.
Hardy son	William	"	Eliz^h	"	b. Feb. 1, 1766.
Selah dau.	"	"	"	"	b. Dec. 14, 1759.
Alsobrook son	"	"	"	"	b. Aug. 20, 1768.
Lucretia dau.	William	"	Lucy	"	b. Nov. 14, 1762.
Littlebury son	Drury	"	Phebe	"	b. Mch. 10, 1764.

R. A. BROCK, of Richmond, Va.]

ROBERT PECKE, minister of the word of God at Hingham in the County of Norfolk, 24 July, 1651, proved 10 April, 1658, by Samuel Pecke, one of the executors. To Thomas, my son, and Samuel, my son, and their heirs forever the messuage wherein I now dwell, situate and lying in Hingham, and an enclosure called the Lady Close (of eight acres). To Robert Pecke, son of my son Robert deceased, twenty pounds at the age of twenty three years. To John Pecke, son of said Robert, ten pounds at the age of twenty two years. To Benjamin Pecke, the youngest son of said Robert Pecke deceased, twenty pounds at the age of twenty two years. To the children of Anne Mason, my daughter, wife of Capt. John Mason, of Seabrooke, on the river Connecticot in newe England, forty pounds to be divided equally and to be sent to my son John Mason to dispose of it for their use. To my son Joseph during his natural life fourteen pounds yearly to be in hands of sons Thomas and Samuel, and I commit said son Joseph to the care of my two sons Thomas & Samuel. To the children of Thomas & Samuel, my sons, five pounds apiece at age of twenty one years. To my now wife Martha Pecke forty pounds within two months after my decease. If I depart this life in Hingham my body may be interred in the church-yard near unto Anne, my wife deceased.

When the will was proved power was reserved to Thomas Pecke, the other executor, to act.   Wootton, 153.

["The Lord and patron of Burgate is Sr Edmund Bacon, Baronet. James Bacon, sonne of Sr James Bacon of Friston, K^nt, was Rector of Burgate in the time of K. Charles, an excellent preacher, but he had a very weake body, he married .... daughter of .... Honeywood Esq. She was grandchild of that famous Mrs Mary Honeywood, so often made mention by devines in regard of her long distresse of con-science, and brought up by her. The husband of yt Mrs Mary Honeywood was a man of 3000£ pr annum, in those times. She was after the death of Mr Bacon married to Mr Robert Pecke Rector of Hingham in Norff. a woman of singular parts."—Add. MS. 15520, British Museum.

This MS. is entitled on the cover, Church Notes for the County of Suffolk, 1655–1665, and, on fly leaf, inside, "Ryece's Collections of the Antiquities of Suffolk;" but this is undoubtedly a mistake. Robert Rice or Ryece, the antiquary, died in 1637-8, as will be seen from his will (which follows). The handwriting shows these Notes to be the work of one of the Candler family.

"John Hale, M^r in Arts, was preacher there [in Mildenhall] in the time of the Long Parliament and there lived in very good esteeme, his father was a citizen of London—hee married Mary daughter of Thomas Sothebie Rector of Combes. She was since his death married againe to Thomas Peck of Prittlewell in Essex—whose first wife was —— daughter of John Rogers the famous preacher of Dedham his 2^d was daughter of —— Caley, this was his 3^d."—Add. MS. 15520 British Muse-um.—H. F. W.

More about the Rev. Robert Peck and his connection with the Bacon family will be found in the REGISTER, xxxvii. 193. Rev. Robert Peck and his brother Joseph came to New England in 1638 (REG. xv. 26) and settled at Hingham. The former returned to England. The latter remained here and has numerous descendants, one of whom, IRA B. Peck, Esq., of Woonsocket, R. I., published in 1868 a large volume on the family (REG. xxiv. 96, 187). The will of Rev. Robert Peck, and that of his father, Robert Peck of Beccles in Suffolk, England, are printed in full by Mr. I. B. Peck, who also gives a tabular pedigree of the ancestors of the two New England emigrants for twenty generations.

The descendants of Anne, daughter of the Rev. Robert Peck and wife of Capt. John Mason, the conqueror of the Pequots, are the subject of an article by the late Chancellor Walworth in the REGISTER, vol. xv. pp. 117-22, 217-24, 318; xvii. 39-42, 214-19.—EDITOR.]

ROBERT RICE of Preston in the County of Suffolk gentleman; "This Seaventh daie of ffebruary In the latter dayes of this miserable world from Christs birth 1637"; proved 16 February 1638 by Sara Allen executrix. My body to be buried in the South side of the Chancell in the church yard of Preston as near unto my wife as conveniently may be. To Mr Thomas Willis, now minister and Vicar of Preston. .... To my reverend and good friend, late minister and Curate in Great Waldingfield, Mr Peachie, now resident in Clare or thereabouts. To my reverend good friend Mr Stanes-bie, sometime minister of Little Waldingfield, and to Mr William Lambert now present minister of Little Waldingfield. To my cousin Robert Hobert of Lynsey in the County of Suffolk, gentleman. To my cousin Mr Wil-liam Munnings, late resident at Sir Henry Myldmayes in the County of Essex. More, I give unto him and his heirs forever, my copyhold meadow in Monkes Illigh in the County of Suffolk, between the common river there and the King's highway leading from Monkes Illigh church to Brent-Elligh, containing four acres, commonly called Skipps meadows, and now in the occupation of Katherine Munninge, widow; he to sell it and divide the proceeds between three of his sisters, Ann, Katherine and Ellen Munninge, so as one half shall go to Anne Munninge, aged, lame and impotent, and the other half to Katherine and Ellen. To Thomas Munning, sometime my servant. To my cousin Robert Doe, of Bardwell.

To my nephew John Appleton, the second son of my loving brother in the law John Appleton of Chilton, in the county of Suffolk deceased, my Latin bossed Bible, of Trimelius, in folio. To William Mills, of Lanham, in the County of Suffolk, painter and glazier, forty shillings, with all my boxes of Painting Colours, with the desire that, so long as he shall live and be able to work, that he do from time to time keep, renew and amend, as need shall require, the decays of colours, words, letters, compartments and forms of those tables, writings and inscriptions which he hath at any time made for me, as they are fixed in the Parish church or chancell of Preston aforesaid. To Zouch Allen the son of my niece Sarah Allen, widow, my customary tenement called Perkins-Bronds, in Preston. To the aforesaid John Appleton my copyhold lands and tenements holden of the manor of Brettenham Hall in the said County of Suffolk. To my loving cousin Richard Kymbould of Braintree in the county of Essex. To my cousins Rice Munning and his sister the wife of Francis Lucas. To Robert Johnson, my godson, and William Johnson, his brother, sometime my servant. To my loving brother-in-law Samuel Appleton, gentleman, now dwelling at Ipswich in New England. To Sarah Allen, sister of Zouch Allen, at the age of twenty one years. To Edmond Betts, of this town, my tenant. My niece Mrs Sarah Allen, widow, to be the sole executrix.   Harvey, 36.

[" Riece was yeoman of the Guard to K. Hen. 7 note y[t] all the kings Guard were gentlemen borne at ye first hee was Capt of Riece banke (?) and came to inhabit in Suff. with little John Vere E. of Oxford. His sone was justice of Peace and setled himselfe at Preston his name Roger he liued in Preston in the dayes of Edw. Mary & Eliza : (thus far Tilletson). Robert Riece his sonne had his education in Geneua in the house of Theodore Beza he liued in Preston in ye dayes of Q. Eliza: k. James and K. Charles and died lamented leauing a good name behind him but sine prole. He was a man very skilfull in Heraldy and set up the Royall armes of England in a faire Table in ye church of Preston in Suff. and in the glasse windowes the coats of very many of the cheife gentry of Suff. in his time where they remaine this 25 of March 1655." Harleian MS. 6071 (Candler's), p. 343, British Museum.
H. F. W.

Samuel Appleton, named in this will, a son of Samuel Appleton of Little Waldingfield, Suffolk, England, was born in that parish in 1586, and was baptized there Aug. 13 of that year. He died in Rowley, Mass., 1670. Messrs. I. A. Jewett (1850), John Appleton (1867) and W. S. Appleton (1873 and 1874) have published books on this family. Mr. Jewett prints the will of Robert Ryece in full.—ED.]

AGNES DARBY, relict of Augustine Darby of Bisley in the County of Surrey (nuncupative), 21 May, 1650, proved 18 June, 1650. To Henry Collier of Horsell, yeoman. He to pay unto Edward Darby in New England ten pounds when he shall come and demand the same. To Richard Darby five shillings. To John Darby twelve pence. To Margaret Lee, wife of John Lee, five shillings. Youngest son Austen Darby. Son John Ellis. Joane Bowbrick, wife of Thomas Bowbrick. Henry Lee a witness.
Pembroke, 90.

[Edward Darby or Derby was of Braintree, Mass. He married Jan. 25, 1659–60, Susanna Hook. Several others of the surname settled in New England. Roger Derby, from Topsham, Devonshire, settled in Ipswich, Mass., about 1671, and among other sons had Richard, born Oct. 1679, who settled in Salem, Mass., and was the ancestor of a distinguished family.—EDITOR.]

RICHARD HOUGHTON, citizen and Merchant Taylor of London, 30 July, 1652, proved 4 August, 1652. To my sister Alice White forty shillings and to her son twelve pence. To my sister-in-law Anne Houghton twenty shillings and to her sons who are now in the Common Wealth of England forty shillings apiece, and to her other son who is now beyond the seas, if he be now living and come home safe and alive within one year after the date hereof, forty shillings. Furthermore unto one of my said sister in laws sons who is now married (a bequest) and to the other son here residing, &c. To my uncle Hanmer twenty shillings and to his children twelve pence apiece. To my cousin Thomas Cooke, living in Fow lane, Southwark, thirty shillings and to his children twelve pence apiece. To Daniel Cooke, where I now lodge, five pounds, whom I desire to be sole executor. George Horne, cordwainer, and Mr Whittle, merchant taylor, to be overseers. A bequest to cousin Anne Cord, widow, and her children. To fifty poor taylors ten shillings apiece; to fifty poor bodiesmakers ten shillings apiece; to fifty poor glovers ten shillings apiece; to fifty poor widows ten shillings apiece. To the two eldest daughters of my executors wife twenty shillings apiece; to his own daughter Mary forty shillings and to Mrs Cooke herself thirty shillings to buy her a ring; and to Daniel Man, to buy him a coat, ten shillings. Sundry other bequests made.   Bowyer, 227.

GEORGE MOODY of Moulton in the County of Suffolk, yeoman, 20 February, 1651. To wife Lydia my mansion house commonly called Fryatts &c. &c. To my cousin Mary Smith thirty pounds in the second year after my death. To my cousin Jonas Alston's wife thirty pounds four years after my decease. To my cousin Alstone's daughter, Ann Alstone ten pounds in the sixth year after my decease. To my cousin Samuel Warren, son of my sister, Margaret Warren, forty pounds in the third year after my decease. To my cousin Clement Warren, son of my sister Margaret Warren, ten pounds in the fifth year after my decease. House to sister Margaret Warren and her son George Warren after her decease. To George Warren's wife ten pounds in the fifth year after my decease. To her daughter Sara five pounds in the sixth year, &c. and five pounds among the rest of her children in the seventh year, &c. To my brother John Salmon's eldest son thirty pounds in the eighth year, &c. Ten pounds to the rest of his children in the ninth year. To Francis Hovell's children five pounds in the tenth year, &c. To Richard Hovell of Ashfield Magna, to Mr Croxen, to Mr Archer, to Mr Chatchpole, to Mr Deaken at Newmarket, to Mr Westwood of Dallam, to the poor in Newmarket, of Gaseley, of Dallum, of Barrow, of Denham and of Moulton. Mr Jonas Alston and John Salmon the younger to be executors. Certain lands to go to brother Samuel Moody in Berry (sic) and to his heirs forever. Mr. Eyres to preach my funeral sermon. The witnesses were Thomas Warren and Nathaniel Eyre.

Administration with the will annexed was granted 3 May, 1654, to Samuel Moody, brother of the deceased, &c. the executors having renounced the trust.   Bowyer, 61.

SAMUEL MOODY, of Mowlton, in the County of Suffolk, Esquire, 18 February, 1657, proved by his son John Moody, executor, 28 June, 1658. To eldest son George Moody, houses, lands, &c. in Mowlton. My late mansion in Bury, where my son George now dwells, the lease renowed in my son's name. A son Henry named. To son John all my lands in Ireland. To Henry lands in Gaywood near Lynn, in Norfolk (forty acres). To daughter Anne in three years after my death or at her day of marriage, and to daughter Elizabeth (with the same condition). To daughter Margaret Westropp, daughter Sarah Cooke and grandchild Mary Browne. To the poor of James Parish in Bury. To Mr Slater, minister in Bury. To the children of my sister Greenwood one hundred pounds in full for the debt which she or her husband claims from my brother George Moodye or his executors or administrators.

The witnesses were Thomas Stanton and Edward Oxborough.

Wootton, 492.

[The following pedigree is from Harl. MS. 6071 (British Museum), p. 512 (or fol. 254).

MOODY.

George Moody of Moulton = ...
famous for his house keeping
and wast and plaine dealing.

- George Moodye of Moulton s. p. = ... daughter of Houill, als. Smith.
- John Moody, went over to New England.
- Samuell Moody = Mary, daughter a wollen Draper in Bury. Alderman, of great power in committees. Justice of the peace since the death of K. Charles, chosen by the Bourugh in Bury into seuerall parliaments in that time. After the death of his Brother he had his father's estate in reuertion. | of John Boldro, Gent. (of St. Edmunds Bury).
- Daughter.

- George Moodey a wollen Draper in Bury. = Anne, dau. of Ambrose Bigge of Glemsford, Gent.
  - Samuel. Ambrose. George.
- John Moody = Anne, one Capt. of foote of the daus. & afterward & co-heirs of serjeant-major ..... of Flowton. of horse in the service of the Parliament. Since a merchant in Ipswich.
- Samuel Moody, a Capt.— Thomas. Henry. all of them s. p.
- Mary = John Browne, Moody, Alderman of eldest Bury this daughter. yeare 1658.

- Margaret Moody, married to Major Westhorp of Hundon.
- Sarah Moody, m. to Wm. Cooke of Bury, a Linen Draper.
- Anne Moody.
- Elizabeth Moody.

H. F. W.

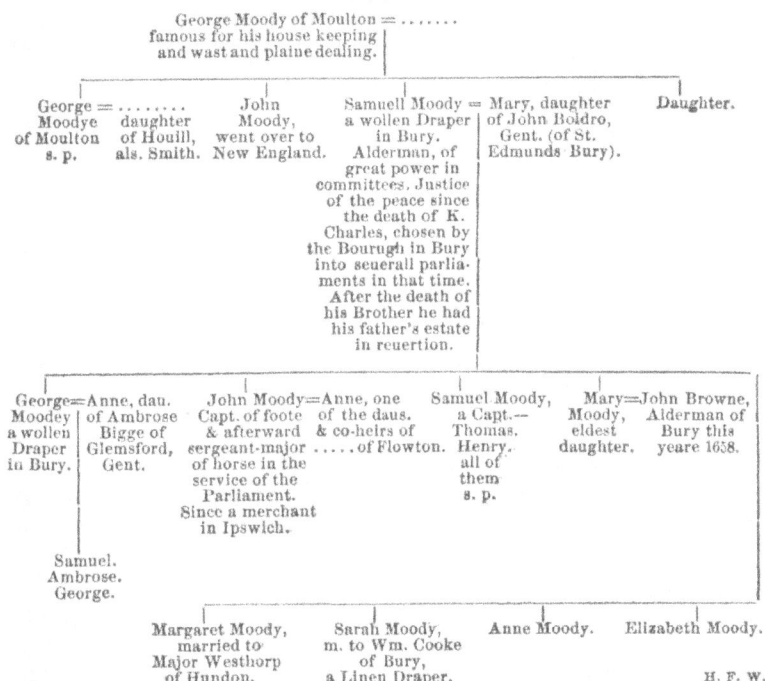

John Moody, according to the Apostle Eliot's records, came to New England in 1633 and settled at Roxbury. His wife was named Sarah. He removed to Hartford, Ct. His widow died in 1671 at Hadley. (See REG. iv. 179; xxxv. 242; Winthrop's New England, ed. 1853, i. 126; Savage's Dict. iii. 225).—EDITOR.]

THOMAS COBBET of Moorton, parish of Thame, in the County of Oxford, 12 November, 1617, proved 11 February, 1617. My body to be buried in the church of Thame. To Thomas Cobbet, eldest son of my son John, five pounds within one year after my decease. To each of the rest of my son John's children forty shillings apiece within one year, &c. To son Raphe Cobbet forty pounds within one year & six months, &c. To Thomas, eldest son of Raphe five pounds within one year and six months, &c., and to each of the rest of son Raphe's children forty shillings (within the same period). To my son Christopher Pytts ten shillings, as a token of my love, and to my daughter Johane Pytts twenty pounds within one year, &c. To each of my god children twelve pence apiece.

Item, I give to my cousin Thomas Cobbett of Newbury forty shillings of good & lawful money of England, to be paid him within one year after my decease. My son John Cobbett to be sole Executor; and my brother John Cobbett and my son in law Christopher Pitts to be overseers and to have five shillings apiece for their pains.   Meade, 10.

[Rev. Thomas Cobbet, of Lynn and Ipswich, Mass., is said by Mather to have been born in Newbury, England, in 1608. (See *Magnalia*, ed. 1853, vol. i. p. 518.) He was probably related to this family.—Editor.]

FRANCIS FAWCONER, of Kingscleare in the County of Southampton, Gentleman, 1 September, 1662, proved 21 May, 1663. To the poor of the parish of Kingscleare three pounds, to be distributed within six days next after my decease. To my cousin Peter Fawconer, son of Richard Fawconer deceased, all my freeland containing thirty acres, more or less, and the barn and timber and wood thereupon growing, in Kingscleare Woolands, which I purchased and bought of James Waite, and all the rents issuing out of the said lands, to the said Peter Fawconer and his heirs forever, and twenty pounds and all my wearing apparel. To his sister Elizabeth Fawconer one hundred pounds.

Item I give and bequeath to my brother Edmond Fawconor that is living in New England two hundred pounds of lawfull money of England. To John Fawkner of Kingscleare twenty pounds. To Alice Person, widow, one hundred pounds. To Elizabeth Fawconer, their sister, forty pounds. More, to the abovenamed Peter Fawconor a joyned bedstead, a bedmatt, a bedcord, a feather bed, a feather bolster, two feather pillowes, a pair of pillowbeares, a pair of sheets of the best, a pair of blaukets, a coverlet and curtains and my great chest, &c. To Alice Person, widow, a brass pot, &c., and all the brewing vessell that I have standing at her brother John Fawconer's house except the brewing tub. To Nicholas Knite of Kingscleare, miller, ten shillings; to Elizabeth, his wife, forty shillings; to her five children that she had by her first husband, that is, to Richard, Francis, John, Daniel and Anthony Fawkoner, twenty-five pounds to be equally divided amongst them, five pounds apiece, at the age of twenty one years. To Elizabeth Fawconer, sister of Peter (some pewter). To my brother in law, John Carter, and to Elizabeth, his wife, each a twenty shilling piece of gold. To John Carter the younger (some furniture standing at Coldhenly House). To Agnes Fawkener, widow, twenty shillings. To Winifrit Waite, wife of James Waite of Kingscleare ten shillings in gold; and to their son James and daughter Katherine Waite ten shillings each. To Francis Friser, of Kingscleare, the elder, ten shillings. To Alice Alle ten shillings. To Christopher Dugdale of Husborne* ten shillings. To his five children that he had, by Master Webber's daughter, one hundred pounds, equally to be divided amongst them, twenty pounds apiece, at age of twenty one years. I appoint John Atfield of Kingscleare, gentleman, overseer, and give him two twenty shilling pieces of gold, and to his wife one twenty shilling piece of gold.

The residue to my sister's son, Matthew Webber, whom I make executor; and it is my will that he should agree with my Lord's officers for the Heriotts that were due to the Lord at my decease and to pay them in money or in goods, as they can agree.

Wit: John Atfiell, Nicholas Bartholomew (his mark).
                                                         Juxon, 60.

* This is probably meant for Hurstborne.—H. F. W.

[The following pedigree of the Fawknor family of King's Clear, to which the testator of the preceding will and his brother Edmund (who settled in Andover, Massachusetts) must have belonged, is from the Visitation of Hampshire, 1634.

Arms.—Sa. three falcons ar., beaked, legged and belled or.
Crest.—A garb or, banded ar.

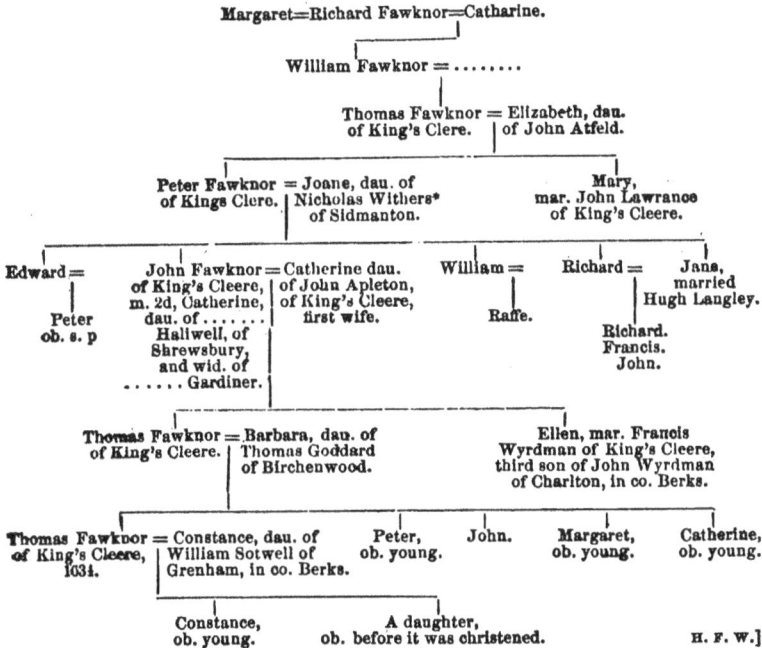

Margaret=Richard Fawknor=Catharine.

William Fawknor = ...

Thomas Fawknor = Elizabeth, dau.
of King's Clere. | of John Atfeld.

Peter Fawknor = Joane, dau. of
of Kings Clere. | Nicholas Withers*
of Sidmanton.

Mary,
mar. John Lawrance
of King's Cleere.

Edward =
|
Peter
ob. s. p

John Fawknor = Catherine dau.
of King's Cleere, | of John Apleton,
m. 2d, Catherine, | of King's Cleere,
dau. of .... | first wife.
Haliwell, of
Shrewsbury,
and wid. of
...... Gardiner.

William =
|
Raffe.

Richard = Jane,
married
Hugh Langley.

Richard.
Francis.
John.

Thomas Fawknor = Barbara, dau. of
of King's Cleere. | Thomas Goddard
of Birchenwood.

Ellen, mar. Francis
Wyrdman of King's Cleere,
third son of John Wyrdman
of Charlton, in co. Berks.

Thomas Fawknor = Constance, dau. of
of King's Cleere, | William Sotwell of
1634. | Grenham, in co. Berks.

Peter,
ob. young.

John.

Margaret,
ob. young.

Catherine,
ob. young.

Constance,
ob. young.

A daughter,
ob. before it was christened.

H. F. W.]

THOMAS FAWNE, 25 December, 1651, proved 17 August, 1652. To Robert Williams, the chirurgeon of the ship called the Peter, one watch and a cornelian ring. To my servant, William Martin, his passage to Virginia and his freedom there and one suit of clothes with black ribbons. To the poor of Skendley† parish in Lincolnshire forty shillings. To Mr Hatch, woollen draper, nine pounds; to Mr Crayford seven pounds; to Thos. Dagger one chest with whatsoever is in it. To my father one pair of silver fringed gloves and one pair of white gloves; to my mother two rings with stones in them. To Mr Murrell, Mr John Richards, Mr Corbin, Matt. Johnson (sundry bequests). To my brother Robert my rapier and belt. To John Younge and John Stone, whom I make executors .... all my debts due to me in Virginia, and likewise the disposing of all my estate now shipped in the ship called the Peter, and the return whereof is to be divided among my brothers and sisters, whereof Mrs Francis White is to have one part. To the seamen two cases of drams.

The witnesses were John Richards and James Frisby.

Bowyer, 220.

* Harleian MS. 1139 (fol. 22), in British Museum, gives the surname Whitacres, instead of Withers, as above.
† This is so written. Probably Skendleby is meant.—H. F. W.

ROBERT NICKOLSON, of London, Merchant, and son of Francis Nickolson, Esq. 10 November, 1651. Ten pounds sterling towards the relief of the English captives in Turkey. Forty shillings to Mr Pickett, sometime minister of Chappell alias Pontibridge, Essex, and twenty shillings to the poor of the said parish. To Capt. Sam: Matthewes of Virginia, Esq. one pair of Buckskin gloves, cost five shillings, and to Mrs Matthewes his wife two pairs of kid skin gloves. To Sam: Matthewes, the son of said Capt., one pair of Buckskin gloves and to his brother one pair of corderont (*sic*) gloves. To Mrs. Mary Bernard of Warwick River six pairs of kid gloves and to her daughters three pairs of gloves apiece. Item fourteen shillings more of gloves or other ware which Stephen Wooderife oweth me. I give unto John Younge, M^r of the ship Peter of London twenty shillings sterling to buy his wife a ring and to himself a buckskin pair of gloves of five shillings. To Mr John Richards two pairs of cordevant gloves and Mr Lockers Sermons. To Mr Thomas Fawne two pairs of cordevant gloves and Leo Afer, a History book. To John Stone twenty shillings, two pairs of Cordevant gloves, all the rest of the syrups and all the books in the cabin. Gloves to Mr Driver, Mr Freizby and Matthew Johnson. To John Corbin my coasting coat, my stuff coat and one turkey waistcoat and two pairs of cordevant gloves. To the seamen one case of Drams. To the steward, boatman, carpenter and gunner all my clothes and bedding, whereof the steward is to have one half. To the poors box five shillings. To Robert and Peter, each of them, one pair of gloves. To Mrs Veheath Land Vernald one diamond ring, one gold ring, the motto *Idem qui pridem*, which said Mrs Veheath Land is daughter to Mrs Mary Vernald of Warwick River, widow. To Mr Murrell and the Doctor, to each of them one pair of gloves.

All the which gifts are to be given and satisfied unto every and several said party or parties by the said John Younge and John Corbin at or near the Barbadoes or at or near Virginia upon demand, if the said John Younge and John Corbin shall think fit. And the said John Younge and John Corbin are to lay out four or five pounds upon my burial at the Barbadoes or at Virginia, &c. All my goods or all goods consigned to me, Robert Nickolson, now shipped in the ship called the Peter, to be sold for the best advantage and the returns to be paid to my father Mr Francis Nickolson, Esq. in Ipswich.

All the rest of my estate to be distributed equally between my brothers and sisters. Eldest brother Francis Nicholson mentioned.

The witnesses were John Richards, Thomas Fawne and John Stone.

The executors named in the will renounced the executorship and letters of administration issued 26 August, 1652, to Francis Nicholson the father, the testator being referred to as late in the parts beyond the seas deceased.

Bowyer, 228.

[I am indebted to Mr. Eccles for the sketch of the Nicholson coat of arms, of which an engraving will be found in the margin, It will be noticed that no colors are indicated on the shield.—H. F. W.

Robert Nicholson was granted 500 acres of land in Charles City County, Virginia, Jan. 3, 1655, Book No. 4, p. 11, *Va. Land Reg. Office.*

The Samuel Matthews mentioned in the will, is presumably "an ancient planter" who was a member of the Council of the Colony of Virginia as early as 1629. In March, 1630, he built the fort at Point Comfort, James river. He served continuously in the Colonial Council or House of Burgesses, and latterly as County-Lieutenant of Warwick County, deriving thence his title of Lieutenant-Colonel. In 1656 he was sent as one of the agents of the Colony to England, and on March 13, 1658, was elected by the assembly Governor of the Colony to succeed Edward Digges. He was an honest, energetic and faithful servant of the Colony, and his death, which occurred in January, 1660, was universally lamented.

The following grants to the name Matthews are on record in the Virginia Land Registry :

Nicholson, Virginia merch!

(ms Harc. 1085. fo. 57)

Thomas Matthews "chirurgeon" 1100 acres in Henrico County, May 11, 1639, Book No. 1, p. 646. Thomas Matthews "chirurgeon" 470 acres in Henrico County, Oct. 10, 1641, Book No. 1, p. 777.

"Captain Samuel Matthews Esq." 3000 acres upon Warwick river, Aug. 20, 1642, Book No. 1, p. 814.

"Captain Samuel Matthews Esq." 200 acres upon Warwick river, Aug. 20, 1642, Book No. 1, p. 815.

"Captain Samuel Matthews Esq." 4000 acres on the North-side of Rappahannock river, Jan'y 6th, 1639, Book No. 1, p. 882.

In regard to the name Barnard, mentioned in the will, it may be said that to Mrs. Anna Barnard was granted 1000 acres in Northumberland County, Apl. 3, 1652, and among the "transports" or "head-rights" was "Mr. Richard Bernard," Book No. 2, p. 306. *Va. Land Reg. Office.* R. A. Brock, of Richmond, Va.]

Thomas Stegge, now bound forth in a voyage to Vergenia, 6 October, 1651, proved 14 July, 1652, by Elizabeth Stegg, relict and sole executrix. •To sister Alice ten pounds per annum during her natural life, to be paid her every half year. To my brother Christophers two daughters twenty pounds apiece, to be paid them within two years after my decease. To my wife's sister Emelion Reade one full sixteenth part of the good ship now called the Seven Sisters, with the profits, &c. I give to my son Thomas Stegg in Virginia all my whole estate in Virginia, as also one quarter part of the Seven Sisters, now bound to Virginia, and all goods and apparel I have in that ship or any other servants and ought else belonging to me ; as also one quarter part of the ship Increase and all that shall accrew unto her for her voyage now at sea ; and for more I leave it to the consideration of his mother. To my daughter Grace Byrd and her children the houses I bought of Mr Neale in Bedlam, as also, after the decease of my wife or at the next marriage of my wife, I give her and her children my houses in the cloisters at St. Katherines that I bought of Mr. Tokely ; also, in like kind and case, I give her and her children my annuity at Elinge, if it so long continue, until the death of my said wife or her second marriage. To Elizabeth Byrd, my daughter's eldest daughter, one hundred pounds if she live until the age of fourteen years. To wife Elizabeth Stegg, during her natural life or widowhood, my whole estate, after debts and legacies are paid, excepting what is directly given away before to my son and houses at Bedlam to my daughter. But in case my said wife should marry again I give her out of my estate eight hundred pounds; and the rest to be equally divided between my two children. Wife Elizabeth to be executrix and loving friend M[r] .... Loton, Mr. Roger Draiton and M[r] Robert Earle to be overseers, and ten pounds apiece to buy them each a cloak.   Bowyer, 202.

[Thomas Stegge, "merchant," was granted 1000 acres of land between "Old man's and Queen's Creeke," January 6th, 1639, Book No. 1, p. 694.—*Virginia Land Records.*—R. A. BROCK, Richmond, Va.]

THOMAS STEGGE of the county of Henrico in Virginia Esq. 31 March, 1669–70, proved 15 May, 1671. To beloved wife Sarah Stegge, for ornaments for her person and as a token of my loving remembrance of her affectionate and tender care for me in sickness and in health (sundry personals) and more one Indian girl named ..... And if she resolve to go for England my will is that she have free power to accommodate herself with bedding, provisions and other necessaries for her voyage without the contradiction of any person whatsoever. And further she is hereby given free power to bestow upon her friends at her departure the value of twenty pounds sterling. I desire M[r] Thomas Grindon of London to pay unto my said wife or her order as soon as conveniently he may after her advice received all such sums of money as are due, belonging or appertaining to me in his hands or custody. To my dearest mother Elizabeth Grindon, wife of M[r] Thomas Grindon, citizen of London, twenty pounds sterling yearly &c. during her natural life. To my loving sister M[rs] Grace Byrd wife of M[r] John Byrd,[1] citizen and goldsmith of London, two hundred & forty pounds due to me in the hands of her said husband, as by his account sent me last year doth appear, and to my said sister one diamond ring given me by my mother when I was last in London, which I promised to give my sister if I died before her. To every child of my said sister and brother Bird of London now living one hundred pounds sterling to each of the sons at the age of twenty one years respectively and to the daughters at the age of twenty one or day of marriage. I give and bequeath all the right, title and interest I at present have or hereafter shall have to part of a house bought by the Honorable Thomas Ludwell Esq.[2] and myself of Henry Randolph and now in the possession of us together with all my interest in the furniture in the house and all lands &c. thereto belonging, to him the said Thomas Ludwell and his heirs forever, requesting him to pay out of the same to the Right Honb[le] Sir William Berkley K[nt], Governor, fifty pounds sterling within six months after my decease, as a token of that unfeigned respect I am and ever shall be obliged to pay his Honor for his many graces and favors.

All other lands, messuages, tenements &c. in Virginia or England to William Bird,[3] eldest son of the aforementioned John and Grace Bird in London, to him and his heirs forever. But because my cousin is yet young and not so well experienced in the transactions of the world I desire my loving wife, for a year or two that she continues in the country, to continue the managing of the estate &c., charging my cousin not to be led away by the evil instructions he shall receive from others but to be governed by the prudent and provident advice of his aunt; further desiring and charging my cousin, in all matters of moment and bargains of consequence, to make his address to the Honb[le] the Secretary[4] for his assistance, whom I earnestly entreat, for the dear friendship we have so long mutually enjoyed, that he will please to continue his kindness to my Remains and accept the trouble of being overseer to this my last Will and Testament.

The witnesses were Henry Randolph,[2] Edward Hill[6] and John Knowles. The above will was proved by the oath of Sara Stegge, relict and executrix. Duke, 69.

["Captain Thomas Stegge, Gentleman," received the following grants of land: 800 acres in Henrico county Dec. 29th, 1662, Book No. 4, page 583; 1280 acs. in Henrico county, on the north side of James river [including the present site of the city of Richmond], January 5th, 1663, and 1850 acres in the same county, December 29th, 1663, Book No. 5, pp. 200 and 528. *Va. Land Rec.* It is recorded in the family Bible of the Byrds of "Westover," that "he was an Officer in King Charles's Army." He was for several years a member of the county court of Charles City, and was a man of prominence and influence.

[1] Of the family of Byrd, Brexton, Cheshire.

[2] The ancestor of the prominent Virginia family of Ludwell [REGISTER, xxxiii. 220]. He was appointed a member of the Colonial Council in 1674. He appears to have been previously Clerk of the House of Burgesses. The following grants of land are of Record: Thomas Ludwell, 961 acres in Henrico county, June 16th, 1663, Book No. 4, p. 599. Thomas Ludwell and Thomas Stegge [they were probably merchants and partners in business], one-half acre in "James Cittie," January 1st, 1667, Book No. 6, p. 223. Thomas Ludwell, 1432 acres in Westmoreland County, October 15th, 1670, Book No. 6, p. 327. His son Philip Ludwell, who was successively governor of North Carolina and secretary of the colony of Virginia, who married Lady Frances (she was thrice married, her first husband being Samuel Stephens; no issue by the first or second marriage), the widow of Sir William Berkeley, and was the ancestor, maternally, of the distinguished patriots of the Revolution, Richard Henry, Francis Lightfoot, Thomas Ludwell, William and Arthur Lee, was a beneficiary in the following grants of land:

Philip Ludwell, 200 acres in Rappahannock county, April 17, 1667, Book No. 6, p. 121; "Collonel" Philip Ludwell, 400 acres in New Kent county, October 22d, 1673, Book No. 6, p. 474. Philip Ludwell, Robert Handfort and Richard Whitehead, 20,000 acres in New Kent county, Oct. 24th, 1673, Book No. 6, p. 467.

There appears to have been a John Ludwell, "planterin," Charles City county in 1662.

[3] According to the family Registry, "The Honorable William Byrd Esquire the first of the name who settled in this Colony was born in 1652 and died in 1704 at 'Westover,' Virg. He came from Brexton in Cheshire to inherit the effects of his uncle Captain Stagg." October 27th, 1673, "Captain William Bird" was granted 1280 acres of land on the north side of James river, "formerly granted Collo. Thomas Stegg, by patent dated January 5th, 1663." *Va. Land Records.* He subsequently received other extensive grants, was a member of the Council, and for a number of years Receiver General of the Colony. He married Mary, daughter of Colonel Warham Horsmonden of "Purley in Essex, England," a member of the Virginia Council.

William Byrd, son of the preceding, was born at "Westover" March 10, 1674; died there August 26th, 1744. He was educated in England; "called to the bar in the Middle Temple, studied for some time in the Low Countries, visited the Court of France and was chosen Fellow of the Royal Society." He succeeded his father as Receiver General of the Colony, "was thrice appointed public agent to the court and ministry of England, and, being thirty-seven years a member, at last became President of the Council." His genius is embalmed in our national literature as the author of the *Westover Manuscripts*, which contain, with other papers, the "History of the Dividing Line between Virginia and North Carolina as run in 1728-29," Colonel Byrd being one of the Commissioners on the part of Virginia. He was the founder of Richmond, Va., which was laid off by Major William Mayo in April, 1737. He married twice. First, Lucy, daughter of Colonel Daniel Parke, Governor of the Leeward Islands; secondly, May 9th, 1724, "Mrs. Maria Taylor, eldest daughter and co-heiress of Thomas Taylor of Kensington, England," born November 16th, 1698, died August 25th, 1771.

William, the eldest son by the second marriage, born September 6th, 1728, died January 1st, 1777, was a member of the Virginia Council; and in 1756 served as Colonel of the 2nd Virginia regiment in the French and Indian war. He was married twice—first, April 10, 1748, to Elizabeth (born October 13th, 1731; died July 14th, 1760), daughter of John Carter of "Shirley," James river; secondly, January 29th, 1761, to Mary, daughter of Charles and Ann (daughter of Joseph Shippen) Willing of Philadelphia, Pa., who survived him. Charles Willing was son of Thomas and Ann Willing of Bristol, Eng.

⁴ Major Robert Beverley, the father of the historian of Virginia.
⁵ Henry Randolph, long the clerk of Henrico county. Joseph W. Randolph, the veteran bookseller of Richmond, is a descendant.
⁶ Colonel Edward Hill, Senior, a member of the Council.—R. A. BROCK.]

REBECCA SAINTBURY of St. Olave Southwark, in County of Surrey, widow, 30 November, 1677, proved 2 January, 1678. To grandson John Leeson my houses in Shoreditch for term of my lease. To Sarah Leechfield twenty shillings, to Susanna Leechfield twenty shillings, to Anne Leechfield, their mother, twenty shillings to buy her a ring. To niece Rebecca Tapley forty shillings. The remainder of my ready money, legacies & funeral expenses being thereout first paid, born and discharged, I give to my grandsons Thomas & James Spicer, equally. All the residue of my estate (excepting twenty pounds which I give unto my niece Elizabeth Griffin⁷ now inhabiting in Virginia, and excepting my iron and brass goods which I give to my grandson John Leeson and granddaughter Anne Spicer, to be divided betwixt them &c., and excepting two silver spoons which I give to the children of my grandson John Tomlinson) I give unto Anne, Elizabeth, Sarah and Mary Spicer, daughters of John Spicer, gentleman, to be divided amongst them, share and share alike. John Spicer, gentleman, to be the sole executor.

The witnesses were Mary Bowder, Ruth Halsey (by mark) and George Miniett.   King, 11.

[⁷ The following early grants of land to the name of Griffin are of record:

Thomas Griffin, 1064 acres in Lancaster county, July 4th, 1653, Book No. 3, p. 79.
Samuel Griffin, 1155 and 1046 acres in Rappahannock county, April 16 and Jan. 1, 1660, Book No. 4, pp. 472 and 473.
William Griffin, 400 acres in Northampton county, December 9, 1662, Book No. 4, p. 570.
Humphrey Griffin, 200 acres "in the south branch of Nancimond river on Matthews Creek," March 11th, 1664, Book No. 5, p. 67.
Richard Griffin, 57 acres in Westmoreland county, September 30th, 1664, Book No. 5, p. 129. Judge Cyrus Griffin, last president of the Continental Congress, was the son of Leroy Griffin and his wife Mary Ann, daughter of John Bertrand and his wife Charlotte Jolly, Huguenot refugees—all of Rappahannock county. The family tradition is that the paternal ancestor of Judge Cyrus Griffin was from Wales. From the christian names of the first two grantees cited above, Thomas and Samuel, which were borne by two brothers of Judge Griffin, and have been perpetuated in succeeding generations, I am inclined to think that they were brothers, and that one or the other of them was the ancestor of Judge Griffin.—R. A. B.]

BATT of Virginia.

[From Pedigrees of Yorkshire Families, West Riding, collected about 1666–67, with additions made 1702.]

Batt of Okewell, near Birstall in the Wapentake of Agbrigg and Morley, bears *Arg. a chev. betw. 3 reremice displayed sable.*

Henry Batt of Okewell in Birstall, lived in the reign of K. Henry VIII., Edw VI., and until second year of Q. Mary; was witness to the last Will and Testament of Sir Henry Savile of Thornhill, K^{nt} of the Hon. Order of the Bath, and had forty shillings yearly annuity for life given him out of his lands, by the said will, and the keeping of his courts. He purchased the manors of Birstall, Heckmondwyke and Heaton, in Bradford dale, with, other lands. He married ...., dau. of .... and had issue—Henry, ——, John.

Henry Batt (son & heir of Henry) married ...., dau. & co.-h. of Mr Richard Wilkinson of Bradford, and had issue—Henry (s. p.), Robert, Richard who lived at Spenn in Gomershall, ... married to Mr Geo. Parry, ... married to Mr Thos Crowle, and Margaret married to Mr Anthony Hopkinson of Birstall.

Robert Batt (son & heir of Henry) was fellow and vice master of University College, Oxford, married Mary, daughter of Mr. John Parry, of the Golden Valley in Herefordshire and had issue—John, William and Henry^s (both lived in Virginia), Robert, Mary married 1st to Mr Reresby Eyre, afterward to Mr Henry Hirst, Elizabeth married to Richard Marshe D^r of Divinity, Dean of York, Rebecca unmarried, Catherine married to Mr Philip Mallory. The said Mary survived her husband and was afterwards married to Mr Richard Rawlinson of Rotheram.

John Batt Esq. (son and heir of Robert) was captain of a foot company in the Reg^t of Agbrigg and Morley, & Justice of Peace in the West Riding; married Martha, daughter of Mr Thomas Mallory, Dean of Chester, and had issue—John, drowned in the Irish Seas coming from Virginia with his father, William, Thomas and Henry in Virginia 1667, and Martha.

William Batt Esq. (son & heir of John) is captain of a foot company in the same Reg^t, Justice of the Peace 1667; married Elizabeth daughter of Mr William Horton & hath issue—William, Gladdhill, John, Thomas died young, Elizabeth, Martha and Judith.

John Batt Esq. (third son and h. of William) is now living 1702; married .... daughter of .... Metcalfe.

Harl. MS. 4630, page 26.

[A partial genealogy of Batte of Virginia was published in the Richmond *Standard*, June 4th, 1881, a copy of which is in the library of the New England Historic Genealogical Society.

The following grants of land are of record to the name:

John Batte and John Davis, 750 acres in Charles river county (now York), April 2nd, 1667, Book No. 1, p. 638.

William Batt, 220 acres on Mobjack bay, September 5th, 1643, Book No. 1, page 901; 182 acres on "Chipoke Creek, called by the natives in the Indian, Paco lacke, in James Cittie county," April 11th, 1649, Book No. 2, p. 161.

Thomas and Henry Batte, 5878 acres "on the south side of James river in Appamattock in Charles Cittie county," August 29th, 1668, Book No. 6, p. 126.

William Batt, 700 acres in Charles City county, April 22d, 1670, Book No. 6, p. 285.

Henry Batte and John Sturdivant, 3528 acres in Charles City, October 28th, 1673, Book No. 6, p. 480.

Thomas Batt and John Bevill, 400 acres in Henrico county, October 25th, 1690, Book No. 8, p. 122.

Henry Batt, 700 acres in Charles City county, and 200 acres in Bristol parish, do., Book No. 8, p. 44.

William Batte, 250 acres in Prince George county, March 22d, 1715, Book No. 10, p. 280.—*Va. Land Records.*

ª Henry gave his estate in England and Virginia to his brother William. The descendants of the last in Virginia include the names of Cox, Poythress, Eppes, Colley, Gilliam, Russell, Maddox, Hinton, Ritchie, Poindexter, French and Friend.— R. A. B.]

HENRY BENSKIN, lately arrived in England from the Plantation of Virginia, 26 September 1692, proved 19 October 1692. Touching the estate which I have in England (having already settled that which I have in Virginia before I left that place) I give & bequeath to my mother Benskin, Mr Alexander Roberts of Shadwell, shipwright and Mr Thomas Whitfield twenty shillings for rings. All the rest to my two daughters, Mary Harman, wife of William Harman of New Kent County, on York River, Virginia, and Frances Marston, wife of William Marston, living upon Shipperhominy River, in James City County, Virginia, equally between them. The said Mr Alexander Roberts and Mr Thomas Whitfield to be executors, &c.

Wit: Benj. Jones, Thomazine Harris, Robert Sandford, serᵛᵗ to Mr Whitfield, Scr.   Fane, 181.

[I fail to find of record any grants of land in Virginia to the testator Henry Benskin, or to any of his surname. The following grants may however be of interest in connection with the names of two of the legatees named:

Henry Harman and John Bishop, 168 acres, 3 perches and 23 poles in Charles City county, Sept. 20, 1683, Book No. 7, p. 305.

Robert Harman, 1200 acres in New Kent county, April 20, 1687, Book No. 7, p. 552.

Thomas Marston, 1300 acres on the north-east side of Chickahominy river, in James City county, Sept. 20, 1691, Book No. 8, p. 211.

Eliza Marston, 349 acres in St. John's parish, New Kent county, April 21st, 1696, Book No. 8, p. 249.—*Va. Land Records.*

The name Marston is quite a common one at the present day in eastern Virginia, while that of Harman is prominently represented in the Valley District.—R. A. B.]

GEORGE WHITTACRE, passenger aboard the good ship called the William, of London, bound from Virginia to London, 13 May 1654, proved 26 June 1654. Seven hogsheads of tobacco to my brother Edward Duckworth, living in the backside of St Clements Deanes hard by the new Inn, London, if the said Edward or his wife be then living. If not to be found, then to William Scott, who is made executor. Some sugar aboard Mr. Webber's ship.

Wit: Solomon Williams, Owen James.   Alchin, 252.

[The Rev. Alexander Whittaker, "the apostle," who accompanied Sir Thomas Dale to Virginia in 1611; married and baptized Pocahontas in 1614, and was drowned in James river in 1616, may be mentioned in this connection. The following grants of land to the name in its various renderings are of record:

Edward Whittaker, 100 acres "adjoining the pallisadoes of middle plantacon," February 8, 1638, Book No. 1, p. 365.

Captain William Whitacre, 90 acres in James Cittie county, June 5th, 1656, Book No. 3, p. 381.

William Whitacer, 90 acres in James Cittie county, March 18th, 1662, Book No. 5, p. 157.

Richard Whittaker, 135 acres in "James Cittie" county, October 22d, 1666, Book No. 5, p. 153; 158 acres in Middlesex county, February 17th, 1667, Book No. 6, p. 275.

William Whitacar, 400 acres in James City county, April 20th, 1680, Book No. 7, p. 25.

Richard Whicker, 300 acres on Knoll's Island, Currituck, Lower Norfolk county, April 20th, 1682, Book No. 7, p. 141.—*Va. Land Records.*
The descendants of one Richard Whitaker, a settler in Warwick county, Virginia, in the 17th century, are now quite numerous in and around Enfield, N. C.—R. A. B.]

JOSEPH WALKER of St. Margarets in the City of Westminster, gentleman, 13 February 1666, proved 27 February 1666. To my kinsman John Walker, now living or being in Virginia in the parts beyond the seas, ten shillings, provided he release & discharge my executors of & from all other claims &c. To my kinsman Andrew Walker, citizen & draper of London, ten shillings (with the same proviso) and to my kinsman Samuel Walker, seaman (under the same condition) ten shillings. All other property to my kinswoman Mary Snow, now the wife of Nicholas Snow, citizen and armorer of London, whom I nominate executrix. Carr, 33.

[Peter Walker was granted 150 acres in Northampton county, September 20th, 1645, Book No. 2, p. 44.
John Walker (probably him of the text), 1000 acres, and 150 acres " on Ware river, Mobjack Bay," January 29th, 1651, Book No. 2, pp. 356 and 357. There are numerous subsequent grants to " Lieut. Collo." John, Henry, Richard and William Walker.—*Va. Land Records.* John Walker was a member of the Virginia Council, 1658–1660.—R. A. B.]

Charta Donationis Georgii Chauncey.

GEORGE CHAUNCEY Sen' of Barking in the county of Essex Esq. 28 November 1621, proved 25 August 1624. I grant, bargain & sell unto George Chauncey, my son, all my goods &c. on condition &c. He to pay, after my decease, to Edward Chauncey my son two hundred pounds, to be paid out of that one thousand pounds which Alexander Williams of Gilston in the county of Hartfordshire doth now owe unto me, to Charles Chauncey my son one hundred marks and Judith Chauncey my daughter three hundred pounds. To Frances Porter my daughter nine & twenty pounds yearly, to her hands and not to any other, for her sole use &c., and not to the hands of Ambrose Porter or to any other for his use. This annuity to be paid immediately after my decease, at Cranbrooke House in Barkinge in the said County of Essex, or at some other place that the said George, my son, and Frances Porter shall appoint the same to be paid. To William Chauncey my nephew five pounds within one year after my decease. To Alice Clarke twenty pounds yearly during such years as are to come in an annuity granted by me to one John Clarke deceased late husband to the said Alice.
If I the said George shall tender at any time during my life the sum of twenty shillings at my now dwelling house in Barking to the use of George Chauncey my son, that then and at all times after this present deed of gift to be frustrate and of none effect.
The witnesses were William Chauncy, Matthew Chauncey & Nathaniel Rowdon (by mark). There issued commission to George Chauncey, natural & lawful son of George Chauncey late of Barking in the County of Essex deceased. Byrde, 62.

JUDITH CHAUNCY of Yardley, in the County of Hertford, spinster, 2 December, 1657, proved 1 March, 1657, by Henry Chauncy and Mountague Lane.
" To my deare and lovinge brother M'r Charles Chauncy minister of gods word and nowe liveinge in newe England Twentie pounds of currant English money which I desire to haue paid and conveyed unto him as soone as

it may be safely done after my decease. And I doe likewise will and bequeath unto my loveinge Cousens Isaac Chauncy and Ichabod Chauncy, twoe of the sons of my said loveinge brother ffive poundes apeece. And I doe giue and bequeath unto the rest of my said brothers children which are nowe in newe England with him (and are sixe in number as I am informed) fforty shillings apeece to be paid to them as soone after my decease as it may conveniently and safely be done."

Bequests are made to loving cousin M[r] Mountague Lane, cousine M[r] Henry Chauncye the elder of Yardley and M[ris] Anne Chauncy his wife, cousin George Chauncy the third son of the aforesaid Henry and godson of the testatrix, said godson's mother, his brother Peter Chauncy and his sisters Anne, Elizabeth and Mary Chauncy, cousins Henry, John and Peter Chauncy, three of the sons of cousin Henry Chauncy, cousin Alexander Chauncy the elder now living in the County of Kent, nephew M[r] John Humberston and his daughter Judith Humberston, Mr. John Sykes, clerk, and his son John Sikes, godson of testatrix, John Starr, son of Edmond Starr, late of London, dyer, and to Thomas Burges whom she had put an apprentice to a tailor. The residue she left to her cousins George Chauncy, Henry Chauncy the elder of Yardley and Mountague Lane.

The witnesses were John Sykes, Hannah North (by mark) and Grace Couch.   Wootton, 109.

ICHABOD CHAUNCEY of the City of Bristoll, Doctor in Physick, 19 March 1688, with codicil made 26 September 1690, proved 17 February 1691. My body to be laid near my children in St. Philip's church yard in the said city. To Nathaniel Wade Esq. Daniel Gwillim, merchant, and William Burgesse, grocer, property in trust. Wife Mary, sons Staunton, Charles & Nathaniel. To brother Nathaniel Chauncy's children. To brother Isaac and to cousin Oziell Chauncy, my cousins Charles, Elizabeth and Isaac Chauncy.   Fane, 138.

Sñia pro Valore Test[i] et Codicilli Ichabod Chauncey nuper civitatis Bristoll, in medicinis Doctor defuncti, Quod coram nobis in judicio inter Mariam Chauncey viduam relictam et executricem in Testamento sive ultima voluntate dicti defuncti nominatam, partem huñoi negotium promoventem ex una et Stanton Chauncey minorem filium naturalem et legitimum dicti defuncti per Josephum Wetham ejus curatorem agentem partem contra quam dictum negotium promovetur etc.

Die Jovis decimo die mensis Decembris Anno Dñi milliñio sexceñmo nonañmo primo.   Vere, 233.

ISAAC CHAUNCY, having by the tender mercy of the most High been preserved in life unto an old age, 26 February 1712, proved 15 March 1711. To son & daughter Nisbet each five pounds. The House I live in, in Little Moorfields &c. Wife Jane Chauncy. To daughter Elizabeth Nisbet my gold non striking watch. To my daughter in law, the relict of my late son Uzziel Chauncy, five pounds. To my grand daughters by her two pounds apiece. To the widow & relict of my late son Charles Chauncy the sum of money due me from the African Company. Reference to the children of said son as infants. Brother Wally, Son Isaac. Wife Jane executrix. Son Nisbet & friend Richard Tailor to aid her.   Barnes, 46.

[We have here abstracts of the wills of George Chauncy, the father, Judith, a sister, and Ichabod and Isaac, sons of the Rev. Charles Chauncy, president of Harvard College. Isaac and Ichabod Chauncy both graduated at Harvard College in 1651, and sketches of their lives, with lists of their publications, are to be found in Sibley's Harvard Graduates, i. 302–9. For a genealogy of the family, see REGISTER, x. 106–120, 251–62, 323–36 ; xi. 148–53. Tabular pedigrees will be found at x. 257 and xi. 148.—EDITOR.

Henry Chauncy, the half brother of Judith and of Charles the president of Harvard College, had a son Henry, who with his wife and children are all mentioned in the will of Judith. His wife was Anna, daughter of Peter Parke of Tottenham, co. Middlesex ; their children were Henry, John, George, Peter, Anne, Elizabeth and Mary. Henry, the eldest of the sons, was the author of the History of Hertfordshire ; he was admitted to Caius College, Cambridge, Eng., 1647 ; to the Middle Temple, 1649 ; Degree of the Bar, 1656 ; Justice of the Peace, 1661 ; called to the bench of the Temple, 1675, and the same year made Steward of the Borough Court in Hertford ; Charter Recorder, 1680 ; Reader of the Middle Temple, 1681 ; the same year he was Knighted ; in 1685, Treasurer of the Middle Temple ; 1688, called by Writ to the State and Degree of a Serjeant at Law.

The details of the Chauncy family history have been gathered by a descendant, William Chauncy Fowler, and published as the "Chauncy Memorials." On p. 312 is given an account of the marriages and children of George ; on p. 313, extracts from the will of Judith ; on pp. 46, 337, pedigree of Isaac's descendants and his will in full ; his grandson, Rev. Charles Chauncy, was the minister of the 1st Church of this city, and his name is perpetuated here by Chauncy Street, where the church was then located ; on p. 78 is a pedigree of the descendants of Isaac. President. Chauncy, like other early presidents of Harvard College, sacrificed his own and his family's pecuniary prospects by his devotion to the college interests ; he had an estate of £60 income given him by a Mr. Lane—probably a relative, of Bristol, England. President Quincy wrote of the early presidents, that " they experienced the fate of literary men of that day,—thankless labor, unrequited service, arrearages unpaid, posthumous applause, a doggerel dirge and a Latin epitaph."

The Chauncy family of England is referred to in the Histories of Hertfordshire by Sir Henry Chauncy, vol. ii. 400 ; Clutterbuck, pp. 60, 189 ; Harl. Soc. Pub. viii. 353 ; Norfolk Arch. So. i. 113 ; Histories of Northamptonshire, by Bridges, i. 119 ; Baker, i. 494.—See p. 312 of Chauncy Memorials.—JOHN COFFIN JONES BROWN.]

FRANCES HANHAM (or Hannam) of Boston in the County of Lincoln, widow, 4 April 7th of Charles (1631) proved by William Hastinges, brother & executor 13 June 1631. To be buried in the parish church of Boston. To the poor of Boston thirty shillings. To Mr. John Cotton and Mr Anthony Tuckney, the ministers, at Boston, to each of them as a token of my hearty affection and true respect unto them, to either of them the sum of twenty shillings, to be paid them presently after my decease. To my brother Mr Ambrose Hayes twenty shillings, within three months &c., to make him a ring. To my brother Thornell ten shillings and to his wife twenty shillings, within three months &c. To my brother Mr William Hastinges of Asterby ten shillings to buy him a ring. To the wife of Mr Thomas Askham & to the wife of Mr Richard Westland ten shillings each within three months &c. To my daughter Pollixena all my rings & jewells & my taffety petticoat. To John Howseman my man servant my sorrel mare &c. To my sister the wife of the said Mr William Hastinges all my wearing apparell not before given. To the widow Yates six shillings eight pence presently.

Item I give to Jonas Horrax, nephew to Mrs Cotton, ten shillings to be presently paid after my decease. Item I give to Mr Thomas Leveritt & to his wife to be paid them within three months next after my decease either of them ten shillings. To Philip Hannam my son, in full of all legacies & bequests given him by the last will of his late deceased father, the sum of two hundred & fifty pounds (at full age of one and twenty). To

Rudyard Hannam my son &c. two hundred pounds & to daughter Pollixena two hundred pounds (at one & twenty). If all my said children depart this life before said ages of one & twenty then to Anne, Frances Pollixena and Pascha Hastinges daughters of my said brother William. Mr
Thomas Askham of Boston to be guardian of Pollixena Mr Richard Westland of Boston guardian of Philip and brother William Hastinges guardian
of Rudyard.   St. John, 73.

[The first wife of the Rev. John Cotton, according to Mather (Magnalia, ed. 1853,
i. 58), " was Elizabeth Horrocks, sister of Mr. James Horrocks, a famous minister of
Lincolnshire." Perhaps Jonas was his son. It is stated in Palmer's Nonconform-
ists' Memorial (ed. 1778, i. 510), that Christopher Horrocks of Bolton in the Moors,
and his family, came to New England with Mr. Cotton. Has any one met with
other evidence of their residence here? They left their son Thomas at Cambridge
University. After taking his degrees he became a clergyman, and after the restoration was ejected from the living of Malden, in Essex.—EDITOR.]

MARY USHER, late of the parish of St. Anne, Westminster, in the County of Middlesex, widow, deceased. Administration on the goods, chattells
and credits pertaining to her estate was granted, 3 April 1739, to Patient
Usher, the Wife and lawful Attorney of James Usher, the natural and lawful son and only issue of the said deceased, for the use and benefit and during the absence of the said James Usher, now at Philadelphia in America.
                                              Admon. Act Book, 1740.

PATIENT USHER, late of Philadelphia in Pennsylvania, in North America, widow, deceased. Administration on her estate was granted 29 April
1749, to Elias Bland, the lawful Attorney of Margaret Kearsley, formerly
Brand, wife of John Kearsley, the niece and next of kin of the said deceased, for the use and benefit of the said Margaret Kearsley, formerly
Brand, now residing at Pennsylvania aforesaid, having first made a sincere
and solemn affirmation or declaration, according to Act of Parliament &c.
                                              Admon. Act Book, 1750.

THOMAS SCOTTOW of Boston in New England, chirurgeon, now bound
forth on a voyage to sea in the ship Gerrard of London, Captain William
Dennis commander, 14 November 1698, proved 4 September 1699. To
my loving sister Elizabeth Savage of New England aforesaid all my real &
personal estate in New England of what kind soever. To my loving friend
Margaret Softley of the parish of St Paul, Shadwell, in the county of Middlesex, widow, all & singular such moneys, salaries and wages whatsoever as is and shall become due to me for my service in the said ship and
all other my goods and chattels and estate whatsoever in said ship to her
own use in satisfaction of what I shall owe and be indebted unto her at
my death ; and I appoint her executrix.
The witnesses were James Richmond, Richard Baddeley & Theo:
Pomeroy.   Pett, 150.

[Thomas Scottow was a son of Joshua Scottow, and was graduated at Harvard
College in 1677. His sister Elizabeth married Thomas, second son of Maj. Thomas
Savage. See Hist. Catalogue of Old South Church, ed. by Hill and Bigelow, page
220.—EDITOR.]

PHILIP GIBBS of the City of Bristol, ironmonger, now bound to Virginia, 26 August, 1658, proved 23 October 1674. To brother Jacob Gibbs.
To brother in law Philip Marshall of Evisham, in the County of Worcester, shoemaker, and his sons Anthony, Philip and Francis Marshall. The
said Philip Marshall to be executor.   Bunce, 113.

JOHN WAYTE of the city of Worcester, glover, 13 August 1691, proved 14 November 1691. My body to be decently interred according to the discretion of my dear and loving wife; and my worldly goods and estate I bequeath in such manner as herein after is expressed, vizt. As for and concerning my land in Pennsylvania which I have impowered Milicent Hoskins to sell and dispose of I give the money to be raised by the sale thereof to my son Benjamin, and five pounds more, for the raising him a stock to be paid him, with the improvement thereof, when he shall accomplish the age of one & twenty years, or have served out an apprenticeship, which shall first come or be. And I give to my daughter Elizabeth the sum of five pounds, to be paid her, with the improvement of the same, when she shall attain the age of one & twenty years or be married, which shall first come or be. And in case either of my said children shall depart this mortal life before the said legacy shall become due & payable, as aforesaid, then I give the whole to the survivor of them. And I give Francis Willis, my servant, ten shillings as a token of my love and to the intent he may be assisting to my wife in all things she desires of him, And my will is my children may be bred up & well educated by my dear wife; and I appoint her guardian to my said children. And all the residue of my goods & chattells, after the payment of my just debts, legacies and educate (*sic*) and breeding up of my said children, I give to my dear and loving wife Elizabeth Wayte, and I do appoint and ordain her executrix and the said Francis Willis executor. Wit: John Lacy, Stephen Cosens, Tho: Taylor.

Vere, 200.

WILLIAM WHITTINGHAM, of Sutterton in the County of Lincoln, yeoman, 22 December 1591, proved 1 October 1599 by Richard Whittingham, son and executor. To the poor of Sutterton ten shillings. Towards the reparation of the church twenty shillings. I give unto Baruke Whittingham, mine eldest son, twenty pounds within one year after my decease. To Anne Pell, my daughter, the wife of Stephen Pell, twenty pounds within one year &c. To Agnes Whittingham, the daughter of my son Richard, twenty pounds at the age of eighteen years or day of marriage. To every of the four children of Robert Harvie of Kirton, yeoman, which he had by my daughter, five pounds at their several ages of eighteen or days of their several marriages, which shall first happen. To the said Richard Whittingham, my son, my "swane marke," called the "Romaine A," marked as it appeareth in the "margent" of this my will.

All the residue to the said Richard, my son, whom I make executor; my body in decent manner to be brought to the earth and buried in the church of Sutterton; and I appoint Anthony Irbie, of Whapload, Esq. supervisor &c., to whom I give forty shillings for his pains in that behalf, advising and charging my sons Barucke and Richard that if any trouble or difference arise between them concerning this my last will and testament, &c. that they be directed therein by my supervisor.

Concerning my lands, I give to William Whittingham, my nephew, one of the sons of Barucke Whittingham, my son, two acres and a half acre of arable land, lying in Bicker in the said County of Lincoln, in the tenure of the widow Rowte, to him and his heirs forever. To Richard Whittingham, my nephew, one other of the sons of the said Barucke, my son, two and a halfe acres in the tenure of Kenelm Philips, in Bicker aforesaid. To Barucke Whittingham, my nephew, one other of the sons of Barucke &c. one acre & a half acre. To Agnes Roote, widow, late wife of William

Roote, deceased, one cottage with the appurtenances in Donnington, for term of her life, the remainder thereof, after her decease, to the uses mentioned in the last will of John Whittingham, my cousin. I give and devise to Richard Whittingham, my son, and to his heirs forever all that my mansion house wherein I now dwell, together with that house at the end of my yard which I had by the gift of my son Thomas Whittingham, and my house called my mother's house &c. (and a lot of other lands and tenements).

Wit: Anthony Irbye, Thomas Landsdaile (his mark), William Bennett.

Kidd, 80.

RICHARD WHITTINGHAM of Sutterton in the parts of Holland, in the County of Lincoln, gentleman, 6 March 1615, proved 18 April 1618. My body to be buried in the Church of Sutterton. To Elizabeth my wife one messuage and twenty acres and one rood in Algorkirke, in Lincoln, lying in seven parcels, which were late my brother William Whittingham's, to wife for term of life, then to the heirs of my body by the said Elizabeth lawfully begotten; and, for fault of such issue, to remain unto William Field, son of George Field of Algarkirke, and the heirs of his body &c.; and, for want of such heirs, then to remain to Elizabeth Stowe, wife of Thomas Stowe of Algarkirke &c. husbandman, and sister of the said William Field, and to the heirs of her body &c.; next to Jane, now the wife of Christopher Passmore, one other of the sisters of the said William Feyld, and to the heirs of her body &c.; then to the right heirs of me the said Richard Whittingham forever. If my wife be with child then to such child nine acres of pasture, in Algarkirke, called Oxholme, late my brother William Whittingham's, subject to the payment of forty pounds, by will of my said brother William, unto the children of Nicholas Thompson of Wigtoft. If wife be not with child then the above to the children of the said Nicholas and to their heirs forever.

All the lands &c. in Sutterton late my uncle Richard Whittingham's (subject and chargeable with my Aunt Whittingham her annuity of forty pounds by the year) unto Hannah Foster, now wife of Christopher Foster, and daughter of Stephen Pell deceased, and to her heirs forever. Sundry lands &c. (after decease of my wife without heirs of her body by me, as aforesaid) to remain to Kellam Harvie, son of Robert Harvie, and to his heirs forever. Other lands to remain to Thomas Harvie of Kirton, son of Robert Harvie, and to his heirs. After the decease of my wife without issue &c. my messuage and twelve acres of pasture in Kirton, in a place called Willington there, unto William Taylor, my cousin of Northkyrne, and to his heirs forever. Other land to Anne Richards, wife of Walter Richards and daughter of Robert Harvie of Kirton, and to her heirs forever. I give and bequeath unto the aforesaid Thomas Harvie, my cousin, and his heirs, one acre of land arable in Sutterton, in a place called Shettlefield, between the lands of William Hewitson, on the North, and my lands, South, &c., in trust &c. I give my revertion, after my Aunt Whittingham's decease, of all my messuages & lands & tenements in Boston, in the said County of Lincoln, to Elizabeth my wife, for term of life; then to the heirs of her body by me &c.; then to Kellam Harvie. To the poor of Sutterton five pounds over and above the ten pounds given by my father. To my servants William Barker and Thomas Handley and John Roote. To Alice Parkynson, Percy Brandon, Fraunce Christian. To the daughter of William Hewitson, my god daughter. To Ellen Diggle, daughter of

Edmond Diggle, clerk, my god daughter &c. I give unto my brother Mellowes his children ten shillings apiece. To William Ingoldsbie, one of the sons of my brother Ingoldsbie, clerk, to be paid at his first commencement, when he shall   bachelor of Art, or within three years after my decease, which shall first happen. To all the rest of my sister Ingoldsbie's children. To Olive Welbie and to all the rest of her brothers and sisters. To my Aunt Whittingham, my Aunt Massingberd, my father-in-law, Mr Doctor Buckley, my brother-in-law, Mr Peter Buckley and to Edward, his son. To Mr. Cotten. To Michael Harbert. To James Wilkinson. To Robert Johnson of Kirton.

My wife to be executrix and residuary legatee, and my friends Mr Thomas Middlecott, of Boston, Esq., Mr Anthony Ingoldsbie, of Fishtoft, clerk, and Mr Edmond Diggle of Sutterton, clerk, to be supervisors.

Wit: Anthony Ingoldsbie, Edmond Diggle & Thomas Knott.

Meade, 28.

[Articles on the Whittingham family, by Mrs. Caroline H. Dall, now of Georgetown, D. C., will be found in the REGISTER, xxvii. 135–9; xxxiv. 34–7. Compare the above abstracts with the parish registers of Sutterton, near Boston, Lincolnshire, in REG. xxxiv. 35–6.

An account of the ancestry of the New England Whittinghams is given in the obituary of Mrs. Mary (Whittingham) Saltonstall, widow of Gov. Gurdon Saltonstall of Connecticut, in the *New England Weekly Journal*, Boston, January 26, 1730. There are important errors in it. The obituary is copied into the REGISTER, xi. 26–7.

It would seem from the will of Richard Whittingham, that he married a daughter of the Rev. Edward Bulkley, D.D., of Odell (REG. xxiii. 303), whose son, the Rev. Peter Bulkley, named in the will, was the first minister of Concord, Mass. Perhaps the Mr. Mellowes also mentioned, was related to Abraham Mellows of Charlestown, Mass. There was a subsequent connection between the Bulkley and Mellows families, Hannah Smith, a niece of the Rev. Peter Bulkley, having married Edward, son of Abraham Mellows (Wyman's Charlestown, ii. 685).—EDITOR.

With one exception the Whittingham family material published before 1880, stands unrivalled for blunders. In the REGISTER (xxxiv. pp. 34–37) Mrs. Dall began the work of correction by printing extracts from the Registers of the parish of Sutterton in Lincolnshire, which had been furnished to her by the curate, Rev. W. W. Morrison. The two wills which Mr. Waters has sent may be most valuable aids towards the discovery of the ancestry of the John Whittingham who married Martha Hubbard. The names correspond exactly with those given from the parish records. So far we stand on secure ground. The evidence is wanting which *proves* John of New England to be son of Baruch, who was born in Sutterton A.D. 1588, and is said to have died there in 1610; possibly Mrs. Dall has this evidence, at any rate she refers to a list of deaths of the Whittinghams of Sutterton, which it is hoped she will contribute to the next number of the REGISTER. I have the strongest doubts of the quotation "From Mad. de Salis, copied from *Alie's* Norfolk"—(vol. 34, p. 36). A *lie* I am afraid it is—as I never heard of the book, and know of no reason to suppose that the record of a marriage on this side of the ocean should have been recorded and printed in a County History of England. The grossest frauds have been discovered in pretended copies from abroad, especially when the American correspondent informed the searcher what he wanted.

Mrs. Dall mentions "William[1] Whittingham with wife Joanna, who was buried at Sutterton Feb. 3, 1540." William,[2] in his will of 1591, mentions "my house called my mother's house," and I should judge that it was so called because William[1] had married an heiress or resident of Sutterton, he having been the first of the name in that locality. The parish records contain baptisms between 1540 and 1570 of the children of Roger[2] and William[2] only. Supposing them to be brothers and sons of William[1] I have made this pedigree, marked with * if mentioned in the will of William,[2] and with † if mentioned in the will of Richard.[4]

William[1] Whittingham m. Joanna ——. They were probably parents of:

Roger,[2] who married and had Margaret,[3] b. 1544; Dorothea,[3] b. 1548; Jane,[3] b. 1549; Anna,[3] b. 1555, and an only son John[3]* (styled cousin in the will of William[2]).

William,[2] will given above, who married and had Thomas,[3*] b. 1540 [who married and had daughters *Agneta*,[4] b. 1570, and Susanna,[4] b. 1572] ; Joan,[3] b. 1546, m. 1569, Thomas Percye; Baruch,[3*] b. 1547, m. 1577, Eliz. Taylor [they had *Baruch*,[4*] b. 1588, *Eliz.*,[4] b. 1593, *William*,[4*] *Richard*,[4*] will given above, m. Elizabeth Bulkley, daughter of Mr. Doctor Bulkley] ; Richard,[3†] b. 1563, m. Mabell, daughter of Francis Quarles (see Harl. Soc. Pub. Vis. of Essex, 1612, p. 271) [they had Agnes,[4*] b. 1590, and perhaps Richard,[4] b. 1610] ; Ann,[3*] b. 1568, m. Stephen Pell*† [they had Hannah Pell†] ; Dorothea,[3] b. 1552, and Almira,[3] b. 1554 ; one of these was the wife of Robert Harvie,*† of Kirton, who had four children,* of whom Kellam,† Anne† and Thomas† are mentioned by their cousin Richard.

John Whittingham, who married Martha Hubbard, had a son William, who married Mary Lawrence ; she died in childbirth, November, 1671. Their son William (5th child) was born November 9, 1671. William, the husband, was probably sick at the time, and hastened over to England to arrange for the legal acquirement of his hereditary property in Lincolnshire ; making a home in Cambridge, co. Middlesex, England, at "Marie le Savoy." His will is dated 25th March, 1672: "Wm Whittingham late of Boston in Massachusetts &c. Gentleman, being sick, gives to his eldest son Richard,—House, Barn, Mill-house, &c. together with 20 acres arable land, and 84¼ acres of pasture, now in possession of Wm Pakey in the town of Sutterboro', in the parts of Holland (low-lands) in the County of Lincoln—gives to son William, one dwelling house and barn, &c. with 42¼ acres of land in tenure of John Trigg ; also One Cottage and barn with 5 acres of land in tenure of Thomas Baily in Sutterboro'. To daughter Mary one messuage, &c. with 18 acres land in tenure of John Wilson and Mr. Baker ;—to daughter Elizabeth one messuage, &c. with 15½ acres of land, also one cottage and 1 acre of land—John Gidny, George Ledman and John Baker tenants ;—to daughter Martha two cottages and 12½ acres of land in the possession of John Pakey, Wm Walker and Richard Gunn,—daughters to have possession at the age of 20 years or days of marriage, &c. &c. Mentions Uncle Nathaniel Hubbard of London, Gentleman ; brother Richard Whittingham ; brother in law John Clark of Boston in New England and his mother Mrs. Martha Eire (annuity to her). Gifts to James Whitcomb of Boston ; cousins Mary Hubbart and Anne Hubbert. Father in law John Lawrence of New York in America, William Hubbert of Ipswich, of America, and said Uncle Nathaniel Hubbard of London, Gentleman, and John Lewine of London Esq. Executors. Proved "Arch. Canterbury" same month and year as dated.—In the certificate he is styled as "formerly of Boston in New England, now of Marie le Savoy of Middlesex." Proved in Boston, New England, 23d July, 1672 ; recorded Suffolk Deeds, vol. 7, p. 224.

I suppose the "town of Sutterboro' " is the same as Sutterton. With proof as to the missing link, consanguinity would be easily established.—JOHN COFFIN JONES BROWN.]

RICHARD BIFIELD minister of the word of God, of Isleworth in the County of Middlesex, 23 August 1633, proved 24 October 1633. To Richard, my eldest son twenty shillings. To the children of the said Richard viz. to Mary twenty shillings, to Timothy twenty shillings, to Sarah Bifield ten shillings and to his other three children Samuel, Anne, & Richard ten shillings apiece. To my son Nathaniel Bifield six pounds and a mark‡ within two years after my decease (and other property). To my grandchild Bathshua Clifford, wife of Mr William Clifford, clerk, twenty shillings, the which twenty shillings the said Mr William Clifford oweth me. To my grandchild Richard Weston four pounds in one year &c. To grandchild Mary Weston three pounds in two years &c. To my loving wife Margaret Bifield twenty five pounds which was owing to me from Edward Browne my son in law deceased and now is due to me from the executors

‡ This amount, commonly written vi£ xiiis iiiid, seems to have been a favorite amount to bequeath previous to the 17th century. It is just ten marks or twenty nobles, and very likely (as my friend J. C. C. Smith, Esq. suggests) would be so read and spoken of, rather than six pounds thirteen shillings and four pence. The noble was one half of a mark, or six shillings and eight pence.—H. F. W.

of his last will and testament. To said Margaret twenty pounds which my eldest son Richard doth owe me. If my son Richard shall depart this life before my wife Margaret his mother aforesaid then the said twenty pounds shall be paid within one month after his decease unto the said Margaret, my wife & his mother. All the rest of my estate, saving my three cloakes and all my study of books which I give and bequeath unto Nathaniel Bifield clerk, my son aforesaid, I leave unto my loving wife Margaret and appoint her sole executrix. Russell, 85.

RICHARD BYFEILD minister of the Gospel, pastor of the church in Long Ditton in the County of Surrey, 15 August 1662, proved 11 June 1665. (The will begins with an interesting confession of Faith.) A reference to a statute or Recognizance of the nature of statute staple ordained & provided for the recovery of debts, bearing date 17 June 1662, taken & acknowledged before Sir Orlando Bridgeman, Knight, Lord chief Justice of His Majestie's Court of Common Pleas at Westminster and a bond of six hundred pounds to Maurice Gethin & John Kay, citizens and merchant taylors of London, for the payment of a debt of five hundred pounds, the security being a messuage or tenement in Ifield in the County of Sussex, now in occupation of John Richardson my tenant.

Bequests are made to "my five daughters" Rebecca, Dorcas, Priscilla, Mary & Debora, to eldest son Mr Samuel Byfeild (inter alia the works of Thomas Aquinas in fourteen volumes and one gold ring which hath engraven on it Thomas Lancashire) and to second son Mr Richard Byfeild. Whereas God hath blessed me with ten children more born to me by my dear & loving wife Mrs Sarah Byfeild which ten children are all now living (praised be the name of our God) —— To my daughter Sarah (at one & twenty or day of marriage), to son Tymothy that fifty pounds given unto me as a legacy by my godly, loving friend Mr Herring, citizen of London deceased. Mention is made of land & tenement in the West end of Little Heath in East Sheene in the parish of Mortlake in the County of Surrey, house &c. in the tenure & occupation of Abraham Baker, a little tenement leased out to Robert Hartwell deceased & now in the occupation of Benjamin Feilder of East Sheene, a tenement in the occupation of John Cooke of East Sheene, a tenement leased to Lucy Northall widow deceased and now in the occupation of Margaret Parker her daughter, in East Sheene, lands lately in the occupation of John Poole of East Sheene, carpenter and other lands. Sons John, Nathaniel & Thomas. To son Nathaniel the three tenements now in the tenure & occupation of William Lytter of Thomas Greaves & of John Best. To son William Wagstaffe forty shillings to buy him books, to daughter Mrs Elizabeth Bowers three pounds, to my three grandchildren the daughters of Mr Robert Goddin, the husband of my daughter Mary deceased, to my grandchild Ann Wickins, my daughter Mrs Ann Wickins, my daughter Mrs Elizabeth Berrow, my two grand children John & Sarah Wright. In the codicil (dated in one place 21st, in another 31st, May, 1664) the testator says, " God hath taken to himself my youngest son Thomas "—" the Lord hath also made a great breach upon us in taking to himself by death our son William Wagstaffe."

The above will was proved by Sarah Byfeild, relict & executrix.

Hyde, 58.

["Richard Bifield, minister, was buried the 30th of Decr 1664." He was rector of Long Ditton, had been one of the assembly of divines, and published several sermons and religious tracts.—Extract from Parish Register of Mortlake, with remarks thereon. Lysons's Environs of London, vol. i. p. 371.

Richard Byfield, M.A., who was ejected from the Rectory of Long Ditton in Surrey, retired to Mortlake and continued to preach to the last sabbath of his life. He died December 26, 1664, aged 67, and was buried in the parish church."—Surrey Congregational History, by John Waddington, D.D. Printed in London, 1866. P. 250.—H. F. W.

Nathaniel Byfield, son of Rev. Richard of Long Ditton, came to New England about 1674, and settled first in Boston and afterwards in Bristol, but returned to Boston, where he died June 6, 1733, in his 80th year (see Lane's Manual of the First Church in Bristol, R. I., p. 74). It is said that he was one of twenty-one children (Savage's Dict. i. 325). Rev. Nicholas Byfield of Chester and Isleworth (Bliss's Wood's Ath. Ox. ii. 323, and Brook's Puritans, ii. 298), whom Brook calls a half brother of Richard of Long Ditton, is more likely to have been an uncle. Nicholas was father of the celebrated Rev. Adoniram Byfield.—EDITOR.]

Notes on Abstracts previously printed.

THOMAS COTTON (*ante*, p. 91):

[Benj. Woodbridge, of Boston, deposes 30 Dec. 1697, that, when I was in London 2 years ago and since, I was often to see Mrs. Bridget Usher the wife of Mr. Hezekiah Usher (lately deceased) who dwelt with her son in law Mr. Thomas Cotton a minister of the Gospel who married her daughter and who had one son living about 5 years old. They dwelt in Hodsdon's Square near Shoreditch. He complained how he was unjustly kept from his wife's portion for about 7 years it being here in New England, and that he would be glad to have relief in that case. (*Mass. Archives*, viii. 66.)—WILLIAM M. SARGENT, of Portland, Me.]

STEPHEN WHEATLAND of the city of Winchester in the County of Southampton, 6 January, 1737, proved 18 June, 1739. To my son Stephen Wheatland, clerk, one shilling. To my daughter Elizabeth Barlow, wife of Henry Barlow, one shilling. To my granddaughter Elizabeth Barlow one shilling. To Henry Barlow one shilling. To my grandchildren Susanna Whitehead, Anna Whitehead, Stephen Wheatland Whitehead and Elizabeth Whitehead and their heirs, and, for want of such heirs, to William Whitehead, my grandson, and his heirs forever, all my freehold messuages and tenements, lands and hereditaments situate, lying & being in the city of Winchester. My loving son and daughter Edward Whitehead & Susanna his wife to be executor & executrix.

Wit: Tho: Cropp, Richard Rimes, James Pledger.

Henchman, 142.

[Possibly there may be some connection between Stephen Wheatland, the testator, and the family from which Henry Wheatland, M.D., of Salem, Mass., president of the Essex Institute, is descended. The name Stephen is found in both. Dr. Wheatland writes to us: "My father, Richard Wheatland, was born in Wareham, England, in 1762. His parents were Peter and Bridget (Foxcroft) Wheatland, who were married about 1752. Their eldest child was born in 1753. We have in Salem the family bible given to my father by his mother, during a visit to England in 1790. It contains the records of the births of the children, 7 sons and 3 daughters, viz.: John, Stephen, Peter, George, Richard, Robert, 2d John, Bridget, Margaret and Anne. My impression is that my father's father was born about midway between London and Wareham, probably in the vicinity of Winchester."

See Gleanings by Emmerton and Waters, p. 130, in relation to William Wheatland, who died 19 Feb. 1575.—EDITOR.]

MEMORANDUM That the tenth daye of July i6ii John Harvard of the pishe of St Sauior in Southwarke wthin the County of Surrey Butcher beinge then sicke and very weake in body but of good memory, beinge moved to dispose of his temporall estate uttered theise or the like wordes in effect (in the presence of us whose names be subscribed) vizt, I give unto Francis Rodgers tenn poundes —— And all the rest of my goodes and estate I giue unto my broth^r Thomas Harvard, and I make my said brother Tho: Harvard my sole Executor, And to witnes the same we haue hereunto sett our handes Tho: Harvard his m^{r}ke Ric^d Yearwood Robert Harvard his m^{r}ke.

The above will was proved 21 July 1611 by Thomas Harvard brother and executor &c.   158, Berry
                                                      (Archdeaconry of Surrey).

Marche the 27. Anno i622.

IN THE NAME OF GOD, AMEN. I Thomas Harvard of the precinct of St Katherins neere the tower of London beinge sicke in bodie but of perfect memory thankes be to God doe ordaine this my last will and testament in manner and forme followinge. ffirst I doe bequeath my Soule into the handes of almightie god that gave it me, and to his sonne Jesus Christ that Redeemed me by whose death and merritts I doe trust onelie to be saved and my Sole receyved into eternall ioye. for my bodie to be committed to the Earthe from whence it came and to be buryed at the discretion of my Executrix hereundernamed And for the rest of the porcion of goodes which the lorde hath lent me duringe my life my will is my welbeloved wife shall fullie and whollie enioy it whatsoeuer and to give unto my children that the lorde hath sent me whatsoever it pleaseth her into whose handes after my decease I coīitt all that my estate and porcion ether in England or elsewhere beyonde the Seas and this I ordaine as my last will and testament and disanull all former whatsoeuer making my deerly beloved wife Margarett Harvarde my sole executrix. In witnes whereof I have hereunto put my hande. The marke of Thomas Harvard.

Subscribed and deliuered by Thomas Harvard in the presentes of us hereunder named   Edmond Swettenham   the marke of Ann Blaton.

PROBATUM FUIT TESTAMENTUM suprascriptum apud London coram venerabili viro magͬo Richardo Clarke legum doctore Surrogato venerabilis viri domini Willimi Bird militis legum etiam doctoris Curie Prerogatiue Cantuarens* magͬi Custodis siue Commissarii ltīe constituti. Vicesimo tertio die mens* Augusti Anno Dñi Millesimo sexcentesimo vicesimo secundo. Juramento Margarete Harvard relicte et executricis dicti defuncti in eodem testamento nominat. Cui Commissa fuit Administracio bonorum iurium et creditorum dicti defunct de bene et fideliter administrañd &c. Ad sancta Dei Evangelia Jurat.   78, Saville.

July the xxvith: 1625

THE LAST WILL AND TESTAMENT of Margaret Harwar* of St Katherines widdowe sicke and weake in bodie but in perfecte memorie thanks be gee geven to god in this manner and forme followeinge; ffirst I bequeathe my soule into the hands of Allmighty god that gave it me, and to Jesus Christ my saviour that redeemed me hopinge and trustinge only to be saved by his merritts death and passion and my bodie I committ to the earth

––––––––––––
* This name in the original will appears invariably as Harvard.—H. F. W.

from whence it came and to be buried att the discretion of my executors
hereunder named And my worldly goodes I bequeathe in this manner and
forme followeinge; ffirst my will and desire is that the howse I now dwell
in, commonly called by the name of the Christopher scittuate and beinge in
St Katherins neere the Tower of London be sould to the best advantage,
And to him or her that will give most money for it, And beinge sould the
money to be devided in this manner followeinge, The money to be devided
between my three daughters Margarett Harward Alse Harward, and Jone
Harward, And if any of my said daughters doe chance to dye before their
legacies come to their hands or growe due, my will is that their parte or
parts shall come to the survivors of those three; Item my will is and I bequeathe unto John Walbank my sonne the some of Twenty Pounds of Currant English money if he be livinge And if it please god that he be dead
then my will is that this Sonne Thomas Walbancke my Grandchilde shall
have it paid him when he comes to lawfull Age. It. my will is and bequeath unto my daughter Susan Walbanck the some of ffive Pounds to be
paid unto her when my said howse is sould It. my will and desire is that
those worldly goodes that god hath blessed me withall shall be equally devided betwixt my said three daughters Jone, Margarett Harward and Alse
Harward parte and parte alike; every one there share; And if any of
them happen to dye before their part come to their hands my will is it shall
come to the survivor or survivo^r. It. my will is and I doe give unto Thomas Wallbanck my grandchild the some of Tenn Pounds to be paid unto
him out of my two daughters porc͞ons Jane and Alse. It. I give and bequeathe unto Thomas Harward the sonne of Thomas Harward my late
husband the some of Tenn Shillins. It. my will is and I bequeathe unto
my frend Edmond Swettenham of East Smithfeild the some of ffourty
shillinges to make him one gould ringe withall to weare for my sake; And
I doe ordaine my daughter Margarett Harward my sole executrix of this
my last will and testamente; And I doe appointe and desire my two lovinge frends Robert Evebancke and Edmond Swettenham my two overseers of this my will and I doe give unto Robert Evebanck for his paines
twenty shillings;   *The marke of Margarett Harward.*

Witnes Edmond Swettenham Rob't Ewbancke The marke of Marie
psons.

PROBATUM fuit Testamentum suprascriptum apud London cor͞a Magis-
tro Thoma Langley Clic͞o Surrogato venerabilis viri domini Henrici Marten Millitis legum doctoris Curie Prerogative Cantuariensis Magistri Custodis sive Commissarii legitime constituti Nono die mensis Septembris Anno D͞ni Millesimo sexcentesimo vicesimo quinto, Juramento Thome Goul-
dan Notarii Publici Procur͞is Margarete Harward filie et executricis in
hu͞moi Test͞o nominat Cui Commissa fuit Administrac͞o bonorum iurium et
creditorum d͞ci defunct de bene et fidelit Administra͞nd eadem Ad sancta
Dei Evangelia Jurat.   91, Clarke.

IN THE NAME OF GOD AMEN. The eight and Twentyth daie of July
Anno D͞ni one Thousand six hundred Twentie five, & in the ffirst yere
of the Raigne of our Soveraigne lord Charles by the grace of God Kinge
of England Scotland ffraunce and Ireland defender of the faith &c. I Robert
Harvard of ye pish of St Saviours in Southwarke in the Countie of Surrey
Butcher, being not well in body but sound in minde in memory (laud and
praise bee to allmightie god therefore) doe make and ordayne this my pre-

sent last will and Testament in manner and forme following that is to saie, ffirst and principally I bequeath and commend my soule into the hands of allmighty God trusting through his mercie and for the meritts of his deere Sonne my lord and Saviour Jesus Christ to haue forgivnes of all my Sinnes, and after this life ended to bee made ꝑtaker of life eu^rlastinge in the kingdome of heaven And I will that my body bee decently and Christianly buried in the ꝑish Church of St Saviours aforesaid, after the discretion of my executrix hereundernamed, And as touching that Temporall estate of goods and Chattles wherewth it hath pleased god of his goodnes to blesse, my minde and will is as followeth vīzt, Inprimis I give and bequeath unto the poore of the ꝑish of St Saviour aforesaid forty shillings and to bee payd and distributed according to the discrecòn of my said Executrix & Overseers hereunder mencòned Item I give and bequeath unto John Harvard my Sonne Two hundred pounds To bee payd unto him when he shalbee accomplish his age of one and Twentie yeres Item I give & bequeath unto Thomas Harvard my Sonne the like soñe of two hundred pounds to be payd likewise unto him when he shall accomplish his age of one and Twenty yeres Item I give and bequeath unto Peter Harvard my Sonne the like soñe of Two hundred pounds to bee payd likewise unto him when he shall accomplish his age of one and Twenty yeres And if any of them my said three sonnes depart this life before his said ꝑte and porcõn shall growe due to bee payd by this my will, Then I give y^e ꝑte or porcõn of him deceaseinge to the residue of them Surviving equallie to bee devided betwixt them, or wholly to the Survivor yf two of them decease And if it shall happen all my said three Children to decease before they shall accomplish theire severall ages of twenty and one yeres as aforesaid Then and in such case I give and bequeath unto my Cosin Thomas Harvard and his Children ffifty pound to bee payd within three moneths next after the decease of the last Child Item I give and bequeath unto Robert Harvard my godson sone of my said cosin Thomas Harvard Ten pounds to be payd unto him when he shall accomplish his age of one and Twenty yeres All the rest and residue of my goods and Chattles whatsoever my debts (if any be) beinge first payd and my funerall expences discharged I give and bequeath unto Katherin Harvard my welbeloved wife whom I constitute ordayne and make full and sole Executrix of this my last will and Testament And it is my will that shee shall haue the use of my said Childrens porcõns for theire educacõn and bringing up untill the same shall growe due to them as aforesaid And I make and ordayne my good neighbour and friend Mr Richard Yearwood Citizen & Grocer of London and the said Thomas Harvard my Cosin Overseers of this my last will and Testament desireing them as much as in them shall consist and lie to see the same ꝑformed according to my true intent and meaneing herein declared And I give unto them for theire paynes to bee taken in seeing this my will performed Twenty shillings a peece to make them rings for a remembrance Provided alwaies & I will and oidayne hereby that my saide wife shall wth sufficient Suerties wthin three moneths next after my decease or at least before shee shalbe espoused or married agayne to any other, enter and become bound in the soñe of one Thousand pounds unto my said Two Overseers, if they shalbe both liveing or to the Survivo^r of them if either of them shallbee deceased, wth condicõn to pay the ꝑts and porcõns of my said Children wch I haue before bequeathed unto them, according to my true intent and meaning herein declared, and at such tyme or times as before is limyted and set downe for the payment thereof, In witnes whereof I the said Robert Har-

vard haue to this my p'sent last will and Testament put my hand and Seale
the daie and yere first aboue written, The marke of the said Robert Harverd Sealed acknowledged and delivered by the said Robert Harverd
for and as his last will and Testament the daie and yere first aboue written
in the presence of Ric: Sandon Scr The m'ke of Richard Rayner.

PROBATUM FUIT Testamentum suprascriptum apud London coram magis-
tro Thoma Langley Clico Surrogato venerabilis viri Domini Henrici Marten militis legum doctoris Curie Prerogative Cantuariensis magistri Custodis sive Comissarii ltime constituti Sexto die mensis Octobris Anno Dni
millcsimo sexcentesimo vicesimo quinto Juramento Katherinæ Harvard
Relicte dicti defuncti et executricis in huiusmodi Testamento nominat Cui
Comissa fuit administrat &c. de bene et fideliter administrando eadem, ad
sancta dei Evangelia Jurat.   111, Clarke.

JOHN ELLETSON citizen and cooper of London 15 June, 1626, proved
the last day of June, 1626. To M' William Quelch, clerk, sometimes minister of S' Olaves in Southwarke, forty shillings, & to M' Archer, minister
of S' Saviours in Southwarke, twenty shillings, within six months after my
deccase if they be then living. To my sister's son Stephen Hall, Bachilor of
Divinity at Cambridge twenty pounds, to be paid him within six months
next after my decease. To my sister Elizabeth Rigate full power and
authority to dispose of the house wherein she now dwelleth for the term of
two years next after her decease conditionally that a pepper corn be paid
yearly therefore to my executrix: The residue of the term of years unexpired of the said house I will and bequeath unto my nephew Robert Elletson, son of my late deceased brother Robert Elletson, his executors and
assigns. To my aforesaid nephew Robert all those my two messuages or
dwelling houses, &c. situate & being in the liberties of East Smithfield in
the parish of S' Buttolph's Algate, to him and to the heirs of his body lawfully to be begotten, and, for want of such issue, to his brother William
Elletson & to the heirs of his body, &c., and, for lack of such issue, to
George Elletson his brother and to his heirs forever, which houses I bought
and purchased of M' Norton, gentleman. And my will and mind is that
my loving wife Katherine Elletsonne shall have her thirds out of the same
during the term of her natural life. Item I give and bequeath unto my
said loving wife Catherine Elletson and her assigns during her natural life
the yearly sum of twelve pounds of lawful money of England to be paid
unto her quarterly and to be issuing and going out of all and singular my
lands tenements and hereditaments whatsoever lying and being in the several parishes of Alverstoke and Rowner in the County of Southampton.
To my sister in law, Mary Elletson, and her two daughters, Elizabeth
Elletson and Margaret Elletson, and their assigns, during the natural life
of my said loving wife Catherine Elletson, the like yearly sum of twelve
pounds, &c. To my nephew George Elletson, son of my said brother
Robert, all that my messuage, barns, lands & commons, &c. called or known
by the name of Hemeleys, situate in the parish of Alverstoke (with remainder first to William, then to Robert, brothers of the said George),
which aforesaid premises I bought and purchased of Thomas Rabenett,
mariner. To nephew Robert my messuage, &c. situate in Brockhurst in
the parish of Alverstocke and Rowner, &c. (with remainder to his brothers
William and George, &c.) which premises I bought of Robert Nokes of
Brockhurst, yeoman. To nephew William my messuage, &c. in Newton

in the parish of Alverstocke, &c. (with remainder to Robert and George), which premises I bought of my brother Robert Elletson. To Thomas Elletson, son of Anthony Elletson, born at Lymehouse in the parish of Stepney, the sum of ten pounds, to be paid him at the age of one and twenty years if he shall be then living. To Robert Wilson in Southwark all such sum or sums of money which he oweth me upon one certain obligation conditionally that he give unto Mr Thomas Foster Bailiff of the Borough of Southwark, as a legacy and bequest from me the sum of three pounds, &c. within three months next after my decease, and three pounds more to the poor of the parish of St Olaves, where he is a parishioner, &c. &c. To my kinswoman Jane Merricke one quarter or fourth part of the good Bark called the Jane of Gosport, with the fourth part of the tackle, munition and apparell, which said Bark is in partnership between her husband Walter Merricke and myself. And I give and bequeath to my sister Mary Ellet son and her two daughters the other quarter or fourth part of the same Bark. To my sister Elizabeth Bygate, widow, twenty pounds yearly & every year during her natural life, to be paid her by five pounds the quarter, or within one and twenty days after the quarter day, out of the tenements which I lately purchased by lease of the wife of James Turner, holden by the masters, brethren and sisters of St Catherine's and which is situate and being in the parish of All Saints Barkin near unto Tower Hill. To my eldest brother George Elletson, dwelling in the County of Lancaster, five shillings, conditionally that he shall give to my executrix a general acquittance of all demands whatsoever from the beginning of the world until the day of the receipt of the same legacy. To my brother William Elletson, dwelling in the said County of Lancaster, ten shillings (on the same condition). To my sister Agnes Stables, the sum of twenty shillings, to be paid her upon lawful demand. To my sister Ellen Towers, dwelling in the County of Lancaster, the sum of twenty shillings (upon lawful demand). I absolutely release and discharge Richard Edwards, dwelling at White Waltham in the County of Berks, of all sum or sums of money which he oweth me, and particularly of one specialty of thirty pounds which I freely forgive him.

Item I give unto my son in law Joseph Knapp and unto Agnes his wife, my kinswoman, all that my house, together with my buildings, yards and appurtenances thereunto belonging, and to his son John Knap after his decease, during the term of a lease which I took of Mr John James, gentleman, paying the rents, &c.; also the goods, household stuff &c in and about the said house, which is in their possession and which I left freely to them at my coming away from Mill Lane. To my said son Joseph Knapp all that my third part and bargains of boards whatsoever remaining in the County of Sussex which is in partnership between Mr Anthony Keeme, Mr Richard Waker and myself, citizens and coopers of London. To the said Joseph my best livery gown and my second cloak. Item I give and bequeath two silver cups, gilded, with my name to be ingraven upon them, to the value of twenty pounds, which shall be bought by my executrix and given to the company of coopers of the city of London within six months next after my decease. To twenty poor people which is in the Almshouse at Ratcliffe twenty shillings to be equally divided amongst them. To Mrs Suttey, my mistress, dwelling at Ratcliffe, over and above the part of the said gift of twenty shillings, the sum of ten shillings.

Item whereas Hugh Horsell of Southwarke, Innkeeper deceased, by his last will and testament did give and bequeath unto his children the sum of six hundred pounds as by his said will appeareth, of the which I have already paid the sum of one hundred pounds to Mary one of the children of the said Hugh Horsell for her legacy, as also the sum of twenty pounds which I gave with Nicholas Horsell, one of the said children, to bind him an apprentice, so that there is remaining now of the said six hundred pounds the sum of four hundred and eighty pounds to be paid unto them as in their said father's will more at large and plainly appeareth. Therefore my desire and meaning is and it is expressly my will that my executrix hereafter named shall truly pay and satisfy unto the children of the said Hugh Horsell or to the survivors of them the said sum of four hundred and eighty pounds in every point according to their father's will and to see them well educated and brought up in all things necessary in the fear of God and in learning. And I do further will that my executrix shall within one month next after my decease enter into obligation of one thousand pounds to my overseers hereafter named in every kind to see these legacies performed and the said children well brought up and educated. To the poor of the parish of Alverstocke and Gosport the sum of twenty shillings. To the poor of the parish of All Saints Barking in Tower Street, twenty shillings. To George Browne my kinsman twenty shillings to be paid upon lawful demand. I absolutely acquit and discharge Richard Graye, waterman, a bill of debt of three pounds which he oweth me. I absolutely acquit and discharge Nicholas Parsons, ostler at the Queen's Head in Southwark, of a debt of twenty and eight shillings which he oweth me. To my kinsman William Hughs and Agnes his wife one hundred pounds &c.

Item I give and bequeath unto my said loving wife Catherine Elletson the lease of all and singular the premises which I hold of the Master, brethren and sisters of St Katherines, together with all the rents and profits that shall arise by reason of the same ; to have and to hold the same lease and the rents and profits thereof unto my said loving wife, Katherine Elletson, for and during the term of her natural life, she paying the rents and performing the covenants contained in the same lease on my part to be performed, the remainder of the years that shall be to come from and after the death and decease of my said wife and the rents and profits that shall arise by reason of the same I give and bequeath unto my said kinsman Robert Elletson, son of my said brother Robert Elletson, and the issue of his body lawfully begotten. And if it shall fortune my said kinsman to die and depart this life before the expiration of the term of years in the said lease granted having no issue of his body lawfully begotten then living that then I give and bequeath the said lease and the benefit and profits thereof arising unto his brother William Elletson, his executors and assigns. The rest and residue of all and singular my goods and chattels whatsoever moveable and immoveable not before by me given and bequeathed, my debts and legacies being paid and my funeral expenses discharged I wholly and absolutely give and bequeath unto my said loving wife Catherine Elletson whom I make and ordain the sole and only executrix of this my present last will and testament, desiring her to see the same in all things performed according to my mind and meaning herein plainly declared, and I do hereby nominate and appoint my loving friends Mr Anthony Kemme, Mr George Preston and Mr Richard Waker, citizens and coopers of London, overseers thereof, desiring them according to my trust in them reposed to be aiding and assisting to my said executrix in the due " exequition " of this my present last will and testament; and I give unto each of them for their pains taking therein the sum of three pounds apiece &c. Provided always that if

my said wife shall not be contented to accept of the said legacies before given unto her and to pay and perform the legacies herein by me bequeathed according to the true intent and meaning of this my present last will and testament then my will is that she shall have only so much of my estate and no more as shall justly belong unto her by the custom of the city of London and then I make and ordain my said kinsmen William Hewes & Robert Elletsonne, son of my said brother Robert Elletson, executors &c.
Wit: William Manbey Scr. Edward Thomas William Hedges.

91, Hele.

RICHARD YEARWOOD of Southwarke in the County of Surrey and citizen and grocer of London, 8 September 1632, proved 6 October 1632, and confirmed by Decree of the Court in the last session of Trinity Term 1633, After my funerals done and discharged I will that an Inventory shall be taken of all my estate in goods, chattells, wares, merchandizes plate and other things whatsoever and be indifferently valued and appraised, and that therewithall the debts which I do owe shall be first duly satisfied and paid. But because the debts which my wasteful son hath brought me unto are so great that I fear much that my personal estate will not be sufficient to satisfy the same or at the least will not be collected and got in convenient time to give that satisfaction which is fit and just much less to pay and satisfy such other legacies as by this my will I have appointed and given I do therefore will, ordain and appoint that my executors hereafter named or the survivor of them with as much convenient speed as they can after my decease for the speedier payment of my debts and discharging of my legacies shall sell and dispose all those my tenements and hereditaments situate lying & being in the parish of S⁺ Mary Magdalen of Bermondsey within the County of Surrey, near the church there, which I purchased of Walter Oliver, being three tenements or houses &c in the several occupations of Thomas Miller Robert Fisher and John Bould their or some of their assignee or assignees. And my will is as well the leases which I bought of the same and which are in being in friends' names as also the inheritance of the said houses be sold for the uses aforesaid by mine executors or the survivor of them and by such other persons and friends who have any interest or estates in the same for my use or benefit. They shall sell &c. all that my tenement &c. in the tenure or occupation of John Blacke, in the parish of Lingfield within the County of Surrey which I bought of Edmond Rofey, and my tenement &c. in the parish of Frinsbury within the County of Kent, now or late in the tenure & occupation of —— Jones, which I bought of Henry Price. I give and bequeath unto Richard Yearwood my son all that my manor or farm with the appurtenances &c. in the parish of Burstow within the County of Surrey, now or late in the tenure &c. of Edmond Rofey &c. to have & to hold during the term of his natural life (then follow conditions of entailment on the issue of the body of the said Richard Yearwood the son). And for default of such issue to Hannah Payne my daughter during her natural life; and after her decease to Richard Payne her second son and the heirs of his body lawfully to be begotten; and for default of such issue to my right heirs forever. Item I give unto the poor of the parish of S⁺ Saviours in Southwark inhabiting within the liberty of the Borough of Southwark whereof I am a parishioner the sum of ten pounds &c. I give unto Mʳ Morton and Mʳ Archer ministers of the said parish forty shillings apiece. I give to William Brayne apprentice with Nicholas King grocer twenty pounds &c. to be paid unto him

at the expiration of his time of apprenticeship.   I give unto Margaret Dallin wife of Christopher Dallin cooper the sum of ten pounds &c. to be
paid unto her in five years by forty shillings a year.   To Hannah Groue
daughter of Richard Groue of Middle Wiche in the County of Chester ten
pounds at day of marriage or age of twenty and one years.

Item I give to Katherine my well beloved wife her dwelling in all that
part of my dwelling house wherein I do now live during so long time as she
shall continue a widow and dwell in the same herself if my lease thereof
shall so long continue, my said wife paying therefore yearly to my executors hereafter named the sum of five pounds per annum by half yearly
payments &c.   And I do further give unto her all such household stuff and
so much value in plate as she brought with her when I married her.   And
I give and bequeath unto my cousin Nicholas King grocer and Margaret
his wife and the longer liver of them the lease of my now dwelling house,
onely I will that my said wife do dwell and continue in such part thereof
as I have before appointed during such time as aforesaid.   To my loving
friend and cousin Mr Stephen Street grocer ten pounds.   The said Nicholas King and Stephen Street to be executors.

The residue and remainder of all my personal estate and which shall remain of my lands and tenements by me appointed to be sold as aforesaid,
my debts being paid and my funeral expenses and legacies discharged, I
will the same shall be distributed and divided by my executors in manner following vizt two third parts thereof unto Richard Yearwood my son
if he shall be then living and that my said executors shall discern him to
be reformed and become a frugal man, and the other third part thereof I
will shall be divided to and amongst my daughter Payne's eight children
now living vizt Edward, Richard, John, George, Anne, Timothy, Susan and
Katherine, and the survivors of them; the same to be paid to their father
for their uses.   And I appoint my loving friends Mr Drew Stapley grocer
and my son in law Edward Payne to be overseers of this my will.   And I
do give to either of them for a remembrance of my love and their pains to
be taken therein the sum of five pounds apiece.

Wit: Thomas Haruard, William Frith William Sheappard John Fincher.

13 march 1661 administration de bonis non was granted to his daughter
Hannah Payne, the executors being dead.   98, Audley.

In the name of God Amen.   I Katherine Yarwood of the parrish of
St Saviours in the Burroughe of Southwarke in the Countie of Surrey
widdowe being at this tyme weake in bodie but of perfect memory praised
be God therefore doe ordayne this my last will and Testament revoakeing
all former wills and Testamentes whatsoever ffirst I bequeath my soule
into the mercifull hands of my Deare Redeemer Jesus Christ the eternall
sonne of God whoe by his holy Spirit as my trust and hope is will p^{r}serve
me to his heavenly kingdome; And my bodie to be interred at the discretion of my executors   And for my worldly goods I thus dispose of them.
Inprimis I give to my eldest sonne John Harvard Clarke all that my messuage Tenement or Inne comonly called or knowne by the name of the
Queenes head in the Borroughe of Southwarke aforesaid with the appurtenances and all my deedes and writeings touching and concerning the same
and all my estate right title interest terme of yeares and demand whatsoever
which I have of and unto the same and of and unto everie part and parcell
thereof.   Item I give unto the said John Hervard and unto Thomas Her-

vard my sonne equally to be devided betweene them all my messuages Tenements and hereditaments whatsoever wth their and every of their appurtenances scituate and being in the parrish of All Saintes Barkeing nere unto the Tower of London whereof I am possessed under two severall leases made by the Master brethren and Sisters of the Hospitall of St Katherine's nere the Tower of London unto John Elletson deceased ; and all my deedes and writeings touching and concerning the same. And all my severall and respectiue estates right title interest terme of yeares and demaund which I have of and unto the same, and of and unto every part and parcell thereof. Nevertheless my will and meaneing is and soe I doe hereby appoint and declare that the said John Harvard and Thomas Harvard their executors Administrators and Assignes shall yearly and every yeare dureing the continuance of the severall tymes in the said severall leases graunted, paye or cause to be payed out of the rentes issues and proffits of the said last mentioned premisses at the feast of the nativity of our Lord God twentie shillings to fower poor people that are reputed of honest conversation dwelling in the parrishe of St Saviours aforesaid by five shillings apeece And that the said John Hervard and Thomas Hervard their executors Administrators and Assignes shall paye or cause to be payed the residue and remainder of the rentes issues and proffites of the said last mentioned premisses unto such of the Children of Hugh Harsall late of the Burrough of Southwarke aforesaid Innkeeper deceased as have not their porçons paied and was given and bequeathed unto them by the last wills & testam^{tes} of the said John Elletson and Hugh Harsall or either of them untill such tyme as the said Children shall have all their said porçons paied unto them and afterwards that the said John Hervard and Thomas Hervarde their executors adm'strat^{ors} and assignes shall enioye the residue of the said rentes issues and proffits of the said last mentioned premisses to their owne proper uses and behoofes equally to be devided betweene them Item I give to my said sonne John Hervard two hundred and fiftie poundes in money And I doe appoint two hundred pounds parcell thereof to be payed wth the moneys due upon one obligaçon of the penall somme of fower hundred poundes bearing date the first daye of this instant moneth of Julie made by my sonne Thomas Hervard unto my Overseer Mr Mooreton for my use condicōned for the payment of two hundred pounds at or upon the first daye of January now next ensueing Item I give to my sonne Thomas aforesaid one hundred poundes in money Item to the Children of my Brother Thomas Rogers I give fortie shillings a peece. Item to the poore of this parrish of St Saviours I give fortie shillinges Item to Mr Archer one of our Ministers I give twentie shillings. Item to M^{ris} Moreton our other Ministers wife I give my best gould wrought Coyfe which of my two best shee please to make choice of Item my Sister Rose Reason and my sister Joane Willmore to each of them I give a ring at the discretion of my executors Item to old M^{ris} Blanchard I give my best paire of Gloves Item to my Cosen Joseph Brocket the younger I give twentie shillings; and to my Cosen Mary Brocket I give my best scarlet Petticoate or the value thereof in money at the discretion of my executors Item I make and ordayne my two sonnes John and Thomas Hervard aforesaid ioinct executors of this my last will and Testament. Item for the overseers of this my last will and Testament I appoint my loveing frend Mr Moreton our minister of St Saviours aforesaid for one, and to him in token of my love I give three pounds and my paire of silver hafted knyves; And for my other Overseer I appoint my Cosen Mr Thomas Hervard Butcher of St Saviours aforesaid and to him like-

wise in token of my love I give three pounds   Item I give to my said exe-
cuto[r] and Overseers eight pounds by them to be bestowed on such Christian poore as they thinke fitt   And I will that all my legacies formerly giv-
en and bequeathed except the two hundred pounds payable by the obliga-
c̃on as aforesaid shalbe paied and deliuered by my executors w[th]in one moneth
after my decease   The residue of all and singular my goods Chattells and
p̃sonall estate after my debts payed and funeralls discharged I give and
bequeath unto my said sonnes John Hervard and Thomas Hervard equally
to be devided betweene them   In wittnes whereof I have unto every sheete
being seaven in number put to my hand and have sealed the same this second daye of Julie in the eleaventh yeare of the reigne of our Soũaigne
Lord Charles by the grace of God of England Scotland ffrance and Ireland Kinge Defender of the faith &c.   Annoq̃ Dñi 1635.   The marke of
Catherine Yarwood.

Memorandum that theis wordes viz[t] porc̃ons in the seaventh lyne and
John in the fourteenth lyne of the fourth sheete were interlyned and afterwards this will was read sealed and published to be the last will and Testament of the said Catherine Yarwood in the p[r]sence of us; Sealed and
published by Katherine Yarwood aforesaid in the presence of us William
Brayne Robert Greaton William Sheap.

PROBATUM fuit Testamentum suprascriptum apud London coram mr̃o
Johanne Hansley Clĩco Surrogato veñabilis viri Dñi Henrici Marten militis legum etiam Dc̃oris Curie Prerogative Cantuar mag̃ri Custodis siue
Com[rii] ltiñe constituti vicesimo septimo die mensis Julii Anno Dñi millesimo sexcentesimo tricesimo quinto Juramentis Johis̃ Hervard et Thome
Hervard filiorum dc̃e defunctæ et executorum in huiusmodi Testamento
nominatorum Quibus comissa fuit administrac̃o omnĩ et singulorũ bonorũ
iuriũ et creditorũ dc̃æ def de bene et fideliter administrando ead[m] &c   Ad
sancta dei Evangelia Jurat.   77, Sadler.

IN THE NAME OF GOD AMEN the fiefteenth daie of July Anno Domini
one thousand six hundred thirtie and six   And in the twelueth yeare of the
raigne of our Soveraigne Lord Charles by the grace of god kinge of England Scotland ffraunce and Ireland Defender of the faith &c   I Thomas
Harvard of the p̃ishe of Saint Olave in Southwarke in the County of Surry and Cittizen and Clothworker of London beinge att this presente sicke
and weake in bodie but of good and p̃fecte mynde and memorie all laude
and praise be given to Allmightie god therefore and consideringe with my
selfe the frailtie and mutabilitie of this present life and the certaintie of
death, And to the end that I may bee the better prepared and settled in my
mynde whensoever it shall please god to call me out of this transitorie life
I doe by the p̃mission of god make and declare this my last will and Testament in manner and forme followinge, That is to saie, ffirst and principally
I com̃end my Soule into the hands of Allmightie god hopeinge aud assuredly
beleevinge through the death and passion of Jesus Christe his only sonne and
alone Saviour to obtaine Remission and forgivenes of all my Synns aud to
be made p̃taker of everlastinge life   My bodie I com̃itt to the earth from
whence it came to be decently buried att the discrec̃on of my executors
here under named, And as concerninge all such worldly goods Chattelles and
p̃sonall estate as it hath pleased god to endue me wth in this life I give and
bequeath the same in manner and forme followinge, That is to saie Inpri-

mis I give and bequeath unto my deere and welbeloved wife Elizabeth Harvard the some of fower hundred poundes of lawful English money to be paied unto her within six monethes next after my decease More I giue and bequeath to my said lovinge all my plate and howsehold stuffe exceptinge only my best standinge bowle of silver guilte and my great Cheste with two lockes Item I give and bequeath unto my said lovinge wife Elizabeth Harvard one Annuitie or yearely payment of thirty poundes of good and lawfull Englishe mony to be yearely due goeinge out issuinge and payable unto my said wife out of all those messuages and Tenementes with thappurtenñces And the rentes issues and proffites of them scituate lyinge and beinge att or neere Towerhill in the parishe of All Saintes Barkinge in London which I hould ioyntly togeather with my brother John Harvard by vertue of a lease to us thereof made by the M[r]. brothers and sisters of the Hospitall of Saint Katherines neere the Tower of London, To have and to hould the said Annuitie or Rente charge of Thirtie poundes p Añ unto my said loveinge wife for and duringe the tearme of her naturall life to be paied unto her att fower feastes or tearmes in the yeare, That is to saie att the feastes of Saint Michaell Tharchangell, the birth of our lord god, Thannuntiačon of the blessed virgin Marie and the Nativitie of Saint John Baptist or within one and twentie daies nexte ensuinge everie of the same feaste daies by equall and even porčons, The first paimente thereof to beginn and to be made att the feaste of the feastes aforesaid which shall first and next happen and come after my decease, or within one and twentie daies then nexte ensuinge with power to distreyne for the same Annuitie in and upon the said tenementes or anie of them, if the same añuitie shall happen to be behinde and unpaied contrary to this my will, Provided that my ffather in lawe M[r]. Nicholas Kinge or his heires att any time duringe the tearme of my naturall life doe assure and conveie unto me and my heires or within six moneths after my decease to my executors hereunder named or to such pson or psons as I the said Thomas Harvard shall by anie writinge under my hand name and appointe, And theire heires and assignes, And to such use and uses as I shall thereby lymitt and declare and in such good sure and sufficiente manner and forme as by learned Councell shall be advised and required All that messuage or Tenement with thappurtenñces and the rente and Reverčon thereof scituate and beinge in or neere Shippyard in the pishe of Saint Saviours in Southwarke now or late in the tenure or occupačon of Owen Jones or his assignes Item I give and bequeath unto such childe or Children as my wife nowe goeth with or is with childe of the some of three hundred poundes of lawfull Englishe money to be paied and deliuered into the Chamber of the Cittie of London for the use of such Child and children within one yeare nexte after my decease to be imployed for the use and benefitt of such childe and children untill they shall accomplishe the age of Twentie and one yeares Item I give and bequeath unto such childe and children as my wife goeth with or is with childe of all that my moitie or halfe parte of the lease of the said Tenem[tes]. with thappurtenñces att or neere Tower hill in the said pishe of All Saintes Barkinge holden of and from the Hospitall of Saint Katherines and the moitie of my rentes and reverčons thereof, And all my estate tearmes of yeares and demaund therein charged with the said Annuity of Thirtie poundes p Añ by me herein before given unto my said wife, Prouided allwaies and my mynde and will is that if my said wife shall not be with childe att the time of my decease, or that such childe and children shall happen to miscarry or dye or departe this life before he she or theie shall accomplishe the age or ages of twentie and one yeares then in such case or cases and not otherwise I doe giue and bequeath unto the severall persons hereunder named the seu'all legacies and somes of money hereunder menc͞oned, That is to saie, To my said lovinge wife one hundred poundes. to my said brother John Harvard one hundred poundes. To and amongst the children of my unckle Rogers fforty poundes To my godsonn William Harvard ffiefteene poundes, To the eldest sonne of my Cossen Thomas Willmore ffower poundes to my Cossen Robert Harvard five poundes to John Brockett the sonne of Joseph Brockett ffortie shillinges, And then alsoe and in such case, I doe give and bequeath unto my said brother John Harvard my said moitie or half parte of the lease of the said Tenementes with the appu'tenn͞ces att or neere Towerhill aforesaid and the rentes and the Reverc͞ons thereof, And all my estate tearme of yeares and demaunde therein charged with the said Annuity of Thirtie poundes p an͞u by me given to my said wife, Item I doe alsoe by this my will give and bequeath unto my said brother John Harvard the sum͞e of one hundred poundes lawfull English mony, and my standinge bowle of silver guilt and my Chest with twoe lockes before ex- cepted, Together with my best whole suite of appell and my best cloake, And all things belonginge thereunto, Item I give and bequeath unto Mr Nichollas Morton Minister and Preacher in the pishe of Saint Saviors in Southwarke the some of fforty shillinges in recompence of a Sermon which I desire he should preach at my funerall, for the better Comforte edifyinge and instruc͞con of such my freinds and neighboures and other people as there shalbe assembled, Item I giue and bequeath unto James Archer Min- ister twentie shillinges, Item I giue and bequeath unto Mr Osney Minister the some of twenty shillinges, Item I give and bequeath unto Mr Clarke Minister the some of twenty shillinges, Item I give and bequeath unto my said ffather in lawe Mr. Nicholas Kinge the some of three poundes to make him a ringe, Item I giue and bequeath unto my Cossen William Harvard the some of Tenne poundes, Item I give and bequeath unto my said Cossen Robert Harvard the some of six poundes, Item I give unto the said Joseph Brockett my seale Ringe of gould, I will that there shalbe distributed by my executors on the day of my buriall the some of ffortie shillinges, that is to saie to and amongst the poore people of Saint Saviours in Southwarke the some of twenty shillings and to And amongst the poore people of the pishe of Saint Olave in Southwarke the like some of twenty shillings Att the discrec͞on of my Executors where moste neede shall appeare.

Item I give and bequeath unto my Mother in lawe Margarett King ffortie shillinges and unto her twoe daughters Margaret and Hanah the like some of ffortie shillinges a·peece to make them Ringes. The rest residue and Re- mainder of all and singuler my goodes chattelles and worldly substance what- soever not herein before given or bequeathed, I give and bequeath in forme followinge, that is to saie, Twoe full third ptes thereof unto such.childe and children as my said wife nowe goeth withall or is with childe of And thother twoe third ptes thereof I fully and wholly give unto my said lovinge wife Elizabeth, and my said lovinge brother John Harvard equally betweene them to be devided pte and porc͞on alike. And in case my said wife shall not be with childe att the time of my decease or that such child and child- ren shall dye before theie shall accomplishe theire age or ages of twentie and one yeares Then in such case I give and bequeath the residue and re- mainder of my estate my debtes funerall expences, and my legacies beinge paied and pformed unto my said lovinge wife and my said brother equally betweene them to be devided pte and porc͞on alike, And my will and mean-

ifige is that the legacies by me in and by this my last will given and bequeathed unto my said wife and such childe and children as she nowe goeth
with or is with childe of is and are in full Recompence and satisfaccon of
such parte of my estate shee they or anie of them shall or may claime or challenge by the custome of the Citty of London, And to the end they shall
make noe clayme or challege thereby, And if they shall make such Claime
or challenge by the said custome Then I will that the said legacies by me
to them given shall cease and bee voide and not be paied, And I doe ordaine and make my said welbeloved brother John Harvard And the said
Nichollas Morton preacher executors of this my said last will and Testament in trust for the due pformance of this my said laste will and the payment of the legacies herein included and given and especially and before
all of such debtes as in right and conscience I shall owe to anie pson or
psons att the time of my decease as my trust is in them, And in recompence of theire paines therein to be taken, I give and bequeath unto either
of them the sume of fiue poundes lawfull englishe mony apeece, And I doe
nominate and appoint my said lovinge ffather in lawe Mr Nicholas Kinge
and my lovinge Cossen Thomas Harvard and my lovinge freind Mr. John
Spencer Merchante to be overseers of this my will desiring them to se the
same pformed accordinge to my true meaning and to be aidinge and assist-
inge to my said Executors with theire best advice And for theire paines
therein to be taken I give and bequeath unto every one of them three
poundes apeece of like mony, And I doe hereby revoke and disalowe of
all former willes and bequestes by me in any wise heretofore made And this
to stand and continewe for and as my last will and testament, In witnes
whereof to this my said last will and testament conteyninge with this sheete,
Nyne sheetes of paper, I the said Thomas Harvard have sett my hand and
seale the daie and yeare first aboue written Thomas Harvard   Sealed and
published by the said Thomas Harvard for and as his last will and testament the daie and yeare abovesaid in the p'sence of me Richard Greene
Scr: Richard Barlowe.

PROBATUM fuit Testamentum suprascriptum apud London coram magr̃o
Willm̄o Sames legum dcōre Surrogato venerabilis viri domini Henrici
Marten militis legum etiam dcōris Curie Prerogatiue Cant magr̃i Custodis
sive Com̄issarii ltim̄e constitut, Quinto die mensis Maij Anno domini mil-
lim̄o sexcentesimo tricesimo septimo Jurament Nicholai Morton Cleric
executorū in humōi testament nominat; cui comissa fuit administracio
omñi et singulorū bonorū iuriū et creditorū dict def de bene et fidļe adᵒ
eadᵐ ad scᵗᵃ dei evang: iurat, Reservata p̃tate similem com̄issiōem faciefid
Johanni Harvard alteri execut etiam in dicto testament nominat cum vene-
rit eam petitur.   69, Goare.

[At last, thanks to the mother that bore him, and who by her careful mention of
him in her will as "my eldest son, John Harvard, clarke," has again, as it were,
brought him to light, we are enabled to lift the veil that for nearly two hundred
and fifty years has hidden our modest and obscure, but generous benefactor, the
godfather of America's oldest University, the patron Saint of New England's scholars; to learn his parentage and birthplace, and to form some idea of his youthful
surroundings.   The will of his brother Thomas, to be sure (discovered by me on
Washington's birth-day, 1884), furnished the first important evidence in regard to
him. It will be noticed in that will, made 15 July, 1636, that he appoints his brother,
John Harvard, and the Rev. Nicholas Morton, parson of St. Saviour's, joint executors; that this will was presented for probate 5 May, 1637, by Mr. Morton alone, and
power granted only to him, a similar power being reserved for John Harvard, the

other executor, *when he should come to seek it.* This seemed to show plainly enough the absence of John Harvard, the brother of Thomas, on that fifth of May, 1637. Well, that was the year of the first appearance of *our* John Harvard on the soil of New England, as shown by the records of Charlestown ; so that probably on that very day in May he was on his way across the Atlantic. The inference then was a reasonable one that the John Harvard named in the will of Thomas Harvard of Southwark and the wise benefactor after whom our ancient University was named were one and the same person. But it needed just the mention of him in his mother's will as " clarke," taken in connection with this fact of his absence at the proving of his brother's will, to put the matter beyond question. Here too it seems as if envious chance had sought to hide him, for in the Calendar of 1637 the name of the testator, which in the record is plainly enough " Harvard," was entered " Haward," a name which might be passed over by any one hunting for the name of Harvard. It was only by *gleaning* that I came upon it.

Again—the Register Books of St. Saviour's, Southwark, the parish in which our benefactor first saw the light, seem to have lent themselves to increase the mystery that has enveloped the English surroundings of John Harvard, as will appear from the following list of baptisms :*

1601 May 31 Marye Harverde d. of Robert, a Butcher.
1602 July 15 Robert Harverde s. of Robert, a Butcher.
1606 September 30 Robert Harvye s. of Robert, a Butcher.
1607 NOVEMBER 29 JOHN HARVYE S. OF ROBT. A BUTCHER.
1609 December 3 Thomas Harvye s. of Robt. a Butcher.
1610 November 1 William Harverd s. of Robert, a Butcher.
1612 September 27 Katherin Harverd d. of Robert, a Butcher.
1613 December 12 Ann Harverd d. of Robt. a Butcher.
1615 April 2 Peter Harvye d. of Robt. a Butcher.

Why, if his name was Harvard, should we accept the baptism of John Harvye as the baptism of our John Harvard? Here again the mother comes to our assistance. It can readily be seen that Katherine Yearwood must have been the widow of Robert Harvard and mother of the John, Thomas and Peter named in his will. It may not appear so evident that John Elletson, whose will I have given in its order of time, had married the widow Harvard before she became the wife of Richard Yearwood. The will of John Elletson makes no mention of any of the Harvard family ; yet no one can read attentively that will and the will of Mrs. Katherine Yearwood in connection with each other, without being forced to the conclusion that Katherine Yearwood must have been the widow of John Elletson and the executrix of his will, and, as such, the successor of his trust in regard to the children of Hugh Horsall, or Harsall, deceased. So convinced was I of this that almost the first object of my quest in the register of St. Saviour's, was the record of the marriage of John Elletson with the widow Harvard. And I soon found it entered thus :

1625 Januarie 19 John Ellison & Katherine Harvie.

Here we find mother and son both appearing under another and the same name, viz., Harvie or Harvye. I found too in the will of Thomas Cox, citizen and vintner of London, made 12 September and proved 21 September, 1613 (79 Capell) bequests made to sundry members of this family (John Harvard's uncles?) as follows': " I give Mrs Herverd als Harvey wife of Mr Thomas Harverd als Harvey of St Katherines Butcher six payre of best sheets," &c.—" I doe give and bequeath unto Richard Harverd als Harvey of St Saviour's parish aforesaid butcher, my now tenant, the sum of ten pounds," &c. A Robert Harvy als Harverde the elder of Rookeby (Rugby) was mentioned by Thomas Atkins of Dunchurch, Warwickshire, in his will, 41st Elizabeth. (48, Kidd.)

The burial of the father of John Harvard is thus entered :

1625 August 24 Mr Robert Harvey, a man, in the church.

The youngest son, Peter, mentioned in his father's will (of 28 July, 1625) but not in the widow's, was buried four days before the father, also in the church, where also Richard Yearwood (a vestryman) was buried 18 October, 1632, and Katherine Yearwood 9 July, 1635. John Harvard's elder brother Robert was buried the very day before his father made his will. Evidently the family were suffering

* The first two children in the list, viz. Mary (bapt. 1601) and Robert (bapt. 1602), were probably the children of Mr. Harvard by his first wife, Barbara Descyn, whom he married 26 June, 1600.

from the visitation of the plague in the summer of 1625. I saw other burials entered, but did not have time to note them. All, however, I think, were buried in the church. As I passed through this venerable edifice, once the place of worship of our modest benefactor, I noticed that the great window in the South Transept was of plain glass, as if Providence had designed that some day the sons of Harvard should place there a worthy memorial of one who is so well entitled to their veneration.—HENRY F. WATERS.]

WILLIAM WARD of the parish of St Savior in Southwarke in the County of Surrey citizen and goldsmith of London 2 April 1624.

My body to be buried within the parish church of St Saviors in Southwark aforesaid. My estate shall be divided into three equal parts or portions according to the laudable custom of the city of London. One of which said third parts of my estate I do give, devise and bequeath unto my now wellbeloved wife Roase Ward. One other third part of my said estate I do give and bequeath unto my loving son Edward Ward and unto my well beloved daughter Roase Warde equally between them to be divided part and part alike (both minors). The other third part I reserve towards the payment of debts, funeral expenses and legacies &c.

To loving aunt Margaret Wood widow forty shillings per annum, in quarterly payments. To the poor of the parish of St Savior's four pounds sterling. To Mr James Archar our minister twenty shillings sterling. To the churchwardens and vestry men of the parish of St Saviors aforesaid of which society I am now a member the sum of six pounds sterling to make a dinner for them. To my good friend Mr Richard Yarwood one silver bowl of the weight of twelve ounces. Item I do give and bequeath unto my brother Mr Robert Harverd and to my friend George Garrett and my cousin William Shawarden to every of them a ring of gold to the value of twenty shillings or twenty shillings apiece in money. The remainder shall be divided into three equal parts or portions, two of which I do give and bequeath unto my said son Edward Ward to be likewise paid unto him at his age of one and twenty years, and the other third part of the said remainder I do give and bequeath unto my said daughter Roase Ward to be paid unto her on the day of her marriage or at her age of one and twenty years, which shall first happen. If both my said children shall happen to die before the legacies by this my last will bequeathed unto them and either of them shall grow due then I do will and bequeath all and every the legacies, herein by me before bequeathed unto my said children, unto my said loving wife Roase Ward and unto my cousin Elizabeth now wife of the forenamed William Shawarden equally between them to be divided &c. And I do make and ordain my said son Edward Warde and my said good friend Mr Richard Woodward executors of this my last will. And I do nominate and appoint the foresaid Robert Harvard, George Garrett and William Shawarden to be overseers of this my will.

This will containing four sheets of paper was read signed sealed and delivered in the presence of us Josua Whitfeild and me William Page Scri. Memorandum that this word Woodward was mistaken in the fifteenth line of this sheet and that according to the true intent of the said William Ward the same was meant and should have been written Yearwood who is the man mentioned to be nominated in the eighth line of the — sheet to be Richard Yearwood and mistaken by me the writer, witness William Page Scri.

Administration was granted to Roase Ward, the widow, during the minority of Edward Warde the son, 5 October 1624.   80, Byrde.

[The foregoing abstract was found in the course of my gleanings nearly a year ago, and preserved on account of its mention of Robert Harvard and Richard Yearwood. It now turns out to be very important as evidence that Robert Harvard's wife Katherine, the mother of our John Harvard, was a Rogers; for in my reading of the registers of St. Saviour's I came upon the following marriage :

1621 Oct 17 William Warde and Rose Rogers.

This I made note of at the time, not remembering this long preserved abstract of William Ward's will, but solely because I recalled that Katherine Yarwood had mentioned a sister Rose Reason, and as I fully believed the testatrix would turn out to be a Rogers, the name Rose Rogers struck me as worth noting. Rose Ward and Rose Reason were probably one and the same person.

Another most important evidence of John Harvard's identity remains to be shown. Knowing that he must have been the owner of landed property, and believing that before leaving for America (in the spring of 1637) he would be selling some of this property, I surmised that some record of such sale would appear in some of the documents preserved in the Public Record Office, although I had been informed that the Record Office had been searched for trace of John Harvard, and that it was hardly worth the while for me to make a search there. However, I laid the matter before my young friend Francis Grigson, Esq. (a son of the late Rev. William Grigson, our former corresponding member), and sought his advice. He said that my surmise was quite reasonable, and that the best field of investigation would be the Feet of Fines. No one could be kinder than he in showing me how to look for the evidence I wanted. After almost a whole day's labor, in which I found many suggestive items bearing on American names, I, at last, found an entry which led me to send for the Feet of Fines of the Hillary Term, 12th Charles I., County Surrey. The following is a copy of the first (and important) part of this document :

Hēc est finalis concordia fca⁾ in cur⁾ Dni Regis apud Westm⁾ in Octavis Purifica-c⁾ois Be⁾ Marie Anno regnorum caroli Dei gra⁾ Angli Scotie ffranc et Hibn⁾ie Regis fidei Defens etc a conqu⁾ duodecimo coram Johe⁾ ffinch Rico⁾ Hutton Georgio Vernon et ffrancisco Crawley justic⁾ et aliis dni Regis fidelibus tunc ibi⁾ p͏rsentibus Int' Johe⁾m Man et Johannam uxo⁾m eius quer⁾ et Johe⁾m Harvard et Annam uxo⁾m eius deforc⁾ de uno mesuagio et tribus Cotagijs cum p'tin⁾ in Parochia Sci⁾ Olavi in Southwarke.

The next day, after a long search, I was able to examine the Concord of Fines, relating to the same transaction, where I hoped to find the signatures of the parties to this agreement, as was the custom. This case, to my great regret, proved an exception to the rule, and I was unable therefore to get a tracing of John Harvard's autograph. However, I was enabled to fix the precise date of the transfer, vizt. 16 February, 12th Charles I. The consideration given by John and Johan Man was one hundred and twenty pounds sterling.

Here we find John Harvard appearing in February, 1636–7, as a grantor of real estate in St. Olave (where his brother Thomas was living) and with wife Ann; surely most important evidence that he was the John Harvard who six months afterwards was in New England with a wife Ann; and the above date of transfer and the date of probate of his brother Thomas Harvard's will undoubtedly furnish the limits of the period of time within which John Harvard left old England to take up his abode in our New England. He must have set sail some time between 16 February and 5 May, 1637. The four tenements thus conveyed were, without doubt, the same as those described in the following extract :

John Man of the parish of St. Olave in Southwarke in the County of Surrey, sea captain, 6 August 1660, proved 25 November 1661.

"I giue and bequeath all those my foure houses or Tenements with thappurtenances thereunto belonging scituate in Bermondsey streete in the parish of S͏ᵗ Olave in Southwarke and County aforesaid which I purchased of one ——— Harbert, being in the occupation and possession of one ——— Greenball or his assignes at yearely Rent of eight and twenty pounds vnto Mary my Loveing wife dureing her naturall life and from and after her decease to the heires of our bodyes lawfully to bee begotten forever and for want of such issue to the heires of the said Mary my wife Lawfully to bee begotten of her body forever."—H. F. W.]   180, May.

In Dei Nomine Amen. The Sixt Daye of the moneth of ffebruary Anno dñi 1637 I John Sadler of Ringmer in the County of Sussex Clerke Compos mentis et Corpore sanus thankes be to God therefore doe make & ordayne this my last will & Testament vizt ffirst I will & bequeath my poore sinfull Soule to God the father Beseechinge him of his mercy to save it for his sonne Jesus Christ his satisfacčons sake And my Body I will to be buryed where & by whome & in what manner God hath appointed. ffor my worldly goodes I will & bequeath them in maner followinge ffirst I will and bequeath to my daughter Anne the wife of John Haruard Clarke Twentie shillinges to be payd her after my decease when shee shall demand it. Item I will and bequeath to my sonne John Sadler Twenty Shillinges to be payd him within a moneth after my death if it be demaunded Alsoe I will and bequeath to the poore of the parish of Worsfield in the County of Salop Twenty shillinges to be distributed amongst them after my death And I will to the poore of ye pish of Ringmer abouenamed the summe of Tenn shillinges to be distributed amongst them after my departure And for the rest of my worldly goodes whatsoever legally bequeatheable I will and bequeath them to Mary my deare and loveinge wife not doubtinge of her good and godly diposeinge of them whome I make the sole and onely Executrix of this my will In wittnes whereof I say In wittnes whereof I haue hereunto sett my hand & seale   John Sadler.

Witnesses hereunto John Shepherd John Legener.

Probatum fuit Testamentum suprascriptum apud London coram ven)-abili viro dño Henrico Marten milite legū dčore Curiæ Prerogative Cant Magřo Custode sive Comissario ltime Constituto vicesimo primo die mensis Octobris Anno dūi Millmo sexcentmo quadragesimo Juramento Marie Sadler Relictæ dicti defuncti et Executricis in hmoi Testamento noiāt Cui Comissa fuit Administračo omniū et singloŕum bonorum iurium et Creditorum eiusdem defuncti de bene et fideliter Administrando eadem Ad sancta dei Evangelia coram Magřo Esdra Coxall Cličo vigore Comissi-onis in ea parte ais emanat Jurat.   Coventry, 128.

[John Sadler, M.A., whose will is given above, was instituted Vicar of Patcham in the county of Sussex, 3 November, 1608, as I have been informed by E. H. W. Dunkin, Esq., who has for years been making careful researches among the records relating to this county. In Patcham Mr. Sadler's children were baptized as follows:

Ann d. of Jn. Sadler, Mary, August 24, 1614.
John s. of Do. .... April 6, 1617.

Afterwards he was settled at Ringmer, where I find he was inducted 12 October, 1626, and was buried there 3 October, 1640.* His son John was a graduate of Emanuel College, Cambridge, M.A. 1638, Fellow of the College, Master in Chancery, Town Clarke of London and Master of Magdalen College, Cambridge, we learn from Cole's Collection (Add. MS. 5851, British Museum). From Le Neve's Fast. Eccl. Angl. we get this confirmed and with further information, under the title St. Mary Magdalene Coll. Masters. John Sadler, M.A., was admitted 1650, and deprived at the restoration.

* The Burrell Collection (Add. MSS. 5697, &c. British Museum), from which I took the above item, gives the date 1642, a manifest error as shown by date of probate of will; besides, Burrell convicts himself in the next line, showing the date of induction of Mr. Sadler's successor, 1640. My friend Mr. Dunkin gives me the entry from the Ringmer Register as follows: " 1640 Oct. 3 buryed Mr John Sadler minister of Ringmer." H. F. W.

In the same MS. Cole gives the admission of John Harvard, P 1631, and the same year Tho. Allen P. June 22, Suff. Mr. Harvard's graduation is shown to be 1635. His pastor, Nicholas Morton, M.A. 1619, born in Leicestershire, was Dixy Fellow and afterwards chaplain of St. Mary Overies, London (i. e. St. Savior's, Southwark).

In the Sussex Archæological Society's Collection (vol. 11, p. 225) is given " A Rolle of the several Armors and furniture with theire names of the clergie within the Arch Deaconry of Lewes and Deanery of South Malling with the Deanry of Battell in the County of Sussex. Rated and appoynted the 11th day of March Aº D'ni 1612 by the Right Reverend father in God Samuell (Harsnet) Lo. Bishoppe of Chichester." I extract the following item : " Petcham, Mr Jo. Sadler, vicar —— a musquet furnished."

As the widow Ann Harvard became the wife of the Rev. Thomas Allen, the following abstract may be worth noting here :

Mense Octobris 1673, Vicesimo Septimo die. Emt. Comº. Thomæ Allen filio nrāli et ltimo Thomæ Allen nup Civtis Norwicen vid def hentis etc. Ad Admistrand bona jura et cred d'ci def de bene etc jurat.   Admon. Act Book 1673, fol. 128.

I cannot refrain from expressing the gratitude I feel towards my brother antiquaries in England for the kindly sympathy and generous assistance I have received from them ; and I desire to name especially Messrs. E. H. W. Dunkin, Francis Grigson, David Jones, Robert Garraway Rice and J. C. C. Smith, who have shown kindness without stint in this matter, as in all other matters connected with my genealogical work in England.—HENRY F. WATERS.]

Testamentatum Georgii ffox.

I do give to Thomas Lower my sadle and bridle they are at John Nelson's and spurrs and Bootts inward leathers and the New England Indian Bible and my great book of the signifying of names and my book of the New Testament of Eight languages and all my physical things that came from beyond the sea with the outlandish cupp and that thing that people do give glisters with and my two dials the one is an Equinoctiall Diall And all my overplus Books to be divided among my four sons in law and also all my other books And my Hamock I do give to Thomas Lower that is at Benjamin Antrobus his closett and Rachell may take that which is at Swarthmore. And Thomas Lower may have my Wallnutt Equinoctiall Diall and if he can he may gett one cut by it which will be hard to do, and he shall have one of my prospect glasses in my Trunck at London and a pair of my gloves and my seale. G: ff: And the flameing sword to Nath: Meade and my other two seals I: Rouse and the other Dan: Abraham And Tho: Lower shall have my Spanish Leatherhood and S: Meade shall have my magnifying glass and the tortoise shell comb and cace. G. ff.

And let Tho: Docra that knoweth many of my Epistles and written Books which he did write come up to London to assist ffriends in sorting of my Epistles and other writings and give him a Guinea. G. ff.

And all that I have written concerning what I do give to my Relations either money or otherwise John Loft may putt it up in my Trunck at John Elsons and write all things down in a paper and make a paper out of all my papers how I have ordered things for them and John Loft may send all things down by Poulesworth Carryer in the Trunck to John ffox at Poulesworth in Warwickshire And lett John ffox send John Loft a full Receipt and a discharge and in this matter none of you may be concerned but John Loft only. And my other Little Trunck that standeth in Benjamin Antrobus his closett with the outlandish things Thomas Lower shall have and if it be ordered in any other papers to any other, that must not stand so, but as now ordered. G. ff. And Sarah thou may give Sarah Freckelton halfe a guinea for she hath been serviceable to me an honest carefull young woman G. ff. Make no noise of these things but do them in the life as I have ordered them And when all is done and cleared what remains to the printing of my Books Benjamin Antrobus and Mary hath one 100 pounds of mine. take no use of them for it when you do receive it And in my chest in Benjamin Antrobus his Chamber there is a little Guilt Box with some gold in it Sarah Meade to take it and let it do it service among the rest so far as it will goe the Box is sealed up.

G. ff.

I do order William and Sarah Meade and T. Lower to take care of all my Books and Epistles and papers that be at Benjamin Antrobuses and att R. R. Chamber and those that come from Swarthmore and my Journall of my life and the passadges and travells of ffriends and to take them all into their hands And all the overplus of them they may have and keep together as a Library when they have gathered them together which are to be printed ; And for them to take charge of all my money and defray all as I have ordered in my other papers and anything of mine they may the my (*sic*) take, and God will and shall be their reward The 8ᵗʰ moᵗʰ 1688.

G. ff.

Thomas Lower and John Rouse may assist you And all the passages and Travels and sufferings of ffriends in the beginning of the spreading of the truth which I have kept together will make a fine History and they may be had at Swarthmore with my other Books and if they come to London with my papers then they may be had either at W: M: Ben: Antrobus his closett, soe it is a fine thing to know the beginning of the spreading of the Gospel, after so long night of Apostacy since the Apostles' days that now Christ reigns as he did in the hearts of the people. Glory to the Lord for ever Amen. The 8ᵗʰ moᵗʰ 1688   G: ff:

30 December 1697: Appeared personally Sarah Meade, wife of William Meade of the parish of Sᵗ Dyonis Back church, London, citizen and merchant Taylor of London, and did declare that she is of the number of dissenters commonly called Quakers; and she did declare in the presence of Almighty God, the witness of the truth of what she said, that she has known George Fox, late of Swarthmore in the County of Lancaster Gentleman, deceased, he marrying with her, the declarant's mother ; and she has often seen him write and is well acquainted with his handwriting and she, having now seen and perused three papers hereunto annexed and marked No 1, 2 & 3, containing the last Will & Testament of the said George Fox deceased, the first beginning thus (I do give to Thomas Lower, &c) and ending thus (" Torkel shel com & case. G. ff."), the second beginning thus (and all that I have written, &c.) and ending thus (the Box is sealed up. G. ff.) and in the margin (give him a guinea), the third beginning thus (I do order William & Sarah Meade, &c.) and ending thus (glory to the Lord forever Amen. G. ff. the 8ᵗʰ mon 1688) she did declare that she did & does verily believe that the same three papers were and are all wrote by & with the proper handwriting of the said George Fox deceased And she farther declared that above a year before the death of the said George Fox (who died on or about the thirteenth day of January in the year of our Lord

one thousand six hundred & ninety) the said George Fox did deliver to her a parcel of papers sealed up & thus superscribed with his own hand, viz (Papers of George Fox which are to be laid up in the Trunk of his at William Meade's and not to be opened before the time) and on the next day after the deceased's death the said bundle was opened in the presence of the declarant and of several other persons and they the three papers hereunto annexed and marked No 1, 2 & 3 were found amongst other papers relating to his concerns.   Sarah Meade.

30 Decembris 1697 dicta Sara Meade fecit declarationem suprascriptam coram me   George Bramston Surr.

30 December, 1697   Appeared personally William Ingram of the parish of St Margaret's, New Fish Street London, citizen & Tallow Chandler of London, aged about fifty seven years, and declared that he is of the number of Dissenters commonly called Quakers; and he did declare in the presence of Almighty God, the witness of the truth of what he said (then follows a declaration similar to the foregoing as to handwriting of deceased testator, &c.).

A similar declaration was made, the same day, by George Whitehead of the parish of St Botolph without Bishopsgate, London, gentleman, aged about sixty years and also of the number of Quakers, &c.

Tricesimo die mensis Decembris Anno Dñi Millimõ Sexcenmõ nonagemõ septima emanavit comico Margaretæ ffox relictæ et Legariæ nominatæ in Testamento Georgii ffox nup de Swarthmore in com Lancastriæ sed in Proâ omniu Sanctoru Lombard Street London dĕfti hentis &c ad administrañd bona Jura et credita dicti dĕfti juxta tenorem et effectu Testamenti ipsius dĕfti (eo quod nullu omnino nõiaverit extorem) declaracone in presentia dei Omnipoteñ juxta Statutum parliamenti in hac parte editum et provisu de bene et fideliter administrañd eadem p dictam Margaretam ffox prius facta.   Pyne, 280.

[George Fox, born in July, 1624, married 27 8mo. 1669, in Bristol, Margaret, widow of Thomas Fell of Swarthmore Hall, Lancashire. She is said to have died at Swarthmore in 1702, near the eighty-eighth year of her age. Of her children by her first husband, Margaret is said to have been the wife of John Rous, Bridget of John Draper, Sarah of William Meade, Mary of Thomas Lower, Susanna of (William?) Ingram, and Rachel of Daniel Abraham.—H. F. W.]

Letters of administration on the estate of the Rev. GEORGE PIGGOTT clerk, late chaplain in the regiment of marines under the command of the Hon. Col. John Wynyard, at Jamaica in the West Indies, granted, 30 June, 1743, to the Rev. George Piggott, clerk, son and lawful attorney of Sarah Piggott, widow, the relict of the said deceased, for the use and benefit of the said Sarah Piggott, now residing at the Massachusetts Bay in New England.   Admon. Act. Book, 1743.

[For this abstract the readers of the REGISTER are indebted to Robert Garraway Rice, Esq., of Acar Lodge, Bramley Hill, Croydon, Surrey.—H. F. W.
The Rev. George Pigot was settled as Rector of St. Michael's Church, Marblehead, 1728; he came to Marblehead from Providence, and in addition to his parochial duties officiated every month in Salem, where in a short time he gathered a congregation of between two and three hundred persons.
In 1730 Mr. Pigot made what proved to be an unsuccessful attempt to regain a right to the Baronies of Morley and Monteagle, to which he was an heir, and requested permission to return to England to attend to the matter, which was evidently not granted. His rectorship ended in 1736. During his rectorship there are recorded 454 baptisms, among them four of his own slaves, 95 marriages, 145 burials. In going from the house of a poor and sick parishioner whom he had been visiting in the winter of 1736, Mr. Pigot fell on the ice and broke his left arm, which

he fractured again the following summer ; his health consequently became broken, and he obtained leave to visit England, and is supposed to have died there or on the passage. His wife was buried in the churchyard fifteen years after.

Samuel Curwen, Esq., in his Diary, writing of Cardiff, 1st August, 1777, says: " After my departure I learnt that a daughter of the late Parson Pigot of Marblehead was an inhabitant of this place."—GEORGE R. CURWEN.

The baronies of Morley and Monteagle in 1686, on the death of Thomas Parker, the third inheritor of the two baronies, fell into abeyance between the issue of his two aunts, Katharine who married John Savage, earl of Rivers, and Elizabeth who married Edward Cranfield, Esq. (Burke's Extinct Peerage, ed. 1846, p. 409). Rev. George Pigot, of Marblehead, wrote to the secretary of the London Society for Propagating the Gospel, August 1, 1730 : " I think it proper at this juncture to notify the Hon'ble Society of one affair which might otherwise deserve their blame : It is that I have made a claim by Mr. Speaker of the House of Commons to be restored to my right to the Baronies of Morley and Monteagle, and that I do not know how soon I may have a call to make out the same. Therefore I request the Hon'-ble Society to give me leave to come home upon a proper invitation." (Bp. Perry's Massachusetts Historical Papers, p. 262.) Mr. Pigot, in a letter Dec. 27, 1734, speaks of having a large family (Ibid. p. 304).

May 1, 1718, " Mr. George Piggott " of Newport was admitted to the freedom of the colony of Rhode Island (R. I. Records, iv. 227). May 5, 1724, " George Pigot " of Warwick was admitted freeman to that colony (Ibid. p. 340). Was either of these the minister ?—EDITOR.

A year or two ago I met at the rooms of the New England Historic Genealogical Society, Rev. Mr. Pigot, an English clergyman, who said he was a descendant of Rev. George Pigot, of Marblehead. He visited the rooms to obtain genealogical information concerning his ancestor. He had an elder brother in Australia who had sufficient property to maintain the dignity of a baron. He wished to obtain documentary evidence to substantiate the claim to the barony which he said was in abeyance in their line of the Pigot family.—JOHN COFFIN JONES BROWN.]

WILLIAM HORSFORDE of Dorchester in the County of Dorset, gentleman, 30 June, 1621, proved 25 January, 1622. To be buried in the church of St Peters. To the poor of the Hospital of Dorchester five pounds. I give & bequeath my house and lands, with the appurtenances, in the parish of St Peter's, in the lane there going towards the Fryery, wherein George Hooper, needle maker, lately dwelt, and which I purchased of Mr Joseph Longe and Thomas Bullocke, unto Joane my wife for the term of her life ; then to Joane my daughter and the heirs of her body, &c. ; then to my own right heirs forever. My daughter Sarah and her husband, my son in law, John Hardey. To their children, John, Jane and Sarah Hardey and the child wherewith my daughter Sarah is now great, one hundred pounds, which was meant to be given unto them by my brother Hugh Horsforde deceased, and one hundred pounds besides. To my daughter Joane Horsforde four hundred & fifty pounds. My daughter Grace, the wife of Thomas Frye, and her children. My friends John Strode of Chantmarrell, Richard Bingham of Melcombe, Richard Kesier and William Clapcott, of Frampton, to be executors. Swann, 27.

[There was a William Horsford, spelled, in other places on the record, Horseford, Hosford, Hosseford, who was an early inhabitant of Dorchester, Mass. He is first mentioned October 8, 1633, when he is styled " Goodman Hosseford "; freeman 1634 ; went to Windsor, Conn. ; was a Commissioner to the General Court in 1637. With his old Dorchester companions and friends, Mr. John Witchfield, and Mr. John Branker " the schoolmaster," he became associated as ruling elders of the church in Windsor. They frequently delivered the weekly lecture before the church. Mr. Savage says, he probably removed to Springfield, and there preached from October, 1652, to October, 1656, " when Moxon gave up in disgust." It seems that he returned to England with his second wife Jane, widow of Henry Fowkes. In 1656, being then in England, he gave land at Windsor to his two children. His wife also gave some of her land to Windsor church and to her husband's children, &c. " In

1671," says Mr. Savage, "she was at Tiverton, co. Devon." William had a son John, whose nine children were living at their father's decease, August 7, 1683. (See Savage, Hinman, Stiles's Windsor.)—WILLIAM B. TRASK.]

MORGAN HOLMAN of Barwicke within the parish of Swyre, in the County of Dorset, gentleman, in his will, dated 19 June, 1614, proved 19 April, 1623, mentions (among others) cousin Humphrey Jolyff, and speaks of land which he lately purchased of Nicholas Darbye, Lawrence and Roger Darbye.   Swann, 33.

BOLD BOUGHEY, Esq., Warden of the Fleete, 17 October, 1669, published and acknowledged by testator the next day. Whereas since my marriage with Jane the widow & relict of William Celey, Esq., by whom I have had no children, and who either hath or pretended to have a reasonable good estate, which I have not wasted or intermedled with; since which marriage I have lived but an uncomfortable life; I do therefore give and bequeath unto my said wife, for her better support and as an addition to her own estate, the sum of twenty pounds per annum, to be paid to her yearly and every year during the life of M^{ris} Challener alias Bamfield, her mother in law, now living, to be paid unto her by my executors by ten pounds at the end of every six months after my decease. To my daughter Martha Boughey the sum of one thousand pounds, to be paid unto her at the day of her marriage, or within such short time after as my executors can raise the same; and in the mean time I give unto her thirty pounds per annum for her maintenance; and if she happen to die before she be married, then I give and bequeath the said sum of one thousand pounds between my two sons John & Bold Boughey. Reference is made to an engagement of John Boughey, son and heir of the testator, to come into partnership with Edmond Peirce, Esq., in the business and office of Wardenship of the Fleete. To my son Bold Boughey three hundred pounds at his age of one and twenty, or when he shall be a Freeman of London and set up his trade of a Linendraper. Unto the poor prisoners of the Fleete five pounds per annum, to be paid on Christmas Eve during all the time that any of my name or family shall be Wardens of the Fleete. To my brother Thomas Boughey one hundred pounds to be paid him within twelve months after my decease. To my two nieces Priscilla and Margaret Roe ten pounds apiece, to put them out to some trades such as my executor shall think fit. To my good friends Mr Robert Leighton, Capt. William Oakes, Sir John Carter, Mr Griffith Boderdo, Mr James Johnsen, Charles Cornwallis, Esq., Mr Samuel Fisher, Mr Richard Beale and Mr Robert Wigmore, forty shillings apiece, to buy them rings. The same to my old servant Christopher Story. To my servant Thomas Corbett the like sum; and it is my desire that he be continued in his place of Tipstaff in the exchecquer so long as he shall " abare " himself honestly. My friends Edmond Peirce, Esq., and William Church, gentleman, to be executors, and to each ten pounds for their pains therein. My loving brother in law Robert Wiggmore, Esq., and Charles Cornwallis, Esq., to be overseers.

The above will was proved by Edmond Peirce, who took out letters 15 November, 1669, and by William Church, 25 June, 1672.   Coke, 133.

[The testator of the above will, although he makes no mention therein of New England or New England people, is clearly enough the writer of the letter bearing date " London, 4th may 1662," and superscribed " For my Deare Sist^er Mrs Elizabeth Harris att Wroxbury These in New England," which was printed in the July number of the N. E. HIST. AND GEN. REGISTER, 1851 (vol. v. pp. 307–8). In it he speaks of his family thus : "our youngest Bro^er Timothy is Chaplaine to the Kings Rigimt of Guards in Dunkirke, Thomas Imployed by me in business, our sister Katherine .... is married to one Mr Thorpe in London, ... our Sist^er Hannah is married to one Mr Wilding and lives in Shrewsbury. Mary is married to Mr Roe, who hath an Imployment under me in London, and lives well, Priscilla is married to an honest minister one Mr Bruce and at present Lives in London, is Chaplaine to mee, at the flcete. Our Sisters, except Katherine, are all mothers of children." .... " I was married but it pleased god to remove my wife by death about foure yeares since : I have only two sonnes and a daughter (viz) John, Bold and Martha living ; my wife was with child of the tenth when she died."

We are told that "Robert Harris & Elizabeth Boffee were married Jan. 24, 1642," in Roxbury.—H. F. W.]

PETER HODGES late of East West Guersey in America, planter, and now in the parish of St Mary Magdalen, Bermondsey, in the County of Surrey, the one & twentieth of July, 1697, proved 21 December, 1697. To my dearly and well beloved friend Elizabeth Willis, of the said parish, spinster, whom I intended for my lawful wife, as well for the natural love and affection I have and bear to her as for divers other good causes and considerations me hereunto especially moving, all those two hundred acres of woodland in East West Guersey in America by me held and granted from the Governour of the said Island, together with the deed or writing by which the same premisses are granted, which is now left in the hands of Thomas Revell of Burrington in East West Guersey aforesaid ; also all my horses, hogs and other cattle whatsoever in the said Island, marked with a half Gad; and also all and singular my estate, both real and personal, as well within the said Island of East West Guersey as any other place or places whatsoever, &c. To all or any of my Relations that shall lawfully claim any estate or interest in the said premisses, &c., I give and bequeath one shilling if demanded and no more. The said Elizabeth Willis to be executrix.

Wit : Joann Pryor Senior, Mary Pryor, Joann Pryor Junior, Hannah Richeson and John Parry Scr. Pyne, 284.

[Burrington should be Burlington. Thomas Revell was at this time a member of the West Jersey Council. See New Jersey Archives, ii. 146 *et seq.*—EDITOR.]

JAMES MONTGOMERY, of James River in Nantzimum in the Island of Virginia, and late chirurgeon of His Majesty's ship St Albans, being sick and weak of body in Richmond in the County of Surrey, 25 August, 1697, proved 24 December, 1697. My body to be buried in such parish as it shall please God to call my soul from thence. To my two loving brothers Robert and Benjamin, all such writings, obligatory bills and accounts which are my property in Virginia aforesaid. To my brother Benjamin one bed. To my brother Robert all the residue of my estate (lands excepted). To Sarah, wife of William Cranbury, of the place above named in Virginia aforesaid, I give and bequeath one warming pan now in the custody of the said Sarah ; and touching all such wages or pay as shall appear due to me for my service performed on board His Majesty's Ship St Albans above nam- ed I dispose thereof as follows (vizt) to my sister Jane and to her youngest son now living, and to her daughters Jane and Elizabeth three pounds apiece, to be paid unto them or either of them on his or her respective marriage day. This money is to be raised out of such pay as shall appear due to me from the Right Honorable the Treasurer or Paymaster to His Majesty's Navy. To my godson James Buxton two pounds, and to his brother Richard one pound ten shillings. To Martha, daughter of my brother Benjamin, five pounds. To my nephews James and Benjamin five pounds apiece. To my nephew Robert Montgomery five pounds.   To Joseph Halford of Richmond in the County of Surrey, chandler, I devise and bequeath one hogshead of tobacco, freight and custom of the same being hereby appointed to be paid by him for the same when arrived from Virginia.   Papers relating to my said ship's affairs, &c. now in the custody of .... Bird of Wapping in the County of Middlesex, Instrument Maker.   My will is that if my executors shall think fit to authorize him their Attorney to receive the money due thereupon or shall recall them out of his said custody that there shall be an allowance of twelve pence per each pound to such person as shall take care in the management and receipt of the same.   My brother Robert and William Wilson of London, merchant, to be joint executors.

Wit: Thomas Ryley, Nathaniel Clark Not. Pub° in Richmond in the County of Surrey.   Pyne, 290.

[Benjamin Montgomery appears as the patentee of 450 acres of land in Nansemond County, October 26th, 1699, Book No. 9, p. 241. The following grants, also of record, may be of interest: Robert Montgomery, Edmund Belson and other inhabitants of Coward Creek, Nansemond County, 850 acres in Nansemond County, April 30th, 1671, Book No. 6, p. 678; Hugh Montgomery, 280 acres in Lower Norfolk County, October 21st, 1687, Book No. 7, p. 615, Virginia Land Records.

R. A. BROCK.]

EDWARD FRAUNCES of Vere in Jamaica but now in London in Great Britain Esq. 24 Dec. 1740.   All my property to my loving brother James Fraunces of Cheapside, London, apothecary.   If he die without issue, lawfully begotten, then all to my cousins Elizabeth Jacquelin now the wife of Richard Ambler of York Town in Virginia Esq., Mary Jacquelin the now wife of John Smith of Gloucester County in Virginia, merchant, and Martha Jacquelin of York Town aforesaid, spinster, equally, share & share alike.   To my negro servant maids Madge & Maria to each an annuity of twenty shillings Jamaica money for & during their respective lives.   To Henry Smallwood, Esq., John Verdon, Esq., Varney Phelp, Esq., and Moses Kerrett, Esq., each a gold ring of twenty shillings value.   My brother James Fraunces, the said Varney Phelp & Moses Kerrett to be joint executors.

Wit: John Hyde, Jn° Harwood, Jn° Hawkesworth.

Proved 3 April, 1741, by James Fraunces, with power reserved for the other executors.   Spurway, 89.

[Edward Jaquelin, son of John and Elizabeth (Craddock) Jaquelin, of county Kent, England, and a descendant of a Protestant refugee from La Vendee, France, during the reign of Charles IX., of the same lineage as the noble family of La Roche Jaqueline, came to Virginia in 1697; settled at Jamestown; married Miss Cary, of Warwick county, and died in 1730, leaving issue three sons (Edward the eldest) —neither of whom married—and three daughters: Elizabeth, of the text, who married Richard Ambler; Mary, of the text, who married John Smith, who is believed to have been a member of the House of Burgesses, of the Council, and of the Board of Visitors of William and Mary College; Martha, who died unmarried in 1804, aged 93 years.   Edward Jaquelin " died as he had lived, one of the most wealthy men in the colony."

Richard Ambler, son of John Ambler, sheriff of county York, England, in 1721, migrated to Virginia early in the 18th century; settled at Yorktown; married Elizabeth Jaquelin and had issue nine children, all of whom died at an early age, except three sons: Edward, Collector of the Port of York; married and left issue. He was a man of consideration in the colony, and when Lord Botetourt came over as Governor he brought a letter of introduction to him from Samuel Athawes, merchant, London (see Virginia Hist. Reg. iii. 1850, pp. 25, 26); John, born 31st December, 1735, Burgess from Jamestown, and Collector of District of York river, died 27th May, 1766, in Barbadoes; Jaquelin, born 9th August, 1742, married Rebecca, daughter of Lewis Burwell, of " White Marsh," Gloucester County, member of the Virginia Council during the Revolution, and long State Treasurer. He left issue : Eliza, married first, William Brent of Stafford County, and secondly, Col. Edward Carrington of the Revolution and member of Congress (no issue) ; Mary Willis, married Chief-Justice John Marshall ; Anne, married George Fisher, of Richmond ; Lucy, married Daniel Call, lawyer and legal reporter, Richmond. Upon the tomb of John Ambler, of Jamestown, Virginia (born 25th September, 1762, died 8th September, 1836), in Shockoe Hill Cemetery, Richmond, Virginia, the Ambler and Jaquelin arms are quartered : Ambler—*Sa. on a fesse or, bet.* 3 *pheons ar. a lion passant guard. gu.* Jaquelin—*On a bird* 3 *roses* (no tinctures discernible).

Much information regarding the Amblers and Jaquelins of Virginia is given in Meade's Old Churches and Families of Virginia, i. p. 97, *et seq.* The descendants of Edward Jaquelin and Richard Ambler have intermarried with the families of Baylor, Byrd, Carter, Nicholas, Norton, Randolph and others of prominence.

R. A. BROCK, of Richmond, Va.]

ANNA COLTMAN of London, widow, 10 February, 1622, proved 25 August, 1623. To my grand daughter Anne Coltman, daughter of my son William, one hundred pounds at her day of marriage or age of twenty-one years. If she die before that time then this sum to her father and his younger daughter Alice and his son Richard, to be equally divided between them. To my son Francis Coltman twenty pounds, to be paid him within three months after my decease.

Item, I give and bequeath unto my son Henry, if he be living, the sum of ten pounds of the lawful money of England, to be paid unto him within three months next after his return from Virginia. Francis my eldest son, William my youngest son. Other legacies to children. To my daughter Margaret, the wife of my son William, a ruby ring of gold. To Ralphe Canning, citizen and ironmonger of London, forty shillings ; and I appoint him sole executor. To his wife a ruby ring of gold. To my friend Mrs. Anne Hebb of London, widow, whom I appoint overseer, forty shillings and a saphire ring of gold. Swann, 78.

SOLOMON STEDMAN of Boston in New England, mariner, 20 October, 1696, proved 1 December, 1697. Henry Cole of St Pauls, Shadwell, Baker, to be my attorney to demand and receive of and from the Right Honorable the Treasurer of His Majesty's Navy and Commissioner for Prize money, &c. &c. I bequeath all my estate to my brother John Stedman.

Wit: Abraham Card, Saml Forrest, John Smith. Pyne, 298.

AUGUSTINE FISH of Bowden Magna in the County of Leicester, yeoman, 7 April, 1646, proved 23 September, 1647, by Christian Fish the relict and executrix. To Thomas Fishe my second son, and to my wife, during her life, and after her life ended to Thomas and his heirs males forever one farm, whereon my eldest son liveth, called by the name of Royses Farm, with all that John Fish had there during my life, both in town and field ;—moreover seven "pastors" in Acharbads which sometimes did belong to Palmer's House in the neather end, I give unto Thomas Fish and his heirs males as aforesaid, with this caution and proviso that he shall pay unto his youngest sister, Elizabeth Fish, one hundred marks at her age of twenty three years or on her marriage day, which shall first happen, if her marriage be with the liking of the overseers and her mother and brother. If Thomas Fish die without issue male his land to return unto Bartholomew Fish. In like manner if Bartholomew die without issue male it is to return to William Fish which is in New England, if he be then living. I give unto Christian my daughter the cottage house wherein "Jhon"

Warde and his sister liveth, with that spot of ground adjoining, bought of Richard Watts, to enter at the death of Jhon Warde, with one cow and five sheep. I give unto Jhon Halliake the eldest son of William Halliake, after his father and mother's decease, the three acres which did belong to Palmer's farm, unto him forever; and all the rest of his other children which will be ruled by parents and grandmother I give five pounds apiece, to be paid at their marriage or at twenty years old. I give unto Bartholomew Fish my youngest son five pounds. I give unto William Fish in New England, if he return, five pounds. Further to my son Thomas Fish, after the lease is expired which now my son John Fish holdeth, called by the name of Waters his close, to my son Thomas and his heirs forever. To my grandchildren at Brigstock, to help to buy every one a sepp,*——— nobles apiece. I also give unto my grand children at Thorpe, in Rutland, three ewes, to be given at the discretion of my executrix. I also give unto my servants half a crown apiece more over than their wages. I make my wife full and sole executrix, praying Thomas Fish my second son, to assist her with his power. I also wish, if be thought good unto my executrix, to give unto my eldest son's children two nobles.

The Test. of Augustine Fishe "Ritten" with his own hand. Intreating these two my sons, Edward Marriat and Robert Sly to be overseers.

Wit: Maurice Dix and William Whittwell.   Fines, 186.

[The William Fish mentioned is probably William of Windsor, Ct. See Savage's Gen. Dict. ii. 161; Connecticut Col. Records, i. 144, 148; ii. 519.—EDITOR.]

JAMES CARTER of Hinderclay in the County of Suffolk, yeoman, Saturday, 8 Sept. 1655. "I give unto the children of my brother Thomas Carter who now is in the new England, to every of them Tenn pounds apeece as Conveyniently as the same may bee raysed out of my parsonall Estate." To the two sons of my brother William Stubbs of Harleston, by his late wife who was my sister, and his two daughters by her, &c. To Frances Edwards, my wife's kinswoman.

Commission was issued 24 October, 1655, to Mary Carter widow of the said James Carter.   Aylett, 391.

[The Thomas Carter mentioned was probably Thomas of Sudbury, who died Aug. 14, 1659. There were at least two others who may have been the man, viz., Rev. Thomas, of Woburn, who died Sept. 5, 1684 (REGISTER, xvii. 51); and Thomas, of Charlestown, who died about 1652. (Wyman's Charlestown, i. 186.)—EDITOR.
Mr. Samuel R. Carter, Paris, Oxford County, Maine, in letter of July 21, 1884, surmises that the Rev. Thomas Carter may have first landed in Virginia (emigrating thence to New England), and that he may have been a relation of John Carter, the ancestor of the well-known Virginia family of the name. There is, however, nothing of tradition or record to substantiate the theory.—R. A. BROCK.]

JOHN COOPER, of Weston Hall (in the County of Warwicke), 21 November, 1654, proved 1 October, 1655, by Elizabeth Cooper, his widow and executrix. To brother Timothy Cooper, now in New England, the sum of thirty pounds, but if it happen that he shall die before this shall be due then to his children that shall be living. To sister Dorcas ten pounds, but if she die, &c. then to brother Timothy if living, if not then to his children. My wife to have the benefit of the said sums of thirty pounds and ten pounds during her widowhood. "Yet notwithstandinge if it shall please god to afflict my wife in anie of his providences towards her that shee hath neede of all that I have as it shall evidently appeare to supply her-

* Interesting as a survival of the Anglo Saxon term for sheep.—H. F. W.

selfe in her want Then my will is that that I have bequeathed to my brother and sister shalbe voyde and shall not be exported from her." Wife Elizabeth to be executrix. Friends Humphrey Hale and John Buttery " to be helpefull to my wife as her occation shall require."

The witnesses were John Sutton & John Buttery. Aylett, 392.

[The Timothy Cooper mentioned was probably the person of that name at Lynn, who died March, 1659, and had sons John and Timothy, and several daughters.—EDITOR.]

JOSEPH TOWNSEND, now of London, gentleman, but late of South Carolina in America, 4 February, 1732, proved 16 August, 1736. Money to be raised to satisfy my brothers in law Mr John Glasse of Cary Street, gentleman, all such sum & sums that I am or shall be indebted unto him together with interest thereon. If any thing remain I give & bequeath the same unto my loving sister Hannah Glass, wife of the said John Glass, in trust, to divide and give the same unto my dear son William Sinclar Townsend and Hannah Townsend, equally to be divided between them, to be paid at their several ages of one & twenty years ; and I desire her to take care of them, &c. My dear sister to be sole executrix, without the control of her said husband.

Wit : Do Strangways G. Thornton, Robt. Thornton. Derby, 185.

JOHN ENDICOTT of Salem in New England, chirurgeon, now resident in London, being bound on a voyage to New England, 12 August, 1689, proved 30 March 1695 by Anne Endicott, his widow. He mentions wife Anne and the child she goes with, brother Samuel, and refers to the will of his father Zerubbabel Endicott. Irby, 208.

[This John Endicott was a grandson of Gov. John Endicott. See REGISTER, i. 336.—EDITOR.]

WILLIAM MARCH of Charlestown in New England, but now residing in the parish of Stepney in the County of Middlesex, mariner, being very sick, &c. makes his friend Mr Richard Robison of Shadwell, shipwright, executor and gives him two guineas. " I can hold my pen no longer." 29 October, 1694, proved 13 September, 1695. The witnesses were Anne Pearce & Jane Willoughby. Irby, 220.

[This William March was the son of Nicholas and Martha March of Charlestown. His mother married for a second husband William Dadey. Administration on this estate in this county was granted to Mrs. Dadey. Inventory, Sept. 12, 1695, £24. See Wyman's Charlestown, ii. 655.—EDITOR.]

Letters of administration granted 11 November, 1633, to John Conant, clerk, uncle on the father's side (*patruo*) of CALEB CONANT, lately in the parts beyond the seas, bachelor, deceased.

Admon. Act Book for 1633, Leaf 204.

JOHN PARRIS of the Island of Barbadoes, Esq., 15 May, 1660, proved 23 October, 1661. To wife Susanna Parris one hundred pounds a year, in quarterly payments ; and I do bind my third part of three plantations in the said Island for performance of the same. To Thomas Parris, son of my brother Thomas, one hundred pounds out of the revenue of said plantations. To Samuel Parris, another son of brother Thomas, one hundred pounds (as before), and to Martyn Parris, another son (a similar bequest). If any of my said three nephews die before they attain the age of twenty one years, the legacies shall remain equally to the survivors. To Sarah

Parris, daughter of my brother Richard Parris, deceased, one hundred pounds to be paid within one year after my decease. To my sister Margaret Bully ten pounds. To my sister-in-law Susanna Parris, forty shillings to buy her a ring. To my sister Rebecca Parris forty shillings to buy her a ring. To Thomas Martaine, son of my cousin Thomas Martaine of this Island, one thousand pounds of Musko sugar within twelve months after my decease. To Hugh Leman, one half piece of fine dowlas, &c. Bequest to James Minge. To Thomas Newman, son of George Newman deceased, fifty pounds at age. To my brother Thomas Parris all my third part of three plantations (as above) as also all my part of the stone house at Reades Bay and land at the Bridge, &c., provided he pay annuity & legacies, &c. To John Parris, eldest son of my said brother Thomas, after the death of his father (all the above real estate), with remainder to Thomas, next to Samuel, then to Marrine (sic) Parris, sons of my said brother. And my said cousin John Parris shall have my gold ring with the signet.

The residue to brother Thomas Parris. Richard Evens, Capt. James Klinkett, Left. Anthony Woodward and my cousin Thomas Martine to be my executors, in trust, until other orders shall be given by my brother Thomas Parris who is at London.

The above will was proved by Thomas Parris, brother of the deceased.

May, 161.

ANNE PARRIS of St Mary Islington, in the County of Middlesex, wife to Thomas Parris now or late resident at the Island of Barbadoes beyond the seas merchant, 9 June, 1665, proved 10 June, 1665. Reference to bond of husband, before marriage, to one Mr William Freeman, in trust for the use of me, for the payment of five hundred pounds, &c. To Samuel Halsey, now an apprentice in —— three hundred pounds. To my loving cousin Thomas Bent, citizen & merchant taylor of London, cousin Frances Ascue & cousin Elizabeth Smith fifty pounds apiece. Their mother, my sister, Elizabeth Smith, my sister Tanser. Others mentioned. Mr Thomas Doelittle & Mr Peter Royle to be executors. Hyde, 65.

[The Rev. Samuel Deane, in his History of Scituate, Mass. (page 320-1), speaking of Thomas Parris, of Scituate, who was born at Pembroke, May 8, 1701. says: " From undoubted documents, now [1831] in the possession of Rev. Martin Parris, of Marshfield, we learn that this gentleman was son of Thomas Parris, who came to Long Island, 1683, from London, from whence he removed to Newbury, 1685, and to Pembroke, Mass., 1697; which latter was son of John Parris, a dissenting minister of Ugborough, near Plymouth, England,—whose father was Thomas, a merchant of London. The last named Thomas had a brother John, a merchant and planter of great wealth, who deceased in Barbadoes, 1660. His original will is in the possession of Rev. Martin Parris."

The testator is undoubtedly the wealthy merchant and planter of Barbadoes referred to by the Rev. Mr. Deane, and the Rev. John Parris of Ugborough must be his nephew John, whom he calls " the eldest son of my said brother Thomas." The late Hon. Albion Keith Parris, the second governor of Maine, was the sixth in descent from Rev. John. (See Historical Magazine, vol. i. (1857) pp. 130-1.)

Mr. Thomas Parris was Assistant Justice in Barbadoes, April 11, 1631 (REGISTER, xxxix. p. 138).

The Rev. Samuel Parris, of Danvers, of witchcraft notoriety, appears to have been the son of Thomas Parris, of Barbadoes, who died in 1673, and who was probably Thomas, a younger brother of Rev. John Parris, also named by the testator. (See REGISTER, x. 34.)—EDITOR.]

JOSEPH WILKINSON of Calvert County in the Province of Maryland merchant, 25 April, 1734. To my brother in law Mr John Skinner an handsome suit of mourning and a mourning ring of twenty shillings sterling price. To my dear and loving wife one full third part of my personal estate. To my daughter Elizabeth one other full third part. To my son Joseph the remaining third part. If my wife be with child then my estate is to be equally divided among all my children. My wife to be executrix. In case of her death my brother in law Mr John Skinner to be executor.

Wit: John Smith, Pos^ths: Thornton, Roger Boyce, Alex^r Lawson.

22 July, 1736, there issued a commission to William Torver the lawful attorney of Mary Wilkinson the widow and executrix of the deceased, &c., to administer according to the tenor & effect of the said will, for the use & benefit of the said executrix, now residing in Maryland.

Derby, 168.

EDWARD PARKS citizen & merchant tailor of London, 28 January 1650 To wife Mary Parks, in lieu of her thirds, fifteen hundred pounds (in various payments) and one third of the plate and household stuff, and all that my freehold messuage or tenement with its appurtenances, &c. which I lately purchased of William Pennoyer of London, merchant, wherein I now dwell, in the parish of Stepney, being the North western part of that great messuage formerly the possession of the Right Hon. Henry Earl of Worcester. My wife to have the education of my children.

If my son Henry Parks shall within three months, &c. and after notice given, release and quitclaim, &c. all his part of all my goods, &c. (according to the custom of the city of London) and release to George Jackson of Sandhurst in the county of Kent all his part of lands, &c. in Maidstone in the County of Kent which I lately have sold to George Jackson, then I give & bequeath unto him three hundred pounds (in various payments). And further I give & bequeath unto my said son Henry Parks and his heirs forever, in consideration as well of the release by him to be made to my brother George Jackson of the lands in Maidstone, &c. all my messuages, houses, lands, tenements & hereditaments situate, lying and being in New England in the parts of America beyond the seas.

If my son Edward Parks, within three months next after notice given him of my death and after he shall attain the age of twenty & one years, release his part of personal estate according to purport of an indenture, dated 26 June 1640, between me the said Edward Parks, of the one part, and Thomas Westby of Fresby in the county of York, gentleman, and Edward Gell of Brimington in the county of Derby Esq., of the other part, then I give and bequeath unto the said Edward three score pounds for his preferment & placing him to apprentice. To my son John five hundred pounds within three months after he attains the age of twenty-one years, and to sons William & Stephen (the same amount with the same limitation). To daughter Elizabeth Parks five hundred pounds at twenty-one or day of marriage. To sons Thomas, Dannett, Francis & Samuel (legacies similar to their brother John's above). To Mark, Francis & Susan Wilcox, three of the children of my sister Alice Wilcox, ten pounds apiece, & to Anne Wilcox another daughter twenty pounds, to be paid, the sons at twenty-one and the daughters at that age or day of marriage. Bequeaths to the widow Brewer, to Martha Wilson now wife of Thomas Wilson, being both my late servants, to my daughter Mary, now wife of Thomas Plampin and my two grand children Thomas and Edward Plampin. Reference to lands in Hadleigh in the county of Suffolk lately bought.

My son in law Thomas Plampin and cousin John Bagnall, both of London, merchant tailors, to be my executors and my brothers Dʳ William Forth and Dannett Forth of London, woollen draper, to be overseers. A Thomas Forth a witness.

The above will was proved 29 January 1650; but the executors having died before fulfilling their trust a commission was issued 29 March 1673 to John Parkes, a son & legatee. He also died before completing his administration, and commission was issued 3 November, 1681, to Mary Cawley als Parkes, the widow relict of said defunct, &c.   Grey, 10.

[A full abstract of this will was printed in a note in Mass. Hist. Soc. Collections, 4th S., vol. vii. p. 385, from a copy obtained for me by Col. Chester. The note was appended to several letters from Edward Parks to John Winthrop, Jr. These show that Parks terms Henry Bright of Watertown his uncle. In the genealogy of the Brights of Suffolk, Eng. (Boston, 1858), we find on pp. 270–71, an abstract of the will of Mrs. Elizabeth Dell, sister of Henry Bright, in which she mentions her nephew William Parks. She also mentions her brother Henry Bright, William Forth and —— Blowers, her sister Martha Blowers, her cousin —— Cawby, Esq., and her nephew Dr. William Forth.

Henry Parks, son of Edward, sold in 1655, his land in Cambridge to John Stedman, and very probably came here for the purpose. This particular branch, however, then ceased to have any connection with New England. But at Cambridge one of the early settlers was Dea. Richard Parke, 1638–1655, whose son Thomas had a son Edward. At Roxbury was William Parke, whose will of 20 July, 1684, mentions only three daughters and their children, brother Thomas Parks of Stonington, deceased, and brother Samuel with his sons Robert and William. Savage says that these three were sons of Robert of Wethersfield and New London, who died in 1665. Very probably this Robert was the man who wrote to John Winthrop in 1629 from Easterkale in Lincolnshire (see Mass. Hist. Soc. Coll., 5th S. vol. i. p. 194), proposing to go to New England.

These *may* have been relatives of Edward Parke, who was clearly allied to Winthrop through the Forths. The family name of Dannett ought also to lead to some trace of this family.

The Alice Wilcox, sister of Edward Parks, recalls the William Wilcockes of our Cambridge, who died in 1653, leaving a widow Mary (Powell) but no children, and a sister Christian Boiden in Old England. A John Wilcox was of Dorchester, 1661, and went to Middletown. The names Wilcox, Hastings, Fox and Hall are in the Leicestershire Visitations, and Wilcox also in Rutland.—W. H. WHITMORE.]

WILLIAM GOORE of Nether Wallop in the county of Southampton gentleman, 9 November 1587. To wife Joane, eldest son William, all my land called Garlacks. To my four youngest sons Richard, John, Nicholas and William Goore the younger all my land in Newington, in the county of Wilts, and in Basingstoke, in the county of Southampton, and two hundred pounds apiece. To my four daughters Agnes, Elizabeth, Barbara and Margery Goore two hundred pounds apiece. The executors to be my eldest son William Gore and Margaret Reade, the supervisors to be John Pittman of Quarley, Thomas Elie, Clerk vicar of Nether Wallop and Leonard Elie of Wonston.

10 May 1588. Emanavit cõmissio Wilłᵐᵒ Sᵗ John armigero marito sororis naturalis et ltiñe dict def et Leonardo Elie generoso uni supervisorum &c. cum consensu Wᵐˡ Gore filii &c. durante minori etate eiusdem Willmi et Margarete Reade als Gore alterius executorum &c.

Rutland, 37.

WILLIAM GORE of Nether Wallop in the county of Southampton, gentleman, 22 January 1655, proved 29 March 1656. Wife Elizabeth to be sole executrix. To the poor of Nether Wallop three pounds to be distributed in one month after my decease. To my wife a portion of my now dwelling house at Garleggs in the parish of Nether Wallop and part of the orchard. To my cousin Richard Hamon. To Amy Singer, daughter of my late sister Margaret, and Jane Singer, another daughter, and Roger Singer, a son. To my cousin Mary Poore the now wife of John Power thirty pounds. To Nicholas & Margaret, son and daughter of my late sister Wallingford, twenty pounds apiece in one year after my decease. To my cousin Nicholas Gore, son of Nicholas Gore late of Farley deceased, ten pounds in one year. To Nicholas Hatchet of Nether Wallop five pounds in one year. My brother in law Mr Robert Sadler, my cousin John Poore and my cousin Richard Miller of Broughton. To the now five children of Richard Hamon forty pounds apiece and to William Poore and Elizabeth Poore, son & daughter of my late cousin William Poore deceased, forty pounds, and to the now children of my late cousin Thomas Singer deceased, forty pounds. To my godson Richard Sherfield, son of my late brother Roger Sherfield, gentleman, deceased. If my cousin Nicholas Wallingford shall have issue of his body or Margaret Wallingford have issue of her body then, &c. To John Gore, son of my late uncle Richard Gore. To my uncle Hugh Mundy.   Berkeley, 110.

[In these Goore wills Mr. Waters is evidently probing the connections of the ancestors of our Merrimac Valley settlers. The villages of Wallop, like those of Choulderton, lie upon the edges of the Counties of Wilts and Southampton, and when Dummer, Saltonstall and Rawson, with their English associates, had arranged for developing a stock-raising town in New England, they arranged also to secure from co. Wilts and its vicinity the transfer of a colony of practical men not only accustomed to the care of live stock, but to the trades which interlaced in the products of a stock-raising community. The matter of first importance was to secure ministers with whom the community would feel at home. Rev. Thomas Parker and his relatives the Noyes family, natives of Choulderton, were secured, and with them the Wiltshire men were glad to join.

In the will, proved 28 March, 1657, the names of many of the Poore family are mentioned as cousins of the testator, and so is Nicholas Wallingford, who came in the Confidence from Southampton in 1638, with others—Stephen Kent, John Rolfe, John Saunders, John and William Ilsley, and more recruits to join their relatives who established the town of Newbury. Joseph Poore, of Newbury, married, 6 August, 1680, Mary Wallingford, daughter of Nicholas, born 20 August, 1663. Anthony Sadler was a passenger in the same vessel. In the Visitation of co. Wilts in 1623 are pedigrees of the Sadler family on p. 63. The son and heir of the family given there is Robert Sadler, born in 1608, who may have been the person mentioned as " brother-in-law " in the will given above.

The will proved in 1588 contains an instance, not uncommon at that period, but a terrible annoyance to genealogists, of two sons having the same baptismal name— *eldest* son William, and four youngest sons, among whom is William the *younger*. The name of Margaret Read recalls the fact that the Read and Noyes family intermarried in the locality of these testators.—JOHN COFFIN JONES BROWN.]

JOSEPH BLAKE of Berkley County in the Province of South Carolina, 18 December, 1750. My whole estate to be kept together until it raises the sum of two thousand pounds sterling money of Great Britain and one thousand pounds Proclamation money, or the value thereof, in the currency of this province, exclusive of the maintenance of my sons Daniel and William and my daughter Ann Blake. After said sums are cleared—to be kept at interest and the interest applied towards educating & maintaining my sons Daniel & William and daughter Ann until they arrive at full age. Then one thousand pounds sterling to my son Daniel, the same to son William and the remaining thousand pounds Proclamation money to daughter Ann. To son Daniel the plantation I now live on called Newington and a tract of land on the Cypress Swamp lying between the lands of Mr James Postell and Barnaby Brandford, part of which I purchased of Mʳ James Postell deceased, the remainder I took up of the King; and that part of my land on Charles Town Neck which lies between the High Road and Cooper River; and fifteen hundred acres to be taken out of my lands on Cumbee River between Mᵣⁿ Hudson's land and the land I bought of Colonel William Bull, the line to run towards Calf Pen Savanah as far back as will take in the quantity of fifteen hundred acres; and a plantation containing five hundred & ninety-seven acres in two tracts bounding on Mᵣⁿ Donings and Mᵣˢ Drake to the North East and to the North West on Mᵣˢ Donings, Mᵣˢ Sacheveralls and Doctor Brisbanes, to the South West on a tract of land which was formerly Mᵣ Dowses but now mine and on Mᵣ Ways, to the South East on Mᵣ Richard Warings. To son William & his heirs forever my plantation containing more or less on Wadmelaw River and new cut, commonly called Plainsfield, lying between lands of Mᵣ John Atchinson and Mᵣ Fuller; and that part of my land on Charles Town Neck that lies between the High Road and Ashly River, bounding on Mᵣ Gadsdens, Mᵣ Hunts & Mᵣ John Humes; and two tracts of land lying between Mᵣ Atchinsons and Mᵣ Stoboes, one tract containing two hundred & thirty acres, the other seventy-six acres; and two tracts of land containing four hundred & forty acres purchased of Stephen Dowse by Mᵣⁿ Jennis, bounding on Mᵣ William Elliott, Mᵣ John Drayton & Mᵣ Graves.

I give and bequeath unto my loving daughter Rebecca Izard, to her and her heirs forever a tract of land containing eighteen hundred & seventy three acres in Granville County on the Lead of Coosaw, Hatchers and Chili Phina Swamp, bounding on James Therrs to the North West; and an Island on Port Royal River in Granville County commonly called Cat Island, containing four hundred acres. I give and bequeath to my loving daughter Ann Blake one thousand acres of land to be laid out by my executors and executrix on the Calf Pen Savanah to be taken out of my lands on Cumbee on the head of the said tracts and an island containing two hundred and eighty-six acres of land in Granville County on the North East side of Port Royal River and on all other sides on marshes and creeks out of the said River. I give all my Real estate, not already given, devised or bequeathed, unto my two sons Daniel & William Blake, all my household goods & plate to be divided between my two sons Daniel & William & my daughter Ann Blake, to each a third. To son Daniel my coach & harness and Prime Thorn, his wife Betty Molly & all their children which they have or shall have. To son William Wally Johnny Molatto Peter Mol Juda & all their children, &c. To daughter Ann Blake Lampset Nanny Patty & Molly child of Hannah & all their children, &c. All the residue of my personal estate (not already given, devised or bequeathed) unto my four children Rebeccah Izard, Daniel Blake, William Blake & Ann Blake, to be equally divided.

I nominate, &c. daughter Rebecca Izard, son Daniel Blake and son Ralph Izard executrix & executors & guardians to my children until they attain the ages of twenty-one years, &c. & to improve the estate of my said children either by putting money at Interest, buying slaves or any other way they shall judge most advantageous.

Wit: Jacob Molte, William Roper, Alexander Rigg.

Charles Town So: Carolina   Secretarys Office.

The foregoing Writing of two sheets of paper is a true copy from the Original will of the Honᵇˡᵉ Joseph Blake Esquire deceased. Examined & certified ℘ William Pinckney Depᵗʸ Secʸ.

11 February 1752 Depositions of John Ouldfield, of South Carolina, planter, & William George, freeman of South Carolina, at present residing in the city of London, gentleman.

The will was proved 20 February 1752 by Daniel Blake Esq. son, &c. &c. Power reserved for the other executors.   Bettesworth, 30.

GEORGE JONES, of the City of Philadelphia in the Province of Pennsylvania, yeoman, having a design by the Permission of the Almighty to pass over the seas, 22 September 1743. To Sarah Toms daughter of Robert Toms twenty pounds current money of Pennsylvania, to be paid her at her age of eighteen years. To Thomas Howard of the city of Philadelphia, joyner, all my right & title of & to my seat in Christ church in Philadelphia. To Mary Howard, daughter of Thomas Howard, ten pounds at age of eighteen. To Andrew Robertson, miller at Wesschicken, my horse, saddle & bridle, my watch & seal thereto affixed. To Kattrine Hinton one hundred pounds immediately after my decease, &c. provided that the said Katrine do not marry till after my decease. To Abraham Pratt, of the city of Philadelphia joyner, twenty pounds, &c. To the children of my brother James Jones deceased, of the parish of St John at Brogmore Green in the County of Worcester in Great Britain, & to my sister Elizabeth Clay, of the city of Worcester, & to her children, all the rest & remainder of my estate, Real & Personal, to be equally divided.

I do nominate & appoint Jonathan Robeson of Philadelphia Esq., Lawrence Anderson, of Philadelphia merchant, and Jacob Duchee, shopkeeper in Market Street, executors.

Wit: William Cunningham, Warwick Coats John Chapman.

14 February 1752 Admon. with the will annexed of the goods & chattells, &c. of George Jones late of the city of Philadelphia, in the Province of Pennsylvania, but at the city of Worcester deceased, lying and being in that part of Great Britain called England only but no further or otherwise, was granted to Elizabeth Clay, widow, the natural & lawful sister of the said deceased & one of the Residuary Legatees named in said will, for that Jonathan Robeson Esq., Lawrence Anderson & Jacob Duchee, the executors appointed in said will, have taken upon them the execution thereof so far as concerns that part of the estate of the said deceased within the Province of Pennsylvania, but have respectively renounced the execution of the said will and their right of administration of the said deceased's estate in that part of Great Britain called England.   Bettesworth, 39.

[Probated in Philadelphia, 1751, Book i. p. 404.—C. R. HILDEBURN, of Philadelphia.]

WILLIAM STOCKTON, Clerk, parson of Barkeswell in the County of Warwick, 2 March 1593, proved 17 June 1594 by Elizabeth his relict & executrix, through her attorney Thomas Lovell Not. Pub. The will mentions brother Randulph Stockton, brother Raphe Stockton, the children of cousin John Stockton, parson of Alcester, the children of cousin Thomas Gervise, son Jonas Stockton, eldest daughter Debora Stockton, wife Elizabeth & daughters Judith & Abigail, cousins John Stockton & Thomas Gervis and Thomas Benyon of Barkeswell yeoman, & John Massame of the city of Coventry, clothworker, to be overseers.   Dixey, 49.

[I suppose the "cousin John Stockton, parson of Alcester," mentioned in the above will, was the father of Patience, wife of Edward Holyoke of New England, whose father, John Holliock, of Alcester in the county of Warwick, mercer, made his will 21 November 30th Elizabeth (proved 31 January, 1587) in presence of John Stockton. If this be so, then Mr. Stockton must have removed before 1607 to Kinkolt in Leicestershire, where he was living (probably as Rector of that parish), as shown by a letter from young Edward Holyoke to his betrothed, dated 21 Nov. 1607. (See Emmerton & Waters's Gleanings from English Records, pp. 57–59.)—H. F. W.]

ROBERT WILCOX, the younger, of Alcester in the county of Warwick, mercer, xiiii October 1626, proved 14 February 1626. To my father M[r] Robert Wilcox, over and above the two hundred pounds due to him by bond, one hundred pounds within one year after my decease (and some chattell goods). To my son Robert fifty pounds to be put out for his best use at his age of xiiii years. My will is that Ann & Elizabeth Heath shall have x[li] between them for the money I received by their brother Richard's will. To each of my sisters xl[s]. To Humfry Bedowe x[s]. To Joane my maid servant xv[s], to Elenor my maid servant x[s]. I give x[li] to be from time to time lent gratis to honest tradesmen at the discretion of M[r] Bay-liffe for the time being, with the assent of my father Wilcox, brother Bridges, brother Holioke and M[r] Jeliffe, or of three, two or one of them so long as any of them shall live, and, after the death of the survivor of them, at the discretion of M[r] Bayliffe for the time being. To mine apprentice xx[s] at thend of his term. The rest of my goods chattells, &c. to Martha, my beloved wife, whom I make sole executrix. The overseers to be my well beloved father in law John Halford and George Jelliffe and my brother Florisell Bovey and I give them ii[s] vi[d] apiece for their pains.
Wit: Samuel Hulford, Edward Holioke. Skinner, 12.

[An article on the Wilcoxes of New England is printed in the REGISTER, xxix. 25–9, but no connection with Robert of Alcester is found. There is probably some relationship between his "brother Holioke" and Edward Holyoke, the immigrant ancestor of the Holyokes of New England, who seems to have come from Alcester (see will of Edward Holliock, 1587, in Emmerton and Waters's Gleanings, p. 57). Two other New England immigrants, William and Richard Waldern (written by descendants, Waldron), were natives of Alcester (see REG. viii. 78).—EDITOR.]

Mr. THOMAS ROPER's will. John West my servant to be set free. Alexander Gill, servant to Capt. Peirce, to be set free or else if Capt. Peirce shall refuse to release him, then that the said Alexander receive two hundred pounds of Tobacco from Capt. Peirce. I give and bequeath all tobaccoes due unto me in Virginia to my brother John Roper in England and that M[r] George Fitz Jefferyes receive it to the use of my said brother. Item a pair of Linen breeches to William Smith of James City. To the said William Smith a waistcoat. To my brother John Roper three hundred and odd pounds of good & lawful money of England, in the hands of my father in law M[r] Thomas Sheaperd of Moine in Bedfordshire. The residue to my brother John Roper. Fifty shillings in money to M[r] Haute Wyatt, minister of James City.
Wit: Haut Wyatt, William Smith, George Fitz Jefferey.
In the letter of administration (5 February 1626) to John Roper Thomas Shepard is spoken of as the natural & lawful father of John, Elizabeth and Constance Shepard, brother and sisters of the deceased on the mother's side (ex materno latere), the letters of administration granted in the month of May 1624 having been brought back and renounced.
Skinner, 11.

[According to a pedigree of the Wyatt family furnished me some years ago by Reginald Stewart Boddington, Esq., London, England, the Rev. Hawte Wyatt (a younger brother of Sir Francis Wyatt, twice governor of Virginia, married 1618, buried 24 August, 1644, at Boxley) was the second son of George and Jane (daughter of Sir Thomas Finch of Eastwell, Knight, by his wife Katherine, elder daughter and co-heiress of Sir Thomas Moyle of Eastwell) Wyat (of Allington Castle, Boxley, and in right of his wife, Lord of the Manor of Wavering, son of Sir Thomas Wyat by his wife Elizabeth, daughter of Thomas Brooke, Lord Cobham, beheaded 11 April, 1554) and Jane (married 1537), younger daughter and co-heiress of Sir William Hawte of Bishopbourne, co. Kent, Knight, and to whom Queen Mary granted the Manor of Wavering) ; inducted after his return to England to the living of Boxley, 3 October, 1632, and Rector of Merston, co. Kent; died 31 July, 1638 ; buried at Boxley.

He was married twice, " *and his issue said to have gone to Virginia.*"

The following document in my possession may be of interest in connection with the immediately preceding paragraph :

" Oct. 29, 1655. This day Pindabake the Protector of the young King of Chiskoyack was at my house [punctuation mine], intending to have spoken with the Governor, then expected to be heer'd, but he came not, & therefore hee desyned to leave his mind with mee, Maj[or] Will Wiat & divers others, as followith, viz: that Wassahickon the —— [illegible] had freely given unto Mr. Edward Wyatt and his heyres, executors, administrators or assigns, all the land from Mr. Hugh Guinn's old marked trees to Vttamarke Creeke, including all Pagan —— [illegible] high Land, being freely given, and with the consent of all the rest of the Indians, it was also agreed among them all that neither the King nor any other of his Indians should sell, alienate or dispose of any land belonging unto them without the consent of Mr. Ed. Wyatt, which was the only business that he had to acquaint the Gov'r therewith in the behalfe of Mr. Ed. Wyat, as we heere doe testify under our hands, this present 29th of October, 1655."

John West

The marke of

[mark]

Pindabake, Protector of
the young King of
Chiskoyake

Signed and sealed in the presence of
all whose names are here subscribed.

Will'm Benett
John West Junior
Toby West

The marke *[mark]* of W[m] Godfrey

The marke of *[mark]* John Talbutt
John King

I find the following grants of land to the name Wyatt and Wyat of record in the Virginia Land Registry Office : Ralph Wyatt, " Gent." Book No. 1, p. 590, lease to Richard Johnson, Roger Davis and Abraham Wood, " planters," " one parcell of Islands," 1636 ; Henry Wyat, Esq., eldest son of Sir Francis Wyat, p. 757, lease for 21 years, of 50 acres in Pasbylaiers James City county for the raising of corn for the better protection of the plantation, Dec. 16, 1641 ; Thomas Wyat, p. 916, 2000 ac. on the south side of the Rappahannock river, " twenty miles up," Sept. 24, 1643 ; George Wyatt, No. 2, p. 54, 250 acres in James City county, April 12, 1642 ; Richard Wyatt, p. 154, 500 acres in Mobjack bay, Aug. 20, 1645 ; William Wyatt, No. 3, p. 4, 400 acres in Gloucester county, April 27, 1653 ; p. 354, 300 acres in New Kent county, June 6, 1665 ; Edward Wyatt and Robert Grig, 4, p. 439, 370 acres in Kingston parish, Gloucester county, April 19, 1662 ; William Wyatt, 5, p. 286, 400 acres in Gloucester county, March 16, 1663 ; Major William Wyatt, p. 439, 1940 acres in New Kent county, May 20, 1664 ; William Wyatt, p. 453, 300 acres in New Kent county, May 20, 1664 ; Anthony Wyatt, p. 510, 282 acres in New Kent county, June 28, 1664 ; Thomas Wyatt, p. 608, 500 acres in Mobjack bay, May 9, 1666 ; William Wyatt, 6, p. 322, 500 acres in New Kent county, June 20, 1670 ; Anthony Wyatt, p. 247, 398 acres in Charles City county, July 24, 1669 ;

William Wyatt, p. 296, 2240 acres in New Kent county, April 17, 1669 ; p. 364, 1900 acres in New Kent county. Oct. 21, 1670 ; 7, p. 32, 850 acres in New Kent county, April 25, 1680 ; Henry Wyatt, p. 123, 649 acres in New Kent county, April 20, 1682 ; John and Richard Wyatt, p. 321, 650 acres in New Kent county, Sept. 20, 1683 ; Nicholas Wyatt, p. 510, 115 acres in Brandon parish [Charles City county?], April 27, 1686 ; John Wyatt, 9, p. 654, 700 acres in King and Queen county, May 2, 1705 ; James Wyatt, No. 10, p. 85, 139 in upper parish of Nansemond county, May 2, 1713 ; Richard Wyatt, p. 247, 285 acres in Charles City county, Aug. 15, 1715 ; Francis Wyatt, 23, p. 635, 377 acres in Prince George county, Nov. 25, 1743 ; Francis Wyatt and Mary Hawkins, No. 28, p. 208, 100 acres in Prince George county, Aug. 20, 1747, and in same, p. 211, 200 acres in Amelia county, Aug. 20, 1747.

Anthony Wyatt was a prominent citizen of Charles City County, Virginia, 1660–70.—R. A. BROCK, of Richmond, Va.]

NICHOLAS JUPE, citizen & merchant Taylor of London, 10 March 1650, proved 13 October 1651. To cousin Benjamin Jupe, his executers & assigns, all my moiety or half part of two houses, &c. in the parish of St Buttolph Aldgate, London, in the occupation of Richard English and Edward Mott, and the house where a stone-cutter did dwell and my own dwelling house and so much of the dwelling house as is now in Mr Finch's occupation,—which I and Richard English bought of Matthew Beanes. To the said Benjamin fifteen pounds and to his brother John & his sister Margaret five pounds apiece. To Anthony and Mary Jupe, equally between them, my half of five houses which were bought by me and the said Richard English, standing in Gravel Lane in the Parish of Saint Buttolph without Aldgate, London, being in one row or rank, they to pay, out of the profits, to Christopher Jupe & Thomas Evans ten pounds apiece within two years after my decease. I give to Simeon Smith my half of four tenements granted by lease from the Hospital of Christ Church London. To Rebecca Smith, daughter of my brother Joseph Smith, my lease of tenements in the occupation of Mr Mason & Mr Harman. To the poor of Bishopsgate, to the minister, Mr Fuller, to the poor of Aldgate. To Richard English & John Euerett & to each of their wives twenty shillings apiece, to Sarah Martin & Mrs Katherine Jackson twenty shillings apiece, to Mr Dye and his wife twenty shillings apiece, to Simeon Smith forty shillings, to Sarah Wilmott ten pounds, to Rebecca Unckles three pounds & to her mother four pounds, to my brother Christopher's daughter Mary five shillings, to my cousin Evans forty shillings, to my cousin Christopher Jupe forty shillings, to cousin John Jupe twenty shillings, to cousin Margaret Jupe twelve pounds, to Anne Foster twenty shillings, to my wife's sister Denton three pounds & to her daughter twenty shillings, to Mr Hedges & his wife twenty shillings apiece, to Edward Smith the elder and Edward Smith the younger and to Elizabeth Smith (certain legacies), to William Harper forty shillings, to Thomas Jackson twenty shillings, more to Benjamin Jupe ten pounds, more to Joseph Smith & his daughter Rebecca Smith, &c. Loving friends Mr Grimes, Richard English & John Everett to be overseers. Simeon Smith to be executor.   Grey, 189.

[At the time of the decease of the testator, the five houses in Gravel Lane above devised were in the occupation of " John Trigg senio^r m^{rs} oakeman ; widdow Izard widdow Bocken and m^r Chambe^{rs} " and the interest of the testator's niece Mary Jupe, afterward Mary Morse, therein, was conveyed with other property by her husband John Morse of Boston in New England, salt boiler, by deed of mortgage dated Nov. 9th, 1654, recorded with Suffolk Deeds, Lib. 2, fol. 180, to Capt. Robert Keaine of said Boston, uncle of said mortgagor, to secure the payment of £32. Capt. Keaine had advanced £15 to pay for the passage of Morse, his wife and his wife's brother, Benjamin Jupe, from New England back to Old England, and the latter sum was to be paid at the Golden Crown in Birchin Lane, London, on or before April 26, 1655, out of the rents belonging to the said wife or brother Benjamin Jupe remaining in the hands of Simeon Smith of Southwark. the executor of the foregoing will, as appears by a bond and order recorded fol. 183 and 184. See also fol. 86 and 182. See note to the will of Benjamin Kaine (*ante*, page 2). See also the abstract made by Stanley Waters of an indenture, found by him in the Suffolk Court Files, dated March 10, 1652, " between Benjamin Kayen of London Esquire, sonne and heire apparent of Robert Kayen of Boston in N. E., Esquire, on the one part, and Simeon Smith, Cittizen and Haberdasher, of London, the executor of the last will &c. of Nicholas Jupe, Cittizen & Marchant Tayler of London, deceased, of the other part." This abstract was published in the REGISTER for July, 1881 (xxxv. 277).—JOHN T. HASSAM.]

FRANCIS NEWTON of London, grocer, 24 August 1660, proved 11 January 1661, now bound out on a voyage to Virginia. To wife Mary Newton six hundred pounds within six months after my decease. The residue to my loving sisters Elizabeth and Susan Newton and loving brother Joseph Newton, equally, &c. Friends John Berry, Anthony Stanford & Joseph Wilson to be executors. Laud, 8.

[See note " Newton of Kingston upon Hull, England," REG. April, 1885, p. 194.—R. A. BROCK.]

RICHARD SMITH, of S*t* Dunstan's West, London, Cook, 13 January 1660, proved 17 January 1661. To be buried in the parish church of S*t* Dunstans in the West. Wife Joane, brother John Smith. To my sister Ann Hawthorne five acres in the possession of John Alley, butcher, of the yearly value of five pounds for her natural life, &c. and then to her two sons John & Nathaniel Hawthorne and their heirs equally. To my brother John Smith the reversion I purchased (after the decease of Anne Henman, widow) of William Backhouse Esq., with remainder to his eldest son Samuel Smith & his heirs male, next to Richard Smith, second son of said brother John, then to the right heirs of the body of the said John Smith. I give and bequeath to William Hawthorne, son of Anne Hawthorne, my sister, the reversion of one pightle called Leachrye or Tan-house Pightle, containing by estimation three acres, in the possession of John Vincent. One third part of land called Welshman's (after my wife's decease) to my loving sister Mary Holloway and the heirs of her body, one third to my loving sister Rachel Horton & the heirs of her body, the remaining third to the children of John Topping begot upon the body of my sister Prudence and their heirs. To my wife the lease or leases of the two houses in Chancery Lane, &c. To my loving friend Mr Robert Hawe of Wokeingham twenty shillings to buy him a ring. To M*r* —— Sedgwick, without Temple Bar, ten shillings to buy him a ring. To the poor of the town of Wokeingham twenty shillings. To the poor of the parish of Wokeingham and dwelling in the said town twenty shillings. Lands, &c. in Wokeingham in the County of Berks. Brother John Smith to be executor & Richard Palmer of Wokeingham Esq. to be overseer.

Wit : L. Astry, George Chapman. Laud, 9.

[The Salem Hathornes, as well as the Hawthornes named above, were allied with a Smith family, the immigrants, William and John Hathorne (REG. xii. 295 ; Emmerton and Waters's Gleanings, pp. 52–5) having had a sister Anne who was the wife of Hugh Smith (*ante*, pp. 43–5).—EDITOR.]

HENRY SEWALL of the parish of S*t* Michael in the city of Coventry, alderman, aged fourscore years or thereabouts, 1 Sept. 1624, proved the last of June 1628 by Margaret Sewall his relict and executrix. To my wife Margaret an annuity or yearly rent charge of eleven pounds, eight shillings, issuing out of certain lands in Ansley in the county of Warwick, granted to me & my heirs forever, and now in the tenure of Elizabeth Throckmorton widow, and all my lands, tenements and hereditaments, with the appurtenances, &c. in the city of Coventry & in Corley and Coundon in the County of Warwick and in Radford Coundon in Urchenfield & Stoke in the county of the city of Coventry. To Henry Sewall, my eldest son, all my lands, tenements and hereditaments, &c. &c. in the hamlet of Radford in the county of the city of Coventry and in Coundon in Urchenfield in the county of the city of Coventry and in Coudon in the County of Warwick, and all my lands, tenements & hereditaments, &c. in Dog Lane in the said city, in the occupation of Richard Baldwyn, a messuage or tenement & one garden, with the appurtenances, in Much Park Street, in Coventry, in the tenure of Henry Critchlowe, draper, and all those messuages or tenements, &c. &c. in the said city in the several occupations of John Harbert, William Heyward, Richard Heyes or Walter Wiggens, and all those three tenements in Little Park Street, in the occupation of Mr Henry Davenport, —— Thorton, Katherine West, or their assigns, after the decease of my wife Margaret, and during his natural life ; then to the heirs of his body lawfully begotten, &c. ; also to the said Henry, my son, a tenement & garden, &c. &c. in Heylane in the said city, in the tenure of Bryan Conigrave.

To Richard Sewall, my younger son, after the decease of my wife Margaret, lands & tenements, &c. in Corley, in the county of Warwick, which I lately purchased of Stephen Hales Esq. with the wyndell thereupon now standing, and other lands, &c. purchased of Richard Patchett, of Martin Whadocke & of Thomas Nicklyn and of Thomas Barre ; also to the same Richard one messuage, &c. in Smithford Street, Coventry, in the tenure of Jefford, barber, and a tenement & certain stables called the Sextree in Coventry.

To my daughter Anne, now the wife of Anthonie Power, my messuage & tenement, &c. &c. in Corley, now in the occupation of me the said Henry, which I lately purchased of Daniel Oxenbridge, and other lands, &c. purchased of Thomas Patchet & of George & Walter Holbech, and two tenements in Bailie Lane in Coventry, one in the tenure of Theophilus Washington, and a messuage in High Street, Coventry, in the tenure of Mr William Hancock, and a messuage in the suburbs of Coventry in the tenure of John Lindon, and a messuage in the tenure of Roger Bird and a tenement in the tenure of Joyce Hobson, a widow and late in the occupation of Lawrence Armeson.

To Margaret, my youngest daughter, now the wife of Abraham Randell, tenements without Newgate in the several tenures of Francis Robinson & Edward Coles, lands, &c. purchased of John Horne of Stoke, gentleman, lands in the tenure of John Wilkinson, & of William, or Thomas, Pywall, that my messuage or tenement & garden in Bailie Lane, in the city of Coventry wherein I now dwell, tenements, &c. in Bailie Lane in the occupation of Roger Dudley, James Knib, William Miller, Edward Malpas, Johane Newland, widow, William Cumberledge & Edward Bissaker, a tenement in Earl Street in the occupation of John Wright, a garden in the occupation of Mr Richard Clarke, a tenement I purchased of John Hammond, Doctor in Physick and tenements in Darbie lane in the occupation of the widow Wothon & the widow Kinsman. Reference also made to tenements in the occupation of Richard Faulkner, Raphe Mellowes, Peter

Baxter, Henry Wetton, Randall Cleaver, Clerk, Thomas Hobson and John Hill. To my loving friend Humphry Burton forty shillings, &c. &c. Wife Margaret to be executrix and friends Mᵣ William Hancock, of Coventry, alderman, and my loving kinsman Reginald Horne, gentleman, to be over-seers. To my cousin John Horne a cloke cloth.

Wit: John Brownell, James Brownell.   Barrington, 63.

[The eldest son of the testator of the above will, Mr. Henry Sewall, came over to New England and was the ancestor of the distinguished family of that name in Massachusetts. In Essex County Court Papers (Book **xxvi**. No. 59) may be found a deposition made 10 April, 1679, by Robert Walker, of Boston, Linen webster, aged about seventy-two years, in which he testified that about fifty-six years before, living with his father in the town of Manchester, in Lancashire, within the realm of England, he did then know one Mr. Henry Sewall who lived at the same town and in the same street with the deponent's father, being his overthwart neighbor, and that afterwards the said Mr. Henry Sewall removed with his family to New England, and there dwelt in the town of Newbury, &c. &c.   H. F. WATERS.

This will furnishes another example of the wisdom of the course pursued by the associated collection and publication of material of this kind. In the introduction to the Sewall Papers, now in course of publication by the Mass. Historical Society, after stating the investigations made by Col. Chester, the main results of whose search was placed in their hands, the editors state that the Sewall family cannot be traced beyond the two brothers (Henry, whose will is here given, and his brother William, both of whom had been mayors of Coventry in England). It is to be supposed that neither the editors nor Col. Chester had the detail which Mr. Waters furnishes your readers, for in the closing paragraphs of the will here given, the mention of his "loving kinsman Reginald Horne, gentleman," who was made an overseer of the will, and the bequest to his " cousin John Horne," furnish direct guides to obtain the name of the father of Henry and William Sewall. It ap-pears from the pedigree of the Horne family, which is given below from the Visitation of Warwickshire, 1619 (see Harleian Soc. Pub., vol. xii. p. 343),* that William Shewell married Matilda Horne, and that her brother John was the father of both Reginald and John, who are mentioned in this will of Henry Sewall respectively as his "kinsman" and " cousin."

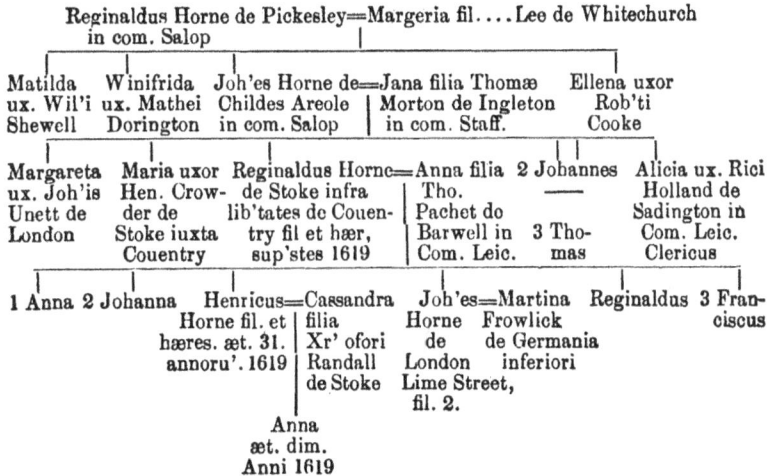

Reginaldus Horne de Pickesley═Margeria fil....Lee de Whitechurch
in com. Salop

Matilda	Winifrida	Joh'es Horne de═Jana filia Thomæ	Ellena uxor
ux. Wil'i	ux. Mathei	Childes Areole | Morton de Ingleton	Rob'ti
Shewell	Dorington	in com. Salop | in com. Staff.	Cooke

Margareta	Maria uxor	Reginaldus Horne═Anna filia	2 Johannes	Alicia ux. Rici
ux. Joh'is	Hen. Crow-	de Stoke infra | Tho.	——	Holland de
Unett de	der de	lib'tates de Couen- | Pachet do		Sadington in
London	Stoke iuxta	try fil et hær, | Barwell in	3 Tho-	Com. Leic.
	Couentry	sup'stes 1619 | Com. Leic.	mas	Clericus

1 Anna	2 Johanna	Henricus═Cassandra	Joh'es═Martina	Reginaldus	3 Fran-
		Horne fil. et | filia	Horne Frowlick		ciscus
		hæres. æt. 31. | Xr' ofori	de de Germania		
		annoru'. 1619 | Randall	London inferiori		
		| de Stoke	Lime Street,		
			fil. 2.		

Anna
æt. dim.
Anni 1619

Judge Samuel Sewall was always sharp in money matters, from the time when he received the dowry upon his marriage with the mint-master's daughter until his

* Was John Horne (otherwise Orne), of Salem, descended from this Warwickshire family ?

death, and whether his visit to his relatives was one of affection or for mercenary motives, it is plain that if he could get an honest penny, he went for it. He evidently had a full copy of this will, and displayed this paragraph from it in his Diary, under date of April 9, 1689 :

" To the said Margaret during her natural Life and after her decease to the Heirs of her Body issuing, and for want of such issue of her body, to remain to the right heirs of me, the said Henry the Testator, for ever."

This extract is followed by a memorandum of the date of Margaret Randall's will, May 4, 1646. If this will could be found it might throw some light upon other relations.

The Judge saw some of the real estate which had been left to his grandfather's sister Margaret, *with the above proviso*, and she had given it to the descendants of her sister Anne, ignoring the rights of the descendants of Henry, her brother, the grandfather of the judge. He told them who he was, and offered to confirm the right (for a consideration?), and he received the emphatic answer that his relatives would not give him 3d. for it.   JOHN COFFIN JONES BROWN.]

NOELL MEW being intended by God's permission to go to old England, 3 August, 1691, proved 4 April, 1700. To my wife Mary Mew, during her widowhood, all my estate, real and personal. But if she sees cause to marry, then she is to have out of my estate in England one hundred and ten pounds sterling in lieu of her dowry, in one year after her marriage, and all the household stuff. To my son Richard Mew all my farm Rockey Farm, &c., with the mulatta boy called George and fifty pounds sterling, he paying each of his sisters five pounds per annum to help bring them up till of age or married, and then to be acquitted of the said payment. To him also my great bible and silver tankard. To my daughter Mary Mew one hundred pounds sterling, &c., an Indian girl called Jenny, one Spanish silver cup, one round silver cup, one silver dram cup with a funnel. To my daughter Patience one hundred pounds sterling, the negro woman Bess, six silver spoons. All my land in West Jarsey to be sold and the proceeds to be equally divided betwixt my said three children. My wife to be executrix and my friends William Allen, Benjamin Newberry and Peleg Sanford to be overseers.

Wit : Richard Jones, Joseph Blydenburgh, Thomas Roberts, William Cload.

Testimony, 22 December, 1692, that the above is a true copy. John Easton Gov[r], John Greene Dep. Gov[r], Walter Clarke, Benjamin Newberry, William Allen, Christopher Almy. In the Probate the testator is called Noell Mew late of Newport in the Colony of Rhode Island and Providence plantations, in New England, deceased.   Noel, 59.

[Richard Mew, of Stepney, merchant, was one of the first twelve proprietors of East Jersey, 1681 (N. J. Archives, i. 366, 383 *et seq.*). Richard Mew, of Newport, R. I., merchant, had an action at law against Jahleel Brenton in 1708. (R. I. Colonial Records, iv. 39. See also iii. 555.)—EDITOR.]

NATHANIEL WEBB of Mountserrett, merchant ——, proved by Robert Webb, Esq., his son, 26 March, 1741. I grant full power and authority to my executors to make & execute a lease to my beloved wife Jane of all my negroes on and belonging to a certain plantation in the parish of S[t] Anthony in the said Island, commonly called Carrolls Plantation, with the house & lands in town (and sundry movables) for her natural life, she paying to my executors in trust for my children the yearly sum of two hundred and fifty pounds sterling. This in full satisfaction of her dower, also the use of half my house in the town of Taunton one half of the furniture, &c. To my eldest son Robert my estate in the County of Somerset formerly under lease to John & Richard Barber of Taunton, and all my houses and lands in said Taunton or elsewhere in England, and five thousand pounds sterling, &c. To my son Nathaniel my plantations in Mountserratt now under lease to John Dyer of the said island, and all my houses & lands in the said island, and my house and land in the town of Bassterre in the island of S⁺ Christophers. Item I give & bequeath to my son John all my lands in the County of Connecticut in New England near the town of Seabrook, they containing about five hundred acres. To my brother John Webb of Abington one hundred pounds sterling, at the same time forgiving him what he owes me. To my brother Harry Webb fifty guineas to buy him a mourning ring. To my executors ten guineas each to buy them mourning rings. To my sisters Anne Stone & Sarah Smith twenty pounds sterling each to buy them mourning & mourning rings. The rest & residue to my five children, Robert, Ann, Ruth, Nathaniel & John.

I appoint William Gerrish, Esq., in London, Isaac Hobhouse of Bristol, merchant, John Paine of Taunton, mercer, Dominick Trant, Thomas Meade, George French and Peter Lee of this Island, Harry Webb of Antigua and my son Robert Webb executors & the guardians of my children.

Spurway, 78.

BENJAMIN PLUMMER of Portsmouth in the Province of New Hampshire in New England Esq. 7 May, 1740, proved 12 March, 1740. To my esteemed friend Mrs Mary Macphederis my gold watch, my negro boy named Juba and a ring of five guineas price. To Theodore Atkinson Esq. my saddle Horse and to him & his wife each of them a gold ring. To M⁺ John Loggin one suit of mourning apparel. The whole of my apparel to be sold for the most they will fetch in the town of Boston. To my honored mother one hundred pounds sterling. The residue to be equally divided amongst my brothers. My brother M⁺ Thomas Plummer of London, merchant & Theodore Atkinson of Portsmouth Esq. to be the executors.

Wit: Arthur Browne, James Jeffrey, Jos⁺ Peirce.

Proved at London by Thomas Plummer, power reserved for Theodore Atkinson the other executor.

Spurway, 73.

[I extract the following from a letter to me from Miss Plumer, of Epping, N. H., dated Nov. 1, 1885, in reply to an inquiry about Benjamin Plumer: "In a note at the end of my father's manuscript genealogy of the Plumer family, my father writes, ' Benjamin Plumer was appointed collector of Piscataway in New England. His commission, of which I have a copy in the handwriting of R. Waldron, Sec⁺, is dated Feb. 11, 1736. It was sworn to before Gov. Belcher, June 8th, 1736. He was perhaps the progenitor of the Portsmouth Plumers. There is a silver vase in the Atkinson family on which is inscribed the deaths of various persons, among the rest that of Benjamin Plumer, Esquire, who died May 8th, 1740, aged 24 years. If this was the collector he was but twenty when appointed.' "—*Com. by George Plumer Smith, Esq., of Philadelphia, Pa.*

In the New Hampshire Provincial Papers, vol. iv. p. 864, is a letter from John Thomlinson to Theodore Atkinson, dated "London, 5 April, 1737." Mr. Thomlinson writes: " Altho the Bearer Mr. Plummer his coming over Collector in your place may be some Disadvantage or Disappointment to you, yet when I tell you I dare say he will prove the most agreeable Gentleman that you could have had, in every respect, you will excuse my here recommending him to your friendship. .... He is a gentleman of good sense and of a very good family and good circumstances." I presume that Plumer was an Englishman.—EDITOR.]

Notes on Abstracts previously printed.

NATHANIEL PARKER (*ante*, p. 8).

[" My god-daughter the daughter of my nephew Bernard Saltingstall."
The pedigree of the Saltonstall family, given in Bond's Watertown, shows that
Bernard Saltonstall was a great-grandson of Gilbert Saltonstall, from whom the
New England family descended, through Sir Richard of Huntwicke. The Bernard
Saltonstall referred to in the will was son of Sir Richard Saltonstall of North Ock-
enden, co. Essex. Susanna, sister of Bernard, married William Pawlett of Cottles
in co. Wilts, who was a grandson of William Pawlett, first Marquis of Winchester.
(See Dr. Marshall's Visitation of co. Wilts, 1623, p. 92.)
                                      JOHN COFFIN JONES BROWN.]

RICHARD PERNE ; RACHEL PERNE (*ante*, pp. 59–61 and 89).

[It was noticed in Rachel Perne's will that she cut off Edward Rawson, our faithful Colonial Secretary, with the proverbial shilling, although she bequeathed to
Rachel, his wife and her daughter, £40.
  By a deed of his recorded in Suffolk Deeds. vol. iii. pp. 413 and 414, he acknow-
ledges receipt of a marriage " portion of £300, which he long since Received with
his wife." This accounts for the omission to bequeath any more of the Perne estate to him on its final distribution by will.   JOHN COFFIN JONES BROWN.]

DOROTHY LANE of London, widow, 17 January, 1605. My body to be
buried in the parish church or churchyard of St Dunstans in the East, London, where I am a parishioner. To Susan Harrys, daughter of my late son
in law William Harrys, late of Wapping in the County of Middlesex, mariner deceased, and of Dorothie my daughter, late his wife, ten pounds. To
George Stake, son of my late sister Elizabeth, thirty shillings. To my cousin
Jeffery Thorowgood twenty shillings. To my cousin Bennet Burton twenty
shillings. To my cousins Elizabeth and Sara Quaitmore, daughters of
Rowland Quaytmore and of my said daughter Dorothie, his now wife, five
pounds apiece. To the said Rowland Quaytmore, my son in law, thirty
shillings to make him a ring. To Helen Averell, late wife of William Averell, Schoolmaster, deceased, my small joyned chair with a back. To the
said Dorothie Quaytmore,* my daughter, and William Harrys, her son, and
to the heirs of the said William Harrys, the son, lawfully begotten, all those
my two tenements and two acres in Saffron Walden in the County of Essex,
which late were Symon Burton's, my late brother's deceased, the said
Dorothie Quaytmore & William Harrys her son to pay out to Samuel
Harrys, son of my said daughter Dorothie Quaytmore, ten pounds upon
reasonable request, within two months next after such day or time as the
said Samuel Harrys shall attain and come to the lawful age of twenty-one
years, and unto Jane and Joane Burton, daughters of my said late brother
Symon Burton of Saffron Walden aforesaid, five pounds apiece within four
years next after such day or time as my said daughter Dorothie & William
her son or her heirs or assigns shall first enter and enjoy the said two tenements, &c. To Susan & Dorothie Harrys, daughters of my said daughter Dorothie Quaytmore (certain bequests). To Mary Quaytmore five
pounds. To my cousin Elizabeth Quaytmore (certain table linen) and to
Sara Quaytmore her sister (a similar bequest). To Mary & Sara Thorowgood, daughters of my cousin Jeffery Thorowgood, twenty shillings. To
Richard Weech of London, merchant, twenty shillings. The residue to my
daughter Dorothie and she and the above named William Harrys the son
appointed full & sole executors. The said Jeffery Thorowgood & Richard

* Rowland Coitmore and Dorothy Harris (widow) married at Whitechapel, co. Mid. 28
March, 1594–5. Elizabeth, their daughter, bapt. 25 Feb. 1595–6.—I. J. GREENWOOD.

Weech appointed overseers. To my cousin Walter Gray five shillings, and to his wife my stuff gown lined with furr.

The witnesses were William Jones, Scr., Jeffery Thorowgood, signum Roberti Powell, shoemaker, and me Richard Perne.

Commission was issued 4 March 1608 to Dorothie Quaytmore, with power reserved for William Harrys, the other executor, &c.

Dorsett, 23.

THOMAS RAINBOROWE of East Greenwich in the County of Kent, mariner, 4 December 1622, proved 23 February 1623. My body to be buried in the church yard of East Greenwich with such solemnity as my executors in their discretion shall think fit. My wife Martha and eldest son William Rainborowe to be executors. Ten pounds to be given for the putting forth of poor children of the parish of Greenwich aforesaid, &c. To said Martha my wife all my plate and household stuff and the furniture of my house and also my one sixteenth part of the good ship called the Barbara Constance of London and my one sixteenth of the tackle, apparel, munition, furniture, freight, &c. of the said ship. To my said son William two hundred pounds within one year next after my decease, and one sixteenth of the good ship Rainbowe of London & one sixteenth of her tackle, &c., one sixteenth of the ship Lilley of London (and of her tackle, &c.), one forty eighth part of the ship Royal Exchange of London (and of her tackle, &c.). To my son Thomas Rainborowe two hundred pounds within one year, &c. To my daughter Barbara Lee two hundred pounds within one year, &c. To my daughter Martha Wood two hundred pounds within one year, &c. To my daughter Sara Porte two hundred pounds within one year, &c.

Whereas I have taken of the Right Honorable Edward Lord Dennie, Baron of Waltham Holy Cross in the County of Essex, by Indenture of Lease bearing date the eight and twentieth day of September Anno Domini 1619, a capital messuage called by the name of Claver Hambury and certain lands, with their appurtenances, situate, lying & being in the said County of Essex, for the term of two and twenty years, &c. and for and under the yearly rent of a peppercorn, &c.; for which said lease I have paid to the said Lord Denny the sum of two thousand three hundred pounds of currant English money; and the said messuage and lands, &c. are worth yearly in rent (de claro) two hundred and twenty pounds or thereabouts, &c. &c. it is my will that there shall be paid out of the rents, profits, &c. to Martha my wife one annuity or annual rent of one hundred pounds, to my son William an annuity, &c. of twenty pounds, to my son Thomas an annuity, &c. of twenty pounds, to my daughter Barbara Lee an annuity, &c. of twenty pounds, to my daughter Martha Wood an annuity, &c. of twenty pounds, to my daughter Sara Port an annuity, &c. of twenty pounds.

The residue of my personal property to my two executors to be divided equally, part and part alike. My dwelling house and lands in East Greenwich shall be sold by my executors for the most profit they can & within as short time after my death as conveniently may be, and of the money arising therefrom one third shall go to my wife Martha, one third to my son William and the other third to my said four other children, Thomas, Barbara, Martha & Sara.

The witnesses were J. W. the mark of John Wotton, of the precinct of St Katherine's, mariner, John Woodward, Not. Pub., and John Brooke his servant.

Byrde, 8

ANTHONY WOOD of Redrith in the county of Surrey, mariner, 13 August 1625, proved at London 3 January 1625 by the oath of Martha Wood his relict and executrix. To wife Martha all my lease &c. in my now dwelling house in Redrith & my part of the good ship Exchange of London & of the Charity of London. To son Richard all my portion of the good ship Rainbow of London & my adventure in her &c. To my sons Richard, Thomas & Anthony five hundred pounds apiece, & to my daughter Sara five hundred pounds, at one & twenty. To my brother John Wood five pounds a year for eighteen years. To my mother Raynborrowe three pounds for a ring. To my brother William Raynborowe five pounds for a cloak. To my brother Francis Port three pounds for a ring. To my brother Thomas Lee three pounds. To my brother Thomas Raynborowe three pounds. To my uncle William Wood & his wife four pounds, for & in remembrance of tokens of my love unto them. I give to my said wife all my lease of certain lands at Waltham which I have & hold from the Lord Denny, &c. My said wife & my said son Richard to be full & sole executors &c., and I name & appoint overseers of this my will my loving friends the wor[ll] Henry Garway & William Garwaye of London merchants.

A codicil made Tuesday the 23[d] of August A.D. 1625 revokes the bequest of his portion of the ship Rainbow to son Richard & bequeaths it to Martha Wood his wife.   Hele, 4.

ROWLAND COYTEMORE of Wapping in the County of Middlesex, mariner, 5 June, 1626, proved 24 November 1626 by Katherine Coytemore, relict and executrix. To son Thomas Coytemore and his heirs, &c. the messuage or tenement, lands, hereditaments and appurtenances in the manor of Milton in the parish of Prittlewell *als*. Pricklewell, in the County of Essex, now in the tenure and occupation of John Greene, &c. and my farm and copyhold land of forty four acres or thereabouts, in the parish of Great Bursted in the County of Essex; wife Katherine to have the use and rents until my son Thomas shall accomplish his age of one and twenty years. To my daughter Elizabeth Coytemore three score pounds at her age of one and twenty years or day of marriage, also the tenement or messuage known by the sign of the Blewboare in the town or parish of Retchford, in the County of Essex, now in the tenure of William Ashwell *als*. Hare. To my son in law Thomas Gray* and his heirs my two copyhold tenements, &c. in Rederith *als*. Rederiff, in the County of Surrey, now in the several occupations of Francis Welby and John Moore. If my children and children's children die before they accomplish their several ages of one and twenty or be married, then my aforesaid lands shall remain, come and be unto my kinsman Hugh Hughs *als*. Gwyn, my sister Elizabeth's son. To my grandson William Ball, son of William Ball, forty shillings. To my daughter in law daughter Dorothy Lamberton forty shillings. To the poor of Wapping three pounds and to the poor of the Upper Hamlet of Whitechapel forty shillings. To the masters of Trinity House, for their poor, ten pounds within one year, &c.

My wife Katherine to be executrix and sons in law Thomas Gray and William Rainsborough of Wapping aforesaid, mariners, to be overseers. The witnesses were Raphe Bower pub. scr. and John Wheatley serv[t] to the said scr.   Hele, 125.

* See Gray and Coytmore Families, REG. xxxiv. 253.—ED.

MARTHA RAINBOROWE of the parish of St Bridget als. Brides, near Fleet St. London, widow, late wife of Thomas Rainborowe, late of East Greenwich in the county of Kent, mariner, deceased, made her will 29 November 1626, proved 23 September 1631. In it she referred to her husband's will & the lease of the messuage called Claverhambury and the disposition of its rents, bequeathed her own annuity among her five children, devised to her daughter Barbara Lee her sixteenth part of the good ship called Barbara Constance and gave the residue of her goods, chattels, &c. to her said daughter Barbara, wife of Thomas Lee, citizen & armorer of London, whom also she appointed sole executrix.

The witnesses were Robert Woodford, Thomas Turner and Tho: Eastwood.   St John, 102.

WILLIAM RAINBOROW of London Esq. 16 July 1638, with codicil of 1 February 1642, proved 8 April 1642. To the Hamlet of Wapping as a stock for their poor fifty pounds ; to the Hamlet of Whitechapel ten pounds, &c. To the Trinity House fifty pounds, with the condition that they give to poor seamen or their widows of the Hamlet of Wapping, every St. Thomas Day, forty shillings. To my eldest son Thomas Rainborowe all those my houses in Southwark purchased of Mr William Gambell and some of them lately built. To my son William Rainborowe those my houses in Gun Alley in Wapping purchased of my father in law Renold Hoxton and also one thousand pounds. To my son Edward twelve hundred pounds. Item I give and bequeath to my daughter Martha Coytmore, the wife of Thomas Coytmore now in New England, the sum of seven hundred pounds, if she be alive at the time of my death. To my daughter Judith Rainborowe one thousand pounds & to my daughter Joane Rainborowe one thousand pounds. All this to be paid to them, by my executors, at their several days of marriage or at their age of one and twenty years, and those that be of age at six months after my decease. To the four sons and one daughter of my deceased sister Sara Port, namely Robert, John, Thomas, William and Martha Porte, two hundred and fifty pounds, that is to each fifty pounds, at twenty one. To my brother Mr Thomas Rainborowe fifty pounds. To my sister Buckridge fifty pounds. To my sister Wood fifty pounds. To my father in law Renold Hoxton and to my mother in law Joane Hoxton ten pounds apiece to buy them each a ring. My executors to be my loving sons Thomas and William Rainborowe and I appoint them to bring up my younger children to their age of twenty one years or day of marriage and to have the tuition of them and be at the charges of meat & drink & clothes & learning. For overseers I desire my loving brothers in law Mr Robert Wood and Mr John Hoxton to have a care that this my will be fulfilled and do give them twenty pounds apiece for their pains. Witnesses Robert Wood and William Ashley.

To my mother in law Jone Hoxton my house at Wapping now in the occupation of Mr Sander Bence, during her natural life, toward her maintenance. To my grand child William Rainborowe one hundred pounds.

Codicil. Whereas the said William Rainborowe hath by his will given to Martha Port fifty pounds the said William Rainborow did about a year since and at other times afterwards declare his mind and will to be that the said Martha should not have or expect the said legacy because he had given her the sum of ten pounds and all her wedding clothes in marriage with William Ashley. Subscribed by witnesses 1 February 1641.

Witnesses to the codicil, John Hoxton, Thomas Hoxton & Mary Bennfes.   Campbell, 51.

STEVEN WINTHROP of James Street, Westminster, Esq., 3 May 1658, proved 19 August, 1658. To wife Judith the house wherein I now dwell, with the house adjoining, lately erected, for her life, and then to all my children. All the rest to my daughters Margaret, Joanna and Judith and such child or children as my said wife shall now be great withall. To my nephew Adam Winthrop, son of my brother Adam Winthrop deceased ; to the children of my brother Deane Winthrop; to my brother Samuel Winthrop's children ; to my half brother John Winthrop's children ; to my cousin Mary Rainborowe daughter of my brother in law William Rainborowe Esq.; to my cousin Judith Chamberlaine, daughter of my brother in law John Chamberlaine Esq.—sundry bequests. " To the poor of Boston in New England one hundred pounds of lawfull money of England upon Condition that the Inhabitants of Boston aforesaid doe build and erect a Tombe or Monument, Tombes or Monuments, for my deceased ffather and Mother upon their graue or graues of ffifftie pounds value att the least, whoe now lyeth buried att Boston aforesaid, according to the Loue and honour they bore to him and her in theire life time." The executors to be my wife Judith Winthropp, my brother in law John Chamberlaine Esq. and Thomas Plampyon, gentleman.

The witnesses were Leo: Chamberlaine, Elizabeth Baldrey and Clement Ragg (by mark).   Wootton, 418.

[In Suffolk Registry of Deeds (Book 8, p. 193) may be found record of conveyance made by Judith Winthrop and John Chamberlain, executors of Stephen Winthrop, 20 April, 1671, to Edward Rainborow of London, of all the said Winthrop's land in New England, consisting of one half of Prudence Island and fifteen hundred acres in Lynn or Salem, &c. This latter property included the well known Pond Farm (Lynnfield), originally granted to Colonel John Humfrey.—H. F. W.

In addition to the ten letters of Stephen W., printed in Part IV. of the Winthrop Papers (5 Mass. Hist. Coll., viii. pp. 199-218) we have found several others, but they are of no importance. Before his final return to England he was Recorder of Boston and a Representative; and, but for the failure of his health caused by sleeping on the damp ground, there is reason to believe Cromwell would have made him one of his generals, as Roger Williams, writing to John Winthrop, Jr., in 1656, says, " Your brother Stephen succeeds Major-General Harrison." By his own desire he was buried with his ancestors at Groton in Suffolk, where were also interred a number of his children, most of whom died young. Only two daughters are known with certainty to have survived him : *Margaret*, who married 1st, Henry Ward, and 2d, Edmund Willey, R. N., and had issue ; and *Joanna*, who married Richard Hancock, of London, and died s. p. During his military service his wife resided partly at Groton and afterwards at Marylebone Park near London, a portion of which estate he had purchased. This gave rise to an absurd tradition, perpetuated in some pedigrees of the last century, that the Winthrops were " of Marylebone Park *before* they settled in Suffolk." Besides his house in James Street, Westminster, he owned, at the time of his death, his father's house in Boston, on the southerly portion of which estate the Old South Church now stands ; this was subsequently sold by his widow, but whether she ever returned to New England I do not know. My kinsman Robert Winthrop, of New York, has a portrait (of which I have a copy) of a young officer of the Stuart period, which has been in our family for generations, and is called " Colonel Stephen Winthrop, M.P." If authentic, it must have either been sent by him as a present to his father before his death, or subsequently procured by his brother John, or his nephew Fitz-John, during their residence in England.—R. C. WINTHROP, JR.]

THOMAS RAINBOROWE of East Greenwich in the County of Kent, gentleman, 24 November, 1668, proved 2 January 1671 by Mary Rainborowe, his widow & executrix. To wife Mary, for life, an annuity bought of Ralph Buskin of Oltham in the County of Kent Esq. one bought of Edward Turner of East Greenwich, gentleman, and all my other goods, moneys, &c.

She to be executrix and to pay two hundred pounds (on a bond which testator made to his mother*). I give to my brother's son Edward Rainborowe twenty pounds, to my brother's daughter Judith Winthrop twenty pounds and to my said brother's daughter Joane Chamberlaine fifty pounds. To the poor of East Greenwich ten pounds. The witnesses were William Richardson & John Fuller. *Eure*, 7.

[The following notes on the Rainsborough family, collected some years ago, will throw light on Mr. Waters's abstracts:

1537.—Reynold Ravynsbye, freeman of the Co. of Cloth Workers, London.

1598.—Roger Rainseburye of Stawley, co. Somerset. Will dated July 24, proved Aug. 23, 1598. Bequeaths to the poor of Kettleford 3-4. To the poor of Ashbrittle 3-4. To his goddaughter Agnes Gover 20s. To each of his other godchildren, not named, 4d. To Edward Blackaller his wife's godson 20s. Residue to wife Honor, whom he appoints executrix, and her friends John Gover and William Golde overseers.—*Book Lewyn*, fo. 68.

1603.—Nicholas Rainbury of Stawley. Will dated April 19, 1603; proved May 4, 1611. To the poor of Stawley the interest of £10,—to be used in keeping them at work. To each of his godchildren, not named, 6s. To Mary, dau. of Richard Wyne 20s. To each of the children of John Grover 12d. To the poor of Ashbrittle 10s. To the poor of Kettleford 5s. To each of the ringers 12d. To Parson John Blackealler 10s. Residue to his sister-in-law Honour Rainsbury, whom he appoints executrix, and William Golde and John Gover, overseers.—*Book Wood*, fo. 46.

Stanleigh or Stowley, Kittesford and Ashbuttel, all in Milverton Hundred.

1615.—Henry Raygnesburye of Culmstock, co. Devon, husbandman. Will dated Feb. 8, 1615; proved March 9, 1615. To his son Henry £60. To daughter Alice R. £80, to be paid to her uncle Christopher Baker, clothier, for her use. To George, son of Andrew Bowreman 10s. To each of his godchildren, not named, 12d. To the poor 20s. Residue to wife Susan whom he appoints executrix.—*Book Cope*, fo. 29.

During the Protectorate the Baker family held the Manor of Columbstock, Hemyoke Hundred, co. Devon.

1636.—Henry Raynsbury, of the parish of St. Austin (Augustine) in London, factor. Will dated March 15, 1636, proved May 8, 1637. To Mr. Stephen Denison, Doctor and Lecturer, of Great All Hallows, 10s, to preach a sermon at his burial, and to the minister of the parish, where he shall be buried, for giving him way to preach the sermon £5. To each poor man and woman of the parish as the church wardens may select 10s. To the parish of Cullumstock, co. Devon, where he was born £100—for the use of the poor forever, the interest to be divided once a year among eight poor men and women. To the poor of Samford Arundel (Milverton Hund.) co. Somerset, £10—for the use of the poor forever. To his sister Alice Wood, widow, of Henryoke, co. Devon, all his inheritage lands in the county of Lincoln, during her life, then to be divided among her five children. To Mrs. Susan Fleming, wife of Mr. John Fleming of St. Austin's, London £100. To their three children, Roland, Mary and Susan, each £10. To each of his godchildren, not named, 20s. To ten poor laboring porters of Blackwall Hall (market for selling woolen cloths), each 10s. To cousin Edward, son of cousin Edward Baker of Henryoke £20. To ten poor servant-maids of Cullumstock, each 20s. Residue to his godson Henry Baker, son of cousin John Baker the elder, of Cullumstock, clothier, when 21 years of age. Appoints the said John Baker executor, and his uncle Christopher Baker, cousin Henry Holwaye, and gossip John Rew, overseers, and gives each of them £5.—*Book Goare*, fo. 59.

The Hundreds of Milverton, co. Somers and Henryoke, co. Devon adjoin.

The parish registers of Whitechapel, co. Mid., which begin in 1558, record the marriage of

Thomas[1] Raineborow and Martha Moole, Nov. 11, 1582.

In Chancery Proceedings, temp. Elizabeth, P.p. No. 23, occurs a bill, filed 1641; Thomas Raynsbury and others, to vacate an annuity charged by George Peirce *plaintiff* on a freehold messuage in Gate Lane, parish of St. Mary Staynings, London, for use of plaintiff's daughter Eliz. Peirce.

Thomas Rainborowe of East Greenwich, mariner, had a lease of certain lands, 28 Sept. 1619, at Claverhambury, co. Essex, from Lord Edward Denny, which manor,

* His mother had been dead many years.

with Hallyfield Hall, &c., had been granted by Henry VIII., 1542, to his lordship's grandfather Sir Anthony Dennye.

His children, baptized at Whitechapel, were :

1. 1583, April 28. Barbara,[2] m. Thomas Lee, armorer, of London, and after Mr. —— Burbridge, or Buckridge.
2. 1584-5, Feb. 21. Elizabeth,[2] d. unm. before 1619.
3. 1587, June 11. William.[2]
4. 1589, Sept. 23. Martha,[2] m. Anthony Wood.
5. 1591-2, Feb. 20. Thomas,[2] d. young.
6. 1594, Oct. 15. Thomas.[2]
7. 1597, June 19. Sarah,[2] m. Francis Porte.

The name is spelled variously on the registers, as Rain(e)borow(e), Rain(e)sborow(e), Raynsborow, Raineburrow(e), Rainsberry, and, though possibly it is synonymous with Ramesbury or Remmesbury [of co. Wilts, &c.), the armorial bearings of the two families do not coincide, the Rainsborowe arms being similar to those of the Raynes, Reynes, or Reymes.

The will of Thomas[1] Rainborowe, mariner of East Greenwich, co. Kent, dated 4 Dec. 1622, and proved 23 Feb. 1623, is given in this article by Mr. Waters, as also that of the widow, Martha Rainborowe, who afterwards resided in the parish of St. Bridget's, London, where she died in 1631.

Before considering the elder son William,[2] it may be briefly stated that the second son—

THOMAS[2] RAINBOROW, bapt. at Whitechapel 15 Oct. 1594, in his will of 24 Nov. 1668, proved 2 Jan. 1671 (as given by Mr. Waters), is styled " of East Greenwich, gent." He evidently died without issue surviving him, though he had a son Thomas,[3] bapt. at Whitechapel, 18 Sept. 1614. The will of his widow is as follows : Mary Rainborow of Greenwich, co. Kent, widow ; dated 11 Feb. 1677, proved 9 Apr. 1678. Whereas she has heretofore expressed her kindness to her brother and sister, not named, to the utmost of her ability, she now gives them but twelve pence. Appoints her niece Sarah Trott, who now lives with her, executrix, and makes her residuary legatee.—*Book Reeve*, fol. 37.

WILLIAM[2] RAINBOROW (eldest son of Thomas[1]), bapt. at Whitechapel, 11 June, 1587. In Nov. 1625, we find him a part owner and in command of the Sampson of London, 500 tons, built at Limehouse, and now granted the privilege of carrying great guns. His name occurs frequently in the Cal. Dom. State Papers. Secretary Lord Edward Conway writes him, 20 March, 1626, relative to taking aboard the trunks, &c. of Sir Thomas Phillips, Ambassador for Constantinople. Letters of Marque were granted 24 Oct. 1627, and finally, when the reconstruction of the navy was paramount with King Charles, the merchantman Sampson, well fortified with iron ordnance, was one of the vessels presented, in Dec. 1634, by the City of London, for his Majesty's service. William Raynisborowe, as one of the inhabitants in the vicinity of the Tower, complained, in the summer of 1627, of the nuisance of an alum-factory erected at the west end of Wapping. Five years later we find his knowledge and experience of maritime matters duly recognized by the Lords of the Admiralty, who in their order of 21 April, 1632, appoint Capt. Rainsborough one of the gentlemen to attend a meeting of the Board on the 26th, to give their opinion concerning the complements and numbers of men to be allowed for manning each of his Majesty's ships.

Jan. 2, 1634-5, the King in Council had expressed his desire that the Merhonour, the Swiftsure, the City of London and other vessels should be presently put forth to sea. The order was confirmed March 10, and the first named vessel was ordered to be fitted out and victualled by April 24 for six months' service, the charge to be defrayed with moneys paid by the several ports and maritime places. To the Merhonour, at Chatham, the Lords of the Admiralty appoint Capt. William Rainborough, March 30, with Capt. William Cooke as Master. This 44 gun vessel (800 tons), sometimes called the May Honora, had been rebuilt and launched, 25 April, 1614, at Woolwich, by Phineas Pett. Other vessels commissioned at the time were the Constant Reformation, Capt. Thomas Ketelby ; the Swallow, Capt. Henry Stradling ; the Mary Rose, Capt. George Carteret ; the Sampson, Capt. Thomas Kirke, &c. &c. ; and these were under the command of Sir William Monson, Vice Adm. in the James, and Sir John Pennington, Rear Adm. in the Swiftsure. Since the death of the Duke of Buckingham in 1628, the office of Lord Admiral had remained in commission, but on May 14, 1635, one of the Navy Commissioners, Robert Bertie, Lord Willoughby de Eresby and Earl of Lindsey, was appointed Admiral, Custos Maris, General and Governor of His Majesty's Fleet, for the guard of the Narrow Seas. He was to defend the King and the Kingdom's honor, which had been lately called in question by a fleet of French and Dutch off Portland, and to exact " the due homage of the sea " from passing ships, and so restore to England her ancient sovereignty of the Narrow Seas ; he was also to clear the neighboring waters of pirates and Turks ; to convoy merchants and others desiring it ; to guard against any infringement of the custom on the part of returning vessels, &c. About the middle of April the Merhonour repaired to Tilbury Hope to receive the remainder of her stores ; and on May 16 the Admiral came on board, the ships meeting twelve days later in the Downs. Rainsborough's vessel, though a good sailer, proved somewhat leaky, and the Admiral was desirous at first of changing to the Triumph ; however, the leaks having been found and her foremast repaired, he concluded she would do well for her present employment, and continued cruizing in her until he brought the fleet into the Downs once more on Oct. 4. Most of the ships were now ordered to Chatham and Deptford, though a few continued out under Sir John Pennington. The Earl despatched his journal of the expedition to the King, and hoped he might, with his Majesty's favor, return home. The Hollanders, who in pursuit of the Dunkirk frigates, had been accustomed to land on the English coast, committing depredations upon the inhabitants, had been checked ; one of their armed bands had been arrested at Whitby, and a vessel of 21 guns had been taken and sent into Hull ; moreover, Capt. Stradling, in the Swallow of 30 guns, being off the Lizard alone, had met the French Admiral Manti with two vessels, who after receiving an admonitory shot apiece, had each struck their flags and topsails, and saluted with three pieces of ordnance.

Writs were now sent to the sheriffs of the various counties of England, to levy money to defray the charge of a fleet for next year of double the strength of that which had just been employed, and attention was paid to the improvement of the vessels in the removal of the cumbersome galleries, as suggested by Capt. Rainsborough. This gentleman, together with one of the commissioners, Sir John Wostenholm and others, was appointed Dec. 9 to inquire into the institution, state, order and government of the Chest at Chatham, as established in 1588 by Queen Elizabeth, with Adms. Drake and Hawkins, for the relief of wounded and decayed seamen, and to certify their doings to the Co. of Chancery.

Towards the close of Feb. 1635–6, a list of Naval Captains, twenty-five in number, was handed in for the year, with Algernon, Earl of Northumberland, as Adm., Sir John Pennington as V. Adm., and Sir Henry Mervyn as Rear Adm. The Earl, in the Triumph, had chose Rainborow as his Captain, with William Cooke as Master, and during the next month he desired the Lords of the Admiralty that his Captain's pay might be made equal to theirs, and that he might have a Lieut., as he had more business to do than any other captain of the fleet. April 9, the ships at Portsmouth were awaiting the arrival of Capt. R. to take them out to sea, the Admiral having promised to send him down for that purpose.

At this time, and for a long series of years previous, England was and had been suffering from a grievous scourge, viz. : the pirates from the north of Africa. So bold and venturesome had they become during the summer of 1636, as to land within twelve miles of Bristol and successfully carry off men, women and children. Their chief place of refuge was the port of Cardiff and its vicinity, whence they carried on their depredations along either coast of the St. George's Channel. No relief, save an occasional collection for the redemption of captives, had heretofore been devised, and numerous were the petitions and statements now being presented to the King and the H. of Lords. The Court was moved to proclaim a general fast, and a sermon was preached in October by the Rev. Charles Fitz-Geffry, of St. Dominick, in Plymouth, from Heb. 13, 3 ; this was printed at Oxford, and entitled, " Compassion towards Captives, chiefly towards our Brethren & Countrymen who are in such miserable bondage in Barberie." A cotemporaneous document reads : " It is certainly known that there are five Turks in the Severne, wher they weekly take either English or Irish ; and that there are a great number of their ships in the Channell, upon the coast of France and Biscay. Whereby it is come to passe that our mareners will noe longer goe to sea, nor from port to port ; yea, the fishermen dare not putt to sea, to take fish for the country. If timely prevention be not used, the Newfoundland fleet must of necessity suffer by them in an extraordinary manner." The greater part of the captives, reported to be some 2000 in number, had been taken within the last two years, and the sea-rovers, most to be dreaded, were the pirates of New Sallee, who had revolted from the Emperor of Morocco, headed by a rebel who was called the Saint. The matter coming to be more seriously discussed, three plans were suggested—peace, war, or suppression of trade. Finally it was proposed that Capt. Rainsborough should be employed in an expedition against Sallee, and he and Mr. Giles Penn (father of the future Adm. William Penn) were called upon by the King, Dec. 28, to give their opinion concerning the particulars. In a letter, some three weeks earlier, Capt. R., then an invalid at Southwold, on the Suffolk coast, states his great willingness to attend the Lords and further their project, as soon as he can set out for London. The plan, which he subsequently submitted, states that to redeem the captives would require over 100,000l., the payment of which would but encourage the pirates to continue their present course. Whereas to besiege them by sea would not only effect the purpose, but give security for the future, or a fleet might be kept on their coast for two or three years, until their ships were worm-caten. That " the maintenance of the suggested fleet would be very much to the King's honor in all the maritime ports in Christendom, &c." He recommends himself to go as Admiral in the Leopard, Capt. George Carteret as V. Adm. in the Antelope, Capt. Brian Harrison in the Hercules, Capt. George Hatch in the Gt. Neptune, Capt. Th. White in the largest pinnace, and Capt. Edmund Seamon in the lesser. The plan was adopted, and, Feb. 20, 1636-7, Sec. Coke writes from Whitehall to the Lord Dep. Strafford : "This day Capt. Rainsborough, an experienced & worthy seaman, took his leave of his Majesty, and goeth instantly to sea with four good ships and two pinnaces to the coast of Barbary, with instructions & resolution to take all Turkish frygates he can meet, & to block up the port of Sally, & to free the sea from these rovers, which he is confident to perform."

March 4 the little squadron was in the Downs and on the eve of departure. The port of Sallee was reached in good season, and the enemy's cruisers, about to start for England and Ireland, were hemmed in and twenty-eight of their number destroyed. A close siege was now maintained, assisted on the land side by the old Governor of the town, and the place was delivered up to the English, July 28th.

The Emperor now agreed to join in a league with King Charles, promising never again to infest the English coasts, and forthwith delivered up some 300 captives, with whom Capt. Carteret immediately returned homeward. Rainsborough, however, on Aug. 21, proceeded to Saffee to treat for about 1000 English captives who had been sold to Tunis and Algiers. Here he remained till Sept. 19, when the Emperor's Ambassador came aboard, accompanied by Mr. Robert Blake, a merchant trading to Morocco, for whom the Emperor had formed a friendship, and who had obtained the position of Farmer of all his Ports and Customs. On the 21st they left the coast, and arriving fifteen days later in the Downs, landed, Oct. 8, at Deal Castle. Detained at Gravesend through sickness, it was not until the 19th that the Ambassador was conducted to London by the Master of Ceremonies, and, landing at the Tower, was taken to his lodgings " with much display & trumpeting." In the procession were the principal citizens and Barbary merchants mounted, all richly apparelled, and every man having a chain of gold about him, with the Sheriffs and Aldermen in their scarlet gowns, and a large body of the delivered captives, some of whom had been over thirty years in servitude, arrayed in white, and though it was night, yet the streets " were almost as light as day." Sunday, Nov. 5, the Ambassador was received by the King, to whom he brought, as a present from his imperial master, some hunting hawks and four steeds, " the choicest & best in all Barbary, & valued at a great rate, for one Horse was prized at 1500 pound." These, led by four black Moors in red liveries, were caparisoned with rich saddles embroidered with gold, and the stirrups of two of them were of massive gold, and the bosses of their bridles of the same metal. An account of the proceedings was printed towards the close of the month, entitled, " The Arrival & Entertainment of the Morocco Ambassador Alkaid (or Lord) Jaurar Ben Abdella, from the High & Mighty Prince Mully Mahamed Sheque, Emperor of Morocco, King of Fesse & Susse, &c."

Great was the enthusiasm created by the successful issue of the expedition, and even Waller was prompted to eulogize the event in the following rather ponderous lines :

> " Salle that scorn'd all pow'r and laws of men,
>   Goods with their owners hurrying to their den ;
>   *   *   *   *   *
>   This pest of mankind gives our Hero fame,
>   And thus th' obliged world dilates his name.
>   *   *   *   *   *

With ships they made the spoiled merchant moan ;
With ships, their city and themselves are torn.
One squadron of our winged castles sent
O'erthrew their Fort, and all their Navy rent:
* * * * *
Safely they might on other nations prey ;
Fools to provoke the Sov'reign of the Sea !
* * * * *
Morocco's Monarch, wondering at this fact,
Save that his presence his affairs· exact,
Had come in person, to have seen and known
The injur'd world's revenger, and his own.
Hither he sends the chief among his Peers,
Who in his bark proportion'd presents bears,
To the renown'd for piety and force,
Poor captives manumis'd and matchless horse."

Even grumbling Master Andrew Burrell, who, in a pamphlet of 1646 condemns the entire Navy, its officers, &c., though he had himself built for them the Marie Rose, "the most sluggish ship " they had afloat, confesseth that Rainsborough's Fleet "performed better service than England's Navie did in 44 years before." The King was very willing and forward to have knighted the gallant Admiral, but he declined the honor, and order was given that he should have a gold chain and medal of the value of 300*l.*; a memorial of loyal service perhaps still extant, "should not very opposite family feelings have melted it down in the days of the Rump," observes Disraeli in his Life of Charles I. An augmentation to the family arms was undoubtedly conferred at the time in the shape of " a Saracen's head couped ppr. in the fesse point."

Meanwhile the raising of funds and supplies for the equipment of the fleet for the following year had again become necessary, and Strafford, writing to the Abp. of Canterbury from Dublin, 27 Nov., says in connection, "this action of Sallee, I assure you, is so full of honor, that it will bring great content to the subject, and should, methinks, help much towards the ready, cheerful payment of the shipping monies." Early in Feb. 1637–8, the list of ships, which were to keep the seas during the following summer, was published, headed by the Sovereign of the Seas. This vessel, launched at Woolwich the preceding year, had been in progress since May, 1635, and surpassed in size, tonnage and force anything heretofore constructed for the English Navy. Thomas Heywood published an account of it, with a view of this " his Majesty's royal Ship, the Great Glory of the English Nation, and not to be paralleled in the whole Christian World," while Marmaduke Rawdon, of York, mentions in his Life,* a visit, in 1638, to the Royal Sovereign, Capt. Rainsberry, then newly finished and riding at Erith, below Woolwich.

Burrell, in his pamphlet before alluded to, condemns the vessel as "an admirable ship for costly Buildings, & cost in keeping ; and, which adds to the miracle, the Royall Ship is never to be used for the Kingdom's good," &c. The Commissioners of the Navy answered in reply : " Capt. Rainsborough, whom Master Burrell confesseth, in his time, was the most eminent Commander in this Kingdom, had the trial of her in the Channel of England, and at his return reported to his Majestie that he never set his foot in a better conditioned Ship in all his life. And as for her Forces, she is not inferior to the greatest Ship in Christendom."†

On Sunday, March 18th, Algernon, Earl of Northumberland, obtained the position of General at Sea, or Lord High Admiral, during his Majesty's pleasure, the King designing to eventually bestow that office upon his younger son, the Duke of York.

That Capt. Rainsborough was ever in active naval service after his cruise in the Sovereign does not appear. He and others, owners of the 200 ton ship Confidence of London, were allowed Feb. 19, by the Lords of the Admiralty, to mount her with 20 pieces of cast-iron ordnance, and, during the fall of the year, together with some 155 other sea-faring men, he signed his consent to a proposition made by the Lord High Admiral and the Att. General, that an amount be deducted from their wages for the establishment of the Poor Seamen's Fund, to be administered by the officers of the Trinity House. The following year, as appears by a paper among the Duke

* Camden Soc. Pub.
† She subsequently did such good service that the Dutch nicknamed her " the Golden Devil."

of Northumberland's MSS., he submitted a proposition, in the form of articles, suggesting that 10,000 pieces of ordnance, with carriages, &c., be kept in readiness to arm 100 collier-ships, which may fight with a great army; stating their superiority for such service. Commission was given, Oct. 20, 1639, to Sir Edward Littleton, Solic. General, Sir Paul Pindar and Capt. William Rainsborough, to inquire into the truth of the statements made in the petition to the Privy Council, by Edward Deacon, who with his goods had been seized and detained in Sallee for debts there contracted by Mr. Robert Blake, as factor for some London merchants; petitioner having come to England, after leaving his son in Barbary as a pledge, in pursuit of said Blake, who, at the time, or immediately subsequent, was one of the gentlemen of the Council.

As William Rainsborough, Esq., he, with Squire Bence, merchant, were members from Aldborough, a seaport of co. Suffolk, in the Fourth Parl. of Charles I., held at Westminster from 13 April to 5 May, 1640; as also in the Parliament which convened 3 Nov. following; that most notable of English Parliaments, before which, a week later, Thomas, Earl of Strafford, was accused of high treason. May 27, 1641, he with others took the oath of Protestation, for the defence of the religion established, of the King's person, and the liberty of the subject; the same having been assented to by both houses on the 3d and 4th of the same month. Aug. 25th Capt. R. was at the head of the committee for taking the whole state of the navy into consideration, and providing ships for transporting the ordnance and ammunition from Hull and other parts of the north. Five days later the merchants' petition for erecting a Company for America and Africa, &c., was referred to Sir John Colpeper and Mr. Pymm especially, assisted by twenty-three other members, among whom was Capt. Rainsborough. The same day he was included in a committee to whom had been referred the Act for making Wapping Chapel parochial. He was also appointed, Sept. 9, a member of the Recess Committee, during the adjournment of Parliament till Oct. 20th; and on Nov. 19, was on a committee for naval affairs, with some other members, including Sir Henry Vane. Three days later it was ordered "that citizens that serve for the City of London and Capt. Rainsborough do inform themselves what shipping are now in the River that are fit to transport the Magazine at Hull to the Tower, and to give an account of it to-morrow morning"; this was in pursuance of a resolution of the 3d.

And so ends his life and public services, for no more is heard of him till Feb. 14, 1641-2, when the Speaker of the House was ordered to issue a warrant to the Clerk of the Crown in Chancery for a new writ to be issued forth for the election of a new Burgess to serve for the town of Alborough in co. Suffolk, in the room and stead of Capt. Rainsborough deceased, and Alex. Bence, Esq., was accordingly elected. On the 17th his body was interred in St. Catherine's (Tower), London. At the time of his decease the Captain was a widower, his wife Judith, a daughter of Renold and Joane Hoxton, having been buried at Wapping, 3 March, 1637-8. The will of William Rainsborow of London Esq., dated 16 July, 1638, with codicil of 1 Feb. 1641 proved 8 April, 1642, has been already given.

1. THOMAS[3] RAINSBOROWE, Esq., of Whitechapel, co. Midd. (William,[2] Thomas[1]), commonly known in history as Col. Rainsborough. A naval captain at first under the L. H. Adm. Warwick; then a colonel of infantry under the Parliament, and finally V. Adm. of their Fleet. A member of the Long Parliament. A more detailed account of this prominent and distinguished individual may be given hereafter. Suffice it to say that the Rev. Hugh Peters, alluding to the services of this officer at the taking of Worcester, that last stronghold for the King (in July, 1646), observes, " and truely I wish Colonell Rainborow a suitable employment by Sea or Land, for both which God hath especially fitted him; foraine States would be proud of such a Servant."* Resisting a seizure of his person on the part of the royalists, he was killed at Doncaster, 29 Oct. 1648, and buried at Wapping, 14 Nov. Administration on his estate was granted, 24 Nov., to his widow Margaret, maiden name probably Jenney.

  1. *William*,[4] eldest son; mentioned in wills of his grandfather 1638, and his   uncle Edward 1677. He was a Captain in the army, it would appear,   during the Protectorate, and judging from the Winthrop Letters (Mass.   Hist. Soc. Col. 5, viii.) was in Boston, N. E., 1673; living 1687.

2. WILLIAM[3] RAINSBOROW (William,[2] Thomas[1]); mentioned in Savage's Geneal. Dic. as being of Charlestown, Mass. Col. 1639; Artillery Co. same year; purchas-

* King's Pamphlets, Brit. Mus., E. 351.

ed 17 Dec. 1640, of Th. Bright, house and land in Watertown, which had been the homestall of Lt. Robt. Feake. Budington mentions his purchase of the old meeting-house. He was evidently a trader or sea-captain. March 7, 1643–4, the treasurer of the Colony was ordered to attend to the discharge of Mr. Rainsborow's debt, with allowance of £20 forbearance for the time past, and the loan of two sachars for two great pieces for one voyage. He had been in England in 1642, when in April his name, and that of his brother Thomas, are found on the list of the proposed Adventurers by Sea, against Ireland. This was the expedition against Galway, &c., whereof, under Lord Forbes, his brother Thomas was commander, and the Rev. Hugh Peters chaplain.

Judging from the discharge of his debt and the loan of cannon, Capt. R. again returned to the old country in 1643–4, and though there are subsequent entries as to the debt, the moneys are always to be paid to parties abroad on R.'s account. He immediately espoused the people's cause and joined that division of the army which was in the west under Lord Essex. Finding himself in a critical position, the Lord General despatched Stapleton, his General of Horse, to Parliament, calling for aid, and on the night of Aug. 30th, Sir William Balfour, his Lieut. General, passed safely through the King's Quarters with 2300 horse, and reached London. Two nights thereafter Essex himself and Lord Roberts fled in a cock-boat to Plymouth, and the following day, Sept. 2, 1644, the commanding officer, Serj. Major General Skippon, surrendered with all the infantry and a few horse. According to a return[*] found in the quarters of Sir Edward Dodsworth, Com. Gen. of the Horse, we find that the cavalry had previously mustered at Tiverton, co. Devon, 39 troops, 420 officers and 2785 men. The first division of 8 troops, 639 men, under Sir Philip Stapleton, Major Gen. Philip Skippon and Maj. Hamilton ; the six troops of the second division (62 officers, 432 men), being commanded by Sir William Balfour, 14 officers, 100 men ; Major Balfour, 9 officers, 77 men ; Sir Samuel Luke (Gov. of Newport Paganel, co. Bucks), 10 officers, 72 men ; Capt. Rainsborow, 9 officers, 57 men ; Capt. Sample, 10 officers, 61 men ; Capt. Boswell, 10 officers, 65 men.

Prestwich's "Respublica" describes the cornet of Capt. Rainsborough's troop as follows : " Azure ; from the sinister base point all over the base, and up to the middle of the dexter side, clouds Argent, shaded with black and crimson ; near the middle or base, a book in pale closed and clasped and covered Or, on the front or side thus : $\frac{VERBUM}{DEI}$; between this book and the dexter side, and a little above the base, an armed arm and hand uplifted, as issuant from the clouds, and as in pale, holding in his hand a Hussar's sword as barrways, and waved on both sides, and the point burning and inflamed with fire proper, hilted Or ; in chief a scroll, its end turned or doubled in, and then bent out and split, and fashioned double like two hooks, endorsed Argent, lined Or, and ends shaded with crimson and Argent, and in Roman capital letters Sable, VINCIT VERITAS. Arms.—Chequered Or and Azure, and in fess a Moor's head in profile, bearded and proper, his head banded with a wreath Argent."

In the list of officers for the New Model of the army, which was sent up from the House of Commons to the House of Lords, 3 March, 1644–5, and approved on the 18th, Col. Sheffield's squadron of horse consisted of his own troop and those of Major Sheffield and Captains Eveling, Rainsborow, Martin and Robotham. He subsequently obtained the rank of Major, and Whitelock informs us of letters received, July 2, 1647, from the Commissioners in the Army, certifying " that the General had appointed Lt. Gen. Cromwell, Cols. Ireton, Fleetwood, Rainsborough, Harrison, Sir Har. Waller, Richard Lambert and Hammond, and Major Rainsborough, or any five of them, to treat with the Parliament's Commissioners upon the papers sent from the Army to the Parliament, and their Votes."

From the Journals of the House of Commons, under date of 27 Sept. 1650, we read that " Mr. Weaver reports from the committee for suppressing lycentious and impious practices, under pretence of religious liberty, &c., the confession of Lawrence Clackson (or Claxton), touching the making and publishing of the impious and blasphemous booke called the ' Single Eye,' and also Major Rainsborrow's carriage " in countenancing the same. Claxton, departing from the established church, appears to have joined all the prominent sectaries of the day, and from a tract of his published in 1660, entitled " the Lost Sheep Found," we gather that much of his trouble and imprisonment resulted from his own licentious behavior, he maintaining that " to the pure all things are pure." He was sent to the house

* Symond's Diary of Marches, Camden Soc. Pub.

of correction for one month and then banished, and his book was burned by the
common hangman. Major Rainsborough, residing at the time at Fulham, was one
of his disciples, " and seems to have been an apt scholar in improving his relations
with the female part of the flock."[*] It was resolved by the House that he be discharged and disabled of and from being and executing the office of Justice of Peace
in co. Middlesex, or any other county within England or Wales.

For almost nine years we hear nothing of him, but on Tuesday, 19 July, 1659, he
presented a petition to the House on behalf of the Sheriffs, Justices of the Peace
and Gentry of the co. of Northampton, and on the same day was made a Commissioner for the Militia for the same county. In accordance with a report from said
commissioners, he was appointed by Parliament, Aug. 9, Colonel of a Regiment of
Horse in co. Northants.[†] After the Restoration, a warrant was issued, 17 Dec.
1660, to Lieut. Ward for the apprehension of Col. William Rainsborough at his
residence, Mile End Green, Stepney (near London), or elsewhere, for treasonable
designs, and to bring him before Secretary Sir Edward Nichols. He was accordingly arrested and confined in the Gatehouse. On his examination next day he declared he was a Major of horse, but dismissed by Cromwell in 1649; that the Rump
Parliament made him a Colonel of Militia-horse, 1659, but nothing was done; that
he had bought 40 cases of pistols for militia, and had since tried to dispose of them.
He gave bond for 500l., Feb. 7, 1661, with Dr. Richard Barker of the Barbican as
security for his good behavior.

His wife's name was Margery, and, as we have seen before, the will of Capt.
Rowland Coytmore of Wapping, in 1626, mentions a son-in-law William Rainsborough, mariner, of Wapping; while the will of Stephen Winthrop, 1658, leaves
a legacy to " cousin Mary Rainsborowe, daughter of my brother-in-law William
Rainsborowe, Esq." From the Winthrop Letters (Mass. Hist. Soc. Coll. 5, viii.)
he appears to have been in Boston, N. E., in 1673, with his nephew William.

3. MARTHA,[3] bapt. at Whitechapel, 20 April, 1617 ; married at Wapping, 14
     June, 1635, Thomas Coytmore,[‡] son of Capt. Rowland Coytmore, an East
     India trader. He came to N. England next year and was wrecked, 27
     Dec. 1644, on the coast of Spain, leaving issue. Her second husband,
     whom she married 4 Dec. 1647, was Gov. John Winthrop, to whom she
     was fourth wife ; he died 26 March, 1649, aged 61. She married third-
     ly, 10 March, 1652, John Coggan of Boston, as his third wife ; he died
     27 April, 1658, leaving issue. Disappointed of a fourth marriage, we are
     given to understand that she committed suicide in 1660.
4. JUDITH,[3] bapt. at Wapping, 14 Sept. 1624 ; married about 1644, Ste-
     phen Winthrop, son of Gov. John W., born 24 March, 1619. He return-
     ed to England 1645, became a Colonel of Horse under Parliament, re-
     ceiving 474l. 10s. per annum, and in 1656 was M.P. for Banff and Aber-
     deen. Resided at time of decease in James Street, Westminster. His
     will of 3 May, proved 19 Aug. 1658, mentions three daughters, Marga-
     ret, Joanna and Judith, as before given. She is mentioned 1668, in her
     uncle Thomas's will.
5. SAMUEL,[3] b.   ob. infs. ; buried at Wapping, 24 Nov. 1628.
6. JOANE,[3] b.   ; m. John Chamberlain, a captain under Parliament ; living in
     May, 1687, a brewer at Deptford, co. Kent. She is mentioned 1668 in
     her uncle Thomas's will. The will of S. Winthrop, 1658, mentions their
     daughter Judith.
7. REYNOLD,[3] bapt. at Whitechapel, 1 June, 1632.
8. EDWARD,[3] bapt. at Whitechapel, 8 Oct. 1633. Richard Wharton, writing
     from Boston, N. E., Sept. 24, 1673, to a kinsman of rank and influence
     in England, suggests that his Majesty should send out two or three frig-
     ates, by the ensuing February or March, with some 300 soldiers, for the
     recapture of New York from the Dutch. That the expedition should be
     assisted by a colonial force, the whole to be under the command of some
     native leader, such as Maj. Gen. Daniel Dennison. He continues : " for
     a more certain knowledge of the constitutions of or government & com-
     plexions of the people I refer you to Mr Edwd Rainsborough an intellig[t]

---

[*] Notes and Queries, 4th Series, xi. 487.
[†] In the limits of Charleton, parish of Newbottle, co. Northants, is a camp and hill commonly called " Rainsborough Hill," supposed to be of Danish origin.
[‡] Katherine, daughter of Thomas and Martha Quoitmore, bapt. at Wapping, 13 April,
and buried 19 April, 1636.

Gentleman who went home three months since. I have requested him to wait on you & communicate w^t I have advised him. .... Mr Rainsborough dwells at Knights bridge & is to be heard of at Mr Whiting's shop upon the old Exchange."* He appears to be the same party whose will runs as follows: Edward Rainborow of Cranford, co. Middlesex, gentleman; Sept. 14, 1677 (proved May 4, 1682), being in good health, but going beyond the seas, do make this my last will, &c. Bequeaths to his wife Christian one fourth of all his real and personal estate during her life. To his dear friend Mary Alcock, widow, for and in consideration of a very considerable sum of money for which he stands indebted to her, one fourth part of his real and personal estate either in England or N. England, during her life; one eighth part to be at her absolute disposal. To son Mytton Rainborow one fourth of all his real and personal estate when twenty-one years of age. To daughter Judith Rainborow one fourth of his real and personal estate until her brother Mytton shall enjoy that part which is given to his mother and also the eighth part given to Mary Alcock. To his nephew William Rainsborow five pounds to buy him a ring. Appoints his wife's sister, Mrs. Sarah Mackworth of Shrewsbury, and Mrs. Mary Alcock of Cranford, executors.—*Book Cottle*, folio 62.

Concerning the New England estate referred to by Edward Rainsborowe in his will of 1677, as above, we have evidence on file in the Registry of Deeds, Salem, of which the following is a summary: Whereas Judith Winthrop and John Chamberlain, two of the Executors of Stephen Winthrop deceased, had by certain deeds of Indenture, Bargain & Sale conveyed to Edward Rainsburrowe of London, merchant, all those parcells of lands lying & being in N. England in America, viz: one moiety of Prudence Island, lying in or near ye bay of Narragansett, in Rhode Island Colony, and all that Farm at Lynn or Salem, containing by estimation 1500 acres more or less, now, considering the great hazard of transmitting ye conveyances beyond sea, the said Executors do acknowledge before a notary public the said deeds of bargain and sale, 21 April, 1671. The document was signed in presence of Nich. Hayward, Not. Pub., Symon Amory, Tim^o Prout sen^r, and his son Wm Prout. Timothy Prout, shipwright of Boston, testified to the same before Dep. Gov. John Leverett, 5 Mar. 1672-3, and the instrument was recorded and compared 5 July following. As late as 21 March, 1695-6, the above was compared with the original and found an exactly true copy of ye record in ye booke of Deeds Lib: 8° Page 195.

Meanwhile John Chamberlain, the sole surviving executor of Stephen Winthrop deceased, having been shown a copy of the instrument above referred to, as being on file in some court in N. England, made oath 31 May, 1687, that he had never signed nor executed any such writing or instrument, nor did he believe that Judith Winthrop, widow & executrix, had made any such conveyance to the late Edward Rainsburrow. This testimony of Mr. Chamberlain appears to have been given at the request of his nephew William[4] Rainsburrowe, son of Vice Adm. Thomas[3] Rainsburrowe, being, we may infer, at the time the only, or at least the eldest, male representative of the family, and acting in the interest of his cousins the children of Stephen Winthrop deceased. Robert Wildey, of the parish of St. Paules Peters, co. Middlesex, cook, and "Thomasine Jenney, of the same place spinster, aunt of ye said William Rainsburrowe," swore to their knowledge of and acquaintance with John Chamberlayn for thirty years and upwards last past; that he and Stephen Winthrop, Esq., whom they had also known, had married two sisters, "this deponent William Rainsburrow's Aunts, and sisters of Edward Rainsburrow in ye above written affidavit named, &c. &c." Nicholas Hayward, the Notary Public, mentioned in the first instrument, swore that he had never drawn up such a paper, and the whole denial was witnessed by four parties on the point of departure from London for New England, and was also compared with the original about nine years later, viz: 21 March, 1695-6. I. J. GREENWOOD.]

EDMUND SPINCKES of Warmington in the County of Northampton, clerk, 2 October 1669, proved 11 August 1671. I give out of that seven hundred & fifty pounds which will be due to me or mine from the heirs or executors or administrators of Thomas Elmes of Lilford Esq. (after the decease of himself the said Thomas Elmes and the Lady Jane Compton),

* Hist. Mag., 1867, p. 299.

to my eldest son Nathaniel Spinckes one hundred pounds, to Seth, my second son, one hundred and fifty pounds, to William, my third son, one hundred & fifty pounds, to Elmes, my fourth son, one hundred & fifty pounds, and to Martha, my only daughter, two hundred pounds. To Nathaniel Spinckes, my eldest son & heir, all that land in Ireland, in King's County, which is now in the possession of the heirs or assigns of Thomas Vincent sometimes alderman of London, which is due to me according to a writing signed by him to that purpose 6 March 1642. Item I give to the said Nathaniel Spinckes all that fifty pounds, more or less, with the profit of it, that is now in the Iron works in New England, acknowledged received by John Pocock then Steward of the Company and living then in London, his Acquittance bearing date March 19th 1645. Item, I give to the said my son Nathaniel all that estate whatsoever it be that falleth to me or shall fall in New England, as joint heir with John Nayler of Boston in Lincolnshire, clerk, to Boniface Burton, now or late of Boston in New England, my uncle and mother's brother and only brother; also my library of books, only such excepted as his mother shall choose out for her own use. To Seth Spinckes, my second son, five pounds at the age of twenty-four years, to William five pounds at twenty-four, to Elmes five pounds at twenty-four and to Martha, my only daughter, five pounds at twenty-four. All the rest to my wife Martha, whom I appoint sole executrix. My loving friend Mr. Saml Morton, clerk & rector of the parish church of Haddon, in the County of Huntingdon, and my much respected cousin Mr Richard Conyer, clerk and rector of Long Orton and Butolph-Bridge in the County of Huntingdon, to be overseers. A schedule to be annexed to the said will &c. that Seth shall have paid him out of the estate that my father Elmes left my wife &c. &c. (So of all the other children.)

18 May 1693 Emanavit commissio Nathanieli Spinckes, clerico, filio et administratori Marthæ Spinckes defunctæ &c. &c.   Duke, 107.

[I presume that this is the " Edmond Spinckes " whose name immediately precedes that of John Harvard in the *Recepta ab ingredientibus* of Emmanuel College (REGISTER, xxxix. 103).

Boniface Burton, whom Mr. Spinckes calls his mother's only brother, died June 13, 1669, " aged 113 years," according to Judge Sewall, who calls him " Old Father Boniface Burton " (REG. vii. 206). Hull in his Diary (Trans. Am. Antiq. Society, iii. 279) gives his age as " a hundred and fifteen years." Both ages are probably too high. Burton's will was dated, Feb. 21, 1666-7, and proved June 24, 1669. An abstract of the will is printed in the REGISTER, xx. 241, and on page 242 are some facts in his history. He left nothing to the family of Mr. Spinckes nor to John Nayler. After bequests to Increase Mather, to his niece Mrs. Bennet, her husband Samuel Bennet and their children, Burton leaves the rest of his property to his wife Frances Burton.

For an account of the Iron Works in which Mr. Spinckes had an interest, see " Vinton Memorial," pp. 463-74. John Pococke is named among the undertakers. —EDITOR.]

GEORGE LUDLOWE[1] of the County and Parish of Yorke in Virginia Esq. 8 September 1655. To my nephew Thomas Ludlow, eldest son to my brother Gabriel Ludlowe Esq. deceased, all my whole estate of lands and servants, &c. that I have now in possession in Virginia, to him and his lawful heirs forever; also my sixteenth part of the ship Mayflower, whereof Capt. William White is commander, which part I bought of Mr Samuel Harwar of London, merchant, only this year's " fraught " excepted, which I have reserved for my tobacco &c. My executor, yearly and every year during the natural life of my now wife Elizabeth Ludlowe, to pay unto her fifty pounds sterling in London. ` My crop wholly this year to be consigned to M[r] William Allen of London, merchant, and one M[r] John Cray that lives at the Green man on Ludgate Hill, whom I make my overseers of my estate in England. Moneys due from M[r] Samuel Harwar at the Sun and Harp, in Milk Street, London. To my brother Gabriel all his children, now in England, one hundred pounds apiece, and the remainder of the money (in England) to my brother Roger Ludlowe's[2] children equally ; and M[r] Thomas Bushrode[3] to be paid seventy five pounds:

Whereas my brother Roger Ludlowe hath consigned divers goods to me as per my book appears, as debts in New England and in Virginia as by his letters and other writings appear &c. To my said brother the hundred pounds I lent him. To my cousin Samuel Langrish three thousand pounds of tobacco &c. To George Bernard,[4] son to Col. William Bernard, my great silver tankard with my arms on it &c. To George Webster,[5] son to Capt. Richard Webster of Jamestown the silver tankard that M[r] Bowler brought in the year 1655. To Col. William Bernard, Major William Gooch[6] and Capt. Augustine Warner[7] ten pounds apiece, and I desire and nominate them to be overseers here in Virginia. To Doctor Henry Waldron all the debt he owes me on book, and the physic I have sent for for him. To M[r] Bushrode five pounds. To my man Archyball a cloth suit &c. To Jane Greeham my servant one year of her time. To M[rs] Rebecca Hurst all the clothes that I have sent for her in full of her time being with me in my house.

Wit: Nicholas Trott, Augustine Hodges.

Codicil:—I Colonel George Ludlowe &c. My nephew Thomas Ludlowe intends to intermarry with one Rebecca Hurst that is at this present living in my house. In that case my will is and my desire that my overseers here in Virginia take into their custody all my whole estate and dispose of the same until they can send into Ireland to my nephew Jonathan Ludlowe, eldest son to my brother Roger, who lives in Ireland at Dublin. Now in case my aforesaid nephew Thomas shall marry with the said Rebecca then it is my will that I give and bequeath unto my said nephew Jonathan all the estate that I did formerly give unto my nephew Thomas Ludlowe and make and constitute the said Jonathan my full and sole executor. Otherwise my former bequest to stand valid and the said Thomas shall enjoy what I have formerly given him to his use and heirs as my executor and heir. 23 October 1655. Witness:—James Biddlecombe.

On the first day of August, in the year of Our Lord God 1656, there issued forth Letters of administration to Roger Ludlow Esq., the father of and curator lawfully assigned to Jonathan, Joseph, Roger, Anne, Mary and Sarah Ludlowe, minors, the nephews and nieces and residuary legataries in this will, during the minority of the said minors; —— —— for that no executor is therein named as touching the said deceased's estate in England.

Berkeley, 256.

Administration on the goods &c. of John Ludlow, late of Virginia bachelor, deceased, granted to his brother Francis Ludlow 15 September 1664.

Admon Act Book p. c. c.

[1 George Ludlow (or Ludlowe), of the text, was a prominent and influential colonist. Grants of land to him, aggregating some 17,000 acres, are of record in the Virginia Land Registry; the first, of 500 acres, " in the upper county of New Norfolk," being dated August 21, 1638. He was long County Lieutenant of York county, and thus by title " Collonell "; Member of the Council 1642–55. There is a tradition that his brother Roger Ludlow was a fugitive in Virginia from Connecticut near the close of the 17th century.—R. A. Brock, of Richmond, Va.

The testator was probably the Mr. George Ludlow whose name appears on the list of those who desired Oct. 19, 1630, to be made Freemen of Massachusetts. He must have returned soon after to the old world, as a petition received from him in England was acted upon by the General Court of Massachusetts, March 1, 1630–31. —Editor.

[2] Roger Ludlow was an assistant of the Massachusetts colony, 1630–4, and was deputy governor in 1634. In 1635 he removed to Windsor, Ct., and was the first deputy governor of Connecticut colony. In 1639 he removed to Fairfield. He was a commissioner of the United Colonies in 1651, 2 and 3. He removed to Virginia subsequent to April 13, 1654, but probably about that time. A full memoir of him by Hon. Thomas Day, LL.D., is printed in Stiles's History of Ancient Windsor, pp. 687-8. Mr. Day styles him the "Father of Connecticut Jurisprudence." We have in this will, for the first time, the names of his children. His daughter Sarah, who is said to have been "distinguished for her literary acquirements and domestic virtues," married Rev. Nathaniel Brewster, of Brookhaven, Long Island, whose memoir will be found in Sibley's Harvard Graduates, i. 73.—Editor.

[3] Thomas Bushrod was a Burgess from York county, March, 1658-9. Richard Bushrod was granted 2000 acres in Westmoreland county, Oct. 15, 1660 (Land Registry, Book No. 4, p. 450). There were probably marriages of members of the Washington family with that of Bushrod, and hence the transmission of Bushrod as a Christian name, instanced in Bushrod Washington, nephew of George Washington, and Justice of the United States Supreme Court.—R. A. Brock.

[4] The name Bernard is of early mention in the records of Virginia. Thomas Bernard was granted 189 acres of land in James City county, January 20, 1641, No. 1, p. 762; William Bernard, 1050 acres in Warwick county, December 16, 1641, No. 1, p. 761; "Collonell" William Bernard, 800 acres in Lancaster county, October 8, 1659, No. 4, p. 372. William Bernard, with title of Captain, was a Member of the Council in 1647, and with that of "Collonell," 1655-58. Captain Thomas Bernard, Burgess from Warwick county in 1644.—R. A. Brock.

[5] Major Richard Webster was a Burgess from James City county, March, 1657-8. Thomas Webster was granted 251 acres in Henrico county, October 20, 1665 (No. 5, p. 519, Land Registry). Lucy, daughter and heir of Roger Webster, dec'd, was granted 250 acres in Hampton parish, Nov 19, 1642. Head rights: Edward Spark, Stephen ———, Thomas Webster, Susan Webster, Book No. p. 857. Lucy, Judith and Jane Webster were granted 500 acres in James City county, July 20, 1646, No. 2, p. 52.—R. A. Brock.

[6] William Gooch, "Gent.," was granted 1050 acres on the south side of the Potomac river, Oct. 18, 1650 (No. 2, p. 251, Land Registry). Captain William Gooch was a Burgess from York county in 1654. Major William Gooch died October 29, 1655, aged 29 years. His tomb in the burying ground at "Temple Farm," York county (where Gov. Alexander Spotswood was also buried), bears the arms of Gooch of Norfolk county, England (of which family was Sir William Gooch, Lieutenant Governor of Virginia, 1727-40), as follows: Paly of eight, ar. and sa. a chevron of the first, between three dogs of the second, spotted of the field. *Crest.*—A greyhound passant ar. spotted su. and collared of the last.

Jeffery Gooch was granted 500 acres in Northumberland county, January 30, 1650 (No. 2, p. 279, Land Registry). The Gooch family, descended probably from Major William Gooch or Jeffery Gooch, as above, has been most estimably represented in Virginia.—R. A. Brock.

[7] Colonel Augustine Warner (son, it is presumed of Augustine Warner) granted 250 acres "called Pine Neck, on New Pocoson," October 12th, 1635 (No. 1, p. 298, Land Registry), born June 3, 1642; died June 19, 1681: Burgess from Gloucester county, 1658, and Member of the Council during the administration of Governor Sir William Berkeley, is buried at "Warner Hall," Gloucester county. The Lewis, Washington and other prominent families have intermarried with that of Warner, which is a favored Christian name in Virginia.

John Lewis, second son of Robert Lewis, from Brecon, Wales, of Abington, Ware parish, Gloucester county, Virginia, married Isabella Warner, "daughter of a wealthy and retired India merchant;" called his seat "Warner Hall," a spacious mansion of 26 rooms, in which was long illustrated the refined hospitality typical of the Old Dominion. This Isabella Warner was probably a daughter of the Augustine Warner, the first grantee as above. — See article, "Descendants of Robert Lewis from Wales," *Richmond Standard*, Feb. 5, 1881.—R. A. Brock.]

JOHN CUTLER of Ipswich in the County of Suffolk, merchant, 10 November 1645, with codicil dated 6 January 1645, proved 29 January 1645. To Robert Cutler, my cousin, youngest son of my deceased uncle Samuel Cutler, one half of my manor of Blofields als Burnivalls and of all lands, tenements, hereditaments, rights, members and appurtenances thereunto belonging &c. in Trimly St Mary and Walton in the said County of Suffolk. If the said Robert die without heirs of his body lawfully begotten or, having such heirs, if the same shall die before they come to the age of one & twenty, then the said half to my cousin Martha Noore, the wife of Raphe Noore of Ipswich, merchant, sister of the said Robert (on certain conditions). The other half to the said Martha Noore. John Smithier of Ipswich, to be assistant to my executor in & about the getting in of my estate beyond the seas and elsewhere. To Elizabeth Smithier his daughter and all the rest of his daughters and to his three sons John, William and Henry and to Nicholas Kerrington, the said Mr John Smithier's wife's brother's son. The said Mr John Smithier and his wife and the longer liver of them shall dwell in my messuage or tenement wherein they now dwell in St Nicholas' Parish, Ipswich, rent free for three years. To Mr Samuel Snelling, son in law to my cousin Mr Ralph Noore, and to my cousin Martha Snelling his wife, and Mary Noore and Alice Noore her sisters and Richard Noore her brother. To my cousin Thomas Cutler Secretary to the Company of Eastland merchants, resident at Ipswich. To Elizabeth Hubbard and Mary Ward, maidservants to my cousin Mr Raphe Noore. To Mrs Ward, widow, late the wife of Mr Samuel Ward, late town Preacher of Ipswich, and to Samuel & to Mr Joseph Ward her sons. To the poor of St Nicholas, Ipswich, to the poor of the parish of Whatfield, near Hadley in Suffolk. To Mr Lawrence, common preacher or lecturer of the said town of Ipswich. Mr John Revett, merchant, to assist my executor in getting in of my estate beyond the seas. To John Cressall, to Johan Nowell. To my cousin Margaret Skinner, wife of Jonathan Skinner, clerk, and all her children now alive. Others named. George Raymond one of the witnesses.   Twisse, 3.

[There were several early emigrants to New England by the name of Cutler :—1. John Cutler, who came from Sprowston in Norfolk, with his wife, seven children and one servant, and settled in Hingham, Mass., in 1637 (REG. xv. 27) ; 2. James Cutler, who settled at Watertown as early as 1634 ; 3. Dea. Robert Cutler, who was here as early as 1636. See Genealogical Record of the Cutler Families, by Rev. Abner Morse, Boston, 1867.
Mr. Samuel Ward named in the will was the author of The Life of Faith. He was a brother of Nathaniel Ward, the compiler of the Massachusetts Body of Liberties. A sketch of his life is appended to the Memoir of Rev. Nathaniel Ward by the editor of the REGISTER. His son Joseph, also named in the will, was rector of Badingham in Suffolk.—EDITOR.]

MARIANE SEVIER of Yenstone, in the parish & peculiar of Henstridge in the County of Somerset, widow, 9 May 1607, proved 26 June 1607. To be buried in the churchyard of Henstridge. To the parish church of Henstridge ten shillings. To the poor folk of Henstridge parish ten shillings. To Deane Haskett, the daughter of Ellis Haskitt forty shillings. To Ellis Haskett's three other daughters and William Haskett his son four pounds, provided if any of them die before they come to the age of one & twenty years or be married then the money to remain to the survivors. To Margaret Sevier, daughter of Richard Sevier, a gown cloth and ten pounds ; to Alce Sevier, another daughter, a gown and ten pounds. To Marie Royall of Henstridge, widow, one featherbed and three pounds. To Annis Harte twenty shillings. To Cicely Royall, daughter of Marie Royall, three pounds; to Richard & to Dorothie Royall, son & daughter of Marie Royall, twenty shillings apiece. To brother in law Reynold Sevier three pounds & to John Sevier, his son, forty shillings. To Dorothie Pennie a gown. To Marrian Harris, wife to Richard Harris, five sheep. To John Moores nine sheep. To the children of John Wollfres nine sheep. To Thomas Seavier the younger nine sheep. To the children of Gregorie Royall four pounds eight shillings and four pence, which money is in the hands of the said Gregorie, the father of the said children. To John & Dorothy Penny, my servants, ten shillings apiece. To Rose Collis, wife of John Collis, three pounds. To Marie Haskett, wife of Ellis Haskett, twenty shillings. To every of my godchildren twelve pence apiece. All the rest of my goods to Gregory Royall, whom I ordain & constitute sole executor &c. The overseers to be Ellis Haskett & Richard Chippman and I bequeath to them three shillings four pence apiece.

The witnesses were John Bryne, William Pittman, Richard Chippman, Ellis Haskett & John Royall.   Huddleston, 62.

KATHERINE SAMPSON, of the parish and peculiar jurisdiction of Hengstridge, in the Diocese of Bath & Wells, maiden, 30 April 1627, proved 14 June, 1627. To be buried in the parish church of Hengstridge. To the said church, in money, twenty shillings. To the poor of the said parish ten shillings. For the love I bear to my cousin Nicholas Locke I do forgive him all the debts that he to me doth owe &c. To my mother my best band of linen and my best apron. I forgive my cousin John Sampson, out of the bond of forty shillings which he oweth unto me, twenty shillings thereof, and the other twenty shillings of the said Bond I do give unto my cousin Susan Sampson. To my sister Joane Sampson one silver spoon. To cousin Mary Sampson, my brother William's daughter, my best gown, my best petticoat, my best hat and sixteen pounds ten shillings which is due to me upon bond from Ellis Hasket and William Haskett, his son &c. To my two sisters Jane & Edith Sampson the residue, and they to be executrices. The overseers to be Richard Sampson the younger & Thomas Morris the younger. Brother Henry Sampson oweth me twenty six pounds. Richard Eburne, vicar, was one of the witnesses. Skinner, 63.

JOHN CARTER of the parish of St Mary Matfellon, alias Whitechapel, in the county of Middlesex, gentleman, 14 February 1691, proved 16 June 1692. To my two attorneys in Barbadoes, Mr Peter Fluellin and Capt. George Paine, twenty pounds each to buy them mourning. To my executors Mr Samuel Shepheard and Mr Samuel Perry twenty pounds each (for mourning). " Item I doe give, devise & bequeath unto my brother RoBert Skelton of New Yorke in America the full summe of five hundred pounds soe soone as Assetts shall come into my Executors hands to that value" &c. on condition that he pay to Samuel Shepheard seventy pounds that he owes to the said Shepheard. To Mr William Shawe, Mr Edwarde Shawe and Mr Francis Shawe, to each six pounds to buy mourning and to each of their wives twenty shillings to buy rings to wear for my sake. The residue to my sister Sarah Slaymaker, wife of Thomas Slaymaker, of the city of Oxford, cook. (By a codicil made the same day bequests to Mr Mark Bedford Whiteing, and his wife and two daughters, Angellick & Annett, to

Alexander Staples Esq and his wife, and son Alexander and *his* wife, and son John and daughter Dorothy. To John Hickman, Elizabeth Hickman, Hannah Hickman and Mary Staples (gold rings). To cousin Elizabeth Carter of Barbadoes, widow and her children Thomazine Gibbs, James Carter, and her other children James, Anne, William, Richard, Jane, Damaris, John & Agnes (gold rings). To cousin John How, of Barbadoes, his wife Elizabeth and daughter Mary, to every of them a gold ring of the value of ten shillings.   Fane, 103.

Mem. that on or about the first day of March 1691 John Lee, heretofore of Charlestown in New England, carpenter, lying sick on board the ship Swallow &c. I desire the captain, meaning and speaking of and to Gyles Fifield, Captain of the said ship, to take care of all my concerns and get in what is due me in England or elsewhere. I give two parts of my whole estate to my two children. The other part I give to the captain and desire he would bestow something of the ship's company. Witness Geo. Robeson, Samuel Boyes. 2 June 1692, the witnesses were sworn.

11 June 1692 Emanavit Commissio Egidio Fifield fidei commissario et legatario nominat in Test Nuncupativo Johannis Lee aliquandiu de Charlestowne in Nova Anglia sed in nave Le Swallow super alto mari deceden &c.
                                                           Fane, 112.

I, William Read of New England in the parts beyond the seas, mariner, have constituted John Harlock of Ratcliff, Stepney, in the county of Middlesex, gentleman, and Elizabeth his wife my attorneys &c. On board the good ship Granado, Capt. Loader commander, on a voyage for Jamaica. 2 October 1691.

Witness Fred. Johnson, Ja* Travers. Proved 12 September 1692.
                                                           Fane, 173.

JOHN SYMONDS of Yeldham Magna in the County of Essex, Esq. 20 March, 1691, with codicil dated 16 February 1692, proved the last of May 1693. I do confirm the jointure made to my wife (Jane) and give her my mansion house called the Poole, &c. Manors of Panfield Hall & Nichols in Panfield & Shalford, in the County of Essex, to my kinsman Mr Martin Carter and his heirs (& other lands). To my niece Elizabeth Pepys all moneys due to her by bond or otherwise by Martin Carter dec^d, father of the said Martin Carter. To my nephew Mr John Pepys, of Cambridge; to my sister Thomasin Pepys; to my nephew Thomas Pepys; to my nieces Anne Whaples and Elizabeth Pepys, to my niece Ellen Bacon. To each of the children of Martin Carter decd. (except the two eldest sons) fifty pounds. To my sister Mrs Judith Burgoyne, to my nephew and godson Mark Guyon, to my niece Jane Guyon, to my nephews Roger and Lucy Burgoyne, sons of Sir John Burgoyne, Baronet. To Mr John Brooke our worthy minister. To the Society of Lincoln's Inn of which I am a member. My wife and sister Thomasine Pepys and nephew John Pepys to be executors.

(In the codicil) to my cousin Mr William Simonds of Ipswich in New England one hundred pounds. To Mr Fisk forty shillings. To my cousin John Carter and his heirs (certain lands). My nephew Thomas Pepys of Felsted. Mr Fisk my chaplain.

Sworn to &c. die Lunæ vizt Decimo die mensis Aprilis A.D. 1693.
                                                           Coker, 86.

The testimony of the witnesses shows that Mr. Symonds had been cursitor for Lincolnshire and Somersetshire.

[John Symonds was the 2d son of John and Ann (Elyott) Symonds, and was born in Yeldham Magna, Sept. 4, 1618. He was a nephew of Samuel Symonds of Ipswich, deputy governor of Massachusetts. See Appleton's Ancestry of Priscilla Baker, pp. 19-102.—EDITOR.]

JANE COAKER of Kingsbridge in the County of Devon, widow, 6 June 1651, proved 1 August 1651. To the poor of Kingsbridge twenty shillings at the day of the funeral. To son Robert Coaker forty pounds within one month after my decease, and I release him of all debts owing unto me, and ten shillings a year to be paid him by my executor so long as they shall live together. To grandson James Coaker, son of William Coaker, my son, all my right &c. in the messuage wherein I live. To grandchild Jane Ball ten pounds within two years after my decease. To son Richard Coaker five shillings, to be paid him at his return into England. To daughter-in-law Agnis Coaker thirty shillings. To daughter Agnis Bound, wife of Thomas Bound, ten pounds within a quarter of a year, and to Jane Kingston five shillings. To daughter Johane Borton (wife of Henry Borton) twenty pounds within one month after my decease and ten bushels of barley malt. To Agnes Risdon, wife of Thomas Risdon, to godchild Thomas Phillipps, to Francis Hingston & to Johane Heyman, my godchildren. To grandchild Jane Coaker forty shillings. To grandchildren Anne Davie and Elizabeth Coaker ten shillings apiece. To grand children Leonard & Francis Kent fifty shillings apiece. To grand children Richard, Henry, Robert, William, Flower and John Coaker ten shillings apiece. To grand child Henry Borton six silver spoons. To grand child Jane Coaker three pounds besides the forty shillings before bequeathed. Residue to son-in-law John Hardie, who is made sole executor. The will was proved by John Hardye.   Grey, 157.

[The foregoing will may refer to Richard Coaker who was of New England in 1640.—H. F. W.

It may not be relevant, but I offer that the following grants are of record in the Virginia Land Registry :—John Corker, 6 acres in James Island, Feb. 10, 1637, Book No. 1, p. 521 ; John Cocker, 1150 acres in Surry county, March 20, 1677, Book No. 4, p. 301.—R. A. BROCK.]

SARAH ELMES, of the parish of St. Saviour's, Southwark, in the County of Surrey, widow 25 August 1653, proved 20 April 1654. To son Anthony Elmes five pounds. To son Radolphus Elmes (now in parts beyond the seas) the sum of ten pounds if he shall be living at the time of my decease. To son Jonathan Elmes ten pounds within one month after my decease. To grand child Jonathan Elmes, son of the said Jonathan, ten pounds, and to such child as Mary, the wife of the said son Jonathan, now goeth withall ten pounds. To son Henry Elmes ten pounds within one month. To my two grand children Curtis and Henry Elmes (minors) sons of my said son Henry, ten pounds apiece. To my two grand children John and Sarah Maries, children of my daughter Margaret Maries, of the parish of St. Saviour's, Southwark, widow, twenty pounds apiece at the age of one & twenty years or day of marriage. To my loving cousin Sarah Best twenty shillings (for a ring) and to sister Elizabeth Sturmey, twenty shillings and good friend Mrs Hamond of Pudding Lane twenty shillings (for rings). Daughter Margaret Maries to be sole executrix and Mr John Chelsham and loving cousin Mr Ralph Collins overseers.

                                              Alchin, 83.

[The testatrix of the above will was undoubtedly the mother of Rhodolphus Ellmes (see Savage), of Scituate, who came in the Planter, 1635, aged 15, and married, 1644, Catharine, daughter of John Whitcomb.

See deed of Rodolphus Emes of Scituate to John Floyd, Oct. 2, 1656, for money lent and paid for passage, in Suffolk Deeds, vol. ii. p. 294.—H. F. W.]

EDWARD WINSLOW, of London, Esq., being now bound in a "Viage" to sea in the service of the Common Wealth, 18 December 1654, proved 16 October 1655 by Josias Winslow, son and executor. All my lands and stock in New England and all my possibilities and portions in future allotments and divisions I give & bequeath to Josia, my only son, and his heirs, he allowing to my wife a full third part thereof for her life. To the poor of the church of "Plimouth" in New England ten pounds. To the poor of Marshfield, where the chiefest of my estate lies, ten pounds. I give my linen which I carry with me to sea to my daughter Elizabeth; and the rest of my goods which I carry with me to sea to my son Josias, he giving to each of my brothers a suit of apparell. Son Josias to be executor and Col. Venables my overseer of my goods in the voyage and my four friends, Doctor Edmond Wilson, Master John Arthur, Master James Shirley and Master Richard Floyd, to be overseers for the rest of my personal estate in England.

The witnesses were Jon Hooper, Gerard Usher servant to Hen: Colbron.

Aylett, 377.

[Edward Winslow, the third governor of Plymouth Colony, was the son of Edward and Magdalen Winslow, of Droitwich in Gloucester, England, and was born Oct. 18, 1595. (See REGISTER, xxi. 209-10, where his pedigree is given.) He was one of the Mayflower passengers. He was appointed by Cromwell one of three commissioners to superintend the expedition against the Spaniards in the West Indies, and died May 8, 1655, on the passage between Hispaniola and Jamaica. An article on his life, by G. D. Scull, Esq., was printed in the REGISTER, xxxviii. 21-6. See also REGISTER, iv. 297; xvii. 159; and xxxvii. 392.—EDITOR.]

JOHN STOUGHTON Doctor "in devinitie" & curate of the parish of St Mary Aldermanbury, London, beginning "Laus Deo the fowerth daie of May 1639" [on which day he died], proved 20 May 1639. To my poor kindred twenty pounds to be disposed of according to the discretion of my wife Jane Stoughton, one of my executors. To the parishioners of the parish of St Mary, Aldermanbury aforesaid five pounds, to be bestowed unto the poor of the said parish.

To my two daughters Jane & Marie five "hundreth" pounds, to say, to my eldest daughter Jane "fower hundreth marks which twoe hundred three score and six poundes thirteene shillings and fower pence, and the remainder beinge twoe C. hundreth thirtie three poundes six shillings and eight pence to my youngest daughter Marie Stoughton, to be paied them att theire age of one & twenty yeares or the day of theire marriage, which shall first happen" &c. If both depart this life before they attain the age specified or day of marriage that then "two hundreth and fieftie poundes thereof shall come unto my wife and two hundred pounds thereof to my nexte of kynn, and twentie fiue poundes thereof to Emanuell Colledge in Cambridge and the other five and twentie poundes to Master Hartlipp a Dutchman."

To four or five persons such as my loving wife & one of my executors shall think fit twenty shillings apiece for a ring, provided Mr Janeway be one of them. The executors to be my dear and loving wife Jane Stoughton and my loving father in law and her father John Browne of Frampton in Dorsetshire Esq. and for overseers Robert Edwards and Edmond Foord of London merchants.

The remainder to my wife Jane Stoughton.

Wit: Robert Edwards   Thomas Davies.   Harvey, 69.

[May 4, 1639, "Dr. Stoughton of Aldermanbury died." See Smyth's Obituary. —H. F. W.

The Rev. John Stoughton was a brother of Israel and Thomas Stoughton, early settlers of Dorchester, Mass. Israel was the father of Lieut.-Gov. William Stoughton. Thomas removed from Dorchester to Windsor, Conn. Rev. John Stoughton, the testator, was also the stepfather of Gen. James Cudworth, of Scituate, New England, and of the Rev. Ralph Cudworth, author of The Intellectual System of the Universe. See articles on Stoughton and Cudworth in the REGISTER, xiv. 101; xxi. 249.—EDITOR.]

MENSE APRILIS 1611.

Thomas Rogers   Vicesimo Septimo die probatum fuit testim̄ Thome
    Sen.   Rogers señ nup de Stratford sup Avon in Com̄ Warwici
                  def heñts etc. Juramento Thome Rogers filii dicti def et
                  exr̃is etc. cui etc de bene etc iurat.   Probate Act Book.

[The will of which the above is the Probate Act, does not seem to have been copied into the Register, which I examined leaf by leaf, with hopes to find it. My friend J. C. C. Smith, Esq., then hunted through the bundle of original wills for that year, but in vain. That the testator was the father of Mrs. Harvard, and grandfather of our John Harvard, there can be no doubt. The extracts from the Parish Register of Stratford upon Avon, together with the wills of his daughters, &c., prove that. Among the Feet of Fines of the Easter Term, 23d Elizabeth (1581), I find a conveyance made to him by one Henry Mace, of two messuages and two gardens with their appurtenances in Stratford upon Avon. He seems to have been a prominent citizen of that borough, as will appear from the extracts I shall give from the records, and, in 1596, while he was holding the office of Bailiff, built the house still standing in High Street, now known as "Ye Ancient House," the best specimen now left in that street, or perhaps in the borough. On the front, under the broad window of the second story, appear these characters:

          T R   1596   A R

In this house, therefore, Katharine Rogers lived from 1596 until her marriage to Robert Harvard, and to it she may have come with her little son John to attend the obsequies of her father. A heliotype of this house illustrates this volume.

                                                                —H. F. W.]

The Parish Registers of Stratford upon Avon commence Anno 1558. By the kind permission of the Vicar, the Rev. George Arbuthnot, M.A., I was enabled to devote the whole of one day, from the close of the morning service to the beginning of the afternoon service, to an examination of them. I took notes of the following marriages:

1562   January 31, Thomas Rogers and Margaret Pace.
1563   November 27, Henry Rogers and Elizabeth Burback.
1566   July 6, Edward Huntington and Matilda Rogers.
1570   October 15. John Rogers and Anne Salsbury.
1579   July 20, William Rogers and Elizabeth Walker.
1581   October 30, Richard Rogers and Susanna Castell.
"   November 5, Richard Rogers and Alee Calle.
1592 (?3) December 30, Antherin Russell and Joyce Rogers.
1596   November 21, William Rogers and Jone Tante.
1600   October 28, John Nelson to Elizabeth Rogers.
1602   April 13, Lewes Rogers to Joano Rodes.
"   October 12, Francis Rogers to Elizabeth Sperpoint.
1603 (4)   January 1, William Smith to Ales Rogers.
1605   " Apriell 8, Robertus Harwod to Katherina Rogers."
1608 (9)   February 6, Henry Stanton to Phillip Rogers.
1609   July 18, Thomas Chestley to Margaret Rogers.

I looked through the record of the marriages down to 1637 inclusive, and found a few other Rogers marriages, which it hardly seems worth the while to print. Thomas, Henry, John, William and Richard Rogers had numerous children baptized and buried. Of these I pick out the children of Thomas.

Baptized.	*Buried.*
Margaret, September 26, 1562.	Margaret, December 1, 1562.
Elizabeth. October 28, 1563.	Johanna, February 21, 1566 (7).
Charles, March 28, 1565.	Alice, October 3, 1568.
Johanna, January 24, 1566 (7).	Anne, July 24, 1581.
Alice, September 2, 1568.	Thomas, August 13, 1584.
Joanna, October 14, 1571.	"Infant," January 15, 1591.
Joyce, February 9, 1572 (3).	Charles Rogers, "homo" March 30,
Ales, September 11, 1574.	1609 (10).
Richard, November 10, 1575.	Thomas Rogers, August 31, 1639.
William, June 8, 1578.	
Edward, February 18, 1579.	
Thomas, July 22, 1582.	
Katherin, November 25, 1584.	
Thomas, June 11, 1587.	
Rose, March 29, 1590.	
Frances, March 10, 1593.	

The burial of Margaret, the wife of Mr. Rogers, I did not find. He evidently married again; for I found the burial of " Alice wyf to Mr Thomas Rogers," August 17, 1608. His own burial is thus given :

1610 (11) February 20, Thomas Rogers, one of the Aldermen.

Thomas Rogers of Stratford upon Avon in the County of Warwick yeoman 27 Aug. 1639, proved at Worcester 21 May 1640. To Anne my beloved wife all that my messuage or tenement wherein I now dwell, with the appurtenances, and all other my lands and tenements whatsoever situate & being in the said town of Stratford &c. to have and to hold for life or until marriage, and, after her decease or day of marriage, to my four daughters Lydia, Alice, Ruth & Hannah & their assigns until Edward Rogers my son shall well & truly pay unto my said four daughters the sum of twenty pounds apiece, and after such payment, then to the said Edward & to the heirs of his body Lawfully to be begotten ; failing such to my right heirs forever. To the poor of Stratford twenty shillings. Towards the repair of Stratford church twenty shillings. John Whinge of Blackwell in the county of Worcester, yeoman to be the executor and my loving kinsman John Woolmer the younger and Henry Smyth of Old Stratford, yeoman, to be the overseers of this my will.

The Inventory of his goods, &c. was taken 1 October 1639 by John Wolmer the younger, gentleman, John Wynge and Henry Smith. The sum total was 86^{li} 13^s 0^d.

The widow Anna Rogers was appointed administratrix with the will annexed and gave her bond 23 May 1640, with Francis Baggott of Witley Parva in the parish of Holt in the County of Worcester, as her surety.

William Smythe of Stratford upon Avon in the County of Warwick mercer, 30 March 1626, proved at Worcester 10 May 1626. To Thomas, my eldest son my shop & the cellars lying in the Middle Row & now in the tenure of William Ayng, butcher, and also my three tenements in the Henley Street, now in the tenures of Thomas Alenn & Thomas Woodwarde and that I late did dwell in, &c. & for want of lawful issue then to

Francis my son & to his lawful issue & for want of such issue to my two daughters Mary & Alice (equally). To daughter Mary twenty pounds to be paid to her within two years after my decease by my son Francis, and in consideration thereof I give to my son Francis the lease of the house wherein I now dwell, &c. To my daughter Alice Smythe all my household stuff, &c. &c. and I make Alice Smyth my said daughter executrix of this my last will & testament, and I make my brother Henry Smythe and John Wolmer overseers, &c.

The Inventory of his goods & chattels was taken 28 April 1626.

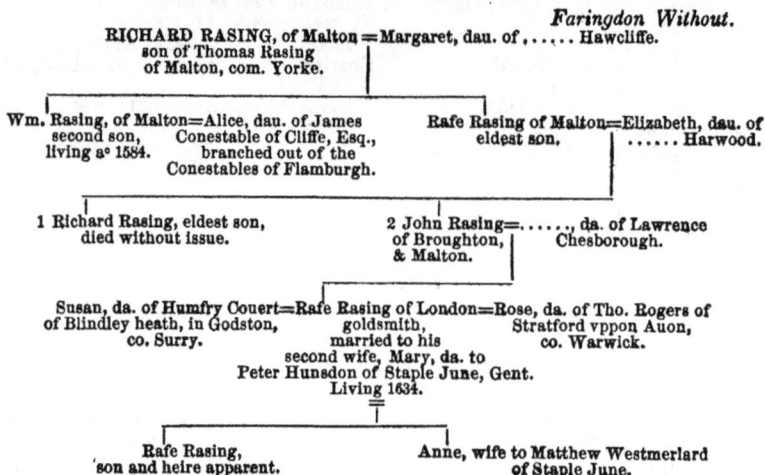

Faringdon Without.

RICHARD RASING, of Malton = Margaret, dau. of , ... Hawcliffe.
son of Thomas Rasing
of Malton, com. Yorke.

Wm. Rasing, of Malton = Alice, dau. of James   Rafe Rasing of Malton = Elizabeth, dau. of
second son,   Conestable of Cliffe, Esq.,   eldest son, ... Harwood.
living aº 1584.   branched out of the
Conestables of Flamburgh.

1 Richard Rasing, eldest son,   2 John Rasing = ..., da. of Lawrence
died without issue.   of Broughton,   Chesborough.
& Malton.

Susan, da. of Humfry Couert = Rafe Rasing of London = Rose, da. of Tho. Rogers of
of Blindley heath, in Godston,   goldsmith,   Stratford vppon Auon,
co. Surry.   married to his   co. Warwick.
second wife, Mary, da. to
Peter Hunsdon of Staple June, Gent.
Living 1634.

Rafe Rasing,   Anne, wife to Matthew Westmerlard
son and heire apparent.   of Staple June.
(Signed) RAIPHE RASING.

[From Visitation of London, 1633–4–5.
Harl. Soc. xvii. 186.]

Mense Junii 1647. Undecimo die emᵗ Comº Rose Reason Relce Radulphi Reason nuᵖ poe Ste Bridgitte als Brides prope Fleetstreete Civitat London deft haben & ad adstrand bona iura et credita dict deft de bene &c. iurat.   Admon. Act. Book. Fol. 76.

[The two forms of spelling this surname are interesting for two reasons; first, as showing the loss of the guttural final *g* sound in Rasing (in connection with which it may be well to note that the crest of this family was a hand grasping a bunch of *grapes*), and, secondly, as illustrating the sound of the diphthong *ea* in *Reason.* I have seen many similar instances showing that in Shakspeare's time the word was pronounced like *raisin.* Recall Fallstaff's play on the word in Henry IV. Part I. Act ii. Sc. 4: "Give you a reason on compulsion! If reasons were as plenty as blackberries I would give no man a reason upon compulsion."—H. F. W.]

IN THE NAME OF GOD AMEN. I Rose Raysings of the Parish of Saint Bride London Widdowe being weake in bodie but of sound and perfect memorie thankes be to God doe make this my last Will and Testament in manner and forme following (videlicet) ffirst I bequeath my soule to Almighty God who gaue it me and my bodie to the Earth from whence it Came to be buried in Saint Brides Church London in Christian decentlike manner as my Executor hereafter named shall thinke fitting. Item I giue to my daughter Rose Haberly the Wife of Anthony Haberly the summe of Tenne poundes and alsoe my best Gowne and petticoate and a payre of Hollande sheetes and one douzen and to her husband twentie shillinge. Item I giue to the Children of my daughter Rose Haberley (that is to say) to Authonie John Mary and Rose I giue fiue poundes apeece But to my Grandchild Elizabeth Haberley who is my God daughter I giue Tenne poundes. Item I giue to Katherine Wilmour my Executors Wife here after named fiue poundes. Item I giue to Joane Wilmour her Kinswoeman fiue poundes. Item I giue to John Wilmour the younger my sisters Grand-Child fiue poundes. Item I giue to my Cousin Brockett's sonne Joseph Brockett in Southwarke fiue poundes and to his Mother twenty shillings to buy her a Ring. Item I giue to Marie Right That Tends me in my sicknes fiue pounds. Item I giue John Corker my Godsonne Twenty shillings and to his Mother and his brother Tenne shillings a peece. Item I giue to William Suthes the sonne of James Suthes twenty pounds to be paid att his age of one and twentie yeares. Item I giue to Master James Palmer formerly the Viccar of Saint Brides London fiue poundes. Item I giue to Master Alexander Baker of Cliffords Inne London Gentleman that Bond wherein Master Morgan and Master Powell stands bound unto my late husband Ralph Raysing which is now in suite in the upper Bench and in the Chancerie and I doe hereby giue power to the said Master Baker to sue in my Executors name for the same provided alwaies That if the said James Suches shall att anie time hereafter trouble my Executor hereafter named for any concerning mee or my late husband Ralph Raysing That then my Legacie to the said Willia Suthes his sonne shall be absolutely voyd. Item I giue to Thomas Smith the sonne of my sister Alice Smith in Warwickshire the summe of fiue pounds. And last of all I make my loueing Kinseman Master John Wilmour of Stratford upon Avon in the Countie of Warwick my full and sole Executor of this my last Will and Testament desireing him to doe all things accordingly as I haue by this my last Will required him. And the remainder of all my goods and Chattells not formerlie bequeath I doe hereby give and bequeath to my said Executor and I doe hereby renounce all former Wills and Testam[ts] whatsoever and doe hereby revoake the same and publish this to be my last Will and Testament and desire that none may stand for my last Will but this and I doe alsoe giue and bequeath to Mistris Susan Annyon Widdowe the summe of Thirtie shillings to buy her a Ring. In Witnes whereof I haue to this my last Will and Testament sett my hand and seale dated This first Day of December in the yeare of our Lord One Thousand six hundred fifty and fower. Rose Raysings Signed sealed published and delivered as her last Will and testam[t] Theise words (videlicet) and alsoe my best gowne and petticoate and a payre of Holland sheetes and one douzen of Napkins and my Bible Kinsewoeman to be paid att his age of one and twenty yeares Avon in the Countie of Warwicke being first interlined in the presence of us Susan Annyon Alex Barker.

THIS WILL was proved in London the twentith Day of June in the yeare of our Lord God One Thousand six hundred fiftie and fiue before the Judges for probate of Wills and granting Administrations lawfully authorized by the oath of John Willmour The Sole Executor named in the aboue written Will To whome Administration of all and singular the goods Chattells and debts of the said deceased was Committed he being first legally sworne truly and faithfully to administer the same. 291, Aylett.

JOH. SADLER clerk M.A. adm., on the resignation of Simon Aldriche, to the Vicarage of Ringmer, 6 October, 1626.

Archbishop Abbot's Reg. p. 2, f. 349[b].

JOHN SADLER was inducted into the possession of y° vicaridge of Ringmer Octobʳ xijᵗʰ 1626.

1640 Oct. 3 buried Mʳ John Sadler minister of Ringmer.

Ringmer Parish Register.

Sussex, Ringmer Vic. John Sadler 14 Nov. 1626 (to Nov. 1628), William Thomas of Lewes and William Michelborne of Westmiston (his sureties).   Compositions for First Fruits.

EDWARD FENNER of Auburne in the County of Sussex (13 July 1603 proved 9 October 1605) wishes his body to be buried in the parish church of Auburne and leaves all to his wife Mary whom he appoints executrix & entrusts the children to her care.   69, Hayes.

License granted 12 May 1613 to the Rector, Vicar or Curate of Stepney in the county of Middlesex to solemnize the marriage between John Sadler, clerk, and Mary Fenner, widow, late the relict of Edward Fenner, while he lived of Auburne in the County of Sussex, gen. dec'd.

Vicar General's Book.

[Albourne is a parish in Sussex near Cuckfield.—H. F. W.]

MARY SADLER of Mayfield in the County of Sussex, widow, 16 January 1645, proved 13 November 1647. " My Corpes to bee interred where ever ytt shall please God by my surviving freindes to dispose of ytt." I do nominate & appoint my daughter Elizabeth James to be my sole Executrix. And I bequeath and give unto her one hundred pounds of money which is in her husband's hands, and such bedding and chests and wearing clothes as I have (saving one chest which is full of linnen and pewter, and other small things). My will is that she shall buy & give to my grandchild Mary Russell two silver spoons of ten shillings apiece price and to Thomas Russell my grandson ten shillings of money. I will & bequeath unto my son John Sadler the money which I have in Mʳ William Michilborne's hands. Item I give unto my grandchild Mary James one chest of linen and pewter except two pair of the sheets and one pair of pillowcoats therein, which I give unto Anne James, and one other pair of sheets which are also in the said chest, which I give unto Elizabeth James my grandchildren. Item I give to each of my son Russell's children not before named in this my will one shilling apiece for the buying them gloves. Item I give unto my daughter Mary Sadler and to each of her children which I suppose to live in " newe " England one shilling apiece. Item I give unto my daughter Anne Allin and to her daughter Mary one shilling apiece, and this I do appoint and intend my last will and testament.   231 Fines.

ALLEN.—THOMAS, son of John Allen, dyer, of Norwich. At school under Mʳ Briggs eight years. Age 15. Admitted sizar litt. grat. July 6, 1624. Surety Mʳ Moore.   Admissions Caius Coll. Cambridge.

THOMAS HERVY, citizen & " Bocher " of London, 16 June 1505, proved at Lambeth 3 October 1505. " I bequeth my soule to god to our blissed lady Virgyñ Mary his moder and to all the holy company of heveñ And my body to be buried in the churchyerd of Seynt Clementes in Candilwykstrete of London on the Northside of the same Churchyerd where the body of William more late Citezein and bocher of London my groundfader lyeth buried. And if it fortune that I dye or decesse owte of Londoñ thañ I will that my body be buried where as it shall please god for it to dispose. Item I bequeth to the high aulter of the said churche of Seynt Clementes for myñ offerynges forgoteñ or negligently w'draweñ in dischargyng of my soule iij^s iiij^d. It I bequeth unto Margarete my wife for hir parte purparte and porcioñ of all my goodes moevable and unmoevable in redy money xl^{li} sterl and all my stuff of household and plate hole as it shalbe the day of my decesse. It I bequeth unto my sonnes Thomas Hervy and Nicholas Hervy and to the Infaunte beyng in my wiffs wombe if she now be w^t childe in redy money xl^{li} evenly to be devided and departed amonges theym and to be deliũed to theym and eũry of theym whañ they or eny of theym shall cõme to their laufull ages or mariages the which money I will my moder mawde Hoppy haue the keping to the use of my said childerñ till they shall cõme to their laufull ages or mariages. And if it fortune any of my said sonnes or the Infañt in my wiffes wombe for to dye or decesse afore they or any of theym shal cõme to their laufull ages or mariages, thañ I will that the parte of hym or theym so decessyng remayne to hym or theym beyng on lyve. And if it fortune all my said childerñ to dye afore they cõme to their laufull ages or be maried thañ I will that my said moder dispose the same xl^{li} to my said childerñ before bequethed for my soule my faderes soule my childerñ soules and for all my goode frendes soules in deedes of almes and of charitie as she shall thinke best for the helth and saluacioñ of my soule. It I will that my saide moder haue the keping of my said childreñ duryng their noonage It I will that the saide Mawde my moder take haue & receyve the proffittes and revenues cõmyng and growying of my fermes called Gubbons and Waltoñs in the Countie of Essex and of my ferme in Madebrokes long mede and Wottons croftes lying in the pisshe of Retherhith in the Countie of Surrey towardes the sustentacioñ and fynding of my said childerñ duryng their noonage and the surplusage of the same revenues and proffittes cõming & growyng of the same fermes I will it be evenly devided and depted amonges my said childerñ and Infaunt by the said Mawde my moder. It I bequeth to my suster Elyñ fflynte the wif of Johñ fflynte all my state and Tñe of years which I haue to cõme of and in my ferme called preestes m̄she sett and lying in the pisshe of Retherhed aforesaid. And I will that thendentur of the same ferme be deliũed unto my said suster incontinent aft^r my decesse. Itm̄ I bequeth unto my cosyñ Thomas Hervy myñ state and termes of yeres which that I haue to cõme of and into the tenementes called the Dogge and the Shippe in Estchepe in the pisshe of Seynt Clementes aforesaid and in seynt Leonardes. And I will that thendentures of the same houses be deliũed unto my said cosyñ Thomas assone aft^r my decesse as is possible. It I bequeth unto my sũnt William Anderby xx^s in money. It I bequeth unto Johñ ffelix xx^s. It I bequeth unto Richard ffelix xx^s. It I will that my moder or hir Executo^{r}s fynde the said Johñ ffelix to gram^r scoole and to writting scole by the space of a yere aft^r my decesse. The Residue of all my goods moevable and unmoevable aft^r my dettes paid my burying done and this my p^{r}sent testament in all thinges fulfilled I geve and bequeth unto the forsaid Mawde my moder she therew^t to doo ordeyne and dispose hir owne freewill for eũmore. Which Mawde my moder I make and ordeyne executrice of this my p^{r}sent testament. In witnesse wherof to this my p^{r}sent testament I haue setto my seale. Youeñ the day and yer̄ aforesaid." 86 Holgrave.

In the name of God amen The xxixth day of the moneth of July In the yere of o^r lord god m^t v^c and viij. I Thomas Hervy bocher of the pisshe of seynt Oluff in Suthwerk in the diocise of Winchester beyng hole of mynde and memory thanked be almighty god sett make and ordeyne this my p[r]sent testament and last will in man[r] and fo[r]me folowing ffirst I bequeth and recomend my soule unto almighty god my creato[r] and savio[r], my body to be buryed in the church of seynt Oluff aforesaid And I bequeth unto the high aulter of the same churche for my tithes & oblacioūs here before necligently paid or forgoten ij[s]. Also I bequith to my moder church of Wynchestre iiij[d] And I geve and bequeth to the aulter of our lady in the said pisshe church of seynt Orluff iiij[d]. Also I bequeth to the ault[r] of seynt Anne there iiij[d]. Also to the aulter of seynt Clement iiij[d]. The Residue of all my goodes and catalles not bequethed nor geven after my fuūall expences dooū and my dettes paied I will and geve unto Guynor my wif she to dispose theym after hir discrecioū as she shall thinke moost convenyent. And of this my present testament and last will I make and ordeyne myū executrice my said wif Thiese witnesses S[r] William Priour Curat of seynt Oluff aforeseid William Bulleyū grocer William Symsoū and other.

PROBATUM fuit suprascript testm corā Dūo apud Lamehith xv° die mens Augusti Anno Dūi Millimͦ quingētesimo octauo Jur Guynoris Relicte et executricis in huiōi testō noiāte Ac approbat & insinuat Et cōmissa fuit admͥistra° omͥ bonorum & debit dicti defuncti prefate executrici de bene & fidelit admͥistrand Ac de pleno & fideli Inuētario citra p[r]imū diem Septembr̃ βx futur exhibend necnō de plano et vero cōmͣpto reddend ad sca dei euͦg in debita iuris forma iurat.   4 Bennett (P. C. C.)

WILLIAM HERFORD citizen & tallowchandler of London, 31 August 1518, proved 10 Nov. 1518. My body to be buried in the parish church of St. Olave in the old " Jure " of London in the same place where my late wife Johan resteth buried. " And I haue bought & payed for the stone that lyeth on her. And therefor I woll haue the same stone layed on my body & I woll have a scripture graveū & fyxed yn the same stone makyng mension off the tyme off my deceasse requiryng the people to pray for me." To the high altar of the same church for tythes & oblations forgotten or negligently withholden iij[s] iiij[d]. Towards the gilding of the tabernacle of S[t] John the Baptist at the south end of the high Altar of the same church xx[s]. Towards the maintenance of Olave's Brotherhood within the same church xij[d]. To the company & brotherhood of Our Lady & S[t] John Baptist Tallowchandlers of London my silver pot. To John Hone my best dagger the sheath garnished with silver as it is. To Richard Chopyn my purse garnished with silver. " It I beqweth to Nicholas Pynchyn my best Jaket." Touching the disposition of my lands & tenements in the parish of St. Stephen in Colemanstreet I will that my wife Agnes Herford shall have them during her life and after her decease they shall remain to my children and to the heirs of their bodies lawfully begotten & for lack of such issue they shall remain to the company of Butchers of London forever, they finding forever in the same church of St. Olaves the day of my decease dirige " on nyght and masse of Requiem on the morne by note dispendyng at eūry such obyte amongyst prestes and clerkes wex Ryngyng off belles & poū people 20[s] foreu[r]. And if the same Company of Bouchers make defaute of and yn kypyng of the same obyte yn man[r] & forme a bouesayd then I woll that the same landes and tenūtes shall full & hole remayne to the cōpany & felyshippe of Talow chaundelers of London foreū they doyng and dyspendyng yerely therfore at an obytt yerly yn man[r] and forme as the forsayd cōpany off Bouchers ar bounde to doo yn kepyng of the forsayd Obyte as they wyll answere before God." ——— To my cousin Richard Baynbery my tawney gown furred with black, to John Kyttelwell & Rob[t] Kyttelwell either of them my single Ray gowns, to John Ryve my best dublett to William Knott my second Dublet, to William Pyper, George Chelsey & James Quick mine apprentices, so that they continue & serve out their terms well & truly to my wife their mistress, to either of them vi[s] viij[d]. when their terms of prenticehood shall be finished. To my god children that at time of my decease shall be living xii[d]. The residue shall be divided amongst my wife & children accordinge to the laws & custōms of the city of London. And Executors of this will &c. I make & ordaine my said wife Agnes & the said Nicholas. To Robert Whetecroft my riding coat.

102 Bennet (Commissary Court of London).

CRISTIANA HARVYE of Shenley in the County of Hertford widow, and John Harvye, son and heir apparent of the said Cristiana, give a bond 30 June 10 Elizabeth, of one hundred pounds, to Lawrence Greene, citizen and cutler of London, that they will carry out an agreement specified in a pair of Indentures bearing date 30 June 10 Elizabeth.

Claus Roll 10 Elizabeth, Part 13.

THOMAS HARVARD of the precinct of S[t] Katherine's near the Tower of London, butcher, conveys to Henry Rawlins of Lee in the county of Essex, mariner 29 January 1621, for the sum of one hundred and fifty pounds already received, all those three several messuages and tenements, with all shops, cellars, rollers, warehouses, backsides, entries, lights, easements, commodities and appurtenances whatsoever to the said three several messuages or tenements, or any of them, belonging, situate, &c. at the North end of Bermondsey Street, near Battle Bridge, in the parish of S[t] Olaves, *als.* tooles in Southwark, &c. now or late in the several tenures or occupations of William Pilkington, William Hatcham and William Fells or their assigns, &c. to be delivered up the 2[d] day of July next. His wife Margaret unites. (What follows seems to indicate that this conveyance is a mortgage.) Claus Roll 20 Jac. I. Part 37.

HILL. 6 H. viij (1514) Apud Westm̄ a die Sci Martini in quindecim dies. Int[r] Johēm Kyrton Nichū Tycheborñ Henr̄ Tyngylden & Johem Fowler quer. et Ricū Harvy & Cristinam uxeñ eius deforc de uno mesuagio & uno gardino cum ꝑtin in Southwerk Et preterea iidem Ricus & Cristina concesserunt pro se & hered ipius Cristine qd ipi warant pdcis Johi Nicho Henr & Johi & hered ipius Johis Kyrton pdca ten cum ꝑtin contr̄ Johem Abbem monastri Sc Petri Westm̄ & successores suos &c. &c.

The consideration was twenty marks of silver.

Feet of Fines, Surrey.

Trin. 10 Elizabeth (1568). Hec est finalis concordia fc̄a in cur Dūe Regine apud Westm̄ in crastino Sc̄e Trinitatis anno regni Elizabeth dei grā Anglie ffranc & hibñie Regine fidei defensoris etc a conqu decimo, coram (&c.), Int Laurenciū Grene quer et Cristianam Harvye viduam & Johem Harvye geñosum deforc de septem messuagiis septem gardinis & una acra trē cum ꝑtin in ꝑochia Sc̄i Georgii in Southwarke etc. Consideration eighty pounds sterling. Feet of Fines, Surrey.

Trinity Term 37 Elizabeth, Essex. Oliver Skinner quer. and Thomas Harvard and Johann his wife, Hugh Gullifer and Anne his wife, William Smarte, Henry West and Margaret his wife and William Spalding and Elizabeth his wife deforc,—for one acre of pasture with the appurtenances in Westham. Consideration 40[li] sterling. Feet of Fines.

Hillary Term 37 Elizabeth, Surrey. Thomas Harvard & Johan his wife quer. and John Leveson mil. deforc,—for three messuages with the appurtenances in the parish of St Olave alias St Toolyes in Southwark. Consideration 160ll st.   Feet of Fines.

Easter Term 38 Elizabeth, Essex. Christopher Poyner gen. quer. and Thomas Harvey & Johan his wife deforc, for one messuage with the appurtenances in Foxyearth & Pentrowe. Consideration 80ll st.
                                                        Feet of Fines.

Easter Term 38 Elizabeth, Essex. John Jefferson and Thomas Smyth quer. and Thomas Harvard & Johan his wife & Henry West & Margaret his wife deforc, for three parts of one messuage, one barn, one garden, one orchard and twelve acres of arable land with the appurtenances, into four parts to be divided, in Westham & Stratford Langthorne. Feet of Fines.

Mich. Term 39–40 Elizth (1597) Surrey. Thomas Harvard quer. and John Anwyke and Alice his wife and William Crowcher (Crowther ?) and Agnes his wife deforc ; for two messuages, two gardens with the appurtenances in the parish of St Olave, Southwark. Consideration 80ll st.
                                                        Feet of Fines.

Easter Term 40 Elizabeth, Essex, David George quer. and Thomas Herverd and Johan his wife and William Spaldinge and Elizabeth his wife deforc,—for one messuage, one barn, one garden, one orchard, twenty acres of land (arable), four acres of meadow and six acres of pasture with the appurtenances in Westham. Consideration 100ll sterling. Feet of Fines.

Mich. Term 22 James I. Surrey. Robert Harverd quer. and Thomas Harverd deforc,—for three messuages, with the appurtenances in the parish of St Olaves in Southwark. Consideration 240ll sterling.
                                                        Feet of Fines.

THOMAS ROWELL of the Parish of Westham in the County of Essex yeoman, 12 August 1583, proved 23 August 1583. My body to be buried in the churchyard of Westham.

"Also I doe giue unto my sonne in Lawe Thomas Harford butcher dwellinge in London one redd cowe and he havinge the said Cowe to giue unto his mother in Lawe the some of xls." To John Bestone my wife's son all my wearing apparell. To Joane my wife all the rest of my goods & I make her Executrix.

Wit. John Hall curate, John Rowell yeoman Richard Cannon yeoman Isabell Spike widow.   306 Bullocke, Consistory Court of London.

Married, 1582, Nov. 19, Thomas Harvarde & Jane Rowell.
                    Register of St Saviour's Parish, Southwark.

JONE HARVARD wife of Thomas Harvard buried June 10, 1599.
                    Register of St Savior's Parish, Southwark.

RICHARD YEARWOOD and Katherine Ellettsone were mard xxviiith of May 1627.   Parish Register of Wandsworth, Surrey.

[This is the third marriage of John Harvard's mother. I am indebted to J. T. Squire, Esq., for his kind permission to extract the above from his MS copy of this Register, and to my friend J. C. C. Smith, Esq., who discovered this important entry.—H. F. W.]

PETER MEDCALFE of the parish of St Olave's in Southwark in the County of Surrey clothworker 24 August 1592, proved 6 September 1592. To Mr Richard Hutton Deputy of the Borough of Southwark my best gown faced with Foynes. To my very friend Mr Thomas Lynne in Pater Noster Rowe my best gown faced with satin. To Richard Barker my gown faced with Budge or Damask at his choice. To Peter Keseler one of my gowns faced with budge. To the poor of St Olave's in Southwark forty shillings To the poor of Redderiffe in the County of Surrey twenty shillings. To my very good friend Mr John Nokes a ring of gold with an agate cut. "Item I giue and bequeathe unto Robert Harvey a boye which I keepe the somme óf ffyue poundes lawfull money of Englande to be paied unto hym at his age of one and twentie yeres. So that he be ordered and ruled by my executrix and that he do liue to accomplishe the age of one and twentie yeres aforesaied." To Symon Harvye my servant my great anvil & two of my best vices with the bellows thereunto belonging. To my other servants viz Francis, Thomas & Peter being my household servants each of them 20 shillings. Others mentioned. Wife Margaret Medcalfe to be executrix.
71 Harrington (P. C. C.).

Admon de bonis non was granted 26 (September) to Christopher Medcalf, the next of kin.

JOHN GUY of the parish of St Saviour in Southwark, in the County of Surrey, brewer (17 June 1625, proved 28 June 1625) bequeaths to Richard Harford citizen & brewer of London the sum of thirty shillings to make him a ring for a remembrance. 64, Clarke.

ROBERT GREENE of the parish of St. Savior in Southwark in the county of Surrey, yeoman (8 November 1645, proved 19 January 1645) appoints as one of the overseers of his will Mr Thomas Harvard of the said parish Butcher, calling him friend & neighbor, and gives him five pounds. In a codicil, made 11 January 1645, he bequeathes unto Robert Harvard son of Thomas Harvard (above) the sum of ten shillings. The testator had a sister Jane Marshall of Billerica, Essex. 3, Twisse.

RAPH YARDLEY citizen & merchant tailor of London 25 August 1603, proved 27 February 1603. After my debts paid and my funerals discharged I will that all and singular my goods chattels & debts shall be parted & divided into three equal parts & portions according to the laudable use and custom of the city of London. One full third part thereof I give and bequeath to Rhoda my wellbeloved wife, to her own use, in full satisfaction of such part and portion of my goods, chattells & debts as she may claim to have by the custom of the same city. One other full third part thereof I give & bequeath unto and amongst my children, Raphe, George, John, Thomas and Anne Yardley and to such other child or children as yet unborn as I shall happen to have at the time of my decease, to be equally parted, shared & divided between them, and to be satisfied and paid to my said sons at the accomplishment of their several ages of one and twenty years, and to my said daughter at the accomplishment of her age of one & twenty years or marriage, which shall first happen, &c. &c. And the other third part thereof I reserve to myself therewith to perform & pay these my legacies hereafter mentioned, that is to say, Item I give & bequeath to the poor of the parish of St Saviours in Southwark where I now dwell twenty shillings, to be divided amongst them by the discretion of the overseers of the poor there for the time being, and to such of the bachelors and sixteen men of the company of merchant tailors London as shall accompany my body to burial twenty shillings for a recreation to be made unto them, and to the Vestrymen of the same parish twenty shillings more for a recreation to be made unto them. Item I give and bequeath to my sister Palmer a ring of gold to the value of six shillings eight pence, and to my cousin John Palmer her husband a like ring to the like value, and to my daughter Earby my first wife's wedding ring, and to my son Erbye her husband my best cloak, and to my cousin Richard Yearwood my black cloth gown of Turkey fashion. The rest & residue of all & singular my goods &c. I wholly give unto my said children &c. &c. Item I give & bequeath to my brother Thomas Yardley a ring of gold to the value of six shillings eight pence. And I ordain & make the said Raph Yardley my son to be the Executor &c. and the said Richard Yerwoode and my son Edward Earbye overseers.

As to my freehold lands tenements & hereditaments I will demise give & bequeath my messuages, lands &c in Southwark or elsewhere unto my said children &c.   24, Harte.

John Hall, Not. Pub., one of the witnesses.

AGNES PARKER of London, spinster, 27 November 1617, proved 9 January 1617. Brother in law Edward Smyth and sister Julian, his wife, Sister Margery, the wife of Thomas Flinte of Litterworth in the County of Leicester, glazier. To Mʳⁱˢ Elizabeth Bygate, sometime my Mʳⁱˢ the sum of twenty pounds &c. To Anne the wife of William Hughes, Elizabeth Turner, the daughter, and Elizabeth Turner, the wife, of James Turner citizen & haberdasher of London. To the poor of all Hallows Barking London where I am now inhabiting. Item I do bequeath to Mʳ John Ellatson & his wife for a remembrance a piece of gold of five shillings & six pence. And likewise to Mʳ William Bygate & his now wife a like piece of gold. And to Mʳ William Turner & wife another piece of gold. To Sarah the wife of Thomas Skinner ten shillings. The residue to James Turner whom I hereby make ordain & constitute my full & sole executor.

122, Vol. 23, Commissary Court of London.

ANN PALMER of London widow, 30 January 1621 proved 31 December 1624. My body to be buried in the parish church of St. Olaves in Southwark in the county of Surrey, where now I am a parishioner, as near the place where my late deceased husband was buried as conveniently may be. I give & bequeath to my son Michael Palmer all such debts duties sum & sums of moneys as are and shall be due & owing unto me at the time of my decease by Jacob Manninge Percival Manninge or either of them or by any other persons by or for them or either of them, all which debts do amount unto the sum of three score and five pounds and twelve shillings or thereabouts principal debt besides all the interest long due, the which money he caused me to lend. Item I give to John Palmer son of my son Michael Palmer three hundred pounds of lawful English money besides I have given to his master the sum of thirty pounds of like money, and unto Andrew Palmer one other son of my said son Michael Palmer twenty pounds &c. and unto Mary Palmer daughter of my said son Michael Palmer one hundred & fifty pounds of like money, and unto Thomas Palmer one other son of my said son Michael twenty pounds &c. & unto Elizabeth Palmer one other daughter of my said son Michael Palmer twenty pounds of like money. To my son William fifty pounds besides I have heretofore given him two hundred pounds and one hundred & fifty pounds before hand, which sums were intended to have been given him for a legacy ; of both which sums I do discharge him, the which may appear partly by his bond of three hundred pounds, dated 19 July 14 James &c. and partly by other writings, and I give him his plate remaining in my hands as a pledge for twenty pounds more, which twenty pounds I forgive unto him also. To John Palmer, son of my said son Michael (sic) two hundred pounds, besides I have given with him to his master the sum of forty pounds. To the said John Palmer, son of my said son William, the lease of my now dwelling house situate upon London Bridge, &c. &c., provided that the said William Palmer, his father, shall, from and after the end of two months next after my decease, until the said John Palmer his son shall accomplish his full age of four & twenty years, have hold & enjoy my said dwelling house, given unto his said son, paying & discharging the rent to be due for the whole to the Bridgehouse and one pepper corn yearly at the Feast of the Birth of our Lord God unto his said son if he lawfully demand the same. Reference made to the will of John Palmer, the late husband of the testatrix, and legacies to John and Mary Palmer, children of Michael, and John Palmer, son of William.

Item I give and bequeath unto my daughter Anne Faldo, late wife of Robert Faldo Esquire, deceased, two hundred and three pounds of lawful money of England and my chain of gold, and unto Thomes Faldo, her son, forty pounds, and unto Francis Faldo, her son, forty pounds, to be paid to my said daughter their mother, and by her to be paid to the said Thomas & Francis when they shall accomplish their ages of two & twenty years. To Anne Faldo, her daughter, forty pounds, and to Jane Faldo, one other of her daughters, twenty pounds, and to Elizabeth Faldo, one other of her daughters, forty pounds, at their several ages of one and twenty years or at the days of their several marriages &c.

To my daughter Elizabeth Fawcett, wife of William Fawcett, gentleman, two hundred pounds, besides four hundred pounds to them formerly given &c. and my bracelets and all my rings of gold &c.

Reference to an Obligation wherein the said John Palmer deceased (former husband of the testatrix) stood bound with the said Michael Palmer (the son) to Mr Jacob Vercelin in the sum of twelve hundred pounds, with condition thereupon endorsed to leave Mary, then wife of the said Michael Palmer & daughter of the said Jacob, if she survive the said Michael, worth in goods & chattels the sum of one thousand pounds &c.

Item I give and bequeathe unto my cousin Anne Streate and to my cousin Ellen Yarwoode twenty shillings apiece to buy them rings to wear in remembrance of me. As touching blacks to be worn at my funeral I dispose them as hereafter followeth, that is to say, I give and bequeathe unto my son Michael Palmer & William Palmer and unto my son-in-law William Fawcett and unto John Fawcett, husband of Jane Faldoe, and to my loving friends & cousins Stephen Streate and Richard Yarwoode and John Grene and Ralphe Yardley, to every of them a cloak of brown blue cloth containing three yards and half quarter in every cloak at twenty shillings every yard or thereabouts. I give and bequeathe unto my cousin Robert Poole a cloak cloth of forty shillings price, to my cousin Richard Hinde a cloak cloth, about forty shillings price and unto his wife a piece of stuff about fifty shillings price to make her a gown. Similar bequests to "my" cousin Nicholas Cowper and his wife, and cousins Anne Streate and Ellen. Yarwood, and to Elizabeth Blinkensopp and Margaret Kinge and to Christopher Blinkensopp and Nicholas Kinge their husbands. Other bequests.

And I do ordain and make the aforesaid Richard Yarwoode & Stephen Streete grocers, "my cosens," full executors &c. and I appoint my loving friends John Grene Esq. and " Richard (*sic*) Yardlye Pottecary my cosen " overseers of this my will and testament, and I give and bequeath unto the said John Grene and Ralphe Yardeley for their pains therein to be taken twenty nobles apiece &c.

In a codicil dated 17 June 1624 the testatrix refers to her daughter Anne Faldoe as since married to Robert Bromfield.   111, Byrde.

Inquisition taken at S[t] Margaret's Hill, S[t] Savior's Southwark in the County of Surrey, 11 March 22 James I. *post mortem* Ralph Yardley, lately citizen and merchant taylor of London Deceased, who was seized, before death, in fee of one capital messuage with the appurtenances called the Horn, lately divided into two several messuages, and situate lying and being in the parish of S[t] Savior in the Borough of Southwark, in the County of Surrey, now or late in the several tenures or occupation of George Fletcher, fisherman, and Lawrence Lunde, or their assigns; and the said Ralph Yardley, being so seized, did on the 25th day of August 1603, 1 James, by his last will in writing, give and bequeath all and singular these premises, in English words, as follows (then follows an extract from the will). And he died, so seized, the 1st day of July 1618, and Ralph Yardley, named in the will, is son and next heir, and was aged at the time of the death of the said Ralph Yardley the father, twenty one years and more ; and the said capital messuage, into two separate messuages divided (as above) with the appurtenances, is held and, at the time of the death of the said Ralph Yardley, was held, of the Mayor, Commonalty and Citizens of the City of London in free soccage, as of their manor of Southwark, in Southwark aforesaid, by the annual rent of two shillings per annum, and is worth clear per annum, during a certain lease made by the said Ralph Yardley to a certain Richard Yerwood, citizen and grocer of London, bearing date 10 July 1603, and during the term of one hundred years, one peppercorn, and after the determination of the said lease will be worth clear and in all events and beyond reprise, three pounds per year.

Chancery Inq. p. m., Miscel., Part 4, No. 130.

[These Yardley items are interesting as showing the connection of Sir George Yardley, the governor of Virginia, to Richard Yerwood, one of John Harvard's step-fathers. I believe a little research would show that these Yardleys were of the Warwickshire family of that name. Richard Yerwood and his kinsman Stephen Street were of Cheshire, I have no doubt.—H. F. W.]

RICHARD BOWMER of the parish of S[t] Saviours in Southwark in the county of Surrey Innholder, 7 January 1593 proved 20 March 1593. My body to be buried in the parish church of S[t] Saviours. To the poor people of the said parish forty shillings and to the poor of the parish of S[t] George in Southwark twenty shillings. For a sermon made at the time of my burial for me (by M[r] Ratliffe if it please him) ten shillings. To the three daughters of Agnes Lackenden widow, viz[t] Joane, Alice and Mary, twenty shillings apiece. To Stephen Lackendon ten shillings, and to my godson, his son, five shillings. To my godson Richard Smyth of Plumpstede in the county of Kent five shillings & to my godson William Cleere of Walworthe five shillings. To my goddaughter Ellyn Beech five shillings. To Thomas Vaugham five pounds and to Henry Vaugham, brother to the said Thomas, three pounds six shillings & eight pence. To Cisly Vaugham, their sister, four pounds. To Richard Emmerson, son of William Emmerson, five shillings.

To Richard Emmerson son of Humfrey Emmerson, five shillings. To Robert Rodes, youngest son now living of Roger Rodes of said parish of St Saviours, goldsmith, three pounds six shillings and eight pence, and to Elizabeth Rodes mother to the said Robert five pounds. To my kinsman Peter Bowmer of Sevenocke in Kent, sadler, ten pounds. To Elizabeth Mitchell wife of Abraham Mitchell feltmaker dwelling at Horseydowne near Southwark, thirty shillings, and to my godson, her son, ten shillings. To Lambert Bowmer of the parish of St Ollifes twenty pounds, and to Robert Bowmer, his son, twenty pounds, also to the two daughters of the said Lambert now living five pounds apiece. To Henry Yonge twenty shillings, to John Yonge twenty shillings, to Gregory Francklyn twenty shillings, to Abraham Allyn twenty shillings, and to every one of their wives twenty shillings apiece to make every of them a ring of gold withall. To Richard Cuckowe ten shillings and to Peter Holmes scrivener ten shillings (for rings) and to Isaac Allen twenty shillings.

" Allso my full intente will and mynde ys : and I doe herebye giue and graunte the lease of my nowe dwellinge house called the queens heade scituate in the sayd parrishe of St. Saviors wythall my Intereste and tytle therein after my decease unto Rose my wife duringe all the yeares therein to come. Provided allwayes and my will and mynde is that the sayd Rose my wife shall haue one years respitte after my decease to pay and dischardge my legacyes herein bequeathed, and therefore I doe appoynte hereby that shee the sayd Rose shall wythin one month nexte after my decease become bounde in good and sufficyente bonde in lawe unto my ouerseers here after nominated in the some of two hundred poundes of lawfull money of Inglande that shee the sayd Rose or her assignes shall well and truly performe fulfill and keepe the tenor of this my will: and pay and discharge: all legacyes and other duetyes by me hereby given and appoynted accordinge to the tennor and true meaninge of this my last will and Testamente."

To the Society of the Vestry of St. Saviors thirteen shillings & four pence. The residue to Rose my well beloved wife whom I make & ordain my full & sole executrix. Thomas Jackson, merchant Tailor, & Miles Wilkinson, Baker, to be overseers. 23, Dixey.

ROSE BOOMER of the parish of Saint " Savyoure " in Southwark in the County of Surrey, widow, 29 March 1595, proved 9 August 1595. My body to be buried in the parish church of St Saviour's where I am a parishioner. To the preacher that shall make a sermon at my funeral ten shillings. To the poor people of the said parish forty shillings, to be distributed amongst them at the discretion of my Executor & the Collectors for the poor there for the time being. To the poor people of the parish of Bossham in the County of Sussex, where I was born, the sum of forty shillings, whereof I will that ten shillings shall be paid to Alice Reade, the widow of Richard Reede (if she be then living) And if she be then deceased then the same ten shillings to be paid to Richard Chapman. To the poor people of St John's house in the city of Winchester forty shillings. To Richard Braxton, son of Cornelius Braxton, the sum of six pounds thirteen shillings and four pence, which I will shall remain in the hands of such person as shall keep him towards his education until he shall be bound apprentice and then delivered over to use for the best profit of the same Richard and the same, with the interest, to be paid him at the expiration of his apprenticeship. And if he happen to decease before the said sum shall come unto his hands then I will to his half brother Edmond Braxton ten shillings & to his sister ten shillings, and the residue to his other two whole brethren both by father and mother, equally. To Richard Mapcrofte six pounds thirteen shillings & four pence, or if he dies to his children (in hands of his wife). To Matthew Barnard the younger, dwelling in York-shire three pounds. To Matthew Barnard the elder ten shillings. To William Hildrop a piece of gold of ten shillings, for a remembrance. And a similar bequest to his brother Barnabie & his brother Richard and to John Hildrop and their sister ——, also to Johane Huskyns, widow, and to her sister the daughter of Edward Hildroppe, and to William Braxton and —— Hardam of Chichester, son of Margery Braxton, and to Richard Wallys of Winchester, to Margaret Bathe, to John Homeade's wife of Win-chester and to Richard Homeade her son, to Mᵐ Bird, to Mistress Denham, to Mʳ Thomas Thorney, of Portsmouth, to John Androwes, to Robert Boomer, to Thomas Vaughan, to his sister Cicely, to Robert Roades, & his brother Henry Clarke, and to my servant that shall attend upon me at the time of my decease, ten shillings. To Johane Allen, my daughter, fifty pounds (and certain household stuff). To Isaacke Allen, her son, & to Rosanna Allen the sum of twentie five pounds each. To my daughter Alice Francklin (certain household stuff).

"Item I will and bequeathe unto Gregorye ffrancklyn my sonne in lawe and the sayed Alice his wife (yf she the same Alice shalbe living at the tyme of my decease) all my Righte title and interest of and in so muche and suche partes and parcells of the mesuage or Inne called the Quenes hed in the parishe of Sainct Savyoure in Sowthwarke aforesayed as I lately demised by Indenture of Lease unto one Oliuer Bowker and of in and to the gatehouse of the sayed Inne nowe in the occupacõn of Bryan Pattenson: The Interest of which premisses I haue and hould by vertue of a Lease heretofore made and graunted by one John Bland unto Richard Boomer my late husband deceased and me the said Rose for diuers yeres yet to haue con-tynewance. Except allwayes and my meaning ys that the sayed Devise by me as aforesayed made shall not extend to certeyne garden plottes lying on the East syde of the Dytche or Common Sewer extending and passing by the Tenter yard and the garden behinde the sayed mesuage. Prouided allwayes that yf the sayed Gregory and Alice shall not permitt and suffer Abraham Allen and Jone his wife Isaacke Allen and Rosanna Allen and theire assignes peaceablye and quietly to hould and enioye the sayed excepted gar-den plottes according to the tenure of suche graunte and assuraunce as I haue lately made unto them That then and from thencefourthe the Devise made to the sayed Gregorye and Alice as aforesayed shall cease and be utterlie frustrate and voyde (any thinge before expressed to ye Contrary notwithstandinge)."

To my daughter Anne Younge the lease of my now dwelling house and of certain grounds at Wallworth and one hundred pounds (and certain house-hold stuff). To my son in law John Younge and Anne his wife towards the buying of their blacks for my funeral four pounds. The same to Gregory Franckling & Alice his wife & to Abraham Allen & Johane his wife. Bequests to others. John Younge to be executor and Thomas Jackson & Myles Wilkenson supervisors.   53, Scott.

GREGORY FRANCKLIN of the parish of Sᵗ Savior in Southwark in the County of Surrey, citizen & sadler of London, 11 September 1624, proved 22 September 1624. My body to be buried within the church of the parish of Sᵗ Savior, at the discretion of Katherine my wife & sole executrix.

To the poor of the said parish forty shillings. To the Wardens of the Company of Sadlers in London four pounds to make them a supper withall.

"Itm̃ whereas I the said Gregory ffrancklin by my deede indented bearing date the Second day of ffebruary in the Thirteenth yeare of the Kings Maᵗⁱᵉ Raigne aforesaid of England ffraunce and Ireland, And of Scotland the Nyne and ffortieth (ffor the Consideracõns in the said deede expressed) did graunte enfeoff and confirme unto Gilbert Kinder Cittizen and Mercer of London All that Capitall Messuage or Inne called or knowne by the name of the Queenes head Scituat and being in the p̃ish of Sᵗ Savioʳ in the Borrough of Southwark in the County of Surr. and one garden to the same belonging To certen severall uses in the said deede expressed As by the same more plainly may appeare, I the said Gregory ffrancklin doe hereby publish and declare that the only cause and consideracõn wᶜʰ moved me to Seale unto the said deede was for that at the tyme of the making and sealing thereof I was a widdower and a sole p̃son, not having any yssue of my body then living nor then intending to marrye. Nevertheles wᵗʰ a Resʳuacoñ unto myselfe in case I did marrye and had yssue, That not wᵗʰstanding the saide deede, or any estate thereupon executed, the power should remaine in me to giue and dispose of the said Inne and p̃imsses at my owne will and pleasure, In such manner as I should thinck fitting. And therefore for significacõn of my will intent and meaning concerning the same, And forasmuch as it hath pleased God that I have marryed the said Katherine my nowe wiffe by whome I have yssue Gregory ffrancklin my sonne and heir who is very young and of tender yeares, unto whome I have but small meanes to conferre and settle upon him both for his educacõn and bringing upp and otherwise wᶜʰ wᵗʰ care I would willingly provide for after my decease, And not minding or intending that my said sonne should be disinherited or deprived of his lawfull right of and to the said Messuage or Inne doe hereby renounce and frustrate the said deede and all thestate thereupon had Togeather wᵗʰ the severall uses and limitacõns therein expressed, And doe declare the same to be of noe force or vallidity at all. And doe hereby giue deuise and bequeath the said Messuage or Inne and garden wᵗʰ thapp̃tenñces to the said Gregory ffrancklin my sonne and the heires of his body lawfully to be begotten, And for default of such yssue unto Gilbert Kinder and Margarett his wife and unto theire heires for ever."

Reference made to a deed indented dated the last day of August 1616 for the jointure of the said Katherine (if she should happen to survive), conveying certain tenements in the parish of Sᵗ Savior in Southwark & in the parish of Sᵗ Sepulchre without Newgate London and confirmation of that deed. Also to the said Katherine the moyty or one half part of the Rents Issues and Profits, when and at such time as the same shall grow due and payable of all and singular those gardens or garden plots with the Alley way or passage to the same leading and used with all the appurtenances thereunto belonging lying and being on the backside of the Messuage or Inne commonly called &c. the Queen's Head &c. now in the tenure or occupation of Isaac Allen Genᵗ or his assigns. And the other moiety or half part of the Rents &c. of the same gardens and premises I give, will and bequeath to the said Gregory Francklin, my son, at such time as he shall accomplish his full age of one & twenty years. And after the decease of the said Katherine, my wife, I give will & bequeath all the said premises unto the said Gregory my son & the heirs of his body lawfully begotten. If my son shall happen to depart this transitory life before his said age &c. (having no issue of his body living) then the said Katherine, my wife, shall freely have, hold, possess & enjoy all & singular the same gardens & premisses &c. for & during her natural life, and from & after her decease then to the Wardens or keepers & Commonalty of the mystery or Art of Sadlers of the City of London & to their Successors forever the moiety or half part of the said gardens &c., And the other moiety &c. to the Governors of the Free School of the Parish of St Saviour in Southwark, aforesaid, and to their successors forever, to this use, intent and purpose only (that is to say) for & towards the maintaining & bringing up of some one child or youth which shall from time to time forever hereafter be born within the said parish.   And I hereby will that such one always may be first taught learned and instructed sufficiently in the said free school and afterwards by them the said Governors and their successors for the time being put forth and brought up in learning, during the term of eight years, so that from time to time such one scholar may attain to the degree of Mr in Arts in one of the Universities of Oxon or Cambridge if such one scholar shall so long continue both scholar and student in either of the same, as by their discretions shall be thought most meet and convenient, whereunto I refer myself.

To the said Katherine, my wife, the lease which I hold of & from the Wardens &c. of the said mystery or Art of Sadlers &c. of all that Messuage or Tenement with the appurtenances &c. called or known by the sign of the Three Kings set, lying and being upon Snowe Hill near the Conduit there, within the parish of St Sepulchre without Newgate London, now in the Tenure or occupation of Josias Curtis, tailor &c.   If she die before the expiration of the term granted by the same lease, then to the said Gregory Francklin, my son, for the time &c. unexpired.   To my said son Gregory my gold seal ring (and other personal property).

Item my special will & meaning is that the said Katherine my wife shall within the space of six months next after my decease well & truly satisfy & pay or cause to be paid unto Ann Parkhurst & Katherine Parkhurst, daughters of Edward Parkhurst, late citizen & merchant tailor of London deceased & of the said Katherine my wife, the sum of one hundred pounds of lawful money of England for the redeeming of the said Gardens or garden plots, and two tenements with the appurtenances thereupon erected, which I mortgaged and stand engaged to pay the said sum by my deed as thereby appeareth.

A bequest is made to John Parvish, "my old servant," and the residue is bequeathed to wife Katherine who is made sole Executrix, and friends Richard Yerwood grocer and Robert Bucke glover are appointed supervisors, and to either of them, for their pains, a ring of gold of twenty shillings apiece is bequeathed.

Witnesses Richard Harrison, Richard Haukins, Antho: Rogers Scr., John Dodsworth, servant to Edrd Jackson Scr.

Probate granted to the widow 22 September 1624.

Decimo quinto die mensis Junii Anⁿ Dñi 1637° Emanavit Comissio Henrico Creswell p̄oe St Bothi extra Aldersgate London aurifabr̄ ad administrand bona iura et crēd d͠ci Gregorii ffrancklyn def iuxta tenorem et effc̃um testī prēd p Catherīnam Creswell al̊s ffrancklyn al̊s Blackleech nup relcam et execūt testī d͠ci Gregorii (iam etiam demort.) non plene ad͞ministrat de bene etc iurat.   73, Byrde.

ANNE WHITMORE of Lambehith in the county of Surrey, widow, 9 August 1624, proved 12 October 1624.   I give all my worldly goods, money, jewells, plate and household stuff whatsoever unto my grandchild

Martha Smith and to the heirs of her body, lawfully begotten, provided always that if the said Martha shall happen to die and depart this life without such issue of her body lawfully begotten then my will is and I bequeath unto my grandchildren Gregory Francklin, Anne Parkhurst & Katherine Parkhurst, the son and daughters of Katherine Francklin, wife of Gregory Francklin, to every of them the sum of ten pounds; also I give and bequeath unto Richard Smith and Thomas Bradbridge, the sons of Anne Bradbridge, my daughter, of Lambehith aforesaid, widow, the like sum of ten pounds and also to the said Anne Bradbridge the sum of forty pounds. And I nominate appoint and ordain the said Martha Smith to be sole executrix &c. And my will is that she shall within six months after my decease give unto her Aunt Katherin Francklin the sum of three pounds sterling to buy her a cup or bowl, in token of my love unto her, and I do appoint my loving friend Mr William Childe to be overseer &c.   118, Byrde.

GREGORY FRANCKLYN 19 February 1635. I do bestow all the estate that is or shall be mine upon my sister Ann, conditionally that she shall help, succor & relieve my mother in all her wants and necessities so far as she is able. And to my sister Kate I give a pair of sheets, a dozen of napkins and a towel, and to my cousin Mrs Martha Marshall a pair andirons, and to Thomas Day a piece of gold of five shillings.

Administration was granted 1 March 1635 to Anne Parkhurst natural & lawful sister of the said Gregory Francklyn of the Parish of St Buttolph without Aldersgate London deceased.   32, Pile.

RICHARD QUINEY, citizen & grocer of London, 16 August 1655, proved 3 January 1656. To be buried at Stratford upon Avon in the county of Warwick, where my father & other my ancestors are interred. One half of my personal estate (having no wife) I bequeath among my five children Richard, Adrian, Thomas, William and Sarah Quiney. To my cousin Dr. Richard Bayley and Master William Wheate forty shillings apiece. To my cousin master George Nash forty shillings, to buy rings. To my brother master John Sadler and my sons in law Edward Pilkington and Thomas Booth and my cousin Richard Chaundler five pounds apiece. To my brother in law William Smith five pounds. To my cousin William Watts and his wife forty shillings apiece. To cousin William Smith & his wife forty shillings apiece to buy rings. To cousins John & Robert Smith ten pounds apiece. To my daughter Ellen Pilkington fifty pounds and to her husband the said Edward Pilkington, ten pounds to buy mourning, to my daughter Elizabeth Cooper ten pounds, to my brother in law master John Sadler and my sister Elizabeth his wife ten pounds, to my son in law Thomas Booth & daughter Ann his wife ten pounds, to son John Lilburne & my daughter Isabell his wife ten pounds, for mourning. To my cousin Charles Watts twenty five pounds when he shall have faithfully served out the term of eight years of his apprenticeship. Ten pounds to be distributed among the children of my cousin Ellen Parker equally. To my cousins John Sadler & William Baker forty shillings apiece, to cousin Margaret Jones forty shillings to buy rings. To my grand child Elizabeth Pilkington ten pounds at one & twenty years of age or marriage, to Gr. children William & Richard Cooper ten pounds apiece at their several ages of one & twenty years. To grand child Richard Booth ten pounds at one & twenty. To such child as my daughter Lilburne now goeth withall ten pounds at one & twenty. To the worshipful

Company of Grocers of London whereof I am a member a piece of plate of the value of ten pounds sterling. To master Watson minister of the Word of God in S[t] Stephen's in Walbrooke, London, five pounds, to master Beane, minister, &c. at Stratford upon Avon forty shillings. To the poor of Stratford upon Avon ten pounds. To my son Thomas my part, share & interest in the Ship called the Seven Sisters, Abraham Reade commander, to be managed for his use until he shall have served out the remainder of his apprenticeship; also several leases estates & interests which I have in the Tyth of Drayton & a certain house at Stratford upon Avon which I hold by lease of the chamber of Stratford upon Avon.

The residue of all & singular my goods chattells, &c. I give & bequeath to John Sadler, Edward Pilkington, Thomas Booth, William Smith & Richard Chaundler, in trust, &c. for my four younger children, Adrian, Thomas, William & Sarah Quiney. To my brother Thomas Quiney, for natural life, an annuity of twelve pounds out of my messuages & lands at Shottery, with the appurtenances, in the County of Warwick; and at the decease of the said Thomas my executors to take out of the said lands the sum of five pounds to bear & defray the charges of my said brother's funeral. (Other lands, &c. bequeathed and devised to his sons.)

Also I give & devise all my land in Virginia in the parts beyond the seas together with all the stock of cattle, servants & other things thereunto belonging unto my said son Thomas Quiney & to his heirs & assigns forever. All my land in Ireland to son Richard. To the town of Stratford upon Avon my two small tenements near the meer side in Stratford towards the maintenance of the Bridge, &c. & for the poor alms men. Son Richard to be executor. If he shall not at the time of my decease be resident in England then my sons in law Edward Pilkington & Thomas Booth to be executors in trust for him in his absence.   Ruthen, 6.

[The testator, it seems, was a brother-in-law of Rev. John Sadler, but whether this Rev. John Sadler was related to the father-in-law of Rev. John Harvard we have no means of ascertaining. Shakspeare's daughter Judith married, Feb. 10, 1615-16, Thomas Quincy, a wine merchant residing in the High Street of Stratford-upon-Avon (See Outlines of the Life of Shakspeare by J. O. Halliwell Phillips, F.R.S., F.S.A., 2d ed. 1882, p. 182). There was a Richard Quiney, son of Adrian Quiney, who about 1598 resided at the Bell in Carter Lane, London (Ibid. p. 579. See also pp. 575-82).—EDITOR.

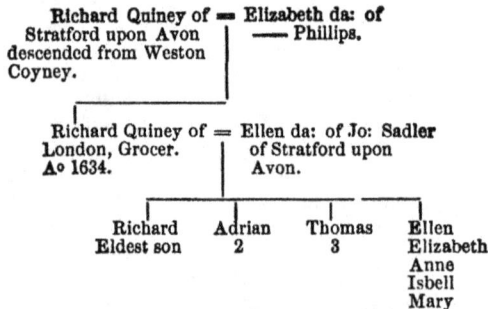

Richard Quiney of ═ Elizabeth da: of
Stratford upon Avon   —— Phillips.
descended from Weston
Coyney.

Richard Quiney of ═ Ellen da: of Jo: Sadler
London, Grocer.   of Stratford upon
A° 1634.   Avon.

Richard   Adrian   Thomas   Ellen
Eldest son   2   3   Elizabeth
                                 Anne
                                 Isbell
                                 Mary

(Visitation of London, 1633, 1634: Harleian MS.
1476, 405: British Museum.)—H. F. W.]

BENJAMIN KEYSAR the elder of Westham in the County of Essex, tanner, 10 April 1650, proved 3 May 1650, by William Salter executor.

Whereas George Keysar my grandfather, late of Layton Buzzard in the

County of Bedford, tanner, deceased, did by his last will & testament give me twenty two pounds four shillings & five pence at my age of one and twenty years as my third part of one hundred marks which my grandfather gave unto the three sons of Benjamin Keysar, &c. and it now remains in the hands of Edmond Keysar my uncle, of London, ironmonger, being the executor of my said grandfather, I give and bequeath ten pounds thereof to my loving brother Gabriel Keysar and ten pounds to my sister Mary Keysar at their several ages of one and twenty years. A bequest to friend William Salter yeoman in the County of Essex, who is to be executor.

Pembroke, 74.

[George Keysar was the name of the tanner who first settled in Lynn, Massachusetts, and carried on his business alongside of Strawberry brook, to the westward of the Water Mill, which itself stood just west of the road now known as Federal Street. He bought the land 19th 1mo. 1649, of Mr. Samuel Bennett who then held the mill property. In October, 1654, he seems to have settled in Salem, buying of Major William Hathorne a lot of land near the South River, as it was often called, or the Harbor, as now termed, at the foot of Burying Point Lane, now Liberty Street. He still retained his estate in Lynn, which passed to Benjamin Keysar.—H. F. W.]

MARGERY COX of Debtford in the County of Kent, widow, 30 May 1656 proved 11 June 1656. To my well beloved brother Giles Webb[1] living now in Virginia, twenty pounds. To my brother William Lews of Titbury in the County of Gloucester ten pounds. To my sister Elizabeth Waight wife of Giles Waight, of Titbury aforesaid, twenty pounds. To William Stone and John Rooper, both of Debtford, five pounds apiece, they being overseers. To the poor of the parish of Debtford twenty shillings. Mary and Elizabeth Waight, daughters of the abovesaid Giles Waight, to be executrixes.

The witnesses were William Huttun, Joane Phillips (by mark) & George Martin. Berkley, 224.

[[1] Captain Giles Webb commanded a company of rangers in Henrico County, Va., in 1692. A Captain Giles Webb died in Henrico County in June, 1713. The last married the widow of Henry Randolph, Jr., Clerk of Henrico County. In his will he mentions a brother Thomas, and his step-son Henry Randolph. The name Webb has been prominent in Virginia. John Webb, "Mariner," was granted 50 acres of land in Accomac County, Dec. 13, 1627. *Va. Land Records*, No. 1, p. 81. Stephen Webb was a Burgess from James City in October, 1644. George Webb was elected, Dec. 17. 1776, by the Virginia Assembly, treasurer of Virginia, to succeed Robert Carter Nicholas, resigned.—R. A. BROCK, Richmond, Va.]

MARK PIERCE, of London, in his will & enumeration of assets dated 10 February 1654 (proved in 1656) mentions forty pounds in the hands of Master Robert Newman,[1] citizen & vintner of London, and ten pounds in money in the hands of Elizabeth Higginson, widow, which I lent to her deceased husband, Theophilus Higginson[2] in New England and ought to have been paid presently at our arrival in England. Berkley, 233.

[Mark Pierce was a resident of New Haven as early as 1639 and as late as 1646 (See New Haven Colony Records, vol. i. pp. 18 and 302). Savage, in his Geneal. Dict., vol. iii. p. 430, says he was of Cambridge 1642, but he is not mentioned in Paige's History of Cambridge.
[1] Probably the Robert Newman who was one of the settlers of New Haven, Ct., and one of the seven pillars of the church there. He resided there as late as 1649 (See New Haven Colony Records, vol. i. pp. 9, 20, 492). Savage, in his Gen. Dict. vol. iii. p. 275, says he returned to England. He thinks he was the Robert Newman whose name is among the passengers in the Mary and John, 1634, printed in the REGISTER, vol. ix. pp. 265-8.—EDITOR.]

[2] Theophilus Higginson, son of Rev. Francis Higginson. See Hist. Coll. Essex Institute, vol. v. p. 34.—HENRY WHEATLAND.

Savage (Gen. Dict. ii. 414) says that Theophilus Higginson, of New Haven, died about 1657, aged 37. This will shows that he was dead three years earlier.—ED.]

THOMAS DUMER of Chicknell within the parish of North Stonham in the County of Southampton, gentleman, 12 April 1650, proved 9 November 1650 by Thomas, John, Robert and Stephen Dummer, his executors. To be buried at discretion of the executors. To the poor in North Stonham and South Stonham and Bishopstoake twenty six shillings and eightpence to every of said parishes. To my wife ten pounds within one month after my decease. To four of my daughters, viz. Susan, Hester, Jane and Mary Dumer, two hundred pounds to either of them at their several days of marriage, &c. To my eldest daughter Joane Nelson, widow, twenty shillings within one year, &c. To my two grand children namely Samuel and Mercie Nelson, son and daughter of my daughter Joane Nelson, fifty pounds apiece at ages of twenty one years. To my daughter Margaret Clements, being my second daughter and now in New England, twenty five pounds, and to her child she now hath twenty five pounds within six months, &c. To my only son Thomas Dumer and his heirs forever all my freehold land of inheritance in North Stonham or elsewhere within the kingdom of England, to have and enjoy at the age of twenty one years. If he die without lawful issue then to my said four first named daughters, being now virgins and unmarried, &c. My beloved kinsmen John Dumer of Townhill, Stephen Penton of Winton, Robert Dumer of Durley, Thomas Dumer of Fairethorne and Stephen Dumer of Bishopstoake to be executors in trust, &c.

The witnesses were Stephen Dumer, Thomas Baylie and Ann Baldry (by mark).   Pembroke, 174.

[For an account of Thomas Dummer, the testator, and his children, see Col. Chester's Dummer genealogy in the REGISTER, vol. xxxv. pp. 269–71. His eldest daughter Joane married Thomas Nelson of Rowley, whose will is printed in the REGISTER, vol. iii. pp. 267–8. His second daughter Margaret married Dec. 25, 1644, Job Clement, of Haverhill, Mass., afterwards of Dover, N. H.

If the testator was the Mr. Thomas Dummer, who was one of the first settlers of Salisbury, Mass. (REGISTER, vol. iii. p. 55; Coffin's Newbury, p. 301), he must have returned early to England.—EDITOR.

In an account against the estate of Mr. Thomas Nelson, deceased, presented to the court held at Salem by Mr. Richard Dummer, the last Tuesday in June, 1656, is a claim for " charges in England, from South-hampton to Yorke & Hull which is 400 miles (18 dayes) [wit]h the hire of three horses & 2 men & Expences y'upon : to Endeauour to gaine the [mon]cy y' due :"

Among the papers also in this case is a copy of a release made the first of July, 1654, by the widow Jone Nelson, who calls herself " of Wecom or Duphy or Dulye neare Southhampton in old England." In 1650 she calls herself of North-stoneham.

Another of these papers is a copy of a bond of Thomas Nelson, dated 15th 12th month, 1641, in which reference is made to the " Contract of marriage betwixt Thomas Nelson of Rowley in New-England gent: & Joane Dumer Spinst: the dafter of Thomas Dummer of Badgely in ould England gent:."

Another is interesting as containing the word " nayther," thus perhaps showing what the sound of this word was as then pronounced.—County Court, Ipswich, March, 1657. Mr. Richard Dummer v. Mr Phillip Nelson. Review.—H. F. W.]

JEREMY DUMMER late agent of His Majesty's Provinces of Massachusetts and Connecticut, in New England, and now resident at Plaistow in Essex, in the Kingdom of Great Britain, 7 June 1738, proved 1 June 1739. In the chief place & before all things I do on this solemn occasion commend my soul to Almighty God and render him Infinite thanks for the many Blessings with which he has been pleased to fill up the short scene of my life, firmly confiding in the Benignity of his Nature that he wont afflict me in another World for some follys I have committed in this, in common with the rest of mankind, but rather that he will graciously consider the frail & weak frame which he gave me and remember that I was but Dust.

As to the Interment of my body I should think it a trifle not worth mentioning but only to desire my executors kindly to invite to my funeral all such New England gentlemen as shall be in London at the time of my decease and to give each of them a twenty shilling ring without any name upon it but only this motto which I think affords a good deal of reflection —*Nulla retro via.*

As to the small fortune I have acquired I bequeath, &c. as follows—To M** Kent where I now live and to Mrs Mary Stephenson lodging in the same house one hundred pounds each and a ring. To my worthy countryman Henry Newman Esq. twenty pounds. To Miss Hook Jacob twenty pounds. To my good kinswoman Mrs Lloyd of New England, formerly Pemberton and Campbell, one hundred pounds. To Dudley Woodbridge[1] of Barbadoes fifty pounds for the pleasure I had in his company when in England. To Commissioner Pearse of the Navy his eldest son by his former wife twenty pounds. Item, I give a fifty pound New England bill to Mrs Burr[2] of New England, and, in case of her death, to her children, as an acknowledgment of a civility I received from her husband at the college, I mean that Burr who was schoolmaster at Charlestown. To Col° & Capt. Mandell, Swedes in London, ten guineas each. To Stephen Whateley of Gray's Inn, gentleman, my little Library, and to my brother Dummer of Newbury twenty pounds New England money to distribute among the poor Indian Squaws that may come a begging at his door in the country. I leave to my sister Dummer her husband's picture set in gold which will be found in my Scrutore. The Bulk of my estate I make no disposition of, being content it should go according to the Act of Assembly in New-England for distributing the estates of Intestates. And lastly I desire that Francis Wilks Esq. and M* Samuel Storke will be my executors and accept of me a small specific legacy, viz[t] M* Wilks the Diamond ring which I usually wear and Mr. Storke my gold watch with the appurtenances. —Made &. published in presence of Benj* Rutland, Ann Silver.

A Codicil, dated 8 April 1739, refers to a deed bearing date 20 March last between the testator of the first part, Dorothy Keant of the second part and Francis Wilks of the third part for the conveying of a house in Clarges street to the said M** Kent "and which I have ordered to be registered" according to Act of Parliament in consideration of the trouble I have given her during a long fit of sickness. I do hereby revoke the legacy I have given her of one hundred pounds in the foregoing will.

Witnesses F. Hutton, James Howgill.

Plaistow 15 November 1738. I desire my executors will give my scrutore to M** Kent, all my wearing apparell to M** Mary and to my coachman a guinea, and the same to each of the maids.   JER. DUMMER.

30 May 1739 appeared Francis Hutton of Gray's Inn in the County of Middlesex, gentleman, and James Howgill of the Middle Temple, London, gentleman, and deposed, &c.   Henchman, 126.

[Jeremy Dummer, the testator, was a brother of Lieut. Governor William Dummer of the Province of Massachusetts. He was the author of "Defence of the New England Charters" (1721). He died in England May 19, 1739, and was buried at West Ham in Essex. See Col. Chester's account of him and his ancestry in the REGISTER, vol. xxxv. pp. 268-9. See also Massachusetts Historical Collections, 5th S. vol. v. pp. xxi.-ii.

[1] Rev. Dudley Woodbridge, probably the eldest son of the Hon. Dudley Wood-bridge, of Barbadoes, was rector of St. Philip's, Barbadoes. He died in 1747. See " Woodbridge Record," compiled by Donald G. Mitchell, from the papers of his brother Louis Mitchell, p. 37 ; REGISTER, vol. xxxii. p. 294.

[2] Mrs. Elizabeth Burr, widow of Samuel Burr, master of the Grammar School at Charlestown, Mass., a preparatory school for Harvard College, which is said to have had a reputation in the New England colonies similar to that of Eton in England. He was born at Fairfield, Ct., April 2, 1679, and died there while on a visit, Aug. 7, 1719. See Todd's " Burr Family " (1878), pp. 148 and 431.—EDITOR.]

NATHANIEL HULTON citizen and Salter of London, 20 July 1692, proved 13 March 1693, with three codicils, the last of which was dated 1 January 1693. To son in law James Greene and his sons James, Richard and John, daughters Margery & Elizabeth Greene ; to Joseph Scriven ; to John Greene, brother of James Greene the elder; to the poor of Newington Green where I live. Wife Elizabeth Hulton ; William Hulton, son of my late kinsman William Hulton deceased; Joseph Hulton son of my late kinsman Adam Hulton deceased; the widow and daughter of the said Adam Hulton ; kinsman Samuel Haward ; Thomas Crompton, son of my late kinsman Adam Crompton deceased & also his second & third sons & two daughters; sister Hulton, widow; the daughter of kinsman George Crompton ; kinsman John Hill; Nathaniel Hill son of Edmund Hill deceased ; kinswoman Elizabeth Hill ; my sister Elizabeth Dickins, widow of John Dickins deceased; kinswoman Ann Prinlott and her two sons now living and her daughter ; Mrs Mary Pickford & her eldest son & her other six children now living ; kinsman Nathaniel Hulton's wife & daughter ; my son in law Thomas Horrocks ; my daughter in law Jane Perry, &c. &c. My body to be interred at Bolton in Lancashire near my father & mother.

In the last codicil he makes a bequest of one hundred pounds to Mr Encrease Mather, minister of the Gospel in New England for the use of the College there of which he is President.   Box 54.

MARY BUTCHER, daughter of Francis Butcher, late of Staplehurst in the County of Kent, Clothier, proved 6 June 1651. Mention made of uncle John Hide, of Sounteine in the County of Sussex, and his daughters Jude & Margaret Hide, brother Thomas Butcher, mother Ann Lambe, father Thomas Lambe, brothers Thomas, James, Christopher & John Lambe (all under 21), uncle Thomas Watersfield & Dorothy his wife, uncle Ninian Butcher & Francis his wife and his two daughters, Mary and Rebecca, Aunt Elizabeth Batherst, widow, cousin Mildred Stace, wife of Captain Stace, Hanna Butcher, wife of Capt. Butcher, and her daughters Elizabeth and Hanna Butcher, Elizabeth Holden, wife of James Holden of Crambroke, Cousin Elizabeth Holden daughter of Richard Holden of Fevershame in Bedfordshire (sic), Mary & Dorothy Lambe daughters of Christopher Lambe late of Westrum and the widow Dupper. Father Thomas Lambe to be executor.   Grey, 109.

[See the will of Ninian Butcher, uncle of the testator, in the REGISTER, vol. xxxviii. p. 415 ; ante, p. 75.—EDITOR.]

ARTHUR SOMNER of Chittlehampton in the County of Devon, fuller, 25 May 1637, proved 10 October 1637. Son John, son Roger (under twenty one), daughter Ales Somner, godson John Somner, my brother John's three other children, my brother William Somner's two children, uncle John Tanner's children. Wife Mary to be executrix and brothers John Somner, William Somner & Lewes Smale to be overseers.

Goare, 129.

[Whether Arthur Somner was related or not to the New England family of Sumner I have no means of determining. William Sumner, of Dorchester, the stirps of that family, came from Bicester in Gloucestershire. See REGISTER, vol. ix. p. 300, vol. xxxvii. p. 237. The name Roger occurs in the Bicester family of Sumner.—ED.]

THOMAS WATERS of Herstmounseux, in the County of Sussex, yeoman, 13 May 1614, proved 11 December 1617. To be buried in the church yard of Herstmonseux aforesaid. To eldest son Andrew Waters fifty pounds within one year after my decease, and, after the decease of Winifrede my wife, six acres of marsh land in the Levell of Horsey & in the parish of Pevensey in the aforesaid county. To son Thomas Waters one parcel of land in the parish of Ashborneham in said county, called Blackland fields, containing five acres, more or less, and forty pounds in one year, &c. I give unto my son Sampson Waters a lease of half an acre known by the name of Lusted's Croft, joining unto Bawley Lane, in the parish Herstmonseux aforesaid, and ten pounds in three years, &c. To Nicholas Waters my brother six pounds that he oweth unto me. To John Waters, my godson, twenty shillings and to the other of my brother's children ten shillings apiece in one year, &c. To Thomas Waters, my godson, son of Andrew Waters, ten pounds & to James, the son of Andrew Waters ten pounds, to be employed to their best advantage within two years after my decease. The residue to my wife Winifred whom I ordain and make sole executrix. Loving friends William Parker, gentleman, and Jerimy Grint, yeoman, of the said parish, to be overseers.
Wit: William Parker, Samuel Parker & Mathy Pinson.

Weldon, 124.

[See Savage. Sampson Waters of Boston.—H. F. W.
Lieut. Edward Waters was granted 100 acres of land in Elizabeth City, Va., "in the precincts of Buck Roe," Oct. 28, 1628. *Va. Land Records*, No. 1, p. 93. William Waters, probably a son, was Burgess from Northampton County, 1654-60. His will is dated 1685 ; died soon after, leaving issue—1. William, Naval Officer for Accomac, 1713; Burgess for Northampton County, 1718; had son William, whose only child Mary married David Meade of Nansemond County; 2. Obedience; 3. Thomas.—R. A. BROCK.]

JOHN KIRTLAND of Tickford in the parish of Newport Pagnell, county Bucks, gentleman, 12 December 1616, proved 1 August 1617. To son Nathaniel all that part of my dwelling house in Tickford wherein I now inhabit sometime called by the name of Emberton's,[1] adjoining to the tenement in tenure of William Coningham and to the house and ground of me the said John Kirtland, sometime Thomas Horton's. Legacies to Mary Kirtland my now wife, sons Francis and Joseph Kirtland, and daughters Abigail, Susanna & Mary Kirtland. To my eldest son John Kirtland the house or tenement sometime Thomas Horton's (next the above) and adjoining a tenement of heirs of William Barton deceased. Wife Mary and her five children (as above). To godson John Kirtland, son of my brother Philip Kirtland, xiiii^s iiii^d and to the rest of the children of the said Philip ii^s vi^d each, to be paid unto the said Philip for their use. To the children of my brother Francis Kirtland ii^s vi^d apiece. To Francis Foster, clerk, ten shillings. Wife Mary to be executrix, friends George Hull and John Horley, inhabitants of Newport Pagnell, to be overseers. Phylipp Kyrtland one of the witnesses. Weldon, 82.

[Probably the family of President Kirkland of Harvard College. A number of settlers of Lynn came from about Olney in Bucks. Sherrington, from which Philip Kirtland of Lynn is said to have come, is only about two miles from Newport Pagnell on the road to Olney.—H. F. W.

President Kirkland was a great-grandson of John Kirtland of Saybrook, Conn., said to be a son of Nathaniel Kirtland, an early settler of Lynn. Philip and John Kirtland were also early settlers of Lynn. (See Chapman's Kirtland Genealogy in the REGISTER, vol. xiv. pp. 241-5, and Lewis and Newhall's History of Lynn (1865), pp. 154-5.—EDITOR.

[1] Paganus de Emberton, of Tykford Priory, Bucks, 1187. Dugdale's Monasti-kon.—JAMES A. EMMERTON.]

JOHN DOWNING of S[t] Clement Danes in the County of Middlesex, skinner, 15 May 1623, proved 7 July 1623. To the poor of the said parish twenty shillings. To my daughter Katherine a ring with a flower de luce which I wear upon my finger. To my daughter Abigail twenty shillings. And moreover my will and meaning is that if my said daughter Abigail shall determine to go to Virginia that upon her going away my executors shall pay to and for use unto the Virginia Company the sum of six pounds towards her charges. To my grand child Sara Smith ten pounds, to be put out to the best advantage by my executors until the day and time of her marriage. To my grand child Katherine Smith and her sister Dorothy Smith twenty shillings apiece, to be paid them at their several marriages, or sooner, at the discretion of my executors. To my grand child Francis Smith forty shillings, at his accomplishment of the age of twenty and one years. To my grand child Sibell Smith twenty shillings, at her day of marriage, or sooner, &c. To my grand child John Smith five pounds towards the placing and putting him forth an apprentice; and my will is that until he shall be fit and capable for service my executors shall maintain him & keep him to school, to write and read. To my son Smith's daughter Mary ten shillings within three months after my decease. To the two sons of my son Drake, vid[lt] to John and Richard, twenty shillings between them, in three months, &c. To my sister Joyce Wilson a seal ring with a faucon in it, which I had of her, and twenty shillings in money, to be paid unto her within three months, &c. To my grand child Abraham Downing ten shillings. To my well beloved son Richard Downing the lease which I hold from and under the countess Dowager of Arundell by the houses now in the occupation of me the said John Downing, together with the shop, &c. of Jane Barkested widow, &c. &c. To my well beloved son Francis Downing twenty pounds over and besides his part of the remainder of my goods, which my will is he shall have within three months after my death. The residue shall be equally shared & divided between my said two sons Richard and Francis Downing and they two to be co-executors.

Wit: Elias Allin, George Courthopp, Thomas Dannett & John Browne, Scr.   Swann, 67.

JAMES RAND, citizen & apothecary of London, 20 June 1685. Legacies to son James and to son Ralph. I have advanced my daughter Mary in marriage. There is a debt owing to me from one William Bancks now or late resident at Virginia, in the parts beyond the seas. My daughter Grace Rand to be executrix. M[r] John Fisher and my son in law Christopher Gould to be overseers.

Wit: Leonard Bates, scr., Robert Burges and George Gittens his servant. In a codicil, dated 26 March 1686, he refers to his daughter Grace as very sick and appoints his daughter Mary Gould executrix in her stead, if she shall happen to die.

The will was proved 3 May 1686 by Mary Gould, wife of Christopher Gould.   Lloyd, 63.

THOMAS DOBSON, citizen and skinner of London, 13 September 1626, proved 30 May 1627, directs his body to be buried in the parish church of St. Michael Bassishawe, makes bequests to sundry people dwelling in Colman Street and to sundry ministers, among whom Mr. Davenport, minister at St Stevens in Colman Street. In a codicil of 11 November 1626 he revokes a bequest of ten pounds made in his Will to his sister Dobson, and bequeaths that sum to Thomas Davenport, son of his neighbor Mrs. Mary Davenport, widow, to be paid to the mother for the use of the said Thomas Davenport. In another codicil, of 13 March 1626, he changes this bequest to one of ten pounds to the widow Davenport and ten pounds to her son Thomas.   Skinner, 46.

Inducco mr̃i Johĩs Davenport clic̃i in artibus probati ad vicariam ecc̃liæ p̃ochiæ Sc̃i Stephĩ in Colman strete cits et archĩñ pʳ vacañ per mortem naǐem mr̃i Samuelis Jerman clic̃i ulti vicarii et incumbents ibm̃ etc emᵗ sub sigillo etc quarto die novembris A° Dnĩ 1624°.

Prob. & Admon. Act Book, Archdeac.
of London, 1611—1626, fol. 190.

Inducc̃o Johis Goodwyn clic̃i in Artibus magr̃i ad vicariam p̃petuam ecc̃liæ p̃och sc̃i Stephañi Coleman streete cits et Archĩñat London def p̃ liberam et spontaneam Resignac̃oem Johĩs Davenport clic̃i ultimi vicarii et Incumbeñ pred̃ ad quam p̃ discretos viros Simonem Laurence Willm̃um Spurtlowe Augustinũ Garland Johẽm Stone Henricum Wood Henricum Austin Ludovicu Roberts et Michaelem Warner p̃ochianos dc̃e p̃oe veros et indubitatos patronos p̃ntatus extitit.

Prob. & Admon. Act Book, Archdeac.
of London, 1626—1637, fol. 139.

[Rev. John Davenport was the fifth son of Henry and Winnifred (Barnabit) Davenport, of Coventry, co. Warwick, where he was born in 1597. On the 9th of April in that year he was baptized in the Church of the Holy Trinity, of which the Rev. Richard Eaton, father of Theophilus Eaton of New Haven, Ct., was rector. He was admitted to Merton College, Oxford University, in 1613, and after passing two years in that college he removed to Magdalen Hall, but the same year, Nov. 15, 1615, left the University and commenced preaching. On the 5th of October, 1624, he was almost unanimously elected vicar of St. Stephen's, Colman Street, London, to which living he was inducted Nov. 4, as the above record shows. On the death of Archbishop Abbot he left London, Aug. 5, 1633, for a hidden retreat in the country, and after waiting three months, finding the messengers of Laud, the new archbishop, were on his track, he crossed over to Holland, landing at Haarlem in November. He resigned the vicarage of St. Stephen's, and John Goodwin was admitted as his successor Dec. 18, 1633. In 1637 he came to New England, arriving at Boston June 26, 1637, with another minister and Mr. Eaton and Mr. Hopkins, merchants, as Winthrop informs us (Hist. of New England, vol. ii. p. 226, 2d ed. p. 272). It is possible that the other minister may have been John Harvard, who probably arrived about this time. It is true that Trumbull (Hist. of Connecticut, vol. i. p. 89) says that Rev. Samuel Eaton accompanied his brother, but it is hardly probable that Winthrop, who gives his brother's name, would omit his. Davenport was the first minister at New Haven, Ct., 1638–67, and was pastor of the First Church of Boston, Mass., 1667, to his death 1670. For further details in the life of Rev. John Davenport, see History and Genealogy of Davenport Family, by A. B. Davenport, 1851, and Supplement to do. 1876; Life and Writings of John Davenport, by F. B. Dexter, in New Haven Historical Society Papers, vol. ii. pp. 205–38; and REGISTER, vol. ix. p. 147. Mr. Waters has much other matter relative to the Davenports, including a will of an uncle of the Rev. John Davenport, who mentions him as at the University. This matter will appear in a future number.— EDITOR.]

JOHN GREENE, late of the parish of Petsoe in the County of Gloucester, Virginia, and now at present of the parish of Sᵗ Butolph's without

Aldgate, mariner, now bound out to sea for a voyage unto Virginia in the good ship Thomas & Francis, Capt. Simmons Commander, 15 April 1685, proved 8 January 1693, by Anne Greene, relict and executrix. He appoints his wife Anne his attorney & the executrix of his will, and mentions six hundred acres in the parish of Petsoe, with certain dwelling houses, &c. given and bequeathed to him by his late father John Greene deceased, now in the tenure and possession of one Wm. Grimes, his undertenants or assigns. He gives and bequeaths unto every one of his relations or near kindred nominated or usually called by any name or names whatsoever, unto each one of them particularly twelve pence apiece, to be paid unto each one of them upon their several demands.

The witnesses were Edward Gibson, Thomas Forne and Thomas Eccleston.   Box (1694).

[Ralph Greene received grants of 50 and 300 acres of land on the north side of York River, July 18, 1650. *Va. Land Records*, No. 2, p. 265. He received subsequently grants aggregating 3500 acres. Oliver Greene was granted 120 acres in Gloucester County, July 24, 1633, No. 3, p. 16, and 450 acres March 30, 1657, No. 4, p. 122. Thomas Greene was granted 270 acres on Elizabeth River, June 11, 1652, No. 3, p. 145. John Green was granted 200 acres on the West Branch of Elizabeth River, June 1, 1655, No. 3, p. 349 (among the " transports " or " head rights " were Richard and Katherine Greene); 350 acres in Gloucester County, Jan. 13, 1661, No. 4, p. 407. There are numerous other grants of record in the 17th century to William, Peter, James and Robert Greene.—R. A. BROCK.]

MILES PRICKETT (by mark) of the parish of Holy Cross near & without the walls of the City of Canterbury, baker, 30 November, 2[d] Charles (1626), proved 30 June 1627.

Whereas there is or will be certain money due to me in consideration of my adventuring into Virginia under the Worshipful Captain Pryn his charge, which goods, if they shall prosper well in the said voyage, I freely dispose of the benefit that shall be due to me unto my brother John Prickett, by him equally to be divided and shifted between my brethren as the same shall come into his hands. To brother William Prickett's two children ten pounds, equally to be divided, &c. as they come to age, which sum of money is now remaining in the hands of my brother Thomas. To brother John nine pounds now remaining in the hands of Jane Prickett my sister & by her due to me. To the son of my said brother John my cloak. To Edward Hollett (certain wearing apparel). Brother John to be sole executor. I give to him and his heirs two hundred acres of land lying in Elizabeth City in Virginia, near Salford's Cricke.

The witnesses were William Brooke, John Slade, Thomas Boudler (by mark) & Edward Turfett.   Skinner, 65.

WILLIAM WHITE of London, linen-draper, 20 August 1622, proved 26 June 1627. I give and bequeath all my lands in Virginia, with all my servants, goods, debts, chattells and whatsoever else I have unto my beloved brother John White of London Esq., whom I constitute and ordain to be the sole heir and executor of this my last Will & Testament. The witnesses were Erasmus Ferior & John Wade.   Skinner, 65.

[George White, " Minister," was granted 200 acres of land on Nansemond River, June 3, 1635. Head Rights: Geo.White, William Moore, John Joyce, Thomas Catchman. *Va. Land Records*, No. 1, p. 240; 100 acres in County of New Norfolk, Aug. 19, 1637. Head Rights: Wife Blanche White, Peter White, Zach. Taylor, No. 1, p. 458; 150 acres do. do. Head Rights: George White, William Moore, John Joyce, Thomas Catchman, No. 1, p. 459; 300 acres in upper county of New

Norfolk, March 6, 1638, No. 1, p. 589 ; John White was granted 50 acres in upper county of New Norfolk, June 10, 1639, No. 1, p. 659. James White and John Richeson 200 acres in Mobjack bay, Aug. 15, 1642, No. 1, p. 810.—R. A. BROCK.]

WILLIAM SAKER of Surrey gentleman, 1 December, 1627, proved 7 December 1627. House & lands in Lambeth to nephew Christopher Saker if he live to be of the age of one & twenty years. If he die before then my cousin John Rayner and his heirs shall have the same. To niece Dorothy Saker one hundred & fifty pounds.

Item, I give my servant Thomas Gregory, if he return alive out of Virginia into England, fifty pounds. To Mrs Machett a piece of plate, which she hath in her custody, of the fashion of a cock, and to Mr Machett two hundred weight of my Virginia Tobacco, to the end he may be assisting to my executors. To Mr Thomas Clarke ten pounds & to Mr John Upton the elder fifteen pounds which he owes me and five pounds to buy him a ring. My executors to be Sir Thomas Jay of the Precinct of Blackfriars, London, Knight, and Nathaniel Finch of Gray's Inn. Wit : G. Hastings & Benjamin Jeay.   Skinner, 117.

PAUL DE REUOIRE, gentleman, born in Savoye, at present in London, sick in bed, 30 November 1627, proved 18 December 1627. Small legacy to a servant. All the rest to good friend Alexander Toriano, minister of the Italian church, who is appointed executor.   Skinner, 118.

[This surname was borne by the ancestors of Paul Revere of Boston, of Revolutionary fame, whose grandfather, Gilbert de Rivoire, a Huguenot, emigrated from St. Foy, in France, and settled in the island of Guernsey. Apollos de Rivoire, son of Gilbert, at the age of thirteen was sent to Boston to learn the trade of a goldsmith. Here he changed his name to Paul Revere, married and settled. His oldest son Paul, above named, was born Dec. 21, 1734, O. S., Jan. 1, 1735, N. S., and died May 10, 1818.—E. H. Goss, *of Melrose, Mass.*]

MARY SYMES, now of Beamister, late of Poorstock, in county Dorset, widow, 7 June 1736, proved 17 November 1738. To be buried in the Church Yard of Poorstock at the end of the chancell there, near my late son in law Mr Bendle deceased, and to the Parson or Vicar of the same parish two guineas for the breaking the ground for my grave and burying me. I give unto my grand son Richard Chichester,[1] now in Virginia (son of my late daughter Elizabeth Chichester deceased) one Bond for one hundred & thirty pounds lately given or entered into by son Chilcott Symes to me and all the moneys, principal & interest now due or to grow due on the same. To John Chichester (son of the said Richard Chichester) eighty pounds sterling within one year next after my decease, and in case he shall not then have attained his age of one & twenty years it shall be paid to his said father in trust for him. To Elizabeth Beer widow and relict of Francis Beer late of Long Bredy, in said County of Dorset, deceased, thirty pounds sterling, in one year, &c. To Mrs Elizabeth Foster, wife of Mr. John Foster of West Milton in the said county, maltster, ten pounds sterling in one year, &c. To my old servant Grace Moores the sum of five pounds sterling. It is my will that in case any right or thing shall happen or accrue to me from or out of the personal estate or effects of my late uncle George Richards Esq., deceased, that the same shall go and be equally divided between my said son Chilcott Symes, my daughter Mary Symes (wife of Mr Arthur Symes of Beamister aforesaid) and my said grandson Richard Chichester. The residue to said son Chilcott & daughter Mary, equally to be divided between them ; and I appoint them jointly to be executor & executrix. Wit : Merfield Cox & Richard Hussey.

In a codicil, of same day, she directs that her silver tankard be exchanged or converted into a flagon or other necessary piece of plate for the communion service of the parishioners of the said parish of Poorstock.   To Dinah, wife of John Darby of Loscombe, Dorothy, wife of John Bailey of Poorstock, taylor, Mary Courtenay, wife of John Courtenay of Poorstock, blacksmith, and Anne wife of ———, formerly Anne Wench, one guinea apiece.   Brodrepp, 272.

[¹William Chichester was granted 220 acres of land in Lower Norfolk County, Va., Sept. 14, 1667. *Va. Land Records*, No. 6, p. 220. The name is extensively represented in Virginia.—R. A. BROCK.]

ANNE NOYES, of Cholderton, in the County of Wilts, widow, 18 March, 1655, proved 20 April, 1658, by Robert Rede, sole executor named in the will. To James Noyes and Nicholas Noyes, my two sons, now in New England, twelve pence apiece and to such children as they have living twelve pence apiece.   To son-in-law Thomas Kent of upper Wallop twelve pence, to his wife five shillings and to their children twelve pence apiece.   To Robert Read of East Cholderton, in County of Southampton, gentleman, all the rest & residue, and I ordain that the said Robert Rede shall be sole executor.

The witnesses were John Tesdale and T. Tesdale.   Wootton, 130.

[Mrs. Anne Noyes, the testator, was, as her grandson the Rev. Nicholas Noyes of Salem states, a "sister of the learned Mr. Robert Parker" (Mather's Magnalia, Bk. iii. ch. 25, Appendix ; ed. of 1853, vol. i. p. 484). She was therefore an aunt of Rev. Thomas Parker of Newbury. Her husband was Rev. William Noyes, rector of Choulderton, Wilts, instituted in 1602, and resigned in 1621 (Savage, iii. 296). Of her sons, Rev. James the eldest, born in 1608, died Oct. 26, 1656, was the colleague of his cousin Rev. Thomas Parker of Newbury ; and Nicholas, who also settled at Newbury, was the father of Rev. Nicholas Noyes of Salem.—EDITOR.]

Notes on Abstracts previously printed.

GEORGE LUDLOWE (*ante*, p. 174.)

[In a note on Roger Ludlow, in the July number of the REGISTER, it is stated that he went to Virginia about 1654.   This assertion was doubtless made on the authority of Dr. Trumbull (*Hist. of Conn.* i. 218), and he based it on what he found in the New Haven records.   Ludlow had hired a vessel to transport himself and family to Virginia, probably intending to take shipping there for England ; for a MS. Roger Wolcott expressly says that Ludlow returned to England, and a deposition of John Webster, dated Dec. 18, 1660, in the Conn. Archives, speaks of "the time that Mr. Ludlow went for old England." If one will examine the printed N. Haven Colonial Records, ii. 69-74, he will find nothing to show that Ludlow went to Virginia, but rather the contrary ; for Manning, the captain of the vessel Ludlow had hired, was arrested for illicit trading with the Dutch, and upon trial, being found guilty, his vessel, in spite of Ludlow's protests was declared by the court to be a lawful prize, and ordered to be sold "by an inch of candell, he that offers most to have her."—CHARLES J. HOADLY, of Hartford, Conn.]

John Rogers the Younger.

OF CHELMSFORD, ESSEX.

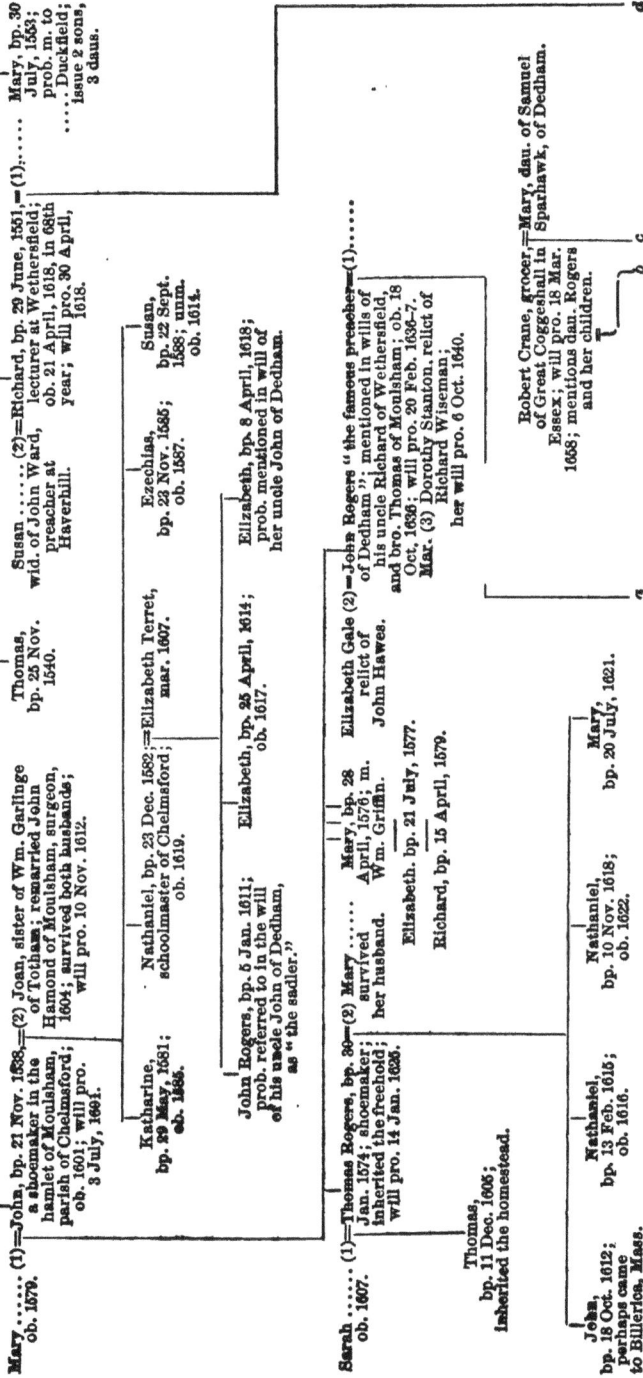

Mary ...... (1)=John, bp. 21 Nov. 1588.==(2) Joan, sister of Wm. Garlinge ob. 1579. a shoemaker in the of Totham; remarried John hamlet of Moulsham, Hamond of Moulsham, surgeon, parish of Chelmsford; 1604; survived both husbands; ob. 1601; will pro. will pro. 10 Nov. 1612. 3 July, 1594f.

Thomas, bp. 25 Nov. 1540.

Susan ...... (2)=Richard, bp. 29 June, 1551,—(1), ... wid. of John Ward, lecturer at Wethersfield; preacher at ob. 21 April, 1618, in 68th Haverhill. year; will pro. 30 April, 1618.

Mary, bp. 30 July, 1553; prob. m. to ....Duckfield; issue 2 sons, 3 daus.

Katharine, bp. 29 May, 1581; ob. 1685.

Nathaniel, bp. 23 Dec. 1582;=Elizabeth Terret, schoolmaster of Chelmsford; mar. 1607. ob. 1619.

Ezechias, bp. 24 Nov. 1585; ob. 1587.

Susan, bp. 22 Sept. 1588; unm. ob. 1614.

John Rogers, bp. 5 Jan. 1611; prob. referred to in the will of his uncle John of Dedham, as "the sadler."

Elizabeth, bp. 25 April, 1614; ob. 1617.

Elizabeth, bp. 8 April, 1618; prob. mentioned in will of her uncle John of Dedham.

Elizabeth Gale (2)=John Rogers "the famous preacher—(1)...... relict of of Dedham"; mentioned in wills of John Hawes. his uncle Richard of Wethersfield, and bro. Thomas of Moulsham; ob. 18 Oct. 1636; will pro. 20 Feb. 1636-7. Mar. (3) Dorothy Stanton, relict of Richard Wiseman; her will pro. 6 Oct. 1640.

Robert Crane, grocer,=Mary, dau. of Samuel of Great Coggeshall in Sparhawk, of Dedham. Essex; will pro. 18 Mar. 1658; mentions dau. Rogers and her children.

Sarah ...... (1)=Thomas Rogers, bp. 30—(2) Mary ...... ob. 1607. Jan. 1574; shoemaker; survived inherited the freehold; her husband. will pro. 14 Jan. 1636.

Mary, bp. 28 April, 1576; m. Wm. Griffin.

Elizabeth, bp. 21 July, 1577.

Richard, bp. 15 April, 1579.

Mary, bp. 20 July, 1621.

Thomas, bp. 11 Dec. 1605; Inherited the homestead.

John, bp. 18 Oct. 1612; Perhaps came to Billerica, Mass.

Nathaniel, bp. 13 Feb. 1615; ob. 1616.

Nathaniel, bp. 10 Nov. 1618; ob. 1622.

a   b c   d

John, eldest=Mary. Samuel=Mary. Daniel=Frances. Abigail=Thomas Bridget=Edmond Martha=...Backler. Nathaniel=Margaret Crane, Samuel Crane,
son, haber-   a clerk.   Teck, of   Anger.   second son,   b. about 1610; of Gt. Cogges-
dasher of   Prittlewell.   came to N. E. came to N. E.   hall, gent.
Colchester   John.   Martha.   1638; pastor of d. in Ipswich   will pro.
in Essex;   Mary.   church in Ips- 21 Jan., 1675-6; 16 Aug., 1670;
will pro. 3   wich; ob. 3 July, adm. granted to mentions sis-
Oct. 1628.   Thomas. John. Abigail.   1655; will pro. eldest son John ter Margaret
                                                                                                 26 Sept. 1655. Rogers, 30 Mar. Rogers and
John, a minor in 1628; living 1640.   1670.   her children.

                                                          John. Samuel. Bridget. Mary.

Mary,   John, b. in Coggeshall   Nathaniel, b. in Assington   Samuel, b. in Assington   Ezekiel, called 4th   Timothy,
bp. in Coggeshall 23 Jan. 1639; Pres. of Harv.   30 Sept. 1632; d. in Ipswich, 16 Jan. 1634-5; d. in Ipswich,   son; d. in N. E.   b. in Ipswich
Feb. 1625; m. Rev. W. Hubbard   Coll.; ob. 2 July, 1684.   N. E. 14 June, 1680.   21 Dec. 1693.   5 July, 1674.   9 Nov. 1638.
of Ipswich; living 1685.

Margaret(1)=Daniel Rogers=(2)Sarah, dau. Ezra, Nathaniel, William(1)=Mary=(2)Adam Harsnett Mary, wid(3)=Ezekiel Rogers=(1)Joan Hartopp, 3 daus.
Bishop.   succeeded his   of John   s. p.   s. p.   Jenkin.   of Cranham, Essex, of Thomas   an eminent   came to N. E.; not
             father at   Everard, cit.   clerk; will pro.   Barker; m.   preacher, came   bur. in Rowley   named,
             Wethersfield.   of London.   16 Sept. 1639.   16 July, 1631; to N. E. 1638.   8 May, 1649.   one m.
                                                                                             bur.   pastor of church   Hasseler.
           Hannah,   Samuel,   Mary,   Issue: John   12 Feb. 1678-9. in Rowley;
           m. Roger Cockington. lecturer at Margaret, and others.   will pro. 23 Jan. 1660;
           Issue: Roger and   Cree Church s. p.   To John the   ob. 26 Mar., 1661.
           Samuel. Had after-   in London.   portrait of   He mentions niece
           ward 2 or 3 husbands.   his grand-   Eliz. Cawton.
                                                     father Rogers.   Mar. (2) a dau. of Rev. John Wilson,
                                                                       who d. with child Feb. 1650.   Issue all dead before 1656.

Daniel Rogers, rector=(1) Dorothy Ball, dau. of
of Wotton in North-   the Mayor of Northampton.
amptonshire; m. (?)
dau. of ... Reading,
counsellor at law.

           William Jenkin,   Mary=Daniel Sutton.   Elizabeth=Thomas Cawton.   Elizabeth.   John   Ezekiel   Anne=..... Clarke, Abigall=..... Taylor.
           of Christ's Church,   Jenkin. Jenkin.   a minister.
           b. at Sudbury, 1612; d. in Newgate 19 Jan. 1684-5.

Daniel, Dorothy.   Sarah=John Bodell. Richard Rogers=Elizabeth, dau. of Charles Humphrey, gent.   Joseph,   Nathaniel. Abigall.   Ezekiel Rogers of Shatford in
s. p.   Issue all dead in 1656.   rector of   and relict of Matthew Browneirg,   s. p.   Essex; m. dau. of
                                               Clopton in Suffolk.   rector of Clopton.   Sir Robert Johnson,
                                                                                                                                   and relict of......

           Humphrey. Elizabeth. Culverwell, s. p. Sarah.

FAMILY OF JOHN ROGERS OF DEDHAM.

IT is with intense gratification that, at last, I am able to answer the long vexed question who was the father of John Rogers, "the famous preacher of Dedham," and to show pretty clearly what was the name of his grandfather, father of the no less famous Richard Rogers of Wethersfield. For more than a score of years has this question been discussed in the New England Historical and Genealogical Register and other publications, without eliciting a particle of positive evidence bearing on this subject. The late Col. Chester, in his memoir of John Rogers the martyr, produced a mass of negative evidence which seemed to refute the wide-spread belief in a descent from that heroic sufferer in the cause of the English Reformation. But all that we actually knew of the family in which so many of our New England people are interested, was what we could gather from the will of Richard, who speaks of his cousin (i. e. nephew) Rogers of Dedham, the inscription on his tombstone, the will of John Rogers himself, his epitaph on the north wall of the chancel in Dedham church, and the Candler pedigrees in the Harleian MSS., British Museum, and in the Bodleian Library, Oxford. Add to these Giles Firmin's Journal and the very significant statement in Nichols's Literary Anecdotes (1812), vol. ii. p. 556 (see Memoir of John Rogers the Martyr, by Col. J. L. Chester (London, 1861), p. 243), in reference to Daniel Rogers, the father of the Rev. Dr. Jortin's mother, that he was "descended from Mr. Rogers, Steward to one of the Earls of Warwick, whose residence was at Lees, near Chelmsford, in Essex, *temp.* Henry VIII.," and we have, I believe, the sum total of our knowledge of this family in England, so far as the genealogical aspect is concerned. In order that we may get our exact bearings at this point of departure, I venture to reproduce the most important of these facts.

The inscription on the tombstone of Richard Rogers of Wethersfield (see Col. Chester's Life of John Rogers, pp. 239, 240) shows that he died 21 April, 1618, in the sixty-eighth year of his age, and was born therefore about A.D. 1551. The following is a very concise abstract of his will, which was published in full in the October number of the REGISTER for 1863 (vol. xvii. p. 326).

RICHARD ROGERS of Wethersfield, Essex, preacher, 16 April 1618, proved 30 April 1618. He mentions John Clarke, a neighbor at the brook, Samuell Waight, a son in law,* Walter Wiltsheir and Jeremy Boozy. To wife Susan all such goods and household stuff as were hers before I married her. I give to my son Danyell my best cloak &c. I give to my son Ezekiell all my Latin and Hebrew and Greek books, but if his brother have not St Austin's Works, I give them him; other books written by myself

---

* Samuel Waite, of Wethersfield, married Mary Ward, either a sister or daughter of Rev. John Ward, of Haverhill (see my Memoir of Rev. Nathaniel Ward, p. 129 ; REGISTER, xxxii. p. 188; also xxxi. p. 160). If this reference is to the same person, as is probable, it is evident that his wife was a *daughter* of Rev. John Ward.—EDITOR.

and all my written lectures and papers I give to sons Danyell and Ezekiell "and to my Cosen Rogers of Dedham" &c. Twenty pounds, out of remainder of my annuities, to wife, and whatsoever shall remain I give it among all my six children. Of the ninescore pounds and twenty marks which Allen Mountjoy gen* owes me I give the said ninescore pounds to sons Daniell and Ezekiell and the twenty marks to my daughter Hasselder's children which she had by her husband now living. Daughter Hasseler again mentioned. To my wife's children forty shillings apiece. To my sister Mary Duckfield's three daughters and her son John forty shillings apiece. To my kinswoman Mary Smallwood twenty shillings &c. To Cousin Daniel Duckfield* twenty shillings. My meadow in Wethersfield lying between the Lords meadow and John Clarke's. Goodman Parker's daughter, the widow Barnard.

My executors to be Cousin Mr John Wright esq. of Romford, in Essex, Susan, my wife, and Francis Longe, my son in law. My brother Cooke and my son Makin to be overseers.

Wit: John Clarke Samuell Wayte.

B. Hamer 314, Consistory Court of London.

The inscription in Dedham church gives us the following dates:

Johannes Rogersius hic, quam prædicavit expectat Resurrectionem

$$\text{Oct 18} \quad \textit{Año} \left\{ \begin{array}{ll} \textit{Dñi} & 1636 \\ \textit{ætatis} & 65 \\ \textit{ministerii} & 42 \\ \textit{Huic Ecclesiæ} & 31 \end{array} \right.$$

$$\textit{Obijt} \; \&c$$

An abstract of his will (also given in full, vol. xvii. of REGISTER, p. 329) is as follows:

JOHN ROGERS, minister of God's word in Dedham, 14 October 1636, proved 20 February 1636. The house I dwell in &c to Dorathie my wife, during her life, and then to John Rogers my grandchild, son of my eldest son John Rogers of Colchester, deceased, and to his heirs, and for default of such heirs to his mother, my daughter in law, for term of her natural life, then to my son Nathaniel and to his heirs male, failing such then to my son Samuel and his heirs male, with remainder to my son Daniel and his heirs forever. To my sister Garood and her children twenty pounds. Item to Sara, Hanna and Marke twenty pounds. To my cousin Webb of Colchester ten pounds, and to John her son ten pounds. To my son Anger's children fifty pounds. To my son Nathaniel's children forty pounds. To son Samuel's son thirty pounds. To son Daniel's child five pounds. To son Peck's children ten pounds. To my daughter Martha's child five pounds. To these poor men, Abraham Ham, Robert Ham, John Ham, John Cannon, Simon Cowper, widow French, John Shinglewood, John Weed, Edmund Spinke, William Wood five shillings each. To my servants, Martin Garood ten shillings, George Havill twenty shillings, Tameson Princett ten shillings, goodman Allen of Santoosey (St Osithe?) twenty shillings, and to Elizabeth, now my maid two pounds. To my cousin

---

* Daniel Duckfield vicar of Childerditch, signs a petition in favor of Mr. Thomas Hooker, preacher at Chelmsford, November, 1629. He died in January, 1653. (See Annals of Evangelical Nonconformity in Essex, by Davids, pp. 156, 360.)—H. F. W.

Elizabeth Rogers ten pounds, and to her brother, the sadler, five pounds. Remainder to all my children in old England. My wife to be sole executrix.

Wit : Richard Backler, Samuel Sherman.

B. Goare 22 (P. C. C.).

The Candler pedigree is in substance as follows :

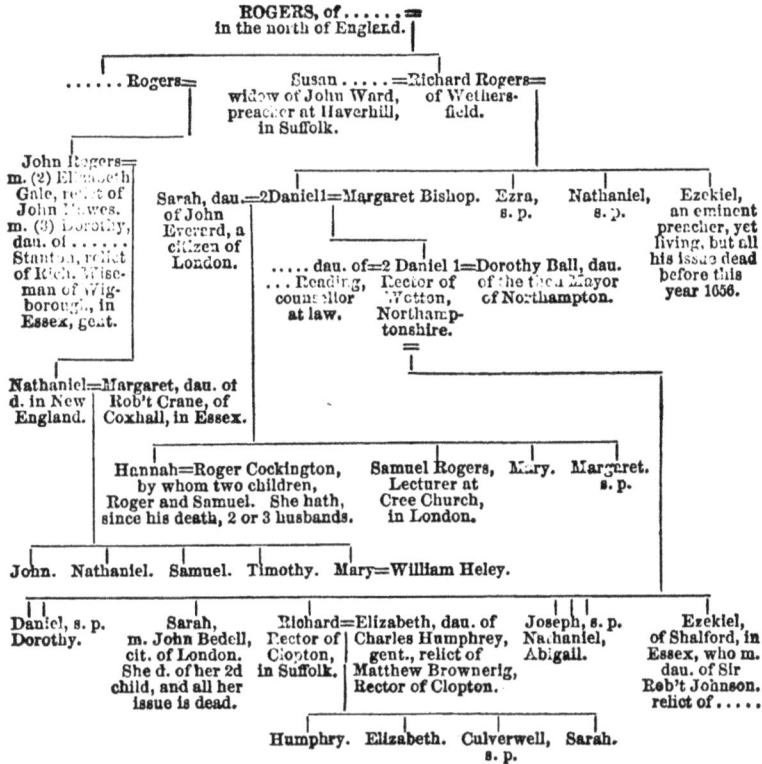

Candler shows the parentage of Margaret, the wife of our Nathaniel Rogers, as follows :

Robert Crane = Mary, dau. of Samuel Sparhawke of Dedham in Essex.
of Coxhall in Essex

Margaret, m. to Nathaniel Rogers, rector of Assington, whence he went into New England.

Besides the pedigree are the following entries by Candler, " closely huddled together," as Col. Chester says :

" Her 2ᵈ Husband was Harsnet clarke."

" William Jenkin, of Christ's Church in London."

" Mary, ma. to Daniel Sutton."

" Elizabeth, m. to Tho. Cawton."

" John, Ezekiel, Anne, to Clarke, a minister."

" Abigail."

All these entries, but the first, Col. Chester was able very clearly to explain. The Rev. William Jenkin, of Sudbury, clerk, married a daughter of Richard Rogers of Wethersfield, and had a son, William Jenkin the younger, of Christ's Church, and daughters Mary, wife of Daniel Sutton, Elizabeth, wife of Thomas Cawton, Anne Clarke and Abigail (Taylor). Probably, therefore, John and Ezekiel were also his children. Col. Chester's suggested explanation of the first entry is probably not correct, as will be seen shortly.

To the foregoing I was able to add sundry new evidence gathered, from time to time, in my gleaning among the wills registered in the Prerogative Court of Canterbury. But it seemed evident that the field of labor should be the Essex wills, whether registered or preserved in the Commissary Court of London, the Consistory Court of London, the Commissary Court of London for Essex and Herts, the Archdeaconaries of Essex and of Colchester, or any of the other various peculiar courts in that county. So, when my researches into the maternal ancestry of John Harvard called for an investigation into the Rogers family and one or two Roses* gathered by me proved to belong to Essex, I eagerly embraced the opportunity and settled down to an examination of the wills of that county, with what result the following notes will show.

JOHN ROGERS of Mulsham in the parish of Chelmsford in the County of Essex, shoemaker, 10 June, 43 Elizabeth, proved 3 July 1601. My body to be buried in the churchyard of Chelmsford by the good discretion of my executrix undernamed. Item I give and bequeath to Joan my well beloved wife all that my freehold messuage or tenement wherein I now dwell, with all the houses, buildings, yards, garden and hop-yard to the same belonging, with their appurtenances, for and during the term of her natural life, and after her decease I give and bequeath the same messuage or tenement and other the premises, with their appurtenances, unto Thomas Rogers my son and to the heirs of his body lawfully begotten. And if it shall happen the said Thomas my son to depart this natural life without heirs of his body lawfully begotten then my will and mind is that the same messuage or tenement or other the premises with their appurtenances shall be and remain to and amongst all my other children and their heirs, part and part alike. Item I give unto the aforesaid Joan my wife and her assigns all those my three tenements, with their appurtenances, that I bought of one John Sames and his wife until my daughter Susan shall come to her full age of twenty and one years, for and towards the payment of the legacies hereafter given to Nathaniel Rogers, my son. And at the full age of the said Susan I give and bequeath unto the said Susan and to the heirs of her body lawfully begotten all those my three tenements, with their appurtenances, before given to my said wife till the said Susan should come of full age. And if it shall happen the said Susan my daughter to depart this natural life without heirs of her body lawfully begotten then my mind and will is that the same three tenements with their appurtenances shall be and remain to and amongst all my other children and their heirs, part and part alike. Item I

---

* I was on the look out especially for any mention of a Rose Rogers, that being the name of John Harvard's aunt.—H. F. W.

give unto my daughter the wife of William Gryffyn the sum of five pounds of lawful English money. Item I give and bequeath to Nathaniel my son the sum of ten pounds of like lawful money, to be paid unto him within two months next after he shall have served the time of his Indenture of apprenticeship by which he now standeth bound for certain years yet to come. Item I give and bequeath unto the aforesaid Thomas my son my standing bed over the hall wherein I usually do lie, with the settle to the same, one feather bed whereon he usually doth lie, with a covering and a blanket belonging to the same, and two pair of sheets, one table, a form and a little cupboard standing in the chamber over the shop, two beds with their furniture, that my servants do usually lie on, one great old table and form, one brass pot and little kettle, one posnet, three pewter platters, two pewter dishes, one pewter bason, two fruit dishes, a copper, an old currying pan and the currying board, all the lasts and other working tools in the shop belonging to my occupation, and my stall and tilt which I use in the market. Item I give and bequeath unto my said son Thomas all my shoes and boots already made and all my leather of all sorts now being bought, upon condition that he pay unto my son John his brother the sum of ten pounds of lawful money of England within two months next after my decease; provided nevertheless that if such shoes, boots and leather as shall remain unsold at the time of my decease shall not amount to the full value of twenty pounds, being valued and prized by four honest and indifferent men, two to be chosen by my said son Thomas and other two by my executrix, that then my executrix shall make up the said shoes, boots and leather to the full sum and value of twenty pounds in ready money at such time as my said son is to pay to his brother John the aforesaid sum of ten pounds by force of this my will. Item I give and bequeath to the aforesaid John my son the sum of five pounds of lawful money of England to be paid to him by my executrix within two months next after my decease. Item I give and bequeath unto the aforesaid Thomas my son the sum of three pounds of like lawfull money to be paid to him by my executrix within two years next after my decease. Item I give and bequeath to the aforesaid Nathaniel Rogers my son all that my copyhold orchard with the appurtenances which I late bought of John Ashbye, to have and to hold unto the said Nathaniel his heirs and assigns for ever according to the custom of the manor of Mulsham Hall, whereof the same is holden.

The residue of all my goods, chattles, movables, household stuff, debts, ready money and implements of household whatsoever not before in and by this my last will and testament given, devised and bequeathed, my debts, legacies being paid and my funeral expences discharged, I fully and wholly give and bequeath unto the aforesaid Joan my wife, whom I make and ordain sole executrix of this my last will and testament.

Wit: John Cooke, Thomas Parker, Michael Newman, Richard Brodway, Urias Spilman.

Commissary of London, Essex and Herts, 1601–2, No. 157.

License granted, 27 September, 1604, to the Rector or Curate of Chelmsford to solemnize the marriage between John Hamond of Moulsham, chirurgeon, and Joan Rogers, late relict of John Rogers, late of Moulsham, shoemaker, deceased.   Vicar General's Book, London.

JOHN HAMOND of Moulsham, in the parish of Chelmsford, surgeon, 24 September 1612, proved 10 November 1612. To wife Joane all the household stuff and other goods which were her own before I married her and twenty pounds to be paid her by her brother William Garlinge. To my son Abraham a house and land called Pypers in Much Baddow, and other land there, with remainder to William, son of said Abraham, and to Thomas, another son. To my son John a house in Moulsham called Cowles. To my daughter Elizabeth forty shillings. To my daughter Margery three pounds. To Mary Barnes, my daughter's child, three pounds. To Richard Edlinge, my daughter Joan's son, forty shillings. To my wife Joane five pounds. To my son Richard five pounds.

Wit: Thomas Rogers, Thomas Jones and Hugh Barker.

Commissary Court of Essex and Herts, 1612.

JOANE HAMOND of Moulsham, in the parish of Chelmsford, widow, 3 November 1612, proved 10 November 1612 (the same day as the foregoing). To my son Nathaniel and to my daughter Susan the twenty pounds in the hands of my brother William Garlinge of Tottham, to be equally divided between them, and also four pounds due by legacy from my late husband John Hamond deceased, also to be divided equally between them. The residue of goods and chattels &c. to my daughter Susan, except an old bedstead, the true, a pan, a chair and some shelves and boards in the buttery which I give to my son in law (step son) Thomas Rogers. Daughter Susan to be executrix. Commissary Court of Essex and Herts, 1612.

THOMAS ROGERS of the hamlet of Mulsham in the County of Essex shoemaker, 23 May, 1st Charles (I.), proved at Chelmsford 14 January 1625. To Mary, my loving wife, my three tenements with all and singular their appurtenances, the which I lately bought of my brother John Rogers of Dedham, clerk, for and during the time or term that my daughter Mary shall attain to one and twenty years or day of marriage; the which my wife shall be contented with. And upon one of those times I will the said Tenements, &c. to my said daughter and to her heirs. But if it shall please God to call her out of this mortal life before she shall come to her several age or day of marriage then I will the same to my son John and to his heirs. And if both of them die before their several ages of one and twenty years then I will the said tenements to the next heirs of me the said Thomas the testator; provided always that if both my said children do die before they come to their several ages my mind and will is that my wife shall have the said tenements for and during her natural life, and after her decease to the next heirs of me the said testator. I further give and bequeath to my said wife twenty pounds of lawful money of England to be paid unto her within three months next after my decease, conditionally that she shall make, seal and deliver to my son Thomas a sufficient release of all her thirds of the house and backsides I now dwell in, at the time of the payment of the said twenty pounds, or else she shall lose the said sum. I give her further all the household stuff in the chamber over the cistern (except the bed and bedsted and furniture therewith), the stuff in the chamber over the Buttery (except one old flock bed). I further give her the bedsted and flockbed in the chamber over the Hall and all the hutches that be mine. I further give her two feather beds and one standing bedsted in the chamber over the buttery and all the moveable stuff in the said chamber. My said wife shall have three chambers in my house until the Michaelmas next after my son Thomas shall be married, viz. the chamber over the Hall, the chamber next the street over the shop, the chamber used for an apple chamber, and the shop, paying therefore to my said son Thomas forty shillings yearly at Michaelmas and our Lady by even portions.

Item I give unto my said son Thomas all that my messuage or tenement I now dwell in situate in Mulsham aforesaid, with all and singular their appurtenances, to him and his heirs for ever, except those the rooms formerly willed to my said wife, upon condition that he pay or cause to be paid unto his brother John thirty pounds of lawful money of England, so soon as he shall come to the age of twenty and two years. The residue to my son Thomas. The executors to be my loving brother John Rogers of Dedham, clerk, and my said son Thomas, to which said brother, for his pains herein, I will and devise by this my last will that my son shall bear his charges in proving of my will and other charges of his expences herein, and give unto him for a remembrance of me one piece of gold of ten shillings towards the making of him a gold ring.

Wit: Petter de Court, Tho. Sherlock Scr.

Commissary Court, Essex and Herts, 1624–5.

Here at last we strike a broad trail, and it becomes evident that this family were at the end of the sixteenth century settled in Chelmsford.

This town, as we learn from Morant, gives name both to the Deanery and Hundred, and is a pretty large and populous place, twenty-nine miles from London. It is seated at the confluence of two rivers, the Can, which flows from the south-south-west, and the Chelmer from the north. From the latter it probably derived its name, which in Domesday-book is written Celmeresfort and Celmeresforda, and in other records Chelmeresford, Chelmerford and Chelmesford; there having been undoubtedly a ford here across the river on the great road from London to Colchester, Harwich and Suffolk County. Close adjoining, on the north-east, is the little village of Springfield, which was the English home of another of our New England families, the Pynchons. A stone bridge over the Can leads directly into Moulsham or Mulsham, a manor and hamlet which before the Conquest was holden by the Abbot and convent of St. Peters, Westminister, and remained in their possession until the suppression of monasteries, when, falling to the Crown, it was granted 23 July, 1540, to Thomas Myldmay, Esq., who built a magnificent manor house, commonly called Mulsham Hall. This hamlet is really a part of the town of Chelmsford, and is but a continuation of its main street. The oldest and most noticeable house on the right, but a short distance from the Bridge, was, I learned, a freehold that had belonged from time immemorial to the Rogers family, and was still owned and occupied by one of that name. I could not but think that this might be the homestead passed down in the preceding wills from father to son, *the birth place of John Rogers of Dedham.*

The Church Registers of Chelmsford go back to A.D. 1538 (when parish registers were first ordered to be kept in England). I spent the latter half of a long summer day in the examination of their contents, while day light lasted, or until nearly nine, P. M. Too late I discovered from internal evidence that the volume which had been handed me was a copy of the original record and made by some rector or curate, who was evidently something of an antiquary, about two hundred years ago. So I offer my notes of baptism with a great deal of diffidence. I found at last the missing volume, but had no time to examine it thoroughly. The parish clerk had fancied it lost.

I found that this family were evidently settled here in Chelmsford as early as the first year noted in the Register, so that it seems needless to visit the Lees or Leighs, with the hope of carrying our history of the family further back by the aid of Church Registers.

There was a John Rogers the elder, carpenter, whose wife Jone was buried in 1540, and a John Rogers the younger, who had a son Richard baptized 29 June, 1551. This I have no doubt was Richard Rogers of Wethersfield (see the inscription on his tomb-stone). Taking this for granted, the problem was to find the baptism of John, the father of John of Dedham and brother of this Richard.

The following were all the baptisms I gathered from 1538 to 1558 inclusive :—

> John, of John Rogers the younger, 21 Nov. 1538.
> Thomas, of John Rogers the younger and Ann, 25 Nov. 1540.
> Mary, of John Rogers joiner (?) and Agnes, 11 Feb. 1542.
> John, of John Rogers and Jone, 19 Oct. 1545.
> John, of John Rogers and Agnes, 10 Sept. 1548.
> *Richard, of John Rogers the younger*, 29 June, 1551.
> Mary, of John Rogers the younger, 30 July, 1553.
> Thomas, of John Rogers, 29 Oct. 1557.
> Ellyn, of John Rogers, 1 Nov. 1558.

Whether John Rogers the younger was the father of all these children it is impossible, without further evidence, to say. Assuming that he had two wives, Ann and Agnes, then all but one are accounted for ; and in that case John the father of John of Dedham and of Thomas the shoemaker was born in 1548. A John Rogers married Agnes Carter in 1541. Coming down to the next generation I found the baptisms of the following children of a John Rogers :—

> Thomas, 30 January, 1574.
> Mary, 28 April, 1576.
> Elizabeth, 21 July, 1577.
> Richard, 15 April, 1579.
> Katherine, 29 May, 1581.
> Nathaniel, 14 December, 1582.
> Ezechias, 23 November, 1585.
> Susan, 22 September, 1588.

The baptism of John, who must have been born about 1569 to 1571, I did not get, though I have note of the baptism of a Johan, son of John Rogers, 9 August, 1579 (the very same year as the baptism of Richard, son of John). If this be our man, then his baptism was postponed nearly ten years after his birth. In New England I have noticed several instances of the postponement of this rite until the individual had even reached the age of manhood. Very likely such cases may be found in English records. At any rate the names of Thomas, Nathaniel and Susan show that we have here the family of John, the shoemaker, while it must have been their sister Mary who was married in 1596 to William Griffyn (mentioned in will of John, the father, in 1601). This John Rogers's first wife was probably Mary, buried in 1579 : and the children born after that year (viz. Katherine, Nathaniel, Ezechias and Susan) were his children by his second wife Joan, who in her will, made 1612, left the bulk of her property to two of them, Nathaniel and Susan. The others both died young, Katherine in 1585 and Ezechias in 1587.

Later on I found the baptisms of the children of Thomas, Nathaniel and Richard, all of Moulsham. Thomas was called a shoemaker, and was, without question, the one who was buried in 1625, and by his mention of his brother John as "of Dedham, clerk," has enabled us to place this family. He seems to have had two wives, Sarah, buried 1607, by whom a son Thomas baptized 11 December, 1605, and Mary who outlived him, by whom he had the following children :—

John, bapt. 18 October, 1612; perhaps died in Billerica, Mass., 25 Jan. 1685–86, æt. 74.
Nathaniel, bapt. 13 February, 1615; d. in Moulsham, 1616.
Nathaniel, bapt. 10 November, 1618; d. in Moulsham, 1622.
Mary, bapt. 20 July, 1621; mentioned in her father's will.

Nathaniel Rogers, of Moulsham, brother of the preceding and of John of Dedham, was called schoolmaster, and, very likely, was master of the Free School in Moulsham, founded by King Edward VI. A.D. 1552. He probably died in 1619, having had by his wife Elizabeth Terret (m. 1607) the following children :

John, bapt. 5 January, 1611; probably referred to in his uncle John's will as "the sadler."
Elizabeth, bapt. 25 April, 1614; d. in Moulsham 1617.
Elizabeth, bapt. 6 April, 1618; adopted, I think, by her uncle John who mentioned her in his will, and mentioned also by the latter's widow, who speaks of her as "my maid Elizabeth Rogers."

Richard Rogers, of Moulsham, called a "Poulter," married Anne Cooke 1613, and had the following children :—

Jeane, bapt. 27 February, 1613.
Mary, bapt. 21 January, 1615.
John, bapt. 28 January, 1618.

Besides all these there was a Thomas Rogers (buried, probably,

1598) who was having children from 1575 to 1580 inclusive. There is no reason to doubt that he belonged to this Chelmsford family.

And there was a William Rogers, who was buried in Chelmsford, 1587, having buried his wife Margaret the year before, who must have belonged to a family of Rogers seated at Stanford le Hope and the neighboring parishes of Fobbinge and Curringham, near the Thames. I have a few abstracts of wills relating to them. One of these, John Roger of Fobbinge, refers to the above, in 1584, as cousin William Roger of Chelmsford, and his wife, and in a nuncupative codicil, made 21 October, 1584, he willed that John Roger his (own) son should remain at Chelmsford, where he then was, until our Lady day next.

There are other references to the name of Rogers on the calendars of Wills and Admons. in Essex County, not yet examined. When they are, we may get more light on the relationship of all these parties. Some of these are as follows :—

John Rogers, 1592.   [bury).
Rose Rogers (widow), 1599–1600 (prob. wid. of Robt. R., of Buttis-
Richard Rogers, 1601–2.
William Rogers, of Colchester, 1618.
Mary Rogers (wid.), of Moulsham, 1626–8.
Richard Rogers, of Moulsham, 1628–31.
Thomas Rogers, of Moulsham, 1639–41.
Jeremiah Rogers, of Chelmsford (test.), 1676–77.
Daniel Rogers, of St. Nicholas, Colchester, 1679–80.
Nehemiah Rogers, Hatfield Brodocke (test.), 1686–7.
Jeremiah Rogers, Chelmsford (adm.), 1686–7.

And in calendars of the Archd. of Colchester,

Barnaby Rogers, of Boxted, 1626–7.
William Rogers, of Bentley Magna, 1638–9.
Elizabeth Rogers, of Witham, 1646–7.
Timothy Rogers, of Tey Magna, 1662–3.
Rachel Rogers, of Tey Magna (Book Symons 46).
James Rogers, of St. Buttolph (Book Symons 43).

Whether this family can be traced farther remains to be proved. I find in Burke's General Armory the following :—

Rogers (Chelmsford, co. Essex; Purton, co. Gloucester; Kent; and Evesham, co. Worcester). *Ar. a chev. betw. three bucks, sa. Crest A buck's head sa. attired or, in the mouth an acorn of the second, stalked and leaved vert.*

In the Visitation of Gloucestershire, published by the Harleian Society, Vol. XXI. p. 141, may be found a pedigree of the family undoubtedly referred to. If of this stock, then, our New England family may surely claim kinship with the protomartyr, by virtue of a descent from a common ancestor. I confess that I am somewhat inclined to think that further research may not only establish this connection, but also trace the ancestry of John Harvard's mother back to the same source.

On the other hand, it will be remembered, Candler says that this family came from the North of England, while the Jertins believed that one of their ancestors was a steward of the Earl of Warwick, without, however, stating which Earl.

Before giving extracts from any other wills, I ought to call attention to a clause in the will of John Rogers the shoemaker (1601), which, taken in connection with a similar one in the will of Thomas Rogers the shoemaker (1625), furnishes a significant bit of evidence to prove that these two stood to each other in the relation of father and son.

John, the father, gave the three tenements bought of John Sames* to his wife for life, then to daughter Susan and the heirs of her body; failing such, then to the testator's other children. Now Susan died young and unmarried, her brother Nathaniel died; whether Mary Griffyn was alive or not I cannot say, but in 1625 Thomas Rogers is found disposing by will of "three tenements lately bought of my brother John Rogers, of Dedham, clerk."

I was fortunate enough to discover the wills of John Hawes, whose widow Elizabeth became the second wife of John Rogers of Dedham, of Richard Wiseman, whose widow Dorothy became his third wife, of Dorothy Rogers herself, who by her conscientious mention of her step-children and their children, adds much to our knowledge of the family; of John Rogers of Colchester, eldest son of the famous preacher of Dedham, and of John Ray† of Stradishall, Suffolk, who calls him brother in law.

Short abstracts of these wills here follow :

JOHN HAWES the elder of St. Lawrence in the County of Essex, yeoman, 7 August 1613, proved 12 October 1613. Mentions son John and Elizabeth his daughter; kinsman John Anthony; Charles Anthony the younger, a sister's son; Martha Anthony, youngest daughter of said sister; Frances, the eldest daughter of sister Alice Anthony; John Olmsted, son of Richard Olmsted and of daughter Elizabeth, Israel their second son, Jedidiah their third son and Elizabeth their daughter; daughter Elizabeth wife of Richard Olmstead, clerk; Julian Veale of Malden, widow; wife Elizabeth.   Commissary Court, Essex, Herts, 1613.

RICHARD WISEMAN, of Much Wigborowe, in the County of Essex, yeoman, 12 October 1616, proved 24 May 1617. To my son Marke Wiseman, at his age of one and twenty years, my copyhold lands and tenements called Sheereinges and Cuckoes &c in Much Wigborowe. My brother Henry Wiseman, of Elsingham, Essex, gentleman, to take charge of said estates &c until then, to collect rents, &c. after the death of Anne Lawrence, widow. My said brother to pay unto my daughter Sara one hun-

---

* There was a John Sames in New England among the early settlers.—H. F. W.

† I have found two or three other wills of this family of Ray, which do not throw any light on the Rogers alliance.

dred pounds, and to my daughter Anne one hundred pounds, at their several ages of twenty years. To my daughter Sara three hundred pounds and to my daughter Anne three hundred pounds, at their several ages of twenty years. To my son Marke one hundred pounds at his age of four and twenty years. To my wife Dorothie my freehold lands, tenements &c in West Mersey, Essex, for and during her natural life, and then to my said son Marke Wiseman forever. To Sir Edward Bullock Kn^t five pounds and to the Lady Elizabeth, his wife, five pounds within one year after my decease. To John Whitacres, gentleman, three pounds six shillings and eight pence within one year after my decease. To Mr Harrison, of Layerdelahay, clerk, one piece of gold of twenty two shillings. To Mr Nicholson of Little Wigborowe twenty shillings. To Christian Bridge, my wife's mother, ten shillings to make her a ring. To Jo: Makyn now servant with William Bond of Colchester, baker, five pounds, at age of four and twenty years. To Matthew London of Colchester, yeoman, five pounds and to Mary his wife, my sister, ten pounds, upon condition that they shall not claim &c anything by force or virtue of the last Will and Testament of Margaret Wiseman, my late mother deceased. To Rachell, Bridgett and Anne London, daughters of the said Matthew London, to every one of them three pounds. To Henry Bridge, my man servant thirty shillings. To my son Marke Wiseman one silver salt parcel gilt, one dozen silver spoons and one silver bowl or cup.

All the rest of my goods and chattels &c to my wife Dorothy, except my gray ambling gelding which I give and bequeath to my said brother Henry Wiseman. Said wife Dorothy to be executrix.

Weldon, 39 (P. C. C.).

DOROTHY ROGERS of Dedham in the County of Essex, widow, 16 April 1640, proved 6 October 1640. She mentions son Mark Wiseman; daughter Sarah Cole, and her children Mary, Samuel, Sarah and Mark; daughter Hannah Hudson and her children John, Samuel, Hannah and Sarah; Sister Garrod and Jeremy Garrod her son; the house where Edmond Spinke lives; Nathaniel Rogers, eldest son of late deceased husband, and Margaret his wife, and their four children, John, Mary, Nathaniel and Samuel; Mary, wife of Samuel Rogers, clerk, another son of deceased husband, and his two children, John and Mary; Frances, wife of Daniel Rogers, another son of deceased husband, and his three children; Abigail, Bridget and Martha, daughters of late husband; the three children of daughter Pecke, Thomas, John and Abigail; the four children of daughter Anger, John, Samuel, Bridget and Mary; Martha, the daughter of daughter Backler; the widow Howchen and widow Reinolds; the wife of John Ham, the wife of Abraham Ham, Michael Ham and the wife of Bezaliel Ravens; her maid Elizabeth Rogers; her god children Robert Webb, Susan Gutteridge and William Thorne; the widow Downes and the widow French; her sister Marshall; John Rogers, her late husband's eldest son's son; cousin Page of Haverhill; and John Garrod of Colchester, her sister's son.

Commissary Court, Essex & Herts, 31, 1641–2.

JOHN ROGERS of Colchester in the County of Essex, haberdasher, 7 July 1628, proved 3 October 1628. To son John one hundred pounds at his full age of one and twenty years. My executrix shall, within three months after my decease, put in good security to Nathaniel Rogers of Bockinge, Essex, my brother, clerk, and Edmond Anger, my brother in law, of Dedham, in said County, clothier, to their liking and content, for the true payment of the said one hundred pounds. My wife Mary shall have the use and consideration of the said one hundred pounds yearly towards the bringing up of my said son John until his said age of one and twenty years. My said wife Mary to be executrix and the said Nathaniel Rogers and Edmond Anger to be supervisors, and to either of them twenty shillings apiece. To every of my brothers and sisters ten shillings apiece for a remembrance. To the poor of Colchester twenty shillings.

Wit: John Rogers,* John Marshall and Tho: Cockerell.

Arch. of Colchester, 11, 1628-9.

JOHN RAY of Stradishall in the County of Suffolk, yeoman, 31 January 1630, one of the sons of Richard Ray, late of Stradishall, deceased. Mentions brother Robert Ray; lands &c in Wichambroke and Stradishall; brother Richard Ray; cousin John Ray of Denston; brother Thomas Ray; John Ray, son of brother Henry deceased; brother Abraham Ray; *brother in law John Rogers, clerk;* brother in law John Benton, clerk; John Ray, son of brother Ambrose deceased; *Elizabeth Page of Haverhill, widow of Michael Page;* Susan Ray, wife of Richard Ray.

Admo^n granted, 30 June 1631, to Ellene Ray relict &c of Robert Ray, brother and executor. St John, 72 (P. C. C.).

EXTRACTS FROM FEET OF FINES.

Between Thomas Cotton gen. *quer.* and William Turner gen., Mary Twidow, John Rogers clerk and Dorothy his wife, *deforc.*, for one messuage, one garden, one orchard, thirty acres of arable land, six acres of meadow, twenty six acres of pasture and four acres of wood, and common pasture for all animals in Goldhanger, Tolshunt Major *als.* Tolshunt Beckingham and Totham Parva. Consideration 100^{li} st.

Mich. 4 Car. I. Essex.

Between Henry Towstall, esq. *quer.* and John Rogers, clerk and Dorothy his wife, *deforc.*, for one cottage, one garden, two acres of arable land, thirteen acres of freshmarsh, and two acres of saltmarsh, with the appurtenances in Fingringhoe. Consideration 60^{li} sterling.

Trin. 11 Car. I. Essex.

The following is an abstract of the will of the Rev. John Ward, whose widow became the second wife of Richard Rogers of Wethersfield.

JOHN WARD, preacher of God's word in Bury St Edmunds, Suffolk, 9 October 1589,† proved 31 October 1598. To youngest son John one hun-

---

* I would suggest that this may be the signature of his father, John Rogers of Dedham.
H. F. W.

† Col. Joseph L. Chester furnished me with a copy of this will which I printed in full in 1868 in my "Memoir of Rev. Nathaniel Ward." In the will as recorded the date is in words, " The nythe daie of October One Thowsand Fyue Hundredth eightie nyne Elizabethe Quadragesimo." Soon after receiving the copy I called Col. Chester's attention to the discrepancy between the regnal and the common year, and suggested that if the year of our Lord had been in arabic numerals instead of words, I should have supposed that the last two figures had been transposed, and that the true date was 1598 instead of 1589. Col. Chester found the original will, and it was as I supposed in arabic numerals, as was also the regnal year. " The year," he wrote, " should unquestionably be 1598, for it is simply impossible that a man writing in the 31st Elizabeth could have written 40th." Besides, Samuel is mentioned in a way that conveys the idea that he was of age, whereas in 1589 he was only twelve years old. *See Memoir of N. Ward*, p. 132.—EDITOR.

dred pounds at twenty one; daughter Abigail one hundred pounds at eighteen, and daughter Mary one hundred pounds at eighteen. To son Samuel all my books and apparell, and to son Nathaniel six score pounds at two and twenty. Wife Susan to be sole executrix. If she refuse then my brother Edward Ward to be executor.

Wit: Lawrence Neweman, John Woodd.   Lewyn, 85 (P. C. C.).

ADAM HARSNETT of Cranham in the County of Essex, clerk, 30 November 1633, proved 13 September, 1639. Mentions wife Mary, widow of John Dawson, daughter Elizabeth Dawson; brothers John Pope of London, salter, and Samuel Harsnett, grocer, executors. To son John the picture of his grandfather Rogers, to son Ezekiel two beer bowls marked with D. R. and E. R., a silver wine goblet marked C. H. and spoons marked M. H. To daughter Anne (certain things which Mr Cotton gave unto her). Daughter Abigail, son Nathaniel annuities to be received out of lands of Grace Reinolds and Elizabeth Fareham of Dublington?, Essex. Mother Mercie Harsnett. Brothers William Harsnett, William White and John Pope. To daughters Tershah and Stanyon five pounds each.   Harvey, 143 (P. C. C.).

The above is evidently the "Harsnet clarke" of the Candler pedigree. I would suggest that he married the daughter of Richard Rogers, widow of William Jenkin, and survived her. He was born, I found, in Colchester, son of Adam Halsnoth (as the name was often spelled), a joiner, by his wife Mercy or Marcey, and was a near kinsman of the well-known bishop, Samuel Harsnett, whose baptism I also found in Colchester under the name of Halsnoth. The will of Adam Halsnoth the elder, joiner, I found among the wills of the Archd. of Colchester (1612–13). He mentions wife Marcey, sons Adam, William, Samuel and Joseph, and daughters Marcey, Tamazin and Elizabeth.

The connection of the Crane family with the Rogers family is shown in the following extracts.

ROBERT CRANE of Great Coggeshall in the County of Essex, grocer (without date) proved 18 March 1658. Mentions wife; refers to marriage contract entered into with brother in law Mr Nathaniel Bacon; lands &c in West Mersey, Essex; son Samuel Crane and his lawfull issue and son Thomas Crane; they to pay my son Robert Crane and his issue; lands &c in Stocke Street, lands in Grt Coggeshall in occupation of myself and William Cottyes, lands in Church Street, sometime Spooners and other estates; refers to a surrender made unto the William Turners (father and son) of Markes Tey &c.

To my daughter Rogers, wife of Nathaniel Rogers, now of New England, clerk, four hundred pounds; to my grand children Samuel, Nathaniel, Ezekiel, Timothy and John Rogers fifty pounds apiece; they to accept of a bond of four hundred pounds made to me from Mr Joshua Foote, now or late of New England, on which there is now due for principal one hundred and fifty pounds, besides use; to daughter Mary Whiting wife of Henry Whiting of Ipswich, two hundred pounds, the remainder of her portion; to my grand children Henry and Mary Whiting one hundred pounds apiece at their ages of one and twenty years or days of marriage respectively; to my daughter Elizabeth, wife of William Chaplyn two hundred pounds ; to my grand children Robert and Mary Crane, children of my son Thomas Crane, one hundred pounds apiece ; to Diana, Elizabeth, Margaret, Frances and Bridget, daughters of my brother Thomas Crane deceased, five pounds apiece; to my kinswoman Frances Stafford,,widow, five pounds ; to Susan Voyse wife of John Voyse of Great Coggeshall, five pounds ; to my three kinswomen, the residue of the daughters of my sister Johan Foulsham, forty shillings apiece ; to Robert Crane, son of my cousin Robert Crane of Braintree, twenty pounds at his age of one and twenty years; to William Fowleger, my servant, for his faithful service &c. thirty pounds ; to my son Samuel all my goods and wares in the shop and warehouses, my debts &c., and the lands and tenements in Lowhard &c had of John Edes, clerk, &c.; sons Samuel and Thomas to be executors.

Proved by the oath of Samuel Crane, the surviving executor.

Pell, 179 (P. C. C.).

SAMUEL CRANE of Great Coggeshall, in the County of Essex, gentleman, —— November, 1669, proved 10 August 1670. To my sister Mrs Margaret Rogers, now of Ipswich, in New England (lands and tenements in various places) for life, and then to her children ; my sister Mary Whiting, wife of M[r] Henry Whiting of Ipswich, Suffolk, and her children ; my sister in law —— wife of —— Daynes, late the wife of my brother Robert Crane ; my sister M[rs] Elizabeth Chaplin, late the wife of M[r] William Chaplin, of Bury S[t] Edmunds ; my brother M[r] William Clopton and his children ; my cousin M[r] Lawrence Stisted of Ipswich, grocer, and my niece Mary, his now wife ; my uncle Mr. Edward Sparhawke and his son Samuel and daughter Sarah Sparhawke ; my kinswoman Mrs. Bridget Andrews, wife of M[r] William Andrews, citizen and cheesemonger of London; John Garwood ; my father in law Mr. Robert Feltham ; my uncle Mr. John Crane, living about Horram in Suffolk, and his son John ; my cousin Cooper, widow, and cousin Burgis, widow ; children of my cousin Robert Foulsam, deceased ; my cousin Robert Crane of Braintree and his son Robert ; my cousin John Sparhawke ; my cousin John Sherman ; my cousin M[r] John Blomfield ; my cousin M[r] John Rogers and M[r] William Hubbard, both in New England; Christian Whiting, daughter of Henry ; Isaac Hubbard; others mentioned. Penn, 97 (P. C. C.).

ROBERT CRANE of Hadleigh in the County of Suffolk, gentleman, 14 May, 18 Charles II. 1666, proved 22 May 1669. My sister Mary Crane to be executrix, to whom all my tenements &c in Kelvedon, in the County of Essex, the reversion of the jointure of my mother in law, the wife of M[r] Robert Andrewes; if my sister die the premisses to be sold by Thomas Goulding and the product to be equally divided betwixt the children of my uncle Whiting and aunt Rogers in New England and the children of my cousin Thomas Goulding ; to the aforesaid Thomas Goulding and his heirs forever my house in Brantray ; my two messuages in Coggeshall to William Fowler and his heirs forever; to William Hawkins my two messuages on Fering Hill ; to M[r] Whiting of Sermer, for preaching my funeral sermon, five pounds ; to the poor of Kelvedon five pounds.

Proved by Mary Stisted als Crane, wife of Lawrence Stisted, sister of the deceased and his executrix. Coke, 51 (P. C. C.).

The following rough table will serve to show the relationship of most of these parties :

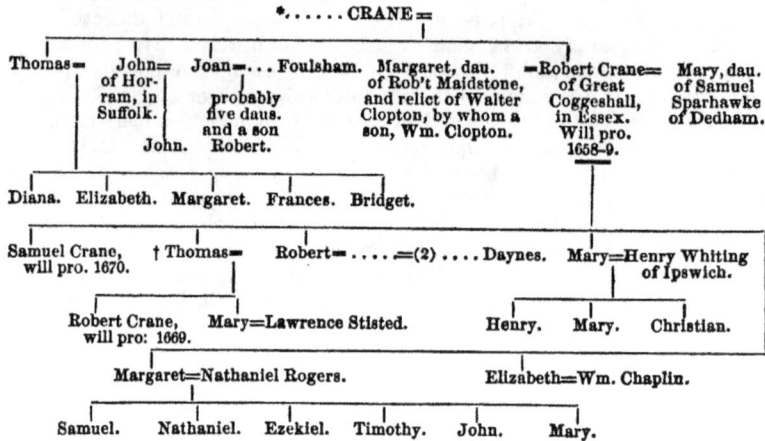

```
*...... CRANE =

Thomas=   John=        Joan=...Foulsham.   Margaret, dau.        =Robert Crane=   Mary, dau.
          of Hor-                          of Rob't Maidstone,    of Great         of Samuel
          ram, in      probably            and relict of Walter   Coggeshall,      Sparhawke
          Suffolk.     five daus.          Clopton, by whom a     in Essex.        of Dedham.
                       and a son.          son, Wm. Clopton.      Will pro.
                    John.   Robert.                               1658-9.

Diana.  Elizabeth.  Margaret.  Frances.  Bridget.

Samuel Crane,    † Thomas=      Robert=....=(2)....Daynes.     Mary=Henry Whiting
will pro. 1670.                                                     of Ipswich.

Robert Crane,    Mary=Lawrence Stisted.      Henry.   Mary.   Christian.
will pro: 1669.

Margaret=Nathaniel Rogers.                   Elizabeth=Wm. Chaplin.

Samuel.  Nathaniel.  Ezekiel.  Timothy.  John.  Mary.
```

The following extracts from the Registry of Deeds of Suffolk County, Mass., refer evidently to the legacy of Robert Crane to his grandchildren, the sons of his daughter Margaret Rogers.

By an Indenture made 24 October 1653 between Joshua Foote, late citizen and Ironmonger of London, then of Roxbury in the County Suffolk in New England, on the one part, and Robert Crane of Coggeshall in the County of Essex within the Commonwealth of England, on the other part, the former made conveyance to the latter of his dwelling house, lately purchased of Joshua Hues, situate in Roxbury, with four acres of land &c belonging, as security on his bond to pay 184£ 7ˢ 2ᵈ, due to the said Crane &c.

Suffolk Deeds I. 335.

Testimony of Samuel Danforth, Thomas Weld William Park and David Richard 1–9–1655 that Nathaniel Rogers of Ipswich and William Barthelmew did enter upon the dwelling house, formerly possessed by Joshua Hewes in Roxbury and since belonging to Joshua Foote deceased and did legally take possession of the said dwelling house &c. and order to give warning that the said house and land in the deed of sale made by the said Joshua Foote unto and for the use of Mʳ Robert Crane &c. 20 October 1653, do legally and properly belong unto Nathaniel Rogers of Ipswich and to his brethren Samuel, Ezekiel and Timothy Rogers of Ipswich.

Suffolk Deeds II. 210.

It seems to me worth the while to add abstracts of the wills of Ezekiel, the son of Richard of Wethersfield, and of Nathaniel, the son of John of Dedham, and certain other notes gleaned in Salem Court House and elsewhere.

---

* Morant, in his History of Essex (reprinted at Chelmsford, 1816), vol. ii. p. 164, refers to will of Samuel Crane of Great Coggeshall, gent., dated Nov. 1609.—H. F. W.

† I have minute of will of Thomas Crane (Essex Co.) 1655 (Book Aylett, 159, P. C. C.), but no abstract at hand.—H. F. W.

EZEKIEL ROGERS " Borne at Wethersfeild in Essex in old England Now of Rowley in Essex in new England " 17 April 1660, sworn to 26 March 1661 Renders praise to God for three special blessings : " fflrst for my Nurture and Education under such a father Mr Richard Rogers, in Catechisme and knowledge of the holy scriptures the want whereof I see to be the main cause of the Errors of the times. Secondly that (whereas till I was aboue twenty yeares of age I made but ill use of my knowledge but liued in a formal profession of Relligion) the lord pleased by occation of a sore sicknes which was like to be death to make me to see the worth and Neede of Christ and to take such houlde of him as that I coolde never let him goe to this houre whereby I am now encouraged to bequeath and committe my soulle into his hands who hath Redeemed it, and my Body to the Earth since he will giue me with these very eyes to see my Redeemer. Thirdly for my Calling even to be a minester of the Gospell the most glorious Calling in the worlde which the lord brought into noth without difficulty for my . . . . ing in the time of the hottest Persicution of that Bloody Hirarchy and being inlightened concerning the euell and snare of Subscrip...n and Cerimonies I was advised to give over the thought of the minestry and to betake my selfe to the study and practise of Phis..ke But the lord mercyfully prevented that ; for though it be a good and Nessecary Calling, I haue observed that the most through these o..e Coruption haue made it to them selues the very Temptation to couetousnes or lust or both, I therefore chose rather to lye hide abo.. a dozen yeares in an honerable famelly exerciseing my selfe in minesteriall dutyes for a bout a dozen yeares after my leaving the uneversity. Then the lord Gaue me a Call to a Publique charge att Rowley in Yorke shire whereby The Gentlenesse of —oby Mathewe I was fauoured both for subscription and Cerimonies and injoyed my liberty in the minestry about seaventeene ..ars in Comforthable sort Till for refuseing to reade that accursed Booke that allowed sports on God's holy Sabbath or lords day I was suspended and by it and other sad signes of the times driven with many of my hearers into New ...land where I haue liued in my Pastorall Office about ———— years with much Rest and Comforth beleeueing the way .. the Churches here to be according to the present light that God hath giuen the purest in the wholle world.

Now Age and Infir...es calling upon me to looke daly for my change I profese my selfe to haue liued and to dye an unfeigned Hater of all the Base Opinnions of the Anabaptists and Antinomians and all other Phrenticke dotages of the times that springe from them which God will ere longe cause to be as doung on the earth. I doe also protest against all the evell ffashions and guises of this age both in Apparr.. and that Generall Disguisement of longe Ruffianlike haire A Custome most generally taken up at that time when the Graue and modest weareing of haire was a part of the Reproch of Christ : as appeared by the tearme of Roundheads and was carryed on with a high hand not with standing the knowne offence of soe many Godly persons, and without publique expression of these reasons for any such libertie taken."

Then follows his disposal of his estate : to wife Mary the dwelling house &c. during her natural life ; to nephew Mr Samuel Stone of Connecticut thirty pounds ; to " my cousen his son John ten pounds ;" to dear brother and fellow officer Mr Phillips five pounds and Aquinas his Sum. in folio ; to my sometimes servant Elizabeth Tenney *ells* Parratt ten pounds ; to loving neice M^n Mary Matosius of Malden in Essex in old England ten pounds ; to loving niece M^n Elizabeth C..ton wife of the Preacher of Roterdam in

Holland ten pounds ; to the wife of cousin Rogers of Billerica five pounds ; sundry gifts to servants ; all his Latin books to Harvard College and some English books, as appears in the Catalogue.

The rest of the estate in lands not given to wife during her natural life, he gives to the Church and town of Rowley upon condition that they pay or cause to be paid &c. unto Ezekiel Rogers the son of Mr Nathaniel Rogers late pastor of the Church of Ipswich deceased the sum of eight score pounds.

The real estate given to wife, for term of her life, after her decease to go to the church and town of Rowley to enable them the better to maintain two teaching elders in the church for ever, on condition that they settle an elder within four years and so from time to time when changes occur by death or removal any other way. On failure of this condition the said houses and lands to be to the use of Harvard College. Wife Mary to be sole executrix.*

The amount of his estate as rendered in the Inventory was over 1535£, of which 400£ was in lands that were Thomas Barker's (his wife's former husband).

This will is on file among the probate papers of Essex County ; but I do not find any copy of it in the Registry or any record of probate or administration granted. In the March term of the Ipswich Court, 1665, Ezekiel Rogers, the son of Mr. Nathaniel Rogers of Ipswich, deceased, brought suit against Mrs. Mary Rogers, the executrix of the above will, for not performing a promise and engagement made to the said Nathaniel in the behalf of his son, wherein the said Mr. Ezekiel Rogers, of Rowley, had obliged himself to provide for Ezekiel the son of Nathaniel, and to make his portion as good as the rest of the sons of the said Nathaniel. The plaintiff in his declaration says that his father for that reason gave him no portion in his estate, except a small pledge of his love, and discharged himself from any care concerning him, and, indeed, looked upon him as the elder brother, though but his fourth son.

This case is valuable and important, since it furnishes evidence that the wife of the Rev. William Hubbard was Mary,† and not Margaret, as all our New England authorities have had it, and thus confirms Candler's statement, made in his account of the Knapp family. I fail to find the least bit of evidence, either that Nathaniel Rogers had a daughter Margaret or that William Hubbard had a

* Rev. Ezekiel Rogers's will is printed in full in the REGISTER, vol. v. pp. 125–8.—ED.
† Candler in his Knapp pedigree gives the name of the husband of Mary Rogers as "Wm. Hobert," and in his Rogers pedigree as "Wm. Heley" (vide REGISTER, xvii. 47). Mr. Waters makes it evident that the surname in the Knapp pedigree (Hobert, i. e. Hubbard) is correct.
William Hubart or Hubbard of the County of Essex, England, who afterwards settled at Ipswich, Mass., married Judith, daughter of John and Martha (Blosse) Knapp, of Ipswich, England (see The Visitation of Suffolk, ed. by Metcalf, 1882, p. 149; REG. xvii. 47). He was father of Rev. William Hubbard, who married Mary Rogers.
The first book in which I find the christian name of the wife of Rev. William Hubbard given is John Farmer's Genealogical Register, published in 1829, where on page 152 she is called "Margaret daughter of Rev. Nathaniel Rogers." Subsequent writers have repeated Farmer's error.—EDITOR.

wife bearing that name. This Mary Hubbard seems to be living as late as 26 March, 1685, when she joins her husband in a conveyance of certain land in Ipswich. The following are some of the depositions filed in this case.

The testimony of MARY HUBBERT.

I can affirme that aft^r my Father Rogers' death my Brother Ezekiell Rogers was very desirous to have lived wth his Cousen Mr Ezekiell Rogers of Rowley & he rendred this as ye reason, w^n sundry complaints were made to his mother against him, that he knew he could please him, if he lived with him, wch he knew he should never doe, unless he lived there, in reg^d that sundry informations would be carried to his Cousen agst him, wch he should be able no otherwise to prevent. And farth^r I know that our friends did endeavour to insinuate so much into my Couzen, but were discouraged therefrom by a report they heard from presseing it over farr, wch report was, that one nere to my Cozen should say, nameing of him by some opprobrious terme, that he should not come there. Also when my Brother lived with him before, he wore his haire longer, by my Cosins sufferance, contrarie to my Fathers desire, then the rest of his Brethren; Farther my Bro: rendred this as the reason why he was not willing to live constantly at the Colledge, because he had not convenient maintenance allowed, my Cosin not allowing above five pound a year at ye most. To the truth of w^t is above written I can attest upon oath if called thereunto.

March 31. 1665.   MARY HUBBERT.

The Deposition of Mrs MARGARET ROGERS aged about 55 yeares.

This Deponent sayth that soon after her husbands death, goeing to visit her cousin M^r Ez. Rogers of Rowly, he told her that he would doe for her son Ezekiel according as here followeth viz. That he would give him his house where he then lived wth severall parcells of land, wch he then mentioned, & shewed ye place of them, altho she had now forgotten the particulars: She thinks also he promised her then to allow 10£ a year towards his education, yet (being long since she cannot speak so punctially thereunto). Further at another time since this Deponent went to the sayd M^r Ez. Rogers to speake wth him about her son Ezekiels hayre, y^t was complayned of, to be too long: but when M^r Ez. Rogers would have had her son bound to let his hayre be no longer then to ye lower tip of his eares, she told him she would never yeild to such a snare for her child, tho he never had peny of him while he lived. Also this Deponent sayd y^t James Baily told her that M^r Ez. Rogers had appoynted him to pay fourty pound to her upon the account of her son Ezekiel, but she never knew but of ten pound thereof paid: Also that she would have been glad if her son Ezekiel might have lived wth her Cousin M^r Ez. Rogers at Rowly, and was troubled that there was no way appearing to have it so, altho her son Ezekiel alwayes about those times seemed very desirous so to doe. The Deponent also saith that Mr Ez. Rogers told her he had appointed James Baily to pay her fourty pound in four years towards the education of her son Ezekiel,   And further saith not

March 3065.   Sworne before me   DANIEL DENISON.

"MATHEW BOYES* of Leeds in the County of Yorke Clothworker aged fifty yeares or thereaboutes " sworn at York 16 Jan'y 1661, makes a deposition concerning the matter.

The testimony of JOHN PICKARD, aged forty three years, made 28 March 1665, is to the effect that he understood from Mr Ezekiel Rogers of Rowly that there were three reasons why he would not give his kinsman more. " 1 Because he refused to dwell wth him. 2 Because he would not keep at Colledge though there he would have maynteyned him. 3 Because he spake to his mother to have his haire cutt, but could not gett it done, And seuerall other things were the mention not here materiall."

Essex Co. Court Papers, Vol. X. Nos. 90–98.

A notable error has been made by all who have written about Ezekiel Rogers, of Rowley. They have all, one after another, stated that he brought over " the wife of his youth," Sarah Everard, who lived here about ten years, and died in Rowley, etc. That he brought over the wife of his youth I do not deny; but that her name was Sarah Everard I can deny with confidence, for I find her provided with another husband, in the person of Ezekiel's eldest brother Daniel, who had by her, as his second wife, four children. Who then was the first wife of Ezekiel Rogers? That he had a wife buried in Rowley about ten years after his coming over is true. Her name, however, was *Joan,* buried 8 May, 1649. This is a strong confirmation of a pedigree which I had constructed in England before I had the opportunity to discover this important fact. I had already been led to give Mr. Ezekiel Rogers a wife Joan by the following evidence which I had discovered in my researches among Wills and Feet of Fines :—

Between Richard Raynton, gen. *quer.* and Ezekiel Rogers, clerk and Johanna his wife, *deforc.*, for one messuage, one garden, nine acres of meadow and six acres of pasture, with the appurtenances &c in Bermondsey. Consideration 100^{li} sterling.   Trin. 11 Car. I. Surrey.

(Feet of Fines.)

THOMAS DAMPIER *als* DAMPORT of Stratford at Bow, gentleman, 26 March 1617, proved 15 February 1627. Mentions son James, daughter Katherine, wife Joane, sister Joane, now wife of John Creed of Shepton Mallett in the County of Somerset, and her sons Matthew, Stephen and John Webb, cousin Marmaduke Moore and daughter Katherine now wife of Hugh Cressie, of London, merchant.

To my daughter in law Joane Hartopp, now wife of Ezekiel Rogers of Hatfield, Essex, gentleman, twenty pounds within six months after my decease.   Barrington, 18 (P. C. C.).

He must have married his second wife (Sarah?), daughter of Mr. John Wilson, very soon after; for Emanuel Downing writes from

* Matthew Boyes was an early settler of Roxbury (REGISTER, xxxv. 24). He was freeman of Massachusetts May 22, 1639 ; removed to Rowley, which he represented in the General Court in 1641, 3, 5 and 50; returned to England as early as 1657. He was father of Rev. Joseph Boyse, of Dublin, Ireland, a famous Puritan author. (See REGISTER, xii. 65.)—EDITOR.

Salem, 24. 12. 1650, to John Winthrop, Jr., "Mr. Rogers of Rowly hath last weeke buryed his wife and childe within a few dayes after shee was brought to bed."

21 Feb. 1621. Ezekiel Rogers, Clerk, instituted to the Rectory of Rowley, void by the death of Henry Pickard, Clerk, on the nomination of Sir Francis Barrington, Baronet.   Institution Books, York.

Extract from a Letter of Robert Ryece to John Winthrop, 1 March, 1636.

"One accidente which I credibly hard, I can not omytte;—While the Bishop his chancelor, Dr. Corbett, was vpon his seate of justice at Bury, newes was broughte hym that Mr. Rogers of Dedham dyed the last nighte. Is he so? sayd the chancelor, let him goe in reste, for he hath troobled all the contry these 30 yeeres, & dyd poyson all those partes for x myle rounde abowte that place,—the manner of whose death is thus reported; whiles the Bishop was at Ipswiche, one daye, havinge occasion to ryde forthe, comanded his servantes to hyer poste horses; who browght hym worde that all the horses were taken vp, by suche as wente to the sermon at Dedham.   Is the wynde at that doore? sayde the Bishop, I wyll soone ease that; & so not long after, as the Commissary synce confessed, he had commande from Canterbury vpon the complaynte of Norwich to stay the lecture at Dedham : wherevpon the Commissary wrote a friendely letter to Mr. Rogers, shewenge hym he had commandemente from Canterbury to require hym to stay his lecture now for a whiles the plague continewed, which by suche concourses was daylie encreased.   Mr. Rogers, beleevinge, as was pretended, stayed his lecture, & after harvest ended, the Doctor & Comissary was moved for renewene of the lecture; the Comissary gave fayer woordes, promysynge uery shortely thay shoolde haue liberty, which after sondry promyses, withowte all in all intention, Mr. Rogers seinge there was a secrett determination wholly to suppresse that lecture, this strooke hym to the harte, hastened all his natural malladies to his vttermost periode."   Winthrop Papers, Mass. Hist. Coll.
Fourth Series, Vol. VI. p. 412.

Extract from a Letter of Emanuel Downing to John Winthrop, 6 March, 1636.

"I was at Mr. Rogers of Dedham his funerall, where there were more people than 3 such Churches could hold: the gallery was soe over loaden with people that it sunck and crackt and in the midle where yt was Joynted the tymbers gaped and parted on from an other soe that there was a great cry in the Church: they vnder the gallery fearing to be smothered, those that were vpon yt hasted of, some on way some an other, and some leaped downe among the people into the Church: those in the body of the Church seing the tymbers gape were sore afrighted, but yt pleased God to honour that good man departed with a miracle at his death, for the gallerie stood and the people went on againe, though not so manie as before; had y^t faln as blackfryars did vnder the popishe assembly, yt would haue ben a great wound to our religion."   Winthrop Papers, Mass. Hist. Coll.
Fourth Series, Vol. VI. p. 47.

Mr. Nathaniel Rogers arrived in New England 17 Nov. 1636.*

* Winthrop's New England, vol. i. p. 205 (2d ed. p. 244).

Concerning his voyage, the following extract from a Letter of Brampton Gurdon to John Winthrop, dated Assington, this 30 of August (1636), seems worth inserting here.

"It hathe faulne out verry hard with the shipe whear in Mr. Nathaniel Rogers imbarked himselff, his wiff who locke for* at the end of 7ᵇᵘʳ, 4 children, & 3 other pore fameles out of this towen; won is Robinson that lived in Litle Waldenfeld, with his wiff & 6 children; they went abord at Grauesend the furst of Jeuen, & have euer scins ben houareng to the Ile of Wite, & this day Mris Crane, their scister, & Mris Rogers mother in law tould me her husband had a letter from them from Plimworth, writ on Saturday scenight. This will fall exceding heui to dyuers in the ship who had mad som prouicyon for their liuelyhod in New England. Thay will be inforsed to spe[nd] it before they goe, & all for want of a constant Est wind. Thay haue had the wind for a day or 2, & then brought backe agayen. Thay haue had dyuers feruent prayers to geue them a good wind, but the tyem is not yet coum for God to haue the prayes of it."

Winthrop Papers, Mass. Hist. Coll.
Fourth Series, Vol. VI. p. 560.

The will of the Rev. NATHANIEL ROGERS, Pastor of the Church at Ipswich, taken from his own mouth, July 3, *Anno Domini* 1655, was proved in court at Ipswich, 25-7-1655. He reckons his estate in Old and New England at about twelve hundred pounds, four hundred pounds of which "is expected from my father Mʳ. Robert Crane in England." He makes the portion of John, though his eldest son, equal only with the others, viz. Nathaniel, Samuel and Timothy, and gives to each one hundred pounds out of his estate in Old England and one hundred pounds out of his estate in New England. To his son Ezekiel he gives twenty pounds, which he may take in books if he pleases. To his daughter he had already given two hundred pounds. To his three grandchildren, John, Nathaniel and Margaret Hubbard, he gives forty shillings each. To his cousin, John Rogers, five pounds, in the hands of Ensign Howlett. To Elizabeth, Nathaniel, John and Mary, children of his cousin John Harris,† of Rowley, he gives twenty shillings each. To Harvard College, five pounds. The remainder he leaves to his wife Margaret, whom he appoints executrix.

The original will is on file in the Probate Registry of Essex County, and a copy of it is preserved among the papers of the case of Rogers *vs* Rogers already referred to.

Mrs. Margaret Rogers died in Ipswich, 23 January, 1675, and admon. was granted to her eldest son, John Rogers, 30 March following (1676.)

Administration of the estate of Margaret Rogers, of Ipswich in

* I am inclined to think that this must refer to her expected confinement. Ezekiel must have been born just about this time.—H. F. W.

† The wife of John Harris of Rowley was named Bridget. I would suggest that she may have been Bridget Anger, one of the children of Edmond and Bridget Anger (see the wills of Dorothy Rogers of Dedham and of John Rogers of Colchester).—H. F. W.

New England, widow, was also granted in England, 21 March, 1677, to William Hubbard, principal creditor.

From her age, as given in her deposition, it would appear that she was born about 1610. Her mother, therefore, could not have been the Mary Sparhawke, daughter of Samuel, baptized 1 February, 1600. (See New Eng. Hist. Gen. Reg., Vol. XIX. p. 125.)

There remains John Rogers, of Billerica, who undoubtedly belonged to this family, as we may learn from the will of Ezekiel of Rowley. The recent history of Billerica, by our associate, Rev. Mr. Hazen, furnishes a good account of him and his descendants. His will can be found on record in the Suffolk Registry (X.—23). It was "declared" 22 January, 1685, and letters were granted 8 June, 1687, to Thomas and Nathaniel, the executors. He gives to Nathaniel one half the house, etc., and to Thomas the other half after the death of the widow, who is to have the use of it. Other bequests to sons John and Daniel, daughter Priscilla, grandchild Mary French (at 21), son George Browne and wife's daughter Mary Browne. He is said to have died 25 January, 1685(6), æt. 74, and was born therefore about 1611 or 1612. On the Tabular Pedigree which accompanies these notes will be found two Johns, either of whom might be this individual, so far as date of birth would indicate. I cannot help thinking that John, the son of Nathaniel, the schoolmaster, was the one referred to in will of his uncle John, of Dedham, as "the sadler," brother to Elizabeth Rogers. This sister, I doubt not, was adopted by her uncle, and was the one mentioned by the widow Dorothy Rogers in her will, as "my maid Elizabeth Rogers." The John Rogers who lived in Billerica was evidently a baker (as I am informed by Mr. Hazen). Whether a man would change an occupation requiring an apprenticehood for another is a question. We have still left John, the second son of Thomas Rogers, who probably was placed by his father to learn some other trade than the ancestral one of shoemaking, in which the eldest son, Thomas, was to succeed him. I am therefore inclined to think that we are to look here for our Billerica Rogers.

It was my good fortune to find in the British Museum two Elegies which seem to have escaped notice hitherto; one in manuscript, which I found in the well known Harleian collection; the other a printed broadside, in a collection known as the Luttrell collection. I found in this latter collection divers other elegies and eulogies which deserve to be known; among them one on the Rev. William Jenkin the younger, I remember, and another on Col. Rainborough.

The two elegies referred to here follow :—

Upon the death of old Mr Rogers of wethersfield minister of god his word, late deceased.

In Rama once a voyce was heard	W^{ch} now in weathersfield doth sound
Of bytter lamentation,	An heavy visitation. ·

He is not now who lately was
    As Rachells children were not
Soe we shall hardly fynd the lyke
    Crye loud therefore & spare not.
The cloudie piller now is gone
    That guyded in the day
And eke ye fire wch in the night
    Did poynt us out the way.
Alas therfore what shall we doe
    Our Moses cannot crie,
Nor stand up in the gapp to stay
    Gods iudgements when they flie.
How shall we passe to Canaan now
    The wildernesse is wide
Soe full of Tygers, Beares & wolues
    And many a beast besyde.
Who shall stand up to plead wth God
    ffor to supplie our neede.
Our waters stand, our Manna feast
    Whereon our soules did feede.
Oh happie it was wth weathersfielde
    And neighboure townes about
When they enioyed y^t worthy light
    Which now is cleane worne out.
Noe greater proofe of loue to god
    Doth Christ himself require
Then was p'formed of this man
    W^th all his hartes desire
W^th wisedome and discretion both
    He fedd Christs lambs indeede
Devydeinge out them portions all
    According to their neede.
To stronge ones he gave stronger meat
    Who better could apply y^t
And to the weaker sort also
    As best might fitt their dyett.
The sicke and feeble ones alsoe
    He nourished paynefully
And evermore his hart did yerne
    To heare ye poore mans crie.
He bound up broken hearted ones
    He did ye hungrie feed
He brought the wandringe home againe
    And did supplie their neede
He sought their peace continually
    He ended all their striefe
Reioyceing neuer more then when
    They ledd a Christian lyfe.
He spared noe labour of the mynde
    Noe bodilie griefe nor payne

That tended to his peoples good
    And to his masters gayne.   [fayle
When strength of leggs and feete did
    On horseback he did ryde
And wheresoeuer he became
    His tallent well emploid.
Soe deerely did he loue gods house
    When Arons bell did call
Noe winde or weather might him lett
    He ventred lyfe and all.
Thus did he leade them forth wth ioy
    To pastures fresh and greene
And to the lyuely water pooles
    As cleere as hath beene seene.
Rare was his order to catechise
    His doctrine sound & playne
And by this holy ordynance
    He many soules did gayne.
Thus hath he spent his vitall breath
    In honour and renowne
His hower is past, his glasse is runne
    And he hath gott the crowne.
And now behold ye shepehards all
    Whom god hath given this station
See here a patterne to behoulde
    fitt for your imitation.
The better sort neede yet to learne
    This patterne to behould
As for the rest, learne you were best
    Looke better to your soulde.
And now Oh woefull weathersfield
    Whose fame soe farr hath sounded
Looke how thou hast received & heard
    And how thy faith is grounded.
And to thy faith and godly life
    As thou before hast learned
W^th out the wch thy faith is deade
    And cannot be discerned.
ffor now the Lord doth call for fruite
    To answere all his payne
And wher he hath bestowed much
    He lookes for much agayne.
Loue thou therefore gods ordynance
    Sell all, that to obteyne
And buy the fielde wher treasure is
    That ever shall remayne
Then thou wth him thats gone before
    Shall Hallelujah singe
And Reigne in heaven for euermore
    W^th Christ our lord and kinge.
                    finis.
                [Harleian MS. 1598.]

A mournefull Epitaph upon the death of that reverend vvorthy Pastor Mr JOHN
ROGERS, late preacher of Gods vvord at Dedham in Essex, vvho departed this
life the 18 of October in the yeere 1636.

                1.   2.   [old,
Come helpe us mourn good Shepherds all,   Come weep and mourne, both yong and
    who love Christs flock indeed   your harts to sorrow move
Helpe us to beg, pleade, cry & call,   Both Sheepe and Lambs all of his fould
    in this our time of need.   shew forth your deerest love.

3.

Our joy is gone, our soules delight,
  our blessed sonne of thunder,
Our valiant champion in Gods sight,
  to breake sinnes boults in sunder.

4.

Our famous light which lately stood
  on hill within our towne :   [abroad,
Whose beames were spread so farre
  is now by death tooke downe.

5.

Those lively christall streames so pure,
  with pastures fresh and greene ;
From us alas are lock't full sure,
  and can no more be seene.

6.

Oh mournefull flocke who art deprived
  of such a faithfull guide ;
Whose drooping soules he hath reviv'd
  Full many a time and tide.

7.

Our faithfull Moses now is gone,
  Which stood up in the breach ;
To stay Gods wrath with many a groane,
  his hands to heaven did stretch.

8.

His life Gods glory did advance,
  his doctrine good and plaine :
And by Gods holy ordinaace
  he many a soule did gaine.

9.

No paine nor labour he did spare,
  the hungry soules to feed,
Dividing out each one his share,
  according to their need.

10.

A person grave, a patron rare,
  most humble, godly, wise,
Whose presence made the wicked feare,
  when they beheld his eyes.

11.

His ears were open and attent,
  To heare the poore mans cry :
And speedily his heart was bent,
  to find a remedy.

12.

To rich and poore, to old and yung,
  most courteous, mild and meeke,
The mourning soules he brought along,
  and comforted the weake.

13.

Much comfort heere his soule posscst,
  his life fame, and renowne,
And now with Saints and Angels blest,
  he weares a glorious crowne.

14.

Where many a soule is gone before,
  Which he through Christ hath gain'd,
His glory shines as Sunne therefore,
  And never shall be stained.

15.

You pastors all of Christ his fould,
  of soules who have the charge,
See here a patterne to behold
  Your duties to your charge.

16.

His faith, his love, his godly care,
  his zeale sinne to suppresse :
His pitty showes to such as were,
  in griefe and heavinesse.

17.

His humble heart did soon make peace,
  by arbitration wise,
All jars and strifes he made to cease,
  twixt neighbours that did rise.

18.

But now those ioyfull dayes are gone,
  which made our hearts so glad,
And comfort brought to many one,
  when sorrow made them sad.

19.

Our Zion temple songs doe cease,
  our burning shining light
Is gone to everlasting peace,
  and bids us all good night.

20.

Our constant Lector twelve dayes fame,
  and ioy of Saints all round,
To which Gods armies flocking came,
  To heare his doctrine sound.

21.

Gods holy Law and Gospel pure,
  he preach't with courage bould,
Whereby he many did allure,
  and brought to Christ his fould.

22.

The poore and hungry soules alway,
  with good things he did fill,
The rich, nor any went away,
  Without Gods mind and will.

23.

Most faithfully he preach't Gods will,
  with wisedome from above,
And left for to direct us still,
  his booke of faith and love.

24.

Gods counsell and the narrow way,
  he clearely did unfold
Without excuse to leave all they,
  That would not be controld.

25.

His proudest foes on every side,
  who sought his deprivation,
He still did overcome their pride,
  by humble conversation.

26.

Against hels force and Satans rage,
  God kept him in his station,
And still preserved him in his old age,
  In *Dedhams* congregation.

27.

From weeke to weeke, from day to day,
 he cryed in our eares :
And this he did without delay,
 the space of thirty yeeres.

28.

In zeale he was a flaming fire,
 yet humble and discreet,
Which made his chiefest foes admire,
 and swadged their malice great.

29.

They often sought for to prevaile,
 to take away our joy,
To quench our light they did assaile
 our glory to destroy.

30.

But God did guard his choice elect,
 who worthy was through Christ,
From dangers all did him protect,
 and tooke home at last.

31.

The time of life that God him lent,
 was three score yeeres and seven,
The greatest part of which he spent,
 to bring soules into heaven.

32.

Oh happy change and blessed gaine,
 good time for him to die :
Vnhappy we that still remaine
 more sinfull dayes to see.

33.

Yet happy now likewise are they,
 which are in state of grace,
And were so wise that in their dayes,
 with God they made their peace.

34.

Now magnifie the providence,
 of Gods election strong,
That he such dayes by sure defence,
 In mercy did prolong.

35.

And now hold fast with diligence,
 the trueths which you have learn'd
And bring forth fruit with patience,
 that grace may be discern'd.

36.

Those graces learne to imitate,
 in him which shine so bright,
So shalt thou live in happy state,
 and pleasing in Gods sight.

37.

A wife hath lost a heavenly head,
 children a father deare,
A losse to all on every side,
 and to his flocke most neere.

38.

His house a blessed *Bethel* was,
 as plainely did appeare :
He lived to see his fruits in grace,
 on all his children deare.

39.

But now alas what shall we doe
 Gods anger to revoke,
Our sinfulnesse have brought us to
 This sad and heavy stroake.

40.

Our sleepy formall carelessnesse,
 in hearing of Gods word :
Vnfruitfull barren heartednesse,
 though we with meanes were stored.

41.

All those that have worne out this light,
 and yet remain all darke,
How shall it now their soules affright,
 to weare this cursed marke.

42.

Now let us all repent and pray,
 with zeale and fervency,
That of the Lord obtaine we may,
 some comfort and supply.

43.

Our King and Counsell Lord preserve,
 and all of each degree,
That from his trueth we may not swerve,
 but therein live and die.

44.

That with him that's gone before,
 a kingdome may obtaine,
And then with Saints for evermore,
 in glory may remaine.

AN EPIGRAM.

In morning wake with God, and beg his
 grace,
Offend not his good spirit in any case,
Hang fast on Christ, cleave closse unto
 his word,
No time forget to weare the christian
 sword,

Run cheerefully your generall is before,
Our blessed captain Christ hath opened
 the doore
Got victory against sin, death and hell,
Eternall life for aye with him shall
 dwell,
Returne my soule, goe foorth unto thy
 rest,
Strange joyes are gone which cannot be
 exprest.

I. L.

FINIS

Printed for the yeere, 1642.
Eulogies and Elegies
        Luttrell Coll. Vol. I.
        British Museum.

INDEX

OF

NAMES OF PERSONS.

INDEX

OF

NAMES OF PLACES.

www.ingramcontent.com/pod-product-compliance
Lightning Source LLC
Chambersburg PA
CBHW080047280326
41934CB00014B/3242

* 9 7 8 1 6 2 8 4 5 0 7 1 2 *